SEE IT ALL AGAIN!

— John Wayne, as Genghis Khan trying to conquer a stubborn woman and winding up merely with half the world.

— Barbara Parkins, Sharon Tate, and Patty Duke popping their pills on screen to the tune of 20 million at the box office.

— Billy Jack magically commanding an eagle to drop from the sky and land on his arm.

— Little Dondi trying to warm your heart and succeeding in turning your stomach.

— Dean Martin as Matt Helm, the private eye who became a monument to screen sexploitation.

— *Eegah!*, the most monstrous monster film ever to give beastly creatures a bad name.

. . . Everything you always wanted to know about Hollywood's most notorious stinkers, including the story behind each film, lines of immortal dialogue, unforgettable performances, special awards, a sampling of critical responses and hilarious anecdotes about the stars and directors. With a special appendix in which nationally known critics list their own nominees for the worst movies ever. Illustrated with more than 100 stills from the films.

Harry Medved   Randy Dreyfuss

THE FIFTY WORST MOVIES OF ALL TIME

(and how they got that way)

by Harry Medved

with Randy Dreyfuss

Angus & Robertson·Publishers

ANGUS AND ROBERTSON • PUBLISHERS

London · Sydney · Melbourne · Singapore · Manila

First published by Popular Library, CBS Publications, CBS Consumer
Publishing, a Division of CBS Inc. in 1978. First published in the
British Commonwealth by Angus and Robertson (U.K.) Ltd,
10 Earlham Street, London WC2H 9LP in 1979.

ISBN 0 207 95891 2 (cased edition)
ISBN 0 207 95892 0 (limp edition)

to the memory of
Isidore Herman—
who knew how to laugh

Photograph credits and acknowledgments: United Artists, Universal
Pictures, American International Pictures, Columbia Pictures, Cinerama
Releasing, Twentieth Century-Fox, RKO Radio Pictures, Republic Pictures,
Allied Artists, Fairway-International, Paramount Pictures, Mosfilm,
Mayflower Productions/Paramount Pictures, Warner Brothers, Astor Films,
Metro-Goldwyn-Mayer, Embassy Pictures.

All photographs from the personal collection of Harry Medved. Photographs
from *Eegah!* courtesy of Arch W. Hall, Sr. The press book from *Robot
Monster* was made available courtesy of Eric Hoffman.

PRINTED IN HONG KONG

ACKNOWLEDGMENTS

Harry's brother Michael Medved was involved in every step of the project and without him this book would not exist. Nancy Medved, who is Michael's wife—and Randy's cousin—did nearly all the typing and editing. Harry's mother patiently endured the insanity of this entire project and dutifully ferried him around town when he was too young to drive himself.

Many others provided important advice and moral support along the way. They include—
Patrick O'Connor, Bruce Akiyama, Dave, Jonathan and Ben Medved, Jordan Rush, Len Hill, Ivor Davis, Bill Ramsey, Leonard Maltin, Briane Murphy, Bruce Rawitz, Bronwen Crothers, Jeff Stolper, Robert Rucker, Ron Herman, Steve Hyman, Jay Ludwig, Frances Jalet, Michael Clark, the Lockmans, Manny, Mo (Berman) and Curly Joe (Berry), Arch Hall, Sr., Greg Tucker, and Gilbert and Evelyn Dreyfuss.

For the background research on each of these films, we used the libraries of the Academy of Motion Picture Arts and Sciences, the University of California at Los Angeles, University of Southern California and Twentieth Century-Fox (Thank you, Jack Yager!).

Viewing the thousands of films considered for this book was made possible by the UCLA Film Archives, the Pacific Film Archives, the Los Angeles County Museum of Art, the Museum of Modern Art, American International Pictures, Inc., the Warner Brothers archives at the University of Wisconsin, the film library of KHJ-TV (with appreciation to Barbara Massey), Audio Brandon Films, Inc., Budget Films, Inc., Swank Motion Pictures, Inc., and the wonderfully wretched Palace Theatre in Long Beach, California.

Special thanks to the Wallace family for their unfailing encouragement and kindness—
And love, most of all, to Muki, who was there to understand when the going got rough.

CONTENTS

INTRODUCTION

Why would anyone in his right mind write a book about bad movies?

It's a fair question. And without making any claims as to our sanity, we'll try our best to answer it.

For several years now, in every sort of social gathering, we've noticed an odd quirk of human nature. When the conversation turns to motion pictures, people show greater enthusiasm in laughing together over films they despise than in trying to praise the films they admire. It may be edifying to discuss the virtues of cinema classics, but listing the oddities in filmic disasters is far more enjoyable. When the subject is bad movies, even the most reticent member of a group will have an opinion and can suggest some beloved turkey for consideration. To appreciate movie greatness—especially in this era of growing sophistication—may require a certain amount of background or patience, but absolutely anyone can recognize a lousy film when he sees one. Bad movies work their magic not on the mind alone, but on the entire body: sitting through a genuinely wretched film can leave you with dizziness in the head, a bad taste in the mouth, agitation in the stomach, and even a rumbling in the bowels.

At this point, we might as well come clean and make an embarrassing confession: we get a kick out of bad films. What's more, we're convinced we're not alone. How else can you possibly explain the continued popularity of TV's "Late Late Shows" unless you assume there are hundreds of thousands of people out there who take a perverse pleasure in some particularly ludicrous entertainments? The determined little cults that surround artistic films cannot compare in stubbornness or passion to the hooting cliques that continually boost such atrocities as *Myra Breckinridge* or *Santa Claus Conquers the Martians*. We know of one California television station which, because of viewer demand, showed *The Horror of Party Beach* every Halloween for nearly a decade. How can quality films boast a following as loyal—or as insatiable?

We hope that the publication of this book will encourage bad-film freaks to come out of the closet and declare themselves. After all, the lure of poor films bears a strong resemblance to the appeal of masterpieces: in both cases, the viewer marvels at the range of human imagination and creativity. After experiencing a beautiful cinematic statement, we stand in awe of the creative spirit that has shaped all the disparate elements into a satisfying whole. When contemplating a terrible film we are also in awe—this time amazed that so many dozens of people could have expended so much time, money, and imagination only to produce such complete and absolute garbage. In screening the candidates for this book, the one thought that came to mind again and again was, "I can't believe that a human being actually bothered to create *this*!" What better monument to human futility—or more profound confirmation of an absurdist view of the universe—than some of the ludicrous fiascoes presented here?

For too long, Hollywood has been sweeping its

most embarrassing disasters under the rug. It's time that these wretched films received the public recognition they deserve as breathtaking achievements in their own right.

SOME GROUND RULES

The hardest part of compiling a list of the worst films is, of course, settling on just fifty titles from among the thousands of movie monstrosities worthy of consideration. In order to narrow the field, we've instituted certain ground rules.

No silent films, for instance, have been considered for this book. It is our conviction that silents are a separate and unique art form, and that judging them alongside talkies would be like weighing apples together with oranges. The style of dramatic presentation, not to mention the level of technical sophistication, changed completely with the advent of sound. The only silents that have survived are the handful of genuine masterpieces. The silent stinkers—and there were thousands of them—have disappeared and in most cases the prints have been lost.

For similar reasons, we have limited ourselves in dealing with foreign films. Our final list of the Fifty Worst includes Italian, Japanese, French, and Russian productions, but we considered only those foreign films that were distributed in the United States. We have studiously ignored such Polish, Mexican, Taiwanese, or other local products that never made their way past the borders of their native lands. For one thing, such films would be extremely difficult for us—and for our readers—to view. Furthermore, it seemed unfair to apply Hollywood standards to the flourishing cheapie film industry in cities like Bombay, India. Since no American distributor has subjected us to these films, we have decided, in the interest of international brotherhood and understanding, to leave them well enough alone.

Travelogues, porno flicks, movies made for television, and U. S. Army training films have also been excluded from competition. Films within these categories serve special purposes—or are produced under special circumstances—which set them apart from purebred Hollywood abortions. Even without such marginal candidates, we still have a remarkably rich crop of bad films to choose from.

In assembling the list, we have attempted to compile a representative cross section of horrible films down through the years. In making our selections, we have divided the films under a few main subheadings:

BIG-BUDGET FLOPS: Films that cost millions of dollars to produce, and that leave you gasping in disbelief at the waste of money. Disastrous ventures such as *Lost Horizon* (1973) and *Zabriskie Point* leap immediately to mind. Such films are nearly as noteworthy for their abuse of talent as for their pathetic squandering of financial resources.

GRADE "Z" ATROCITIES: Films like *Eegah!*, *Robot Monster*, and *Swamp Women* achieved the same low quality as the major studio flops—and at only a fraction of the cost. Tens of thousands of "B" and "C" films have been made over the years, but only a legendary handful have been so thoroughly lacking in entertainment value to qualify for our list. Most low-budget films have some shortcomings, but the shoestring productions nominated here can boast nothing but shortcomings. The competition among these grade "Z" films for places on our list was particularly fierce.

OVERRATED ART FILMS: A few so-called "art films" are so tedious, so mannered, and so patently fraudulent that they could not escape mention in this book. Though praised by critics, such films leave audiences bored and furious, and their tendency to take themselves with the utmost seriousness only makes matters worse. Pictures such as Eisenstein's *Ivan the Terrible* and Resnais's *Last Year at Marienbad* are the most controversial choices in our book, but we hope that abused viewers everywhere, forced to endure such "classics" because of their inflated reputation, will applaud their selection on our list.

IMPLAUSIBLE ODDITIES: Would you believe *The Terror of Tiny Town*—a 1938 musical Western with an *all-midget* cast? What about a science-fiction saga called *Santa Claus Conquers the Martians*? It is hardly surprising that such films turned out miserably—what is surprising is that so-called professionals ever bothered to make them in the first place.

POPULAR "TRIUMPHS": The voice of the people is not always the voice of God—at least not so far as we're concerned. Anyone's confidence in the public's taste and good sense would be shattered by the fact that films such as *Valley of the Dolls, The Omen,* and *The Trial of Billy Jack* have proven so enormously successful. Perhaps the popularity of such films proves our earlier point—that this country is crawling with bad-film aficionados, many of whom may not even acknowledge the designation.

EGREGIOUS EXAMPLES: No book on the worst films could be complete without a jungle movie, a Japanese horror epic, a singing-cowboy saga, a violent blacksploitation film, and a spaghetti Western. Hundreds of awful films have been made within each of these categories, and we have selected one of each as an egregious example. Since we have not seen every jungle film of the last forty years, we cannot say with absolute certainty that *Daughter of the Jungle* is *the* worst one ever made. Nevertheless, it does come close enough to that distinction to merit inclusion here. The same is true of *Godzilla Versus the Smog Monster, Twilight on the Rio Grande, Trouble Man,* and *The Return of Sabata.* Such movies are presented in this book as prime representatives of hackneyed and ridiculous film formulas.

TARNISHED STARS: How could we ignore the 1956 adventure film, *The Conqueror,* in which John Wayne stars as Genghis Khan? Not to mention the 1959 biblical epic *Solomon and Sheba* with Yul Brynner struggling to play King Solomon. Ridiculous casting has provided the silver screen with some of its most ludicrous moments, and there is a special fascination in watching major stars disgrace themselves before our eyes. Try as you may, you will never forget Hedy Lamarr as Joan of Arc in *The Story of Mankind.* Yet most embarrassing of all was Shirley Temple's role in the 1947 melodrama *That Hagen Girl.* America's Little Sweetheart, then eighteen years old, was forced to play an unhappy orphan girl thought to be Ronald Reagan's illegitimate daughter.

OLDIES BUT BADDIES: No, the Golden Age of Hollywood was not pure gold. Along with those delightful Frank Capra, John Ford, and Howard Hawks creations came laughable turkeys such as *Parnell* (1937) and *The Goldwyn Follies* (1938). Some of the worst of the old films, like D. W. Griffith's *Abraham Lincoln* (1930) and Alfred Hitchcock's *Jamaica Inn* (1939), were actually perpetrated by distinguished directors. The inclusion of such classic bombs in this volume should demonstrate that bad films are by no means a recent invention; they have a long and honorable history.

As far back as 1926, in fact, British critic Iris Barry wrote in *The Spectator,* "I recommend the smaller and obscurer of the picture houses to the film lover's attention. . . . They teach one how incredibly bad the worst films can be. There is a sort of perverse pleasure to be got out of a really unspeakable film. Joys unknown to the casual frequenter of picture houses are open to habitués who note with glee how many famous stars are shockingly inept." Ms. Barry was a prophet far ahead of her time. What a rich harvest of bad films we have enjoyed in the fifty years since she made her observations! In selecting the very worst from among these, we have been guided by the sage advice of another critic, Frank Rich of the *New York Post.* In sending us his own nominations for the list, Mr. Rich pointed out that "a worst film can't be any mediocre movie, but must be a movie that is *both* atrociously made and philosophically ridiculous—a merging of form and content, as it were."

We do not claim to have seen every poor film ever made, but in researching this project over the last two years we have endured nearly two thousand of them—an achievement for which we surely deserve some sort of cinematic Purple Heart. We freely admit that our choices are highly subjective. Our list is hardly final or definitive, and we want very much to hear the opinions of others. We have asked several distinguished critics to assemble their own lists of the worst films, and their responses are reprinted in the appendix to this book. Also in the appendix is a ballot for you, the reader, to fill out. Please send us your personal nominations, and the results of this Worst Films Poll will be reported in subsequent editions of our book. New films come out every year that deserve to be considered for the list, and so we are determined to maintain our flexibility as we look ahead to future stinkers. We know all too well that the horizons for bad films are unlimited—as boundless as the reach of human imagination and incompetence.

Walter Huston as Abraham Lincoln ponders weighty issues: "Ah! The blood it takes to hold this union together."

ABRAHAM LINCOLN (1930)

Directed by: D. W. GRIFFITH
Written by: STEPHEN VINCENT BENÉT and GERRIT J. LLOYD
Produced by: JOSEPH SCHENCK
Featuring: WALTER HUSTON, UNA MERKEL, KAY HAMMOND, E. ALYN WARREN, HOBART BOSWORTH, FRED WARREN, HENRY B. WALTHALL, FRANK CAMPEAU, LUCILLE LA VERNE, IAN KEITH, JASON ROBARDS, SR.

United Artists

The Critics Rave

"The Wonder Film of the Century about the Most Romantic Figure who ever Lived."
—Promotional Leaflet for *Abraham Lincoln*

"Totally dull . . . unbelievably slow dialogue. . . . It is difficult to understand why contemporary critics were so impressed by this dull, episodic, overlong production. . . . Griffith appears to use Mrs. Lincoln as a substitute for the Negro comic relief of many of his other productions. . . . Nor does Una Merkel help; her portrayal of Ann Rutledge must qualify as the worst example of miscasting in the history of the cinema."
—Anthony Slide, *The Films of D. W. Griffith*

"No new insights were presented, and the results were waxworks."
—Robert M. Henderson, *D. W. Griffith*

"Static. . . . No feeling for the movie medium. There were so many moments of absurd sentimentality that the whole carried little weight."

—Lewis Jacobs, *The Rise of the American Film*

"A nightmare of the mind and nerves."

—D. W. Griffith

Plot Summary

Lightning crackles above a humble log cabin and we hear a baby's wail. Mrs. Lincoln proudly holds up her newborn boy, who looks for all the world as if he were a pineapple in diapers. "I think I'll call him—Abraham!" she exclaims, just before collapsing on her bed. In a quick transition from diapered pineapple to Walter Huston, we see youthful Abe working as a clerk in Illinois. In between chores (which are absurdly portrayed by having Huston hammer a tiny peg into a gigantic log), Lincoln spends his free time with Ann Rutledge, the village belle.

In the big love scene that follows, Abe tells Ann that he has been longing for her in the same way that a child longs for gingerbread. Finally, he pops the question and asks her to marry him. She replies, "Well, you know I've been intending to for a long while." Abe stammers, his eyes nearly popping from their sockets. "You mean . . . !" "Yes, Abe," she answers, "you've got your gingerbread."

Unfortunately, Griffith blows his chance for classic comedy by letting Ann Rutledge die just three minutes after her initial appearance on screen. She expires in Lincoln's arms while "The Sweet By and By" is intoned by an off-key chorus in the background. Abe throws himself on Ann's muddy grave, and Griffith throws us headlong into Abe's future—using the novel motif of an hourglass to show that time is passing.

Abe now is married to Mary Todd. He is a practicing attorney in Springfield and decides to run for the United States Senate. This leads to the Lincoln-Douglas debates—one of the film's most ludicrous charades. For several minutes we hear such witty exchanges as: "If the Southern states want to secede, let them alone" (*applause*) and then Lincoln's reply, "I say—the Union must be preserved!" (*even greater applause*). The forensic style of the entire scene is strongly reminiscent of

the famous "Certs-is-a-candy-mint—No-Certs-is-a-breath-mint" debate of a later era. Adding insult to inanity, the makers of this film pointlessly alter Lincoln's immortal line "A house divided against itself cannot stand" to "A house divided against itself must fall."

Lincoln is elected President and survives many hardships. To portray the beginning of the Civil War we are treated to totally predictable scenes of Union troops marching off to "The Battle Hymn of the Republic," followed by an equally snappy sequence showing Confederate soldiers going off to "Dixie." There's the inevitable sentimental scene in which Lincoln pardons a young soldier, while we hear some Negro spirituals in the background. The President, while preparing battlefield strategy, suddenly comments, "Ah! The blood it takes to hold this Union together." While he is pacing the floor one night in the White House, Mrs. Lincoln kneels to put slippers on his feet. He suddenly and inexplicably gets a brainstorm that changes the course of history. "I've got it, Mary!" he exclaims. "I've got a man to win this war—and his name is . . . Grant!"

Finally the war is over, and Lincoln is free of his torment. He decides to take it easy and plans an outing to Ford's Theater. Little does he know that John Wilkes Booth (played in the Snidely Whiplash manner by Ian Keith) has a plot up his sleeve. Lincoln arrives at the theater, and the audience leaps to its feet demanding, "Speech! Speech!" In this absurd revision of history, the President obliges them by offering part of his inaugural address. Finally he settles down to enjoy the play, while we settle down to enjoy the spectacle of the assassination. After the shooting, to make sure we didn't miss the action, Griffith has several members of the audience call out, "Mr. Lincoln has been shot! Mr. Lincoln has been shot!" while one man solemnly (and somewhat prematurely) intones, "Now he belongs to the ages."

The films ends with a long shot of a scale model of the Lincoln Memorial. The camera pans onto the model of Lincoln's statue as we hear a choir singing "The Battle Hymn of the Republic" and a sunburst appears behind Lincoln's marble head. To complete the festivities, bells ring out for a "triumphal" conclusion. Such an inspiring moment was not seen again for thirty years, until Walt Disney designed his "Great Moments with Mr. Lincoln" attraction for Disneyland. The only difference between the two interpretations of Lincoln was that Disney's robot gave a far more life-like performance than did Walter Huston in this film.

Unforgettable Performances

Walter Huston is an outstanding actor, and he struggles manfully to make a creditable presentation here. The odds are too much against him, however: costume designer Walter Israel, for instance, has placed stilts in his boots and a ridiculous stovepipe hat on his head. The hat is about sixteen inches in height and Huston constantly pulls things out of it. He also has trouble walking, and it makes no sense at all to portray Mr. Lincoln as if he were a cripple.

In a further attempt to make the young Mr. Lincoln live up to his advertised billing as "the Most Romantic Figure who ever Lived," Huston is coated with a thick layer of white, chalky make-up, complete with lipstick. He could easily pass for the Scarecrow in *The Wizard of Oz*. As the great man grows older, Griffith and Huston obviously strained to show Lincoln as a down-to-earth, simple person, but the net effect was to make him appear simpleminded. Huston lopes around, furrows his brow in constant confusion, and seems as clumsy and slow-witted as Jed Clampett in "The Beverly Hillbillies."

Una Merkel's performance as Ann Rutledge is very simply beneath contempt. Historians now recognize that this entire episode in Lincoln's youth is actually little more than a myth, and certainly no real individual could fall in love with the young lady who is presented here. Merkel's Ann is a composite of Shirley Temple, Gidget, and Zasu Pitts, and in most screenings the audience will welcome her death with audible sighs of relief.

Immortal Dialogue

Love Scene:
ABE: Every time I dream, your face gets mixed up in it.
ANN: Does it really, Abe? I know that's just flattery, but I love it.

* * *

Death Scene:
ANN: I know the truth, dear. I'm going to die.
ABE: No, no, you won't dear. I won't let you!
ANN: We must be brave . . . it's getting so dark and lonesome! (A saccharine chorus of "Sweet By and By" comes up in the background.)
ABE: Oh, Ann! I love you so!

* * *

The President's Marital Life:
MARY LINCOLN (putting slippers on his feet): Abraham Lincoln! Will you ever learn to keep your feet in shoes!

Young Abraham Lincoln takes on Jack Armstrong in a thrilling moment from D. W. Griffith's epic film biography. Who do you think is going to win?

15

The Noble Resolution of a Born Leader:
ABE: I've hung my hat, and here it stays till they
    knock it off with a bayonet. From now on,
    Mary, *I'm* going to run this war!

*   *   *

(An aide approaches General Lee and suggests
    that they surrender.)
LEE (furiously clutching his sword): Surrender?!
    My poor army! Why, I'd rather die a thousand
    deaths than ...
AIDE (pacifying him): There, there, General.
    You must lie down and rest.

*   *   *

The Story Behind the Film

D. W. Griffith's earlier Civil War epic, *The Birth of
a Nation*, was one of the greatest silent films ever
made. It was only natural for him to turn to the
same era as subject matter for his first experiment
in talkies. Originally he planned to make a screen
version of Stephen Vincent Benét's *John Brown's
Body*, which had won a Pulitzer Prize for poetry.
But Griffith's producer Joseph Schenck, not noted
for his taste in poetry, turned down the idea. When
Griffith suggested making a biography of Lincoln
as an alternative, Schenck decided that the Great
Emancipator was surefire box office, and the project went forward.

At first, Griffith dreamed of collaborating with
Carl Sandburg on the screenplay, but Sandburg's
price was too high. Eventually, the director hired
Benét, who agreed to do the screenplay with one
stipulation: he was to work exclusively with Griffith. Unfortunately, much of Benét's original
script was discarded and revised by Schenck.
Griffith was in poor health while the film was in
production, and much later he described the entire project as "a nightmare of the mind and
nerves." After the shooting was finished he had to
retire to his Texas retreat to regain his strength.

The final version of *Abraham Lincoln* was
edited by John Considine, Jr., a Schenck employee. Nonetheless, Griffith insisted on claiming
full responsibility for this ridiculous film. The
credits proudly proclaim that it was *"PERSON-
ALLY DIRECTED BY D. W. GRIFFITH."* The
credits also reveal that the production manager
for the film was a gentleman most appropriately
named "O. O. Dull."

Perhaps the most astonishing thing about *Abraham Lincoln* is the amount of first-rate talent that
was wasted on the project. In addition to Griffith,
Benét, and Huston, William Cameron Menzies
served as the film's art director. Later, Menzies
did the art direction for *Gone with the Wind*, as
well as directing the classic *Things to Come*.

The Balance Sheet

On November 5, 1930, *Abraham Lincoln* opened
in New York to laudatory reviews and by the end
of the following year the film turned in a modest
profit. In the 1940s, the film was released in 16
mm. for classroom use. With all its historical inac-
curacies, it is hard to imagine any responsible
teacher making use of the film, and it is even
harder to envision their use of the "educational"
handbook that was distributed along with it. This
handbook features stills from Griffith's film. There
is a shot of Lincoln cuddling up to the dying Ann
Rutledge, for instance, with the captioned question, "How does tragedy affect interest in the pho-
toplay?" There is a still of Lincoln pacing back
and forth, thinking up strategies, with Mary on
her knees trying to put on his slippers. The question here is, "How does this scene show dramatic
suspense?" Another picture features John Wilkes
Booth sitting in a saloon with his co-conspirators,
all frowning, with grimacing faces. The caption
reads, "What emotions do these faces express?"
Another interesting question might be: "What do
the faces of the audience express after viewing this
film?" Unfortunately, the answer might be unprin-
table.

*We are given a taste of naked
realism as the passengers panic
aboard their crippled 747. That's
Myrna Loy crouching behind her
seat in the foreground. Take special
note of the inspired performance
by the black gentleman at the
extreme right in this photo.*

16

AIRPORT 1975 (1974)

Actress Nancy Olson heightens the dramatic tension in Airport 1975.

Directed by: JACK SMIGHT
Written by: DON INGALLS
Produced by: JENNINGS LANG
Music by: JOHN CACAVAS
Featuring: CHARLTON HESTON, KAREN BLACK, GEORGE KENNEDY, GLORIA SWANSON, EFREM ZIMBALIST, JR., SUSAN CLARK, HELEN REDDY, LINDA BLAIR, DANA ANDREWS, ROY THINNES, SID CAESAR, MYRNA LOY, ED NELSON, NANCY OLSON, LARRY STORCH, MARTHA SCOTT, JERRY STILLER, NORMAN FELL, CONRAD JANIS, BEVERLY GARLAND, AUGUSTA SUMMERLAND, GUY STOCKWELL, CHRISTOPHER NORRIS, KIP NIVEN

Universal Pictures

The Critics Rave

"American film making at its shabbiest, most unimaginative, most exploitive. Nothing about *Airport 1975* is good; no actor in the cast of dubious luminaries even tries to be. . . . It is to be wished that everyone in the film would go away—violently. . . ."

— Jay Cocks, *Time*

"Processed schlock . . . a box of rotten candy for movie junkies and TV dipsos. . . . Even technically, the picture is a shambles. . . . The audience kept breaking up over the hackneyed editing. Probably everybody will have some reason to hiss this picture. . . . Hissing is more expressive than anything that happens on the screen."

— Pauline Kael, *The New Yorker*

"This sequel to the financial blockbuster *Airport* doesn't even have a wing and a prayer."

— Paul D. Zimmerman, *Newsweek*

"Cheapjack moviemaking. . . . True sequels rarely live up to the originals, but this one manages to live it down. . . . A 107-minute plug for the Boeing 747. . . . Jack Smight's direction matches the hiccupping story line."

— Judith Crist, *New York*

"Discriminating audiences may find the story beyond credibility and some of the dialogue inane and they will be absolutely correct."

— *Film Bulletin*

"It's kind of a *Lost Horizon* with wings. . . . Airborne buffoonery. . . . *Airport 1975*, unlike its predecessor, crashes on takeoff. . . . It's appropriate that the 747 in this turkey takes off from an airport called Dulles. Try not to see it on a plane because it might force you to walk out."

— John Barbour, *Los Angeles*

Plot Summary

A crowded jumbo jet leaves Dulles Airport in Washington, D. C. On board we find such typical, down-home Americans as the famous movie star Gloria Swanson (Gloria Swanson), a lovely teenager awaiting a kidney transplant (Linda Blair), the wife and son of the airport operations chief, two nuns, a couple of drunks, and the usual assortment of stock characters. These include individuals who are billed in the script as "Needlepoint Woman," "Funeral Director," "Frightened Woman," "Hostile Man," "50th Anniversary Celebrator," "Dowager with Dog," and, naturally, a "Rock Star" plus two "Rock Singers." This entire precious cargo is headed for Los Angeles on a routine flight. But we know there is high adventure and bone-rattling drama ahead, don't we, kiddies?

As our 747 floats serenely across the continent, a worried Dana Andrews is on the ground at another airport. He is debating whether he will fly his small private plane that night, even though the rain is pouring heavily and his tummy doesn't feel too good. He goes through with it and takes off. Suddenly, in midair, he dramatically grabs his stomach, squints his eyes, and makes gurgling sounds. These actions are supposed to represent Andrews having a massive heart attack. He loses control of the plane, which proceeds to go crazy. The small craft zooms upward toward the unsuspecting jumbo jet and crashes right into the cockpit. BLAMMO! (You can almost see the flashing pop-art caption.) Naturally, as any first-year student of aerodynamics can tell you, whenever a small private plane stumbles into the cockpit of a 747, this causes one of the co-pilots to be sucked right out of his seat and go flying off into the wild blue yonder. The other pilots are either dead or blinded, though the plane itself seems to be doing fine. One of the stewardesses, Nancy (Karen Black), runs up to the cockpit to see what the mild disturbance was all about. When she sees the gaping hole in the side of the cockpit, she exclaims, "Oh, my God!" while the studio orchestra throbs "Uh-Oh!" for dramatic effect.

Thinking quickly, the plucky stewardess gets in touch with airport authorities through the radio in the cockpit. She manages to reach Murdock, (Charlton Heston), her lover of six years, who also happens to be an ace pilot. Over the radio, Murdock gives her some elementary flying lessons, and Nancy gamely steps behind the controls, blinks back her tears, and tries to steer the plane to safety. Finally, she turns the whole great big giant plane right around all by her little teeny-weeny self. The audience sighs in relief, for they think that the film is finally over. But boy-oh-boy, do we have a surprise or two coming up. Since Nancy cannot possibly land the plane all by herself (after all, Karen Black is noticeably cross-eyed), Murdock decides to meet her for a dramatic midair rendezvous. A helicopter flies in the direction of the crippled plane with our hero dangling from a long string. Mr. Heston then jumps in through the gaping hole in the cockpit and coolly greets his girl friend. Murdock lands the big bird at the Salt Lake City airport, and the all-star cast quickly runs out of the plane and off the screen, as if they can hardly wait to leave this movie. Nancy and Murdock, however, walk slowly down the loading ramp, embracing each other, as the camera follows them for a touching freeze frame. And now a word from our sponsor.

Unforgettable Performances

Karen Black is well cast playing a stewardess under normal circumstances: she offers coffee, tea, or milk with just the right touch of bored, transparently phony sweetness. She also does well at flirting with one of the co-pilots—precisely the sort of sparkling, witty byplay at which Ms. Black seems to excel. As the film progresses, however, and she is called upon to display emotion, our heroine flounders. The close-up showing her horror as she first glimpses the hole in the cockpit suggests nothing so much as a busy housewife who has just noted, much to her chagrin, that the family dog has committed an indiscretion on the carpet. Later, whimpering and sniffling and struggling to be brave, Ms. Black does provoke audience reaction: one does not so much want to slap her cheek and urge her to get hold of herself as one wants to grab her firmly around the neck and strangle her.

Charlton Heston, meanwhile, portrays a swinging, macho, self-confident pilot, who slinks around as if to the music of a burlesque house orchestra. In one scene he is wearing dark glasses, and he generally refers to Nancy as "bay-bee." Yeah, cool daddy, very hip! In his frantic effort to shake the solemn religious associations of some of his previous roles, he begins to suggest Dean Martin.

Linda Blair is responsible for many of the film's most "inspirational" moments—she is everyone's favorite character, the cute little thing who is on the verge of death, flying to Los Angeles for a kidney transplant. While the other characters seem unable to look at her sorry plight without choking back their tears, Linda remains excruciatingly chirpy and cheerful. She is comforted by a musical nun, played by Helen Reddy. Sister Reddy whips out her guitar in mid-flight and belts out a power-of-positive-thinking song that sets all the passengers to tapping their feet and beaming like beatific idiots. "It is easier for a camel to go through the eye of a needle than for a Hollywood nun to enter into the Kingdom of God." (Matthew XIX, 24)

Karen Black, the heroic (if cross-eyed) stewardess in Airport 1975: *"There's no one left to fly the plane! Help us! Oh, my God . . . help us!"*

Immortal Dialogue

1ST PILOT: I hear we expect a bumpy ride tonight.

2ND PILOT: I used to know a stewardess who thought that was sexy.

1ST PILOT: You're weird, you know that?

* * *

(Two nuns are waiting aboard the 747, as an ambulance races onto the airfield.)
1ST NUN: Look, Sister, an ambulance!
2ND NUN (Helen Reddy): Oh, I hope it's not serious! (She then kisses the crucifix hanging around her neck.)

* * *

(Janice Abbot [Linda Blair] is carried on a stretcher to the plane.)
MOTHER: Please, Janice. Remember what the doctor said—you must lie still, very still.
JANICE: I know, Mother, but it's so exciting! People are so interesting!

* * *

AIRPORT ATTENDANT (commenting on the unfortunate Janice): The poor kid! She's in Washington and her kidney is in Los Angeles.

* * *

(Nancy tries to reach the Salt Lake City airport after the accident.)
NANCY: Salt Lake . . . Salt Lake! This is Columbia 409! It's Nancy Pryor . . . stewardess. Something hit us! All the flight crew is either dead or . . . or badly injured! There's no one left to fly the plane! Help us! Oh, my God . . . help us!

* * *

The Story Behind the Film

With all the fanfare and the all-star cast, *Airport 1975* cost less than $3 million. Jennings Lang, the film's executive producer, accomplished this by hiring mostly television technicians to work on the film. The script by Don Ingalls, a veteran TV writer, was originally submitted to Universal's television division for consideration as a made-for-TV film. Lang liked the script and thought he could pass it off as a feature film. Jack Smight, a director who had recently specialized in made-for-TV movies, was assigned to the project. John Cacavas, the composer of the "Kojak" theme, was asked to write the film's musical score. To top it off, many of the big names in the all-star cast were basically TV actors. The only passengers who were missing were Ricky Ricardo and Uncle Miltie.

An actual 747 as well as seven other airplanes were used in the filming. Universal also constructed a set resembling the cockpit of a 747. The publicity for the film read, "Every dial, light, and switch is an exact replica, even to the air-worthiness certificate," which was posted near the door of the cockpit.

The Balance Sheet

Airport 1975 was Gloria Swanson's first film in twenty-two years and she insisted on writing all her own lines. Perhaps someone had warned her in advance about the skills of scriptwriter Ingalls. When asked why she stayed away from films for such a long time, Ms. Swanson replied, "I was holding out for a picture I could take my grandchildren to see, something exciting and contemporary without senseless violence." Well, Gloria, we hope it was worth the wait.

Certainly for its producers, *Airport 1975* was well worth the trouble. Much to the disgust of all major critics, the film proved immensely popular and grossed somewhat more than $25 million. With this sort of profit potential, Universal decided to continue cashing in on the *Airport* formula. Next we will be treated to a sequel to this sequel—*Airport 1977*—in which an all-new airplane, piloted by Jack Lemmon, stumbles into the Bermuda Triangle. Apparently, all that is necessary to assure a film's whopping success is to recruit a star-studded cast and to keep them up in the air, flying around and around for a while. We look forward to innumerable *Airports* of the future, *Airport 1979, 1981,* and so forth, finally culminating in *Airport 1984,* in which a convent basketball team hijacks an SST as a protest against Big Brother, while the passengers are saved by a heroic puppy in the baggage department who holds on to the severed left wing with his teeth. It's so exciting! People are so interesting!

ALAKAZAM THE GREAT! (1961)

(Original Title: SAIYU-KI)
1961

Directed by: TAIJI YABUSHITA and OSAMU TEZUKA
Written by: OSAMU TEZUKA, KEINOSUKE UEKUSA, LOU RUSOFF, and LEE KRESEL
Produced by: HIROSHI OKAWA and LOU RUSOFF
Music by: LES BAXTER
Featuring the voices of: FRANKIE AVALON, DODIE STEVENS, JONATHAN WINTERS, ARNOLD STANG, STERLING HOLLOWAY

American International Pictures

The Critics Rave

"*Alakazam the Great!* is a wild, nonsensical, hack-chop-you're-dead fairy story. . . . The hero is an emetic little monkey (U. S. adapters thoughtfully assigned Frankie Avalon to provide his voice) who sets out to conquer the world."

—*Time*

"This Japanese cartoon has an American commentary, dubbed voices and music. . . . Much of it is derivative of second-grade Disney. . . ."

—*Monthly Film Bulletin*

"Grueling . . . ponderous."

—*Motion Picture Herald*

"Wild . . . not likely to put Disney out of business."

—Philip T. Hartung, *Commonweal*

"Bomb: Lowest Rating! . . . Dull. . . . Japanese cartoon with American actors doing voices might

Alakazam (the voice of Frankie Avalon) comforts his monkey girl friend, Dee-Dee (the voice of Dodie Stevens). Prince Amat, Alakazam's spiritual counselor, looks on approvingly.

have been more appealing in Japanese. Bad excuse for children's entertainment."

—Leonard Maltin, *TV Movies*

Plot Summary

Alakazam (an animated character whose voice is provided by Frankie Avalon) is a magical monkey who is about to become king of all the animals in Majutsoland. Before receiving the crown, he is required to jump over a high waterfall and into the water below in order to prove his courage. Alakazam is worried about performing the feat and tells his monkey girl friend, Dee-Dee (the voice of Dodie Stevens), "I'm not sure I'm gonna like this, but when you gotta—you gotta!" Alakazam goes through with it successfully. He is made king. Next we see Alakazam in his palace wearing a little kingie crown. He is entertained by

a horde of sexy monkey belly dancers (hubba, hubba)—each one of them wearing an Arabian veil and carrying a giant leaf.

Realizing his power, he turns out to be extremely arrogant—and Alakazam the Great becomes more like Ivan the Terrible (q.v.). He is so arrogant, in fact, that he challenges the human king of Majutsoland, King Amo, to a magic contest. King Amo (who bears a strong resemblance to Buddha) beats Alakazam and locks him up in a cave with bars. Dee-Dee constantly trudges through snowstorms to see her beau. The sweet little thing brings with her, on every one of their meetings, a present for Alakazam: chestnuts. On one visit, she treads her way through a blizzard and suddenly faints from exhaustion. It looks as if she is doomed, until a halo appears from over the mountains. It's Queen Amas, wife of King Amo, and she says to Dee-Dee, "Your life will be saved. Love like yours deserves to be rewarded." Dee-Dee is rejuvenated and Alakazam's prison magically disappears. Our hopes that the two monkeys will live happily ever after and that we can leave the theater are quickly dashed as Queen Amas puts a condition on Alakazam's release: he must go on a pilgrimage with Prince Amat (a bald-headed fellow adorned with bright red lipstick), son of Queen Amas and King Amo. On this pilgrimage, Alakazam must learn humility.

On their travels, Alakazam and Prince Amat meet several villains. They meet a talking pig with heavy eyebrows. (Gee, we thought only monkeys talked.) The pig's name is Sir Quiggley Broken

King Gruesome's evil wife throws daggers at Sir Quiggley Broken Bottom (the voice of Jonathan Winters) in one of the stirring action sequences from the Japanese cartoon Alakazam the Great!

Bottom (Jonathan Winters), a member of the McSnarl Brothers Gang, and he is suavely dressed in a violet bathrobe and large boots. They also meet Max Lulipopo, a giant bare-chested cannibal with pearl necklace. His voice is provided by the ubiquitous Arnold Stang, straight from the classic *Dondi* (q.v.). Instead of killing these two villains, Alakazam decides to invite them along on the pilgrimage. Suddenly we hear Dee-Dee's voice happily blurt onto the sound track: "Alakazam, you're learning humility."

Meanwhile, King Gruesome (an orange-eyed bull), king of all ogres, has decided to kidnap Prince Amat and demand a ransom from King Amo. He hires Philo Fester, a pointy-eared midget with red hair who has a spike protruding from the top of his head and who wears a leopard-skin loincloth. King Gruesome contacts Fester through a cosmic television set and Fester proceeds to kidnap Prince Amat. Gruesome explains why he wants to have the prince kidnapped with a line to delight children of all ages. "I need that ransom money. That queen of mine wears a mink stole like nylon."

Prince Amat is finally recaptured by the pilgrims. Fester gets his comeuppance and in tears he pulls the spike out of his head and decides to help the good guys. Alakazam meets King Gruesome and they perform a bullfight in midair above an erupting volcano.

All this animation is supposed to be artistic. It consists of a lot of glitter, weak drawings, and red backgrounds. Alakazam finally kills King Gruesome and returns to his homeland. He is personally congratulated by King Amo and his wife. This calls for a celebration! Fireworks are ignited and confetti is thrown as Alakazam, Prince Amat, the pig, and the cannibal walk through a crowd of cheering monkeys. Alakazam finds Dee-Dee lying sick in her bed. He yells, "Dee-Dee, I've returned to you!" and Dee-Dee joyously cries, "Oh, you're back!" Alakazam lovingly tells her, "I'm never going to leave you again! I'll stay and we can rule this kingdom together!" As our film finally ends, the narrator (Sterling Holloway) comments, "Now wouldn't you just know that it would end like this? Everyone living happily ever after and all that." It just sort of warms your heart, doesn't it?

Unforgettable Performances

Perhaps the producers of this film deliberately selected actors of the dubious stature of Frankie Avalon as the only performers who could possibly match the relentless banality of the animation. The content of the drawings suggests a retarded twelve-year-old wandering aimlessly through the San Diego zoo while under the influence of a massive overdose of LSD. The splashy use of color indicates that the artists for this film had just been given an exciting new box of crayons and quickly proceeded to run amuck; staining every available surface violet, guava, mauve, or "passion fruit," without sympathies for the headaches they would produce in viewers.

Frankie Avalon as the voice of Alakazam provides such classic lines as "I command you to disappear" and "You get me, buddy?!" Actually, Alakazam is a real cool character. He constantly sings hip songs that are accompanied by choruses of "Alkay, Alko, Alakazam!" and "Sing this magic tune," and dresses in a small karate coat that reaches to his hips. Otherwise, from the waist down, Alakazam is *totally naked!* (In a kid's movie, too!) Avalon recites his lines like a restless child taking his first reading lesson. Most actors who do the voices of cartoon characters have the courtesy to put a bit of enthusiasm into their roles. But with Avalon, even a simple line like "Oh, yes!" sounds as if it was delivered by someone muttering in his sleep.

Dodie Stevens plays Dee-Dee, Alakazam's monkey sweetheart. The boy and girl monkeys in this film do have distinguishable differences. The girl monkeys are colored pink and have eyelashes, lilies on top of their heads, and are developing modest little pre-pubescent breasts. The boy monkeys are colored light brown and have bigger noses than the girl monkeys. Who is Dodie Stevens? At the time the film was made, she was a fifteen-year-old singing star who had made it big with her hit recording of "Pink Shoe Laces." (She was known as "The Pink Shoe Laces Girl.") Ms. Stevens tries to sound innocent and charming, but she instead suggests a primate Kate Smith.

Jonathan Winters in his first movie role supplies the voice for Sir Quiggley Broken Bottom, a talking pig.

Immortal Dialogue

DEE-DEE and ALAKAZAM (breaking into song):

> *Alkay, Alko, Alakazam.*
> *Happy and carefree—*
> *That's how I am.*
> *If you want sunshine*
> *All the day long,*
> *Sing this magic song.*
> *If you want rainbows*
> *Chasing the moon,*
> *Sing this magic tune.*

*   *   *

(Alakazam plans to visit Merlin the Magician's castle.)
DEE-DEE (pleading to Alakazam): Take me with you!
ALAKAZAM: It's no place for women. Besides, magicians don't like girls. They saw them in half!

*   *   *

KING AMO (seeing Alakazam): So you're Alakazam! We meet at last! . . . No one until now has tried to challenge me to a contest of skill.
ALAKAZAM: Well, you know, I, uhh, I—I think it's like this: you old guys should make way for the younger generation. You get me, buddy?

*   *   *

More singing:
ALAKAZAM, BROKEN BOTTOM, LULIPOPO, and PRINCE AMAT sing to pass the time away on the pilgrimage:
> I never give up
> I never give up
> Singing the magic words: ALAKAZAM.
> Ali—the great!
> Ali—the great!

*   *   *

The Story Behind the Film

Alakazam the Great! was the first of a three-picture deal between Toei Films of Tokyo and American International Pictures. Toei planned to make two other cartoons that American International would distribute in America. They were *Ali Baba and the Seven Wonders of the World* and *Sinbad the Sailor.*

American International head James H. Nicholson first saw *Alakazam* when he visited Japan and stumbled into a local movie house on a rainy day. He thought that marketing the cartoon in the United States would be very profitable, since besides Disney's, there were few animated features. He bought rights to the film's foreign release and promptly Americanized his product. Six minutes were cut from the original print and the entire score was altered. By dubbing the film the whole story line was changed. Lou Rusoff wrote a new screenplay and changed the Japanese religious myth theme that ran throughout the film, providing a whole new "be good to your neighbor" theme. The original may have avoided the inanities of the specific score and script inflicted on American audiences, but it suffered from the burden of the garish, clumsy, pretentious animation—surely enough in itself to qualify the film for anyone's list of the worst-ever children's movies.

The Balance Sheet

The film's American International Pictures pressbook claimed, "No greater line of items has ever been made for the special promotion of a full-length cartoon feature." True enough: the imagination lavished on the promotional campaign clearly exceeded the creativity employed in making the film itself. Some of the items made available were: "a nine-inch *Alakazam the Great!* washable plush monkey, in full color"; "a 9 X 12 inch full color *Alakazam the Great!* jigsaw puzzle"; "all rubber washable *Alakazam the Great!* hand puppets"; "*Alakazam the Great!* metal-plated magic rings, with full color picture"; "specially autographed 5 X 9 pictures of Frankie Avalon and Dodie Stevens"; and other delights. Theater owners playing the film could rent an eleven-foot helium balloon to fly 150 feet over the theater. The balloon proudly announced: "Alakazam Is Coming to Town."

The pressbook also generously suggested: "Offer a special screening of *Alakazam the Great!* to your local children's hospital, orphanage, or other sick or underprivileged children's facility. Supply free ice cream and candy, etc., at the screening with the cooperation of the local confectioner, and invite the press to observe and photograph children's reactions for excellent public service stunt and favorable publicity." Apparently, the publicity men had no confidence that the children would be amused by the film, so they insisted that the kids be bribed with ice cream in order to ensure positive reactions.

Alakazam the Great! received the *Parents' Magazine* Family Medal for September of 1961. This auspicious beginning led American International to believe that the film would be a total success; they had already planned to buy two more Japanese cartoons. However, they later "dropped the whole idea," according to *Variety*. The paper reported that *Alakazam the Great!* "turned out to be a disappointment in the domestic market, despite the fact that AIP invested a sizable amount of loot in completely re-editing the pic.... Pic also did poorly in the foreign markets in which it played. It was banned in Norway and Denmark because of the horror elements." Hats off to the Scandinavian censors for recognizing an unmitigated horror when they see it.

SPECIAL AWARD

The Dr. Pavlov Animal-Torment Award goes to American International Pictures for their incredible suggestions for simian exploitation. In their desperate need for publicity, AIP came up with the disgusting idea of exhibiting actual monkeys in theater lobbies. Their suggestion read as follows: "'Brothers' of Alakazam the Great (tame squirrel monkeys) are available for any of the following seat-selling slants, a special lobby exhibit or any other promotion, through an animal wholesaler in Los Angeles, California, at the low price of only $20.00 each, *including a cage*, F.O.B., Los Angeles. These pet monkeys, perfect for a household pet, will make wonderful exhibits and/or giveaways in your city. Contact American International Pictures Publicity Department, 1416 North La Brea Ave., Hollywood 28, Calif., for full details. Allow two weeks or more for orders to come through. The kids will *love* this one!"

Imagine for a moment the experience of these pathetic monkeys, trapped amid the popcorn and noise in theater lobbies, facing hordes of disappointed children streaming out of this film. Nice going, American International! If the kids hate *Alakazam*, then try bribing them with ice cream, and if that doesn't work, let's use caged monkeys. If that one bombs too, guys, why don't you just try caging the kids?

*Matt Helm (Dean Martin)
prepares for a dangerous mission
in* The Ambushers. *The film
featured a bevy of starlets billed
as "the Slaygirls."*

*Dean Martin subtly turns his
amorous gaze on co-star Janice
Rule. Critic Judith Crist wrote that*
The Ambushers *"just about reaches
the nadir of witlessness, smirky
sexiness and bad taste."*

THE AMBUSHERS (1967)

Directed by: HENRY LEVIN
Written by: HERBERT BAKER
Based on the book by: DONALD HAMILTON
Produced by: IRVING ALLEN
Music by: HUGO MONTENEGRO
Featuring: DEAN MARTIN, SENTA BERGER, JANICE RULE, JAMES GREGORY, ALBERT SALMI, KURT KASZNAR

Columbia Pictures

The Critics Rave

"The makers of the Matt Helm series starring Dean Martin appear to be proceeding under the theory that off-color jokes, a leering star, and scantily clad females will make money at the box office. They may be right. But for someone who demands that the jokes be funny as well as dirty, that Martin give some semblance of an acting performance, and that a spy script (who stole the flying saucer?) be intelligent, *The Ambushers* hits a new low."

—William Wolf, *Cue*

"Lowest rating! . . . The first two of Dino's 'Matt Helm' epics were *The Silencers* and *Murderers' Row*. This is the worst of the lot."
—Steven H. Scheuer, *Movies on TV*

"The sole distinction of this vomitous mess is that it just about reaches the nadir of witlessness, smirky sexiness and bad taste—and it's dull, dull, dull to boot."
—Judith Crist, *TV Guide to the Movies*

"Martin at times becomes a caricature of himself playing himself, and comes across as a male Mae West . . . tedious plot resolution right out of old serials. . . . Acting, writing, and direction are pedestrian, to say the most."
—Art Murphy, *Variety*

27

"Plot, jokes, and gadgets are all below par."
—*Monthly Film Bulletin*

"Seasonal junk. . . . There's absolutely nothing special about Dean Martin's new vehicle, *The Ambushers,* except its air of tired stupidity and professional staleness. . . . Completely lustreless . . . a lot of hand-me-down gags, some third-rate, suggestive dialogue, and leftovers from the James Bond bonanza."
—Howard Thompson, *New York Times*

"James Bond movies are spy spoofs with some sexual innuendos on the side. Matt Helm movies consist of sexual innuendos with a vague attempt at spy spoofing on the side. *The Ambushers* is the most blatant and inane of the lot."
—Moira Walsh, *America*

Plot Summary

A United States flying saucer is stolen by a power-hungry beer manufacturer who lives in Acapulco. There is only one man who can retrieve it: Matt Helm (Dean Martin), a constantly slushed top secret agent who works for I.C.E., a special training center for American spies. He travels to Mexico with Sheila Sommers (Janice Rule), the country's leading authority on flying saucers, and it is their job to fly the missing saucer back to the States. While in Acapulco, they enjoy a tour of the brewery that has captured the flying saucer. Suddenly, Matt and the tour guide are pushed by mysterious hands into a huge vat of beer. The guide gluggingly informs Matt that he can't swim, but Dino advises him, "Drink your way to the bottom." With Sheila's help, Matt finally climbs out of the bubbling beer vat—none the worse for wear. They then find out that the brewery doesn't have the flying saucer after all and begin searching through Mexico.

We see them asking a series of Mexican villagers (straight off the set of *Zorro*) if they have seen anything suspicious hovering in the vicinity. These excursions give us some relief from the infantile plot, as we are treated to a travelogue of sleepy villages and majestic mountains. Finally, Matt and Sheila find the saucer conveniently parked on a railroad track. Sheila gets in to make sure it's the right flying saucer (perhaps she will

check the registration), but without warning, the mysterious craft takes off down the railroad tracks at lightning speed. Sheila can't find the brake, so in order to save the day, Matt pursues the saucer by sliding downhill at about sixty miles an hour with his rear end on one of the tracks. (Okay, Dino, whatever turns you on.) This sequence is depicted by Dean Martin's wildly waving his arms and swaying crazily back and forth in a small studio backed up by one of the worst process shots we have ever seen. Matt finally latches onto the saucer, pulls Sheila out of it, and they both jump out in the nick of time. The space craft runs off a cliff and smashes to pieces on the beach below. Now, since there is no more flying saucer, no one can debate who stole it. As a result, Mexico and the United States are at peace once more, and a grave international crisis has been averted (whew!). Matt goes back to his apartment and reaches for a bottle of beer.

Unforgettable Performances

Dean Martin's acting is so inept in this film that even his impersonation of a lush seems unconvincing. If nothing else, we had a right to expect that Dino would resemble an "entertaining" drunk—the sort of lovable inebriate who amuses us with his wit, his flair, or a silly gesture or two. Instead, Martin gives us a sodden, hopeless boozer—the sort of slow, plodding, pathetic character who drinks alone in a remote corner of the bar, teetering at the verge of blacking out and voiding himself. In Dino's defense, it should be noted that he does an excellent imitation of an aging walrus—complete with grunts and a lot of deep breathing. He also takes long pauses in his speech, as if trying to hold back impending belches. Finally, we have his frequent giggles, suggesting nothing so much as a ruined man attempting to laugh off his distress.

Meanwhile, poor Janice Rule struggles through her role as Sheila Sommers. Her assignment is a difficult one: how can she possibly handle a script that presents her as a feckless piece of meat and subjects her to leers, sneers, and double entendres that would embarrass even a sex-craved twelve-year-old? Ms. Rule answers the challenge by smiling bravely through every insult, but the grueling nature of her effort suggests a cigar-store Indian with make-up and a high-fashion wardrobe. She grits her teeth as if telling the audience, "There is nothing you will get from me except my smile, rank, and serial number."

Even less animated than Ms. Rule are the celebrated "Slaygirls," the female bit players who bounce through this film in various states of undress. These young ladies are about as graceful as meatballs and as sensual as department store mannequins. Based upon their performances here, their acting is somewhat below the standard usually observed in Playtex bra TV commercials. Their main function, aside from set decoration, is to pant and slobber every time Dean Martin appears, in a losing effort to convince us that the star is virile and irresistible. Nice try, ladies.

Immortal Dialogue

A Course in Self-Defense:
FEMALE INSTRUCTOR (holding a ray gun): This little gadget here dissolves metal electronically. Easy to conceal, extremely effective in times of danger.

(She points the gun and dissolves the belt buckle on Dean Martin's pants. The pants immediately fall to the ground.)

1ST FEMALE STUDENT: That's when the danger usually starts!
2ND FEMALE STUDENT (suggestively): I like my way better!

     ❊   ❊   ❊

MATT HELM: Oh, when you say you're a "38" you ain't just kidding!
LINDA: It's not a gun, Mr. Helm. It's the new weapon they gave me, developed right here in our labs.
MATT: Developed pretty well, too!
LINDA: May I point out . . .
MATT: You already do!
LINDA: . . . that that's why you're here. To become familiar with our latest equipment.
MATT: You're right. An agent should always keep *abreast* of the times!

     ❊   ❊   ❊

(Matt's secretary, Lovey Cravesit (yes, that's really the name in the script), brings him his supplies.)
LOVEY: I think I've got everything you want.
(Camera zooms in on her behind.)
MATT: Yeah!!!

     ❊   ❊   ❊

MATT'S BOSS: Matt, have you ever seen a flying saucer?
MATT: Is that your way of offering me a drink?

     ❊   ❊   ❊

(Matt and Sheila are secluded on a mountaintop.)
MATT: We have a long wait ahead of us, so let's get comfortable.
SHEILA: (purring) How comfortable?
MATT (complaining): It's broad daylight!
SHEILA: What's the matter with a broad in daylight?

     ❊   ❊   ❊

ORTEGA (toasting): Cheers!
GIRL (also toasting): Skoal!
MATT (reasoning): Sure it's cold. It's got ice in it.

The Story Behind the Film

To lend their project a touch of class, Columbia Pictures hired Oleg Cassini—who at the time was Jackie Kennedy's personal designer—as the film's "director of fashion design." He supervised every detail of color, fabric, make-up, hairdos, jewelry, furs, and styles for every member of the cast. Cassini had not designed for films since 1939, and even a cursory glance at the surface of *The Ambushers* will tell why. Cassini seems no more sympathetic to women than the other geniuses behind this film, and he dresses his actresses to look like stewardesses or, at other times, like tour guides at Disneyland.

Another one of Cassini's important responsibilities involved the recruiting of the Slaygirls. He personally handpicked these lovelies in a twelve-week tour around the world. In order to assure broad appeal, the Slaygirls represented a number of different countries, including Japan, England, Denmark, Italy, Germany, Sweden, and Australia.

The director of *The Ambushers* was Henry Levin, who was responsible for another Matt Helm film, *Murderers' Row*. In addition, Levin has to his discredit one more sickening spy spoof (without Matt Helm), called *Kiss the Girls and Make Them Die*. Levin's string of turkeys from the 1960s include *Genghis Khan, Honeymoon Hotel,* and *Where the Boys Are*. For *The Ambushers,* Levin enjoyed the support of a composer whose music blends perfectly with the quality of the rest of the film. Hugo Montenegro subsequently executed the ostentatious score for that other classic *Hurry Sundown* (q.v.). Before turning his attention to films, Montenegro had composed for television and penned the abominable theme to the series "I Dream of Jeannie." His score for *The Ambushers* suggests a garish meld of the Monkees and Herb Alpert's Tijuana Brass.

The Balance Sheet

The film was advertised with the lines "They're All Trying to Get the Best of Matt Helm in the Best Matt Helm of All" and "Matt Helm Rides Again with the Slaygirls Dressed to Kill in *The Ambushers*." The studio suggested that theater owners "line up your own group of Slaygirls to parade with display board in and around the theater. Hold a beauty contest for the local Slaygirl of the week for each week the film plays." Through careful planning, Oleg Cassini's fashions from the film, part of the "new wave" look, were available in stores around the country when the film was released in winter of '67.

The Ambushers turned in an outstanding profit and proved to be very popular—demonstrating once again that it is impossible to insult the intelligence of the moviegoing public. The film grossed (no pun intended) $4.7 million. It was the third in the Matt Helm series and was followed by *The Wrecking Crew* (1969), after which the beloved secret agent finally turned in his cocktail glasses and sixth-grade jokebooks and sank slowly into the west. In an attempt to revive the incomprehensibly popular spy, a Matt Helm series with Tony Franciosa appeared on television. Thankfully, the series was short-lived.

Richard Burton as Leon Trotsky registers his displeasure after he is struck by assassin Alain Delon.

THE ASSASSINATION OF TROTSKY (1972)

Directed by: JOSEPH LOSEY
Written by: NICHOLAS MOSLEY
Produced by: NORMAN PRIGGEN and JOSEPH LOSEY
Music by: EGISTO MACCHI
Featuring: RICHARD BURTON, ALAIN DE-LON, ROMY SCHNEIDER, VALENTINA CORTESE, GIORGIO ALBERTAZZI, LUIGI VANNUCCHI, DUILIO DEL PRETE, JEAN DESAILLY, SIMONE VALERE, CARLOS MIRANDA, MIKE FOREST

Cinerama Releasing

The Critics Rave

"Atrocious . . . tritely psychologized pretty pasteboard nonsense. . . . About as lively as a Hollywood biography of the thirties."
—Stanley Kauffmann, *The New Republic*

"Cockamamie . . . a ridiculous movie. . . . Another miserable Richard Burton performance—his Trotsky resembles nothing so much as Lionel Barrymore playing Dr. Gillespie. How about Burton and Desi Arnaz, Jr., in a revival of the Kildare series. . . . *Trotsky* is a strange little fiasco. . . . In time you give it up as a bad joke, and the murky solemnity of it all becomes rather funny. . . . What a hopeless movie!"
—Gary Arnold, *Washington Post*

"Trotsky was an extremely public figure. Given the vast amount we know about him, it is inexcus-

able to present him as a foxy grandpa mouthing platitudes. . . . We get lots of crazy acting and lots of the aimless camera movement which director Joseph Losey passes off as style."
—Richard Schickel, *Life*

"Character assassination. . . . *The Assassination of Trotsky* has the faintly instructional air of a classroom filmstrip. By contrast, the movie assassination is staged like a scene out of some Hammer horror epic."
—Jay Cocks, *Time*

"Poor Trotsky comes off as a windy fool. . . . A good part of the blame for Trotsky's absurdity must be borne by the actor who plays him—Richard Burton, who gives each phrase such an exaggerated sense of importance that he either intensifies triteness or indeed, at times, supplies it. Director Joseph Losey must also be held accountable."
—Joy Gould Boyum, *Wall Street Journal*

"Features Burton with spectacles and chin whiskers and Welsh accent, chanting (in person, in voice-over, and on Dictaphone rolls) pithy sayings from Leon Trotsky, and Alain Delon, writhing with symptoms of haute-psychopathia behind dark glasses and blank expressions, as his assassin. . . . There are all the clichés of melodrama. . . . Losey succeeds in making fact seem like lurid fiction."
—Judith Crist, *New York*

"A sorry mix of bad history and worse invention. . . . Trotsky most of the way sounds like a pompous pedant. . . . His assassin in a trench coat and smoked glasses belongs to comic opera."
—Charles Champlin, *Los Angeles Times*

"Reduces the complex tragedy of Trotsky to bull."
—Bruce Williamson, *Playboy*

"A very odd project indeed."
—Roger Greenspun, *New York Times*

"Not for anyone who knows, or cares, anything about Leon Trotsky."
—Pauline Kael, *The New Yorker*

Plot Summary

Leon Trotsky (Richard Burton), noted revolutionary, is living in exile in a heavily guarded Mexican compound, complete with alarm system, watchtowers, and about a hundred armed bodyguards. He lives out his last days by talking to his precious "bunny rabbits," talking to his friendly chickens, talking to his potted plants, and talking to a Dictaphone machine which records his memoirs. Occasionally he also talks to his wife, Natalya (Valentina Cortese), whom he calls "my only one, my faithful one, my eternal one. . . ." (Sigh!) He has another friend named Gita (Romy Schneider), his secretary, who is in love with a mysterious young businessman named Frank Jacson (Alain Delon). Jacson, a fan of Josef Stalin's, actually has a plan to assassinate Trotsky and is using his girl friend as an introduction to the old revolutionary.

Gita and Jacson, we soon learn, are quite a fun couple. On one of their dates, they go to the bullfights, where we see a fiesta of slaughter with the assassination of the bull used as a symbol for the upcoming assassination of Trotsky (who, in this film, bears a certain likeness to the bull, we'll have to admit). We are treated to shots of banderillas being plunged into the bull's body. Finally the animal keels over, a river of blood spurting from its mouth. As if this weren't repulsive enough, we later see Mexicans peeling off the bull's hide. Then its flesh is neatly carved like a char-broiled steak. This must be, as Arthur Knight pointed out in the *Saturday Review*, "The ugliest and most superfluous bullfight ever presented on the American screen." Olé!

One of Jacson's Stalinist buddies, Felipe, is anxious to get rid of Trotsky. Felipe is played with meaningless finger gestures by Duilio Del Prete, the no-talent Italian lover boy who went on to star in the disastrous *At Long Last Love* (q.v.). He organizes an unsuccessful raid on Trotsky's house; one of Trotsky's playmates, Sheldon, is killed during the raid. When Trotsky hears this, he breaks into tears, like a small boy losing his puppy dog.

Jacson later asks his girl Gita if she will introduce him to the "great man" and she finally consents. But first, Jacson has to be properly outfitted for the meeting. In order to avoid suspicion, he

Alain Delon, dressed in his best assassin's suit, prepares to enter Trotsky's heavily guarded compound. His appearance fails to arouse suspicion, and he is given free entry.

wears a pair of menacing dark glasses, greasy slicked-back hair, a drooping porkpie hat, and an old trench coat. It's as if he had just walked out of *Mad* magazine's comic strip "Spy *vs.* Spy." The guards at Trotsky's fortress decide that Jacson looks innocent enough and they let him by. When the two principals finally meet, Trotsky notices Jacson playing with the bunny rabbits. "You like rabbits?" asks Trotsky. Jacson, with a childish grin, affirms that he does. Trotsky shows him one of his furry white baby bunnies and the two become friends.

On one of his later visits to the Trotsky household, Jacson decides to bring with him a king-size ice pick, which he hides in his trench coat.

Sitting at his desk, Trotsky reads an article written by Jacson for the old man's approval. Jacson produces the ice pick from under his coat, raises it, and—chunk! The theater audience bursts into spontaneous applause. Before anyone responds on screen, however, the two men stare at each other for several moments. Then Trotsky decides to shriek and to stagger around the room with bloodied skull. This goes on for about five minutes. He is rushed to the hospital and soon dies.

Later, the police hold Jacson and ask him over and over again for some sort of identification. He is questioned by Salazar, a police chief, who is played bewilderingly by Giorgio Albertazzi, the "acting" robot from *Last Year at Marienbad* (q.v.). (Strange how these names keep reappearing, isn't it?) It seems that Jacson can't remember his own name and he stubbornly keeps silent. Finally he prepares to speak, and despite our expectations that he will announce, "My name—José Jiménez," we hear him say simply that he is the man who killed Trotsky. And so the movie ends on a perfect note of "heavy" meaning, as the members of the audience stream out to the lobby with assassination on *their* minds. Joseph Losey and Richard Burton, beware!

Unforgettable Performances

Publicists for this film announced that Richard Burton lost thirty pounds in order to prepare for his role as Trotsky. This may have been true (frankly, we doubt it), but his ample torso still seemed such a far cry from the ascetic dimensions of the famed revolutionary that the costume designers felt compelled to cram the hapless star into a rather obvious corset. At times, this apparatus makes it difficult for him to breathe and in general Mr. Burton resembles a stuffed cabbage. Burton is not to blame for the talky, awkward script but he is to blame for all the instances of misplaced emphasis and shameless overacting. At times, his performance suggests Elmer Gantry rather than Leon Trotsky. To demonstrate moments of inspiration while writing his memoirs, Burton's Trotsky raises his head high in the air and waves around the pair of spectacles he clutches in his hand. Later in the film, when a bull in a bullfight is introduced as the symbol for Trotsky, Burton tries his best to imitate the animal. We see him going into fits of snorting and coughing in bed; then we cut to shots of the bull in the arena, panting, dripping blood, and acting sick just like Burton . . . get it? The star's most hilarious moment, however, comes when his skull is punctured by the assassin's ice pick. His delayed reaction is supposed to increase the dramatic effect, but it only highlights the palpable phoniness of the whole scene. When he finally does react, his outrageous bellowing closely resembles the screams of Godzilla ferociously pouncing on his deadly foe in *Godzilla Versus the Smog Monster*

(q.v.). After wobbling briefly on his feet, Burton begins running around the room. He ends up leaning against the door with popping eyes and blood splattered over his face and goatee. His heavy breathing suggests only that he is now exhausted from his own histrionics.

It is hard to believe that anyone could compete with the great Burton in terms of a ludicrous performance, but in this film Alain Delon nearly outdoes the master. He portrays Trotsky's maniacal assassin with so much twitching and eye rolling that the audience in the screening we witnessed began to laugh and snicker every time Delon appeared. At one point, when his girl friend is talking to him, he sits perfectly still in his chair without blinking or answering. In other scenes he talks to himself while smoking a cigarette clasped between his fingers. He takes the cigarette and nervously tosses it to the ground about three times in the film; we're glad to know that he learned some meaningful gestures in acting school. In one segment, we see him discarding his cigarette and running up to a tolling church bell. He grabs the bell's clapper and swings madly from it as the screen shows a freeze frame of his feet suspended in midair. Bats in his belfry, right? Later, when Delon prepares for the assassination, he is dressed precisely the way any comic-strip assassin would dress, complete with trench coat and dark glasses. As William Wolf in *Cue* magazine observed, he is "such an overly suspicious-looking character that you wouldn't let him in to fix your TV set. The cautious Trotsky admits him into his study to commit murder."

Immortal Dialogue

(Trotsky talks to Jim, a devoted bodyguard, and reminisces about the good old days.)
TROTSKY: It's hard living with an old revolutionary. You should have been with us when we stormed the Winter Palace! With Lenin in Moscow in the early days! What happiness to be alive—to be fighting then!

○   ○   ○

(Gita tries to start a conversation with her catatonic boy friend, Jacson.)

GITA: You're in a fine state! God, has someone cut your tongue off? (Pause.) Why do you get like this? Is it the altitude you're in—or is it something you've eaten?

*　　　*　　　*

(Trotsky speaks with another bodyguard, Sheldon.)
TROTSKY: Sheldon?
SHELDON: Yes.
TROTSKY: How long have you been with me, Sheldon?
SHELDON: A month.
TROTSKY: I depend upon loyalty, Sheldon. All around the world lies a cold silence. But the truth, Sheldon, they cannot silence *that*!

*　　　*　　　*

(Gita and Jacson enjoy a lovers' quarrel.)
GITA: If you go I'll kill myself. . . . Frank! I don't know who I am! I don't know who you are!
JACSON: You're Gita.
GITA: Leave me alone!
(On the morning of his assassination, Trotsky takes several deep breaths and sniffs at the cacti in his garden.)
TROTSKY: Ah! It's a long time since I've felt so well! Today I could climb mountains.

*　　　*　　　*

(Natalya, Trotsky's wife, has long nagged him about going to a barber. He is now in a hospital bed after having an ice pick buried in his head.)
TROTSKY (to Natalya, breathing heavily): You see, the barbers also come. Natalya, don't let them undress me. I want you to undress me.

The Story Behind the Film

The Assassination of Trotsky was very loosely based on two books: *The Great Prince Died* by Bernard Wolfe and *The Mind of an Assassin* by Isaac Dan Levine. Supposedly director Joseph Losey spent over two years researching the film in Mexico. During that time he must have developed an excellent suntan. Publicity for the film claimed that Losey talked to Trotsky's grandson, many of Trotsky's guards, and the prison psychiatrist who examined the assassin before his trial. There is no evidence in the film—not even circumstantial evidence—that such careful research took place.

The screenplay was written by Nicholas Mosley, son of Sir Oswald Mosley, the celebrated British fascist leader, and Lady Cynthia Mosley, a onetime Trotskyite and Labour M.P. Coming from that sort of mixed marriage, it's no wonder that poor Nicholas is confused.

The film was shot in Mexico and at the Dino De Laurentiis studios in Rome. A censor representing the Mexican government was on the set at all times and the finished film had to be approved by Mexican censors before it was released. The film's final production budget was $2.5 million—a modest sum considering the high-powered international stars who decorated the cast. It should be

Richard Burton in The Assassination of Trotsky: *"Another miserable . . . Burton performance—his Trotsky resembles nothing so much as Lionel Barrymore playing Dr. Gillespie."*

noted—much to Losey's credit—that his original choice for Trotsky was not Burton, but Dick Bogarde. Fortunately for his reputation, that excellent actor managed to steer clear of this pretentious stinker.

Joseph Losey once commented, "The productiveness of the director-actor relationship depends on the degree to which the actor trusts the director. Unless the actor feels he can safely risk everything he has to give without making himself ridiculous, he won't try. . . . He'll play safe until he knows that the director will not let him make a fool of himself." After a quick glance at the reviews of his ridiculous performance as Trotsky, we wonder if Richard Burton would ever again "safely risk everything" with director Losey.

The Balance Sheet

On several occasions, Joseph Losey tried to remove his name from films he actually directed. He asked that his name be erased from the edited Italian version of his film *Figures on a Landscape*. Losey also demanded that his name be removed from the credits to *Secret Ceremony* when it was edited for television. The producers of *Eva* cut up the final print and again he asked that his name not be connected with the film. In all these instances, Losey proved unsuccessful in his attempts, and his reputation was sullied in spite of his efforts. With *Trotsky*, however, for some incomprehensible reason, he seemed positively proud to attach his name to the credits. In publicizing the film, Cinerama Releasing boasted, "Losey takes pride in his accomplishments and fights tenaciously for artistic control. There is no question that when *The Assassination of Trotsky* opens it will be proudly proclaimed a Joseph Losey film." Apparently, Cinerama wanted to leave no doubt as to who was the responsible party.

The film received its American premiere on October 13, 1972, at the New York Film Festival, and naturally proved one of the least popular selections on the program. It went on to a shaky three-week run in New York, and an even weaker reception in the rest of the country. The dramatic ad line, "For One Moment, They Hold History in Their Hands. With One Terrible Blow, They Make It," did nothing to save the film from the ignominious fate it so richly deserved. We originally caught the film during its first (and only) week at a theater near San Francisco. By the end of the showing, the restive crowd was registering its displeasure by hooting every other line, laughing at the "dramatic" highlights, and literally throwing popcorn boxes and candy wrappers in the direction of the screen.

SPECIAL AWARD

The Flak of the Year Award goes to Richard Burton's public relations man, whoever that might be, who manages somehow to keep the public convinced that Burton is a distinguished actor despite his seemingly endless series of screen disasters. Most major actors and actresses make one or two bad films in the course of a career. But it has been Burton's astonishing achievement to turn out one bomb after another with machine-like precision and regularity. In addition to this film, his screen dis-credits have included: *Boom!*, *The Sandpiper*, *Bluebeard*, *The VIP's Staircase*, *Hammersmith Is Out*, *The Rains of Ranchipur*, *The Klansman*, *The Comedians*, and that monumental turkey, *Cleopatra*. Congratulations, Richard, and keep up the good work.

The Italian singing-acting "discovery" Duilio Del Prete belting out a song about brighter tomorrows in Peter Bogdanovich's At Long Last Love. Perhaps critic John Simon best summed up Mr. Del Prete's unique appeal: "... with his thick accent and thin talent, he has as much charm as a broomstick with a smile painted on it."

AT LONG LAST LOVE (1975)

Directed by: PETER BOGDANOVICH
Written by: PETER BOGDANOVICH
Produced by: PETER BOGDANOVICH
Music supervised by: ARTIE BUTLER, with sixteen songs by COLE PORTER
Featuring: BURT REYNOLDS, CYBILL SHEPHERD, MADELINE KAHN, DUILIO DEL PRETE, EILEEN BRENNAN, JOHN HILLERMAN, MILDRED NATWICK

Twentieth Century-Fox

The Critics Rave

"The Turkey of the Year Award"
      —Michael Goodwin, *Take One*

"If this Peter Bogdanovich fiasco were any more of a dog, it would shed. . . . A movie that has been bombed by even the pushover critics and rejected by every film bootlegger. . . . The film cost $6 million—it looks like Fox spent $100 on Bogdanovich, $900 on Burt Reynolds and $5,999,000 on singing and dancing lessons for Cybill Shepherd."

      —John Barbour, *Los Angeles*

"*The Big Blooper of 1975.* . . . a colossal ego trip that leaves everyone stranded, actors and audiences alike."

      —Bruce Williamson, *Playboy*

"May be the worst movie musical of this—or any—decade . . . resounding dud. . . . Sitting through this movie is like having someone at a fancy Parisian restaurant who neither speaks nor reads French read out stentoriously the entire

Some of the precise, pinpoint choreography from At Long Last Love. *From left to right, Duilio Del Prete (watching his feet), Cybill Shepherd (watching Duilio Del Prete's feet), Burt Reynolds (doing stretching exercises), and Madeline Kahn (thinking about her next role).*

Those dancing fools—Eileen Brennan, Cybill Shepherd, and Madeline Kahn—living it up in the unforgettable powder room sequence from At Long Last Love.

long menu in his best Arkansas accent, occasionally interrupting himself to chortle at his cleverness. . . ."

—John Simon, *Esquire*

"A shameful failure . . . infantile . . . relentless vapidity. . . ."

—Pauline Kael, *The New Yorker*

"One of the Ten Worst Films of 1975."
—*Harvard Lampoon*

"One of the Ten Worst Films of 1975 . . . a bit of a mess. . . . Starring Cybill Shepherd and Burt Reynolds, who have, between them, four left feet and who sing with a gallantry that reminds me of small children taking their first solo swim across the deep end. . . ."

—Vincent Canby, *New York Times*

"The most perverse movie musical ever made . . . a colossal, overextravagant in-joke. . . . Every time his stars open their mouths or shake their legs, they trample on Cole Porter's grave . . . when the leads break into song and dance at a nightclub or a cotillion, the extras just stand there like goons, staring off into space; it's like watching a musical unfold within *The Night of the Living Dead.*"

—Frank Rich, *New Times*

"This Cole Porter coloring book, mounted with great expense and no taste, is one of those grand catastrophes that make audiences either hoot in derisive surprise or look away in embarrassment.

In dancing [the stars] resemble a troop of hikers trying to extinguish a campfire. The sets and costumes are of such resplendent ugliness that they go beyond campiness. . . ."

—Jay Cocks, *Time*

"This is failure so dismal that it goes beyond failure. The musical is not trash, exactly. Its rottenness lies in the pretension and inflated ego behind its conception, in its pandering to film-buff nostalgia, and in some of the sorriest casting ever to sink a production. . . ."

—Hollis Alpert, *Saturday Review*

"I think we bombed!!"
—Burt Reynolds, star of the film

Plot Summary

Michael Oliver Pritchard III (Burt Reynolds) is riding on the outside of his Rolls-Royce, hanging from the door. Pritchard is a rich heir who is bored with his 1930s life. Suddenly the car comes to a stop and Pritchard is thrown off wildly. He knocks over a woman and falls into her lap. They introduce themselves; she is a Broadway singer-comedienne named Kitty O'Kelley (Madeline Kahn). They immediately fall in love.

Johnny Spanish (Duilio Del Prete) is an Italian card shark who constantly breaks into song and discusses the current affairs of Little Orphan Annie. He obviously can't sing, and one of his poker-playing buddies forecasts audience response by saying, "Don't you hate a happy Italian?"

Johnny meets Brooke Carter (Cybill Shepherd), a spoiled heiress, at the racetrack, and offers to give her a ride in his car. As he croons to himself, Brooke asks, "You sing?" Johnny enthusiastically replies, "Oh, yes!" but the audience knowingly moans, "Oh, no!" The girl also happens to sing off-key, so they immediately fall in love.

Conveniently enough, Kitty O'Kelley and Brooke Carter were old school chums and they run into each other at one of Kitty's performances. They each introduce their newfound lovers and decide to get together at Pritchard's mansion. Brooke brings along her maid. The maid meets Pritchard's chauffeur-butler and they immediately fall in love.

The two rich couples go around to parties and dances and usually end up singing. This gives them an excuse to warble most of the sixteen (yes, that's right, sixteen) Cole Porter songs featured in the film and also to twitch spastically with their legs in actions that are supposed to resemble dancing. One of the songs sung by both the butler and the maid at the mansion is "But in the Morning No." As if it isn't bad enough the first time, the song is repeated *twice*.

Complications begin as the lovers slowly lose interest in one another and are more attracted to each other's lover. They finally switch lovers at a ball when the bandleader announces "Change partners!" After this film, the actors should have changed their names instead.

Unforgettable Performances

Leading critics have waxed so eloquent in reviewing the stars of this film that we could hardly improve on their descriptions.

Burt Reynolds "sings like Dean Martin with adenoids and dances like a drunk killing cockroaches."

—John Barbour, *Los Angeles*

Duilio Del Prete, as a merry Italian lothario, "might conceivably play a street arab, but in a sophisticated role, with his thick accent and thin talent, he has as much charm as a broomstick with a smile painted on it, and turns every Porter lyric into a verbal jigsaw puzzle we are supposed to piece together on the wing."

—John Simon, *Esquire*

"Duilio Del Prete, an Italian discovery, sings as if he came to paint the mansion and stayed on to regale the company with wobbly impersonations of Louis Jordan and Maurice Chevalier."

—Bruce Williamson, *Playboy*

"Duilio Del Prete (in the second male lead), an Italian with no voice, makes the elegant English of Cole Porter sound like pig Latin."

—Frank Rich, *New Times*

Cybill Shepherd is "a leading lady who can neither sing nor dance and who apparently thinks badinage is something you put on a small cut."

—Vincent Canby, *New York Times*

"Cybill Shepherd plays a poor little snotty rich girl with a notion of sophistication that is underpassed only by her acting ability. (I will not even sully my pen by making it describe her singing and dancing.) . . . In fact, she comes across like one of those inanimate objects, say, a cupboard or a grandfather clock, which is made in certain humorous shorts to act, through trick photography."

—John Simon, *Esquire*

"Her singing voice, which is as sing-songy as her speaking voice, causes one to yearn for the days when Marni Nixon dubbed in the songs of every tone-deaf Hollywood leading lady. . . . As for Shepherd's dancing, the best to be said is that it may not be recognizable as such: when this horsey ex-model starts prancing around, she tends to look as if she's fighting off a chronic case of trots."

—Frank Rich, *New Times*

"Cole Porter's music seems so effortless that some people think the songs can be sung by almost anybody. But 'almost' does not include Cybill Shepherd, the former (and future) model. . . ."

—Gene Shalit, *Ladies' Home Journal*

Immortal Dialogue

(Rodney, Michael Pritchard's manservant and chauffeur, is driving Pritchard in his Rolls-Royce, early in the morning.)

PRITCHARD: What time is it, Rod?

RODNEY: Six, sir.

PRITCHARD: Six?

RODNEY: Six.

PRITCHARD (lackadaisically): Ummm. I'm sick of six.

RODNEY: Sir?

PRITCHARD: Why isn't it seven? Or even eight?

RODNEY: Well, it was just five recently, sir, and six comes before seven. And eight.

PRITCHARD: Oh, yes. I suppose there's a logic to that somewhere. But it's too tiring to think about.

❈   ❈   ❈

(Brooke and her maid go to the races.)

MAN AT RACETRACK: Dames don't belong down here!

BROOKE'S MAID: Aw, go suck an egg!

❈   ❈   ❈

JOHNNY SPANISH: Did she get home safe? . . . Little Annie Orphan!

RODNEY: You mean the figure in the comics?

JOHNNY: Of course! She has been trying to return to her Daddy Warbucks for three weeks. Is no her *real* Daddy, because she is orphan—she no have Mama or Daddy.

❈   ❈   ❈

True Wit:

PRITCHARD (to Johnny Spanish): You know, Mr. Spanish, I've been thinking. You remind me of someone I'm quite fond of.

JOHNNY: Oh, yes—who?
PRITCHARD: Me.

⁂ ⁂ ⁂

The Story Behind the Film

Director Peter Bogdanovich is a past master at the deliberate imitation of 1930s entertainments. In his previous films *What's Up Doc?* and *Paper Moon* he scored immense popular triumphs by carefully revamping the old style and format. In *At Long Last Love,* he resolved to try the same approach and hoped to succeed on a grand scale. After all, with Cole Porter's ever popular songs, a host of lavish sets and costumes designed to appeal to the national nostalgia craze, and a big-name star like Burt Reynolds, how could he miss?

What Bogdanovich failed to consider was the mysterious jinx associated with the Cole Porter lyric that provided the film's title. The song "At Long Last Love" had been conceived under the most unpleasant circumstances imaginable. Cole Porter had been out riding one afternoon when his horse fell on top of him, breaking the composer's legs. While Porter waited for help to arrive, he composed the song in order to divert himself from his agony. Since that time, the song proved a hex to anyone who dared perform it. Bogdanovich's film has hardly served to break that string.

During the production of the film much was made of the fact that this was the first movie musical since 1932 in which all the songs were recorded live. Bogdanovich went to great lengths in working with his actors and technicians to achieve this feat, and then carefully supervised the later dubbing of the orchestrations. This was no doubt a daring and a noble effort, but judging from the results in the film, it will probably be another forty-three years before anyone tries it again.

Critics who panned this effort as a Bogdanovich ego trip would have been even more enraged if the director had gone ahead with his original plans for casting the film. At first he wanted to play the male lead-Burt Reynolds role himself, so that he could star opposite his girl friend and roommate Cybill Shepherd. He explained, "I was going to sing and dance and star with Cybill, but, Christ, the critics would kill me, so I'm using Elliott Gould." Nice try, Peter—but Gould shied away from the project and, at long last, Burt Reynolds was chosen for the part. His main qualification, it would seem, was that he was even less talented as a dancer-singer-actor than Peter Bogdanovich.

The Balance Sheet

Mention of *At Long Last Love* sparks people in the movie industry into talking disaster—and they don't mean flaming office buildings or crippled airplanes. The film cost Twentieth Century-Fox more than $6 million and has grossed a mere $1.5 million as a return on the investment. The studio tried its best to salvage this catastrophe: the film opened as the Easter attraction at Radio City Music Hall, but closed in less than a month. The heavy advertising proclaimed "A New Kind of Musical with 16 Great Songs!" and used the title of one of the Cole Porter songs to announce "It's the Top!" The promotional campaign was so elaborate, in fact, that one critic remarked it was too bad the studio couldn't release the various advertisements instead of the film. As it turned out, the only consolation for the producers of this film was that it offered a massive write-off for tax purposes.

THE BIG NOISE (1944)

Directed by: MALCOLM ST. CLAIR
Written by: SCOTT DARLING
Produced by: SOL M. WURTZEL
Featuring: STAN LAUREL, OLIVER HARDY, DORIS MERRICK, ARTHUR SPACE, ESTHER HOWARD, VEDA ANN BORG, BOBBY BLAKE, FRANK FENTON, JACK NORTON

Twentieth Century-Fox

The Critics Rave

"A *Groan.* . . . Even the most devoted patrons of Laurel and Hardy films will probably balk at the comics' latest cut-up, *The Big Noise.* . . . It has about as much humor in it as a six-foot hole in the ground. . . . The boys fumble weakly with old business for an hour and a quarter—and that is that. Once, long ago, it was funny to see them joust with wet paint and folding beds. But now it is dull and pathetic. And they don't even seem to care."
—Bosley Crowther, *New York Times*

"*The Big Noise* will have a tough time making the grade as comedy entertainment. . . . The laughs are few and far between. Flimsy yarn, drawn out to feature length with generous padding."
—*Independent Film Journal*

"Fails rather dismally. . . . From any comic consideration, it represents the last stop on a dead-end street."
—Howard Barnes, *New York Herald Tribune*

"A concoction of silly situations that may have been comical in their time; but certainly not in

Some of the "hilarious hijinx" in The Big Noise. *As critic Bosley Crowther observed, this film "has about as much humor in it as a six-foot hole in the ground."*

43

this day and age. Practically every gag the fat boy and his partner use in this melange has been used on the screen before. . . . An obviously poor screenplay."

—Variety

"Sank to a new low . . . probably the worst of all the full-length Laurel & Hardy films . . . pale and tedious."

—William K. Everson,
The Films of Laurel and Hardy

"Abominable by any standards. . . . Not only unfunny, but for anyone who loves Laurel and Hardy, very sad."

—Leonard Maltin, Movie Comedy Teams

Plot Summary

Stan Laurel and Oliver Hardy are janitors who work at a detective agency. Late one night af-
ter everyone else has left, the phone rings and they pick it up. On the line is an inventor named Alva P. Hartley, who wants to hire two detectives to guard his newest top-secret invention; a super-bomb that will allow America to win the war. (The film was prophetic in spite of itself.) Laurel and Hardy are so interested in this job that they decide to impersonate detectives and go out to Hartley's home. When they get there, they soon learn that they will be served a turkey dinner. In the dramatic highlight of his performance, Hardy's face lights up like that of an eager hog. What follows is a "hilarious" scene at dinner in which they are served turkey, mashed potatoes, Brussels sprouts, carrots, cranberry sauce and lemon meringue pie—all in the form of dehydrated pills, which they handle using tweezers as utensils (yuk, yuk). To show their frustration, the two stars spend several minutes making sour faces at each other.

Next door to inventor Hartley lives a gang of criminals. Somehow the gangsters find out about the bomb and want to steal it. Laurel and Hardy hide the bomb in an accordion and run off to the airport with it while the crooks follow closely behind. When our heroes reach the airport they hide inside a plane with the precious bomb. The plane they choose, however, is a radio-controlled target plane used by the Army to train its anti-aircraft gunners. After the plane takes off, one of the wings is quickly shot off. The fun-loving louts wisely decide to bail out, using parachutes they find on the plane. As they prepare to jump they spot a Japanese submarine in the ocean just below them. Hardy, a true patriot, drops the bomb on the submarine and scores a direct hit. And just think . . . it all started out when they tried to impersonate two detectives! (yawn). The dunderheads are commended for their heroic action in destroying the submarine, and everyone lives happily ever after. Believe it or not, that's all this film has to offer over the course of seventy-four minutes. But after all, it was wartime, with shortages in everything. Apparently Twentieth Century-Fox had already used up its ration of plot ideas before this dud was made.

Unforgettable Performances

In this film it is hard to determine who is worse—Stan Laurel or Oliver Hardy. In the last analysis we must recognize their harmonious teamwork and judge them equally bad. They walk through their parts with all the finesse and enthusiasm of two nervous schoolboys imitating the famous Laurel and Hardy for a sixth-grade talent show. In *The Big Noise*, Stan Laurel's whimpering and whining finally (and definitively) cross the border from the amusing to the purely irritating. His behavior and mannerisms are of the sort which would provoke any parent to child abuse. The familiar goony smiles suggest that what he is really doing is trying to quiet his hiccups . . . as if even he had a hard time digesting this moronic script.

Meanwhile Oliver Hardy's performance suggests a grouchy baby who has been awakened by colic from its afternoon nap. Not wishing to exert himself, Mr. Hardy relies on his bulging belly to produce laughs. It most certainly wobbles around impressively every time he appears on screen, especially when he wears his size 58 pajamas. This sort of humor, however, only carries him so far: after all, those who get off on obesity would do better to attend a local Weight Watchers meeting than to pay good money to see this film.

Esther Howard plays Aunt Sophie, the overweight, wealthy widow who casts loving eyes on the eligible Ollie. Apparently the producers of this film, hoping that one fat person could produce laughs, assumed that two fat people romantically interested in one another would provide double-bellied entertainment, ho-ho! They hardly reckoned with the deadly effect of Ms. Howard's wooden and inane screen presence. She fails miserably even in her attempt to provide us with a poor man's Margaret Dumont. As a caricature of a caricature she emerges only as a cipher, despite her frantic efforts to overact. From this film, Ms. Howard went on to a small part in *Dick Tracy Versus Cueball* (q.v.) and other similarly exciting screen ventures.

Immortal Dialogue

(Inventor Hartley has just acquired a valuable painting.)

OLLIE: My, what a beautiful picture.

HARTLEY: Yes—that cost a lot of money. It's a Vandyke.

STAN: A what?

HARTLEY: Vandyke. You know what a Vandyke is.

STAN: Oh, yeah—my uncle had one but he had to have it shaved off. You see it got—

OLLIE (shoving him): Shh!

STAN: What?

OLLIE: Vandyke was a painter—not a beard!

*　　*　　*

(Stan is bemused by Mr. Hartley's crazy inventions.)

STAN: You know what?

OLLIE: What?

STAN: I've got a clue. I think Mr. Hartley is just a little bit cracked. Well, I ought to know.

OLLIE: All inventors are like that—they're eccentric. They're not like you and me. They're different.

*　　*　　*

(Aunt Sophie falls in love with Ollie.)

SOPHIE: Oh, Mr. Hardy, you look so much like Romeo! Do you know, Mr. Hardy, you remind me so much of my dear departed husband.

OLLIE: Really?

SOPHIE: Would you like to see my album?

STAN (answering for Ollie): We'd love to.

OLLIE: Shh! Two is company!

*　　*　　*

(One of the desperate criminals shoves a gun into Ollie's bulging stomach.)

DUTCHY (to Stan): If you don't tell me where the bomb is I'll plug your friend here so full of holes he'll look like a Swiss cheese!

The Story Behind the Film

The Big Noise was shot in Arcadia and Monrovia (for the airport scene), California. In publi-cizing the film, the stars wanted to make clear that they were doing their best to aid the U.S. war effort. Stan Laurel reported, "We cut out automobile chases and food-wasting gags when the war first started, and with The Big Noise we decided to slash every gag that might conceivably have bearing on wartime wastages and destruction." He failed to comment on the gratuitous waste of film represented by this entire project. Because of the pious pretensions associated with the production, the crew on the film applied the rule that any destructive scene left for the sake of "story content" must be filmed in one take, so that no more than one wardrobe was ruined in a single gag. Apologists for Laurel and Hardy suggest that this might account for the amateurish production values in so many of the film's scenes.

One of the few distinctions of this dismal film is the fact that The Big Noise marked the first screen appearance of the popular song "Mairzy Doats." Stan Laurel plays it on his accordion before the bomb is hidden there. During production, the set of The Big Noise was continually besieged by players from other films who hoped to learn from the "antics" of the two masters in action. The only thing they might have learned is that it's best to stay away from scripts like this one.

The Balance Sheet

Producer Sol Wurtzel chose The Big Noise as his last (and least) film for Twentieth Century-Fox after thirty years with the studio. Even the moguls at Twentieth, not always noted for their perspicacity, realized that they had a turkey on their hands this time. The film ran on the bottom of dreary double bills when it was released. It provoked general disgust among critics and is now considered by most Laurel and Hardy enthusiasts to be the team's worst film. Laurel and Hardy went on to make three other films after this one—Nothing But Trouble, The Bullfighters, and Atoll K. None of them were particularly distinguished, but at least they represented steps up from The Big Noise. It was released in France under the title Quel Pétard! The English translation of that is What a Bomb! We certainly agree.

Phyllis Diller made her major film debut as Bob Hope's maid in Boy, Did I Get a Wrong Number! *An example of their sparkling repartee:*
  DILLER: How do you want your eggs?
  Poached, fried, or raw?
  HOPE: Scrambled—like your head.

Cesare Danova threatens old Ski Nose in Boy, Did I Get a Wrong Number! *"It Looks Like a Hopeless Case for Bob Hope This Time."*

BOY, DID I GET A WRONG NUMBER! (1966)

Directed by: GEORGE MARSHALL
Written by: BURT STYLER, ALBERT E. LE-WIN, and GEORGE KENNETT
Produced by: EDWARD SMALL
Music by: RICHARD LA SALLE and BY DUNHAM
Featuring: BOB HOPE, ELKE SOMMER, PHYLLIS DILLER, CESARE DANOVA, MARJORIE LORD, KELLY THORDSEN, BENNY BAKER, TERRY BURNHAM, JOYCE JAMESON and HARRY VON ZELL

United Artists

The Critics Rave

"Bomb: Lowest rating! . . . Absolutely painful. . . . *Boy, Did I Get a Wrong Number!* . . . They sure did: result is worthless film that should be avoided."

—Leonard Maltin, *TV Movies*

"Wretched . . . a store of one-line gags that often sound like a prelude to a friendly word from his sponsor."

—*Time*

"Feebly scripted and limply directed, this unhappy comedy does no credit to anyone involved in it."

—*Monthly Film Bulletin*

"A many-hued package of obvious and largely unfunny situations . . . dull . . . juvenile. . . ."

—A. H. Weiler, *New York Times*

"Lowest rating! . . . Poor Bob Hope entry . . . the script offers little in the way of funny lines."
—Steven H. Scheuer, *Movies on TV*

"Bottom-of-the-barrel. . . . Three scriptwriters are credited. They seem to have been vying to see who could write the worst jokes. Corny lines drop like bricks all over the place. . . . Phyllis Diller must contend with throwing away lines that should have really been thrown away, along with the film."

—*Cue*

"*Boy, Did I Get a Wrong Number!* . . . Boy, did he! . . . Flat, generally unfunny story. . . . Hope diehards may tolerate it. Others will find it a pain."
—Howard Thompson, *New York Times*

"It Looks Like a Hopeless Case for Bob Hope This Time."
—Advertisement for the film

Plot Summary

Didi (Elke Sommer) is a world-famous sex queen who comes to Hollywood in the hope of playing her first serious dramatic role. In the past, she has raised audience temperatures with her steamy bubble baths, but when she finds that her new Hollywood script calls for another sexy soak she is hurt and disappointed. She runs off the studio set crying, "No more bubble bath!" and runs into her dressing room. Her boy friend is also the director of her film. His name is Pepe Pepponi (Cesare Danova), the famed European filmmaker. Aggravated by taking too many bubble baths, Didi then runs away and hides. A newspaper headline reads DIVINE DIDI DISAPPEARS.

Meanwhile, Tom Meade (Bob Hope), an unlucky real estate agent (would you buy a used house from this man?), is placing a call to his wife at the beauty salon. He wonders out loud, "What are they doing to my wife that's taking her so long? Teasing her follicles?" At that moment, the switchboard operator mixes up the phone number of the beauty salon and connects Meade with a hotel instead. The Divine Didi happens to be in that very hotel, and Meade is somehow connected to her room. When Meade speaks to her, he realizes that he is speaking to the bubble-brain, bubble-bath queen. He slobbers into his telephone receiver, "You're her! You're that dame! The biggest thing in bathtubs since rings!" She admits her true identity and tells Meade that she needs a small secluded place to stay. Meade comes up with the brilliant idea of letting her stay in a backwoods cottage that he's been trying to sell. He reasons that after Didi has stayed there the place will become a national tourist spot and maybe even a shrine. Then it would be easy to sell the cabin to someone. He describes the house to her: "And what a view! All you can see for miles and miles is—miles and miles!" Meanwhile, Meade's housemaid (Phyllis Diller) has been listening to his conversation on an extension line.

Much later, Pepe Pepponi discovers that Didi is living in the cabin. Pepe and the police tirelessly search for her, but she is nowhere to be found. They do find her car at the bottom of the lake and find some blood on the floor in the cabin. They assume that she has been murdered and their first suspect is—yep!—Tom Meade. They bring Meade to the cabin and force a confession out of him. His housemaid speeds down to the cabin on her motorcycle. While the police aren't looking, she escapes with Meade. Meade drives off in one of the police cars, and a chase ensues. This lame sequence suggests that the makers of this film were still stumbling over technical problems solved successfully by the Keystone Kops some fifty years before. Not only does the chase fail in its role as the comic highlight of the film but it even fails to generate the thrills provided by a fourth-rate driver training film.

The chase ends as all the cars drive into a warehouse that is filled, inexplicably, with bubbles. Apparently Didi was in the back seat of Meade's car all along and is not dead. Thank goodness! The automobile in the lake was a result of a car accident and the blood that was found on the cabin's floor was from a small cut she got on her finger. Everybody is happy. Didi and Pepe Pepponi embrace and they decide to get married. Pepe promises her that he'll never direct another film which will require her to take a bubble bath. All of a sudden, Meade's housemaid emerges from the warehouse bubbles, trying to look seductive.

She shouts to Pepe, "You! If you're looking for another bubble girl, I'm ready!" The words "The End" flash on the screen as bubbles fall from the air on top of the entire cast. A more appropriate ending would be to have a *Godfather* hit man walk onto the set and gun down the entire cast.

Unforgettable Performances

In *Boy, Did I Get a Wrong Number!* a movie producer complains, "All I ask is that someday they invent a way we can make pictures without actors!" Considering the acting in this film, that would be a fantastic idea.

When Bob Hope first appears, a jazzy big-beat band plays the film's theme song, and Hope almost swivels his hips in time to the rhythm. He enters the film with a large grin on his face as if he expects to be greeted with a round of applause, but he would be fortunate if he received only a few catcalls and hoots. In this film, he delivers his one-liners holding a drink in one hand and waiting for giggles from the audience, but they never materialize. "Don't lose your head" (ha, ha,) "you might" (get ready for this) "you might need it" (chuckle) "for—HALLOWEEN!" (hee, hee.) At times, even a few supporting players look at each other in astonishment at Hope's horrible delivery.

Throughout the film Phyllis Diller constantly laughs as if she were a wild orangutan. She's not much of an orangutan, mind you, and not much of an actress either. Her lines are shot straight into the camera while she guffaws noisily at the splendid wit of the scriptwriters. Her delivery suggests a drunken amateur auditioner for a third-rate radio play. In one of her worst scenes we see her listening to a rock 'n' roll song on the radio while scrubbing dishes in the kitchen. Suddenly she takes some plates and starts waving them around. We finally realize that she is trying to do a Watusi while holding a plate in each hand. She begins to rub her behind with one of the plates and leers suggestively at the audience.

Asking Elke Sommer to play a flighty French sex queen is like asking a Doberman pinscher to play a poodle. She tries her best to give her German accent a hint of Gay Paree, but the result is

Bob Hope tries to hide "bubble-bath queen" Elke Sommer from his unsuspecting wife Marjorie Lord.

an unintelligible garble that suggests only an Esperanto accent. She constantly begins her sentences with "Didi" instead of "I." For instance, "Didi not take bubble bath!" She appears to have prepared for this role at a school of international elocution in which Dondi (q.v.) is the chief instructor. Ms. Sommer also gets a chance to throw a couple of temper tantrums; these usually result from taking too many bubble baths. When she gets mad, the hilarity begins. She yells as if she were a sick sea lion in mating season. In a scene with Bob Hope, she goes berserk and stomps her feet on a newspaper on the floor, crying, "Men! Men! Men!" As Hope leaves the room, she flings some paraphernalia at the door and falls to the ground. On all fours, she pounds her fists and kicks her feet into the rug furiously. After five minutes of this, she stops and says dumbfoundedly, "But what am I yelling at Monsieur Tom Meade for?"

Immortal Dialogue

PEPE (angrily to Didi): Who discovered you? Who made you the Divine Didi?
DIDI: I made myself Didi!

＊ ＊ ＊

DIDI (after getting harsh treatment from Pepe):
You know that I am of royal blood! Everybody
knows that Didi comes from a noble line!
PEPE: You come from a noble line, all right. A
noble line a sailor gave your foolish mother!

＊ ＊ ＊

(Didi is a little worried about living alone in
Meade's cabin.)
DIDI: What if something goes wrong?
MEADE: Well, everything's practically new; ex-
cept the water pipes hum a little, but they're on
key.

＊ ＊ ＊

MEADE'S HOUSEMAID (Phyllis Diller): How
do you want your eggs? Poached, fried, or raw?
MEADE: Scrambled—like your head.

＊ ＊ ＊

HOUSEMAID (noticing lipstick on Meade's
cheek): What's this?
MEADE (suddenly noticing it): I hope it's
blood.
HOUSEMAID: If your wife sees it, it will be.

＊ ＊ ＊

(Meade's pre-teen daughter has picked up some
new lingo.)
DAUGHTER: Gee, Mom, you look real groovy.
Gee, Dad, you look real beat.

＊ ＊ ＊

DIDI (getting mad at Tom Meade): You get
away from me, you phony-baloney! You liar
you!

＊ ＊ ＊

MEADE (to housemaid): What kind of a mood
was Martha in when she got home?
HOUSEMAID: She was so mad at you I couldn't
tell.

MEADE: Well, at least she still loves me enough
to hate me.

＊ ＊ ＊

The Story Behind the Film

Phyllis Diller makes her major film debut in *Boy,
Did I Get a Wrong Number!* Before this film
she had appeared in a cameo role in Elia
Kazan's *Splendor in the Grass* and had co-
starred with Jack E. Leonard in a quickie
called *The Fat Spy.* Bob Hope actually helped
discover her—and so must bear much of the responsibility for all the pain she has inflicted
since.

The film was based on an original story by
George Beck. Three screenwriters—Bud Styler,
Albert E. Lewin, and George Kennett—labored
(Huff! Puff!) over the screenplay. Edward
Small (his last name is always printed in BIG
letters in the credits) served as producer. He
also helped assemble that timeless bomb *Solomon
and Sheba* (q.v.).

The Balance Sheet

Boy, Did I Get a Wrong Number! was released in
June of 1966. Among the phrases in the advertising campaign was "No More Bubble Bath,
She Screamed." The distributor, United Artists,
suggested that the theater managers could set
up an old bathtub in the lobby of the theater.
Then a local bikini girl might be persuaded to
"bubble-bathe" for the edification of the theater's patrons. Another suggestion was the idea
of a Phyllis Diller hairdo contest. After all, this
was the era of the Beatles and the hair revolution, and the producers may have figured that
any insanity might catch on. Astounding as it
seems, *Boy, Did I Get a Wrong Number!* did
exceptional business at the end of its run. It
grossed more than $4.4 million and was the
last—and very much the least—Bob Hope film to
make big money. It must have been all those bikini girls splashing away in the theater tubs.

BRING ME THE HEAD OF ALFREDO GARCIA (1974)

Gig Young brings frightening intensity to his role as a hired killer in Sam Peckinpah's Bring Me the Head of Alfredo Garcia.

Directed by: SAM PECKINPAH
Written by: GORDON DAWSON and SAM PECKINPAH
Story by: FRANK KOWALSKI and SAM PECK-INPAH
Produced by: MARTIN BAUM
Music by: JERRY FIELDING
Featuring: WARREN OATES, ISELA VEGA, GIG YOUNG, ROBERT WEBBER, HELMUT DANTINE, EMILIO FERNANDEZ, KRIS KRISTOFFERSON

United Artists

The Critics Rave

". . . turgid melodrama at its worst. . . ."
—*Variety*

". . . an all-out preposterous horror. . . . Peckinpah clearly doesn't lack talent; what he lacks is brains."
—John Simon, *Esquire*

". . . an exercise in manic machismo . . . so witless you can't believe it was made by the man who directed *The Wild Bunch*."
—Vincent Canby, *New York Times*

"*Bring Me the Head of Alfredo Garcia* is a catastrophe so huge that those who once ranked Peckinpah with Hemingway may now invoke Mickey Spillane. Sam recently told an interviewer, 'I used to hit people . . . now my right hand feels like mush.' So does this film."
—Michael Sragow, *New York*

Warren Oates is so deeply involved in his search for the head of Alfredo Garcia that he fails to notice the evil menace that looms up behind him.

". . . ragged and desultory . . . a private bit of self-mockery."

—Jay Cocks, *Time*

"*Alfredo Garcia* is the work of a talented filmmaker who has grown more and more childish with time . . . should fail to rouse most audiences out of a stupor."

—Frank Rich, *New Times*

"A Peckinpah (pecker-in-paw?) adventure in full color and full buzz (flies try to feast on a bloody head wrapped in cheesecloth). Lots of shoot-outs, fuck-ups, one attempted rape, and one picnic . . . it seemed to be painted on as the film ran through the projector."

—Rosalyn Drexler, *Vogue*

". . . the only kind of analysis it really invites is psychoanalysis. . . ."

—Joy Gould Boyum, *Wall Street Journal*

"Few movies are as tedious. Bring me the head of the studio that released this one."

—Gene Shalit, *Ladies' Home Journal*

Plot Summary

A young, pregnant woman sits on the bank of a small lake; ducks paddle gently through the leaf-sprinkled water, smaller birds twitter in the lush foliage, and a soft voice is heard humming to the tinkle of a Mexican guitar. But no, this is not a Walt Disney nature film (the photography isn't nearly good enough), this is another Sam Peckinpah line-'em-up-shoot-'em-down-but-in-slow-motion pseudo-Western.

A man appears and tells the young woman that her father wants to see her. She enters a nineteenth-century Mexican hacienda, where her father, El Zefe (Emilio Fernandez), is waiting behind an imposing wood-carved desk. "Who is the father?" he demands coldly in Spanish. When his daughter refuses to reply, he nods to his henchmen, who rip open the girl's blouse and then break one of her arms. As we hear the bone snap, she agonizingly yells, "Alfredo Garcia!" Now the Latin American top banana turns to his toughest-looking honchos and coolly announces, "Bring me the head of Alfredo Garcia" (clever way to get a title, yes?).

Suddenly we are greeted by zooming sports

cars and Lear jets, and we realize that this movie takes place in the present. El Zefe promises $1 million for Alfredo's head, and gangster upon gangster assembles to hunt the bounty. Two homosexual hoodlums (Gig Young and Robert Webber) enter a dive in Mexico City and find our hero (for lack of a better word), Bennie (Warren Oates). He is sitting behind the bar playing the piano, sporting a nubby set of whiskers and enormous smudged sunglasses. He has lived in Mexico for six years but speaks no Spanish (and very poor English). The gay gangsters offer Bennie $10,000 for the head of Alfredo Garcia.

Bennie runs home to tell this exciting news to his girl friend, Elita (Isela Vega), a lady of *la noche*. Elita, who had known Garcia on a "professional" basis, informs Bennie that poor Alfredo has already been killed while drunk in an automobile accident. Does that mean that the next hour and a half is going to be spent hunting down a corpse, bringing back the severed head, and collecting a reward? You bet your sweet vomit bag it does. And along the way, Elita is almost raped by two motorcycle-riding toughies straight out of a Hell's Angels movie,

Bennie has to kill off everyone else competing to find Garcia's noggin, and Elita is eventually killed, too. By the time Bennie goes to collect the reward, he has killed so many people that he can't stop until he finds out why the head is so important. He kills the merry mobsters who sent him out in the first place, then their higher-ups, and finally he even plugs old El Zefe, who wouldn't even take the head (and who could blame him?). It's unfortunate that El Zefe's henchmen gun Bennie down, because he had so much momentum going that he would otherwise have gotten right to the person really responsible for the whole fiasco: Sam Peckinpah.

Unforgettable Performances

One would never guess that a two-hour movie could seem like an entire weekend. All the action shots are in slow motion. Cars slam into each other with the force of sponge rubber, victims ooze blood and guts having the consistency of molasses, and when anyone is shot down he falls as if he was tumbling through outer space.

Warren Oates doesn't help the speed of this picture either. He—speaks—very—slowly, attaching great emphasis to words such as "and," "the," and "by." He meanders around as if drunk—which may have been the only way they could get him to make the movie. He is seldom aroused to anger, and when he does finally lose his temper (as in the scene with the motorcycle riders), he says things like, "You guys are definitely on my shit list." After Elita is killed, he makes the long ride back home alone, with the head of Alfredo Garcia wrapped in a burlap pillowcase rolling around on the front seat of the car. As he drives he talks to it as though it were his best buddy. He takes a swig of vodka, then pours the rest onto the head and mutters heartily, "Have a drink, Al!" He stops every once in a while at a motel or bar to give the head a shower and change the ice it's packed in, as if he were changing diapers on a baby. But despite his care in keeping ol' Al's head on ice, the flies (which play a starring role in this movie) swarm around persistently. Since everything else in this film moves so slowly, the flies buzzing around at full speed manage to upstage the entire cast, including Warren Oates.

Isela Vega, the "romantic" lead, seems to have difficulty keeping her clothes on. Her constant, methodical disrobing is about as sexy and provocative as a peephole view of a women's wrestling team locker room. Every time she gets Bennie into a motel room—wham! off with the clothes. When Kris Kristofferson comes to rape her, zip, zip!—off comes the blouse. Her behavior, one would think, should make Oates just a little suspicious of his honeybunch, but perhaps he's already so infatuated with the cranium he's after that he just doesn't notice.

Emilio Fernandez as El Zefe is one of the great "nodders" of all time (albeit not as great as the audience nodding off to sleep). He has his henchmen so well trained that they act at the slightest twitch of his head. One twitch might mean, "Bring me my cigars!" while another means "Break my daughter's arms!" One shudders to think what would happen when he only nods yes.

Kris Kristofferson makes a cameo appearance as a Hell's Angels type hood. Looking somewhat like a hirsute pickle (one wonders if he really has a chin under that beard), he attempts to rape Ms. Vega, but is so surprised when she whips her blouse off of her own volition that he's stricken with impotence. A good whiff of this picture would do that to the best of us.

Immortal Dialogue

BENNIE (to the head of Alfredo Garcia, rolling around on the car seat): Al, it wasn't your fault. I'm sorry.

*   *   *

Love Scene (under a tree while a Mexican guitar strums in the background):
ELITA: Have you really thought about marrying me? I mean seriously.
BENNIE: Yes I have.
 (Long pause.)
ELITA: How come we've never married?
BENNIE: I don't know.
 (Longer pause.)
ELITA: Ask me, Bennie. Ask me.
 (Excruciatingly long pause.)
BENNIE: Will you marry me?
ELITA: (sobs effusively.)

*   *   *

BENNIE (to Elita): He loved you . . . think he'd care if his head could bring you everything you wanted?

*   *   *

ELITA: Bennie, I don't know how you're gonna get money from a dead body . . .
BENNIE: I take 'em the proof . . . his head.
ELITA: How, Bennie? You're mad!
BENNIE: He's dead! Shut up! I'm sick of it now, the whole way 'round. Listen—the Church cuts off the feet, fingers, and any other goddamned thing from the saints, don't they? Now Alfredo's our savior—he's the saint of money, and I'm going to borrow his head.

The Story Behind the Film

While *Bring Me the Head of Alfredo Garcia* was in production it caused a scandal in Hollywood. Director Peckinpah was quoted as saying, "For me, Hollywood no longer exists. It's past history. . . . Look at M-G-M—it's now in the hotel business, and maybe their old directors can get jobs as bellhops. . . . I've decided to stay in Mexico because I believe I can make my pictures there with greater freedom." Peckinpah was accused of making a "runaway" film, one that is shot in another country because the labor there is cheaper. The National Conference of Motion Picture and Television Unions condemned Peckinpah for his "disgraceful attitude" toward making films in the United States. Peckinpah denied the charges, saying, "This isn't a runaway production. The entire story is set in Mexico. They don't even know what the film's about. They don't seem to understand that pictures have to be made with people and places all over the world. It's a disgrace for the unions to have made such accusations. If they want to boycott me for making pictures in Mexico, let them." He added that another one of his films, *Pat Garrett and Billy the Kid*, was shot in Mexico "because they thought it would be cheaper south of the border. That could have been called a runaway production, not this." The National Conference formally censured Peckinpah for his remarks, but they withdrew their threat to picket the film. They left that task to outraged audiences who had seen the movie.

From the looks of the film, Mexican labor isn't the only thing that's cheap. Microphones bob in and out of the picture. Every room used appears to be the same one with different wallpaper. As well, the same motley band of Mexican peasants appears everywhere, like Coca-Cola and McDonald's.

The Balance Sheet

Bring Me the Head of Alfredo Garcia earned a hefty $578,596 by the end of its fourth week, and rose to number nineteen before sinking into a well-deserved oblivion.

Some officials cited the film as the end of the star system. Kris Kristofferson, who usually earns $150,000 per picture, Gig Young, who gets $125,000, and Robert Webber, $75,000, all made the film for minimum pay. Judging from their performances, though, even that was too much.

West Germany, the country that banned *Enter the Dragon*, a maladroit martial arts film featuring Bruce Lee, confiscated the Peckinpah film because it was a "glorification of brutality." The Perónist government in Argentina banned the film, condemning it as "offensive to morals and good behavior." The film is hardly deserving of that much attention.

The promotional campaign—as with so many of the Fifty Worst—was ambitious. One ad called the film a "New Classic in the Mold of *Treasure of the Sierra Madre*," but in truth the only similarity is that they both take place in Mexico. The same advertisement sums up the case for this movie by saying, "It's Got Guts." And blood. And flies. And sadism. And naked women. But no point, no sense, and no sensibility.

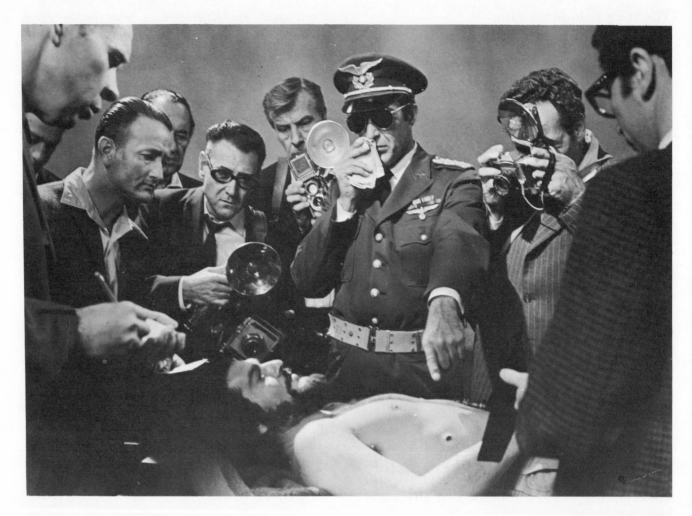

A colonel in the Bolivian army
shows reporters the bullet-riddled
body of Che Guevara. For actor
Omar Sharif, who portrayed the
famed revolutionary, this is the
most convincing moment of his
performance.

Omar Sharif as Che Guevara and
Jack Palance (yes, Jack Palance) as
Fidel Castro co-star in the insipid
historical melodrama Che! As
Guevara so well expresses it in one
of the film's many poetic lines:
"The peasant is like a wild flower
in the forest, and the revolutionary
like a bee. Neither can survive or
propagate without the other."

CHE! (1969)

Directed by: RICHARD FLEISCHER
Written by: MICHAEL WILSON and SY BART-
LETT
Produced by: SY BARTLETT
Music by: LALO SCHIFRIN
Featuring: OMAR SHARIF, JACK PALANCE,
CESARE DANOVA, ROBERT LOGGIA,
WOODY STRODE, BARBARA LUNA, FRANK
SILVERA, ALBERT PAULSEN, LINDA
MARSH, PERRY LOPEZ

Twentieth Century-Fox

The Critics Rave

"Stinkeroo. . . . All this movie inspires
toward the Cuban Revolution is excruciating
boredom, accompanied with nausea."
—Roger Ebert, *Chicago Sun-Times*

"Grotesque . . . unbelievably contrived. . . ."
—David Pirie, *Monthly Film Bulletin*

"A flop. . . . Omar Sharif can no more in-
terpret the fiery revolutionary than Elvis Presley
could portray Lenin. . . ."
—Sherwood Ross, *Christian Century*

"Perfectly awful. . . . A sort of Dumb Kid's
Comic Book History of What a Five-Year-Old
Might Think Happened in Cuba and Brazil
maybe. You don't have to see *Che!* to disbelieve
it."
—Judith Crist, *New York*

"A script that never rises above banality. . . ."
—William Wolf, *Cue*

"More like grave robbers than biographers. . . ."
—*Playboy*

"A notably asinine bit of Hollywood claptrap. . . . It's a stupid, offensive film about an interesting, important subject. Everyone connected with it deserves censure."
—Steven H. Scheuer, *Movies on TV*

"The cost in dollars was 5 million. And I hope Fox loses every penny of it. Director Fleischer's galumphing attempt to substitute monkey glands for ideology. . . ."
—Raymond A. Sokolov, *Newsweek*

"The consistency of strained spinach . . . actually seems to diminish the sum total of knowledge with which one enters the theater. . . . A timeless, placeless jumble. . . ."
—Vincent Canby, *New York Times*

"It is a pity that the actors could not grow insight or force along with their beards. If anyone doubts Che's death he has only to look at the celluloid coffin that bears his name."
—*Time*

"BOMB: Lowest rating. . . . one of the biggest film jokes of 1960s. However, you haven't lived until you see Palance play Fidel Castro."
—Leonard Maltin, *TV Movies*

"Frequently becomes ludicrous . . . laughable. Retakes should have been done on numerous scenes in which the lighting by photographer Charles Wheeler seems more appropriate to a comedy than a political drama. . . ."
—*Variety*

"Goes at the pace of a drugged ox . . . it hasn't an ounce of political or historical sense in its nut."
—Penelope Gilliatt, *The New Yorker*

"The film is so bleached, so thoroughly castrated, there isn't much fun in mocking it."
—Stanley Kauffmann, *The New Republic*

. . . AND our special recognition for the lonely courage of *Los Angeles Times* critic Kevin Thomas, who wrote:
"Fairly absorbing . . . a well-structured, well-directed effort. Palance and especially Sharif are forceful . . . a commendable undertaking reflecting a concern for topicality all too rare in Hollywood."

Plot Summary

Che! opens with a shot of Guevara's bullet-riddled body—Omar Sharif's best acting in the film. The basic structure (if you can call it that) is quickly established as we are treated to a series of "cinéma vérité" interviews with ninth-rate actors representing people who knew the famed Cuban revolutionary. These actors narrate the film, talking directly into the camera, their faces solemn, saying things like, "Let me tell you something," or "Excuse me for a moment," or "If you tell anyone I said this, I'll call you a liar."

With more of this brutal realism still to come, we go back to the beginning of Che's revolutionary career, as he hikes in the jungle with Castro's revolutionary troops. These smiling louts seem considerably less earnest than the Caribbean revolutionaries who appeared in Woody Allen's more recent film *Bananas*. Fidel Castro (Jack Palance) furthers the resemblance by yelling to his cadres, "You've committed every blunder in the book."

Che is the mid-mannered army doctor who finally makes it big with his fellows by heaving a Molotov cocktail into an enemy structure. This is followed by a "witty" sequence (but who needs comic relief here?) in which Che yanks out one of Castro's teeth. A bottle of Metaxa is used as a pain reliever. After this experience, Castro orders Che to give up his career in medicine and concentrate on revolution. . . . When a girl asks Che how he feels about the suggestion, Sharif replies, "How can I answer that? Maybe Fidel knows me better than I know myself."

With such incisive reasoning, how can the revolution fail? Che and Fidel march into Havana, but the charms of the big city are no match for their jolly days in the jungle. As Che comments pensively, "It took two years to reach Havana, and after two days I'm sick of it."

Tired of playing second fiddle to an actor so obviously incompetent as Jack Palance, Che decides to pack his bags and clear out. In an interminable scene, possibly suggested by the polular "Can This Marriage Be Saved?" column in *Ladies'*

Home Journal, Fidel pleads for understanding: "Che, Cuba needs you! I need you." They stand side by side on a balcony, gazing meaningfully at one another until Che concludes, "This conversation is pointless. Goodbye, Fidel." In a last desperate attempt to keep him in Cuba, Castro shouts, "I see it all now! You want it to be your own show—all the way!" but Che walks out and slams the door. Apparently the marriage cannot be saved. Castro, almost in tears, stumbles back to his chair, and like an alcoholic wife, reaches for his bottle of brandy.

Next Che leads a starving band of revolutionaries in Bolivia. In one of the narrative interviews an actor asks the audience, "Do you realize what chronic malnutrition does to a man?" Guevara at this point is also suffering from a terrible case of asthma—a true historical fact, folks. To make sure that we all get the point we see Sharif constantly huffing and puffing, sustaining enough heavy breathing for a dozen obscene phone calls. With all this noise he is an easy target for a Bolivian patrol, and is soon captured. He has an incisive debate with a Bolivian officer who disapproves of Che's revolution. The officer reasons, "You cannot cure the illnesses of the universe with blood and violence," to which Che responds, "Can you cure the illnesses of your people with cruelty and oppression?"

To prove his point, the officer introduces Che to a local goatherd with a white scraggly beard, dressed as if he just emerged from a midday nap on a park bench. The officer asks the old man why he turned Che over to the authorities when Guevara was actually planning to liberate all the kindly old peasants. "To free *me*? From what?" the old man asks. "Nobody asked me what I want! Ever since you come to these mountains with your guns and your fighting, my goats—they not make milk. You frighten them. You stink of death." By now the Bolivian officer is tired of the whole movie, and in order to expedite its end, executes Che with five shots from his revolver.

We now return to the opening scene, with members of the press standing around Guevara's corpse, snapping photographs. A reporter asks the colonel in charge if he can explain why so many people are gathered in this place. The colonel responds, with the movie's last harrowing words, "You're an American journalist. Why do people in your country flock to see a dead gangster?" Why indeed.

Unforgettable Performances

At the opening of the film Omar Sharif's impersonation of Che's dead body is entirely credible. Unfortunately, this high point is spoiled as his voice comes onto a sound track, murmuring Che's "philosophy," in tones reminiscent of a sleepwalking Desi Arnaz.

In discussing his approach to his role Sharif admitted, "Having this facial resemblance, I'm trying not to do much more. I'm taking all the craft from the acting, just leaving the bare bones." This is all too painfully true. The most zealous impression Sharif can render under all that make-up is that of a melancholy circus clown—complete with drooping eyes and a gigantic frown. At times he has all the convincing mannerisms of a wind-up toy.

In this film Jack Palance indeed bears a strong resemblance to Fidel Castro; in fact, his make-up seems to have been done by Madame Tussaud. At time it seems she may have also served as his acting coach. His voice sounds somewhere between James Cagney's and Marlon Brando's. He constantly puffs up his cheeks, closes his eyes, beams a daffy grin, and looks as if he is about to fall asleep. It was rumored that during the production Palance requested changes in the script to reduce Castro's "buffoonery." Apparently he gave up at some point and decided to act his part as a natural fool. One can easily imagine him wearing cap and bells throughout the movie. In the filming of one of Castro's more dramatic public speeches, four hundred Puerto Ricans were used as a listening crowd. Joseph Morgenstern of *Newsweek* attended Palance's re-enactment and reported that "the crowd keeps mostly mum except for giggles."

Immortal Dialogue

FIDEL (watching Che fall behind on a hike): Stragglers are sure to die, don't you know that?
CHE: I'm not a straggler. I'm your rear guard.
FIDEL: No you're not, you're the company doctor. See what you can do for the men with blistered feet. You've got ten minutes.
CHE (noticing the enemy planes flying over-

head): It's too late for chiropody. The buzzards are already circling.

*   *   *

CHE (instructing the hapless rebel army): The peasant is like a wild flower in the forest, and the revolutionary like a bee. Neither can survive or propagate without the other. There is one essential difference between us and the bees, however. In this hive, I *will not* tolerate drones!

*   *   *

CHE (explaining why he must leave Fidel): When we lost the missiles, Cuba lost its promise. My departure is long overdue.
FIDEL: Yes, I know, I know! You've told me! Things are moving too slowly for you here. You've told me a dozen times! . . . Che, sometimes I don't understand you!

*   *   *

INTERVIEWEE (reflecting about Che): Sometimes, I loved him. Sometimes, I hated him and wanted to kill him. But I always respected him.

*   *   *

CHE (asking one of his Bolivian revolutionaries if he is a traitor): Are you one of them, Antonio? You know, you reek of disenchantment.
ANTONIO: Yes, I am disenchanted. . . .
CHE (slapping him): Why you degenerate!
ANTONIO: Degenerate? You're a fine one to talk! . . . You don't love my people—you despise them!
CHE: Get out of my sight!

The Story Behind the Film

Che!, a Twentieth Century-Fox release, cost $6 million. It was originally planned as a project by Darryl F. Zanuck (Fox's president) when he realized the "tremendous appeal" of Guevara's life story. Zanuck hired Sy Bartlett (who had a record of long associations with Latin American peoples, and spoke Spanish fluently) to produce the film. Bartlett interviewed over one hundred people who had some connection with Che. The author of *Twelve O'Clock High* and *The Big Country*, Bartlett wrote his screenplay based on these in-

terviews. Richard Fleischer, the director of such other wonderful films as *The Vikings, The Boston Strangler, Soylent Green, Mr. Majestyk, The Don Is Dead, Tora! Tora! Tora!, Dr. Dolittle,* and *Mandingo* (need we continue?), agreed to direct the film and said that he thought of Che Guevara as "a handsome, sexy guy."

The film's Cuban scenes were shot in Ponce, Puerto Rico, and the Bolivian scenes at the Twentieth Century-Fox ranch in Malibu, California. During the filming in Puerto Rico, three hundred townspeople were hired to play themselves and one hundred were hired to play guerrillas. The hundred partisans were given costumes, beards, weapons, and cigars in order to make them look authenic. The cigar bills eventually ran up to $100 a day. Realism was stressed down to Jack Palance's nose, which was made specially by a German make-up man, and replaced on each day of shooting.

The Balance Sheet

Che! is that rarest of birds: a major studio film that proved a complete bomb critically as well as at the box office. The production cost of *Che!* was $2.8 million, and the film grossed only $2 million, a loss of $.8 million. When released, it was advertised with the lines "Separates the Man from the Myth" and "With a Dream of Justice, He Created A Nightmare of Violence!" The film was almost unanimously panned by the critics. *Filmfacts*, a magazine devoted to summaries of and critical response to new films, analyzed the reactions of twelve major film critics to the film. The result: zero favorable, one mixed, and eleven negative. The audiences didn't like the film much either. It was banned in Mexico and picketed in New York. A week after its opening, seven Molotov cocktails were thrown over the wall surrounding the Twentieth Century-Fox Studios on Pico Boulevard in West Los Angeles. In downtown Los Angeles, two men set fire to a theater where the film was scheduled to run. Two sticks of dynamite had been thrown into the theater, but the fire had been extinguished before the dynamite could be kindled. It is impossible to determine whether this hostile response was inspired by political—or artistic—considerations.

THE CONQUEROR (1956)

A HOWARD HUGHES PRESENTATION
Directed by: DICK POWELL
Written by: OSCAR MILLARD
Produced by: DICK POWELL
Featuring: JOHN WAYNE, SUSAN HAYWARD, PEDRO ARMENDARIZ, AGNES MOOREHEAD, THOMAS GOMEZ, JOHN HOYT, WILLIAM CONRAD, LEE VAN CLEEF

RKO Radio Pictures

The Critics Rave

A moment of sizzling passion between Genghis Khan (John Wayne) and the Princess Bortai (Susan Hayward). Quoth the Duke: "I feel this Tartar woman is for me, and my blood says, take her!"

"A substandard horse opera featuring John Wayne as Genghis Khan, Susan Hayward as his hot but reluctant bride and almost all of the Utah beyond Salt Lake City as the Gobi Desert. History has not been well served and neither has the popcorn public."

—Robert Hatch, *The Nation*

"A technicolored cloud of charming horsemen, childish dialogue and rudimentary romance. It is simply an Oriental Western. An illusion persists that this Genghis Khan is merely Hopalong Cassidy in Cathay. Should get a few unintentional laughs. . . ."

—A. H. Weiler, *New York Times*

"Wayne . . . portrays the great conqueror as a sort of cross between a square-shootin' sheriff and a Mongolian idiot. The idea is good for a couple of snickers, but after that it never Waynes but it bores. . . . The terror of two continents takes almost two full hours to win one girl, so the script just skips the conquest of Asia. It apparently wasn't very important, anyway."

—*Time*

"The most preposterous piece of casting since the same actor turned up last year as a German raider captain. A well-nigh perfectly horrible example of Hollywood's prostitution of history. . . . It is full of Minsky-oriented dancing girls and passion and sadism for their own sakes, and its script is strictly a Grade B Western set in Asia. Its performances are ludicrously bad."

—Moira Walsh, *America*

"Pure Hollywood moonshine. . . . When the film is not concerned with Mr. Wayne's skirmishes with the Tartar's daughter—she keeps trying to slit his throat and chop his head off even after he has declared that she is his wife—it's occupied with mad cavalry charges in what purports to be the Gobi Desert. You never saw so many horses falling down in your life. Still, even though their tumbling is far superior to the antics of the actors, it presently becomes tiresome. Susan Hayward, cast as Mr. Wayne's cutie, seems a rather odd Tartar, what with her red hair and fair skin. But then, Mr. Wayne seems a rather odd Mongolian."

—John McCarten, *The New Yorker*

"As a story, it's just about as silly as they come. As literature, it's strictly on the comic strip adventure level. . . ."

—*Cue*

"Unfortunately, money can't buy basic ingredients like a good script. . . . When the principals go into their tent or palaces to talk things over in flowery dialogue like twelfth-century Omar Khayyams, *The Conqueror* becomes a comedy rather than an epic adventure film. . . ."

—*Los Angeles Mirror-News*

"Absurd. . . . The intimate scenes sound more like those of high-school students declaiming than real-life historical characters."

—Philip T. Hartung, *Commonweal*

"A series of headlong mounted encounters—one of which looks very much like another—interrupted by intervals of treachery, torture, and an occasional spot of Oriental dancing, Grauman's Chinese style. . . . It must have required a

great deal of time to create a movie picture that is so full of action without motivation, spectacle without humanity, sound and fury without point. . . . After all, Genghis Khan was something more than a scowling, barbaric oaf."

—John Beaufort, *Christian Science Monitor*

"The script, by Oscar Millard, is so hopeless only one actor had enough craft integrity to even try (John Hoyt, who played a shaman). The others, including John Wayne, Susan Hayward, and Agnes Moorehead, didn't even bother to dissimulate their disinterest. . . . Pretentious. . . . A fatuity."

—*Films in Review*

"*The Conqueror* was a debacle. Critics hooted it down and audiences laughed at it."

—Maurice Zolotow, *Shooting Star:
A Biography of John Wayne*

"A monument to bad taste. . . . One of Wayne's worst. . . . He . . . simply shudders when anyone mentioned this film."

—Alan G. Barbour, *The Films of John Wayne*

Plot Summary:

The Tartar princess Bortai (Susan Hayward—that's right, redheaded Susan Hayward) is traveling by royal caravan across the Gobi Desert. Suddenly a cloud of dust appears on the horizon and the thunder of approaching hoofbeats is heard. Is it Errol Flynn and the 7th Cavalry? Close, but no cigar. It's Duke Wayne as the Mongolian brigand Temujin, along with his ruthless horde of bored extras. Wayne blinks his eyes, and looks around for the stagecoach, but when he finds only an Oriental caravan he naturally orders his men to begin a massacre. Bortai scolds him for slaughtering her best guards (after all, those bloodstains will never wash out of the livery) but Temujin just stares at her, grunting and licking his chops. We wonder whether he is planning to eat her or rape her, but this being Hollywood in the mid-1950's he does neither. He merely seizes her in his brawny arms and falls head over heels in love. He decides to propose marriage, but since Bortai needs time to make up her mind, the Conqueror kidnaps her in the interim.

In the scenes that follow, Bortai passionately resists Temujin's grubby advances, and tries to murder him at every opportunity. At times, their domestic squabbles resemble a caveman version of "I Love Lucy." Temujin, however, is not about to give up. After all, as John Wayne eloquently declares, "I am Temujin—barbarian—I fight! I love! I conquer—like a barbarian! . . . The world? I will take it! The woman? I will tame her!" In the interest of achieving this worthy goal, our hero drags his unwilling captive (not to mention the unwilling audience) to his grand palace to watch his dancing girls perform. The show that follows bears an odd resemblance to Las Vegas' Flamingo Review and no wonder it fails to seduce Bortai, or anyone else.

Finally Bortai concedes that her brute captor means business and in one of the more dramatic switcheroos since Christine Jorgensen came out of surgery she throws herself willingly at his feet. "To reach his arms I'd betray my people into Mongol bondage!" she warbles. Her father, a Tartar leader, is furious when he hears of this latest development. After all, Temujin never even came over for dinner to meet the family. The angry Papa mounts a massive campaign to discipline his lusty son-in-law. It just so happens that this same Tartar chief had previously murdered Temujin's father, so the resulting gigantic battle is something of a grudge match. Okay, Duke, let's win this one for the Gipper. On the eve of the big game, Temujin prays for victory. "Eternal skies," he begs, "send me men!" The eternal skies do the best they can, and send him whole squadrons of stumbling horses. Every other second in the battle sequence we see a mount keeling over, and this spectacle is surpassed in hilarity only by the piercing moans of the dying extras. To no one's surprise, the final score shows Temujin 63, Tartars 14, and the fans give him a standing ovation. Since our barbarian hero is too old for the Heisman trophy, his followers award him instead the honorary title Genghis Khan. It is with this glorious handle, and the beauteous Bortai in his saddlebags, that our hero rides off into the sunset and onto the pages of history.

Unforgettable Performances

In this film, John Wayne does his part for East-West understanding by combining slanted eyes and a droopy Charlie Chan moustache with the slow drawl and bowlegged stride of his role in *Fort Apache*. To make sure that no one misunderstood his ridiculous intentions, the Duke announced beforehand that "*The Conqueror* is a Western in some ways. The way the screenplay reads, it is a cowboy picture and that is how I am going to play Genghis Khan. I see him as a gunfighter," We'd hate to put him up against Paladin, because this particular gunfighter is so slow on the draw—particularly when it comes to picking up his lines. Wayne does most of his communicating through a series of grunts. Perhaps the director forgot to explain to him the difference between a Mongol and a mongoloid. For his tender love scenes with Bortai, Wayne resorts to the "me Tarzan you Jane" school of romantic patter. For this remarkable performance, Wayne received memorable support from the RKO costume department. Often he wears an Eskimo shirt and baggy pants. At other times he dons a metal helmet with a spike on top, an Arabian sheet that flows from his helmet to his shoulders, and a necklace that more closely resembles a Mexican bandito's ammunition belt. Mr. Wayne is perhaps a little too old to be dressing up for Halloween.

As Bortai, Susan Hayward succeeds in striking a number of risqué poses. She suggests an inexperienced model going through her paces for a still photographer rather than a motion picture actress in a starring role. Considering her formidable natural assets, it is hard to believe that Miss Hayward nearly succeeds in making herself undesirable, but her portrayal of a hot-blooded and untamed princess suggests a grouchy wife who has just gotten up on the wrong side of the bed with her hair full of curlers and a hangover to boot.

Agnes Moorehead, as Temujin's mother and the wise old Mongol matriarch, nearly manages to steal the show. Her imitation of a talking prune is absolutely extraordinary.

Immortal Dialogue

(*Temujin's Mother Complains About Her Boy*:)
MOTHER (Agnes Moorehead): My son has won the world; still he must conquer that red-headed Jezebel!

    ❄   ❄   ❄

BORTAI: The Conqueror? Mighty armies cannot stop him! But one touch of my lips. . . . Yes, he captured me—but he cannot tame me!

    ❄   ❄   ❄

TEMUJIN (to Bortai's Tartar father): While I live, while my blood burns hot, your daughter is not safe in her tent!

    ❄   ❄   ❄

Duke Wayne in the most unforgettable role of his career —as Genghis Khan, the fastest sword in the East.

Our boy Genghis avenges his father's murder in mortal combat with the evil Kumlek (Ted De Corsia). Just one of the many stirring action scenes from Howard Hughes's production of The Conqueror.

(*Bortai tries to escape from Temujin's flaming passions.*)
TEMUJIN (threatening her): I stole you! I will keep you! Before the sun sets you will come willingly to my arms!

    ❄   ❄   ❄

(*Temujin is surrounded by menacing enemies.*)
TEMUJIN: Come and take me, mongrels—if you dare! . . . While I have fingers to grasp a sword, and eyes to see your cowardly faces, your treacherous heads will not be safe on your shoulders! For I am Temujin, the Conqueror! No prison can hold me! No army defeat me!

    ❄   ❄   ❄

(*Temujin's mother disapproves of his aggressiveness.*)
MOTHER: She will bring woe to you and your people, my son! A woman made wife against her will can be a dangerous foe!
TEMUJIN: For good or ill—she is my destiny.

    ❄   ❄   ❄

(*Temujin soliloquizes about his lust for Bortai.*)
TEMUJIN: I feel this Tartar woman is for me, and my blood says, take her! . . . There are moments for wisdom and moments when I listen to my blood; my blood says, take this Tartar woman!

    ❄   ❄   ❄

(*Bortai tries to kill Temujin.*)
BORTAI (while lunging at him): For me, there is no peace while you live, Mongol!
TEMUJIN (recognizing how awfully cute she

looks when she's mad): You're beautiful in your wrath!!

＊   ＊   ＊

The Story Behind the Film

Long before this film was actually made, John Wayne had committed himself to an RKO project with former actor Dick Powell directing. One day Wayne strode into Powell's office and happened to pick up a script that was lying around called *The Conqueror*. The Duke quickly decided that he loved the material, and he later told Powell that he wanted to change their original plans and do that picture. "At first I was surprised," Powell recalled. "Wayne as the barbarous Genghis Khan? I asked him if he was serious and he said he was. I was unprepared for the situation but John was insistent. . . . Who am I to turn down Wayne?"

To prepare for his role, Wayne went on a crash diet and at one point was gobbling Dexedrine tablets four times a day. Susan Hayward took her part somewhat less seriously. She was quoted as saying, "I had hysterics all through that one. Every time we did a scene, I dissolved in laughter. Me, a red-haired Tartar princess! It looked like some wild Irishman had stopped off on the road to Old Cathay."

The Conqueror was the last film personally produced by the legendary Howard Hughes. It was also the most expensive production to date for Hughes's RKO Radio Pictures. The palace scenes and other interiors were shot on a sound stage. For their Gobi Desert, director Powell and his helpers searched over eight states by plane, helicopter, car, and half-track until they found the "perfect location." It was St. George, Utah. Indians from a nearby reservation were used as extras in the film to portray the Mongolian hordes. After all, anthropologists tell us that American Indians were probably descended from Central Asian peoples, so why not? The Indians received $10 a day on foot, $12 a day when they rode horses, and their presence on location must have made Wayne, the veteran cowboy star, feel right at home.

RKO paid the state of Utah to construct fifteen miles of special roads to reach the remote canyons used in the filming. An army of more than 560 RKO craftsmen and actors were brought back and forth to their motels by more than a dozen school buses. (Where were the anti-busing protesters when we really needed them?) Sixty huts, which comprised the Tartar village, were constructed in Hollywood and then transported all the way to Utah. Accommodations were made for 900 horses, 500 oxen, 200 goats and sheep, 12 snakes, 4 pumas, 2 camels, a black leopard, a dancing bear, and John Wayne. No animals or men were hurt during the entire filming and a representative from the SPCA was on the set at all times. One man did, however, rip his pants.

In the course of the film, Susan Hayward danced on screen for the first time in her career. To prepare for this epochal event, the star received six weeks of dancing lessons. It looked as if the make-up artists at RKO would require a similar length of time to prepare Wayne for his part. Director Powell was naturally the first one privileged to catch a glimpse of the Duke's new image. When asked by reporters how Wayne looked as Genghis Khan, Powell replied, "Murderous. Just murderous."

The Balance Sheet

It was John Wayne who first came up with the brilliant idea that *The Conqueror* should receive its world premiere in Moscow. After all, much of the action of the movie was supposed to have taken place in what is now present-day Russia. Moreover, a U.S.S.R. premiere might give the Duke a chance to punch out a few prominent Commies. Before RKO could go ahead with these grandiose plans, the Russian Embassy in Washington, D.C., demanded an advance, private screening. After viewing the film, the Soviet diplomats said "*Nyet!*" to the whole idea of a Moscow performance. Subsequently, the film was banned in Russia. This angry reaction had nothing to do with artistic considerations. The Red bureaucrats simply decided that the story of a love affair between a Mongol and a Tartar would prove too inflammatory for Russian audiences.

As it turned out, the film received premieres in thirty different world capitals: no one ever accused Howard Hughes of being a piker. Wayne attended the London premiere, and then went on to lend his name to many of the dozens of shoddy promotional gimmicks adopted by RKO. One such idea suggested posting a picture of John Wayne at the Traffic Control Department of each city in which the film played. The illustration would bear the caption, "JOHN WAYNE—THE CONQUEROR—SAYS YOU CAN CONQUER AUTO ACCIDENTS—BY DRIVING CAREFULLY." The `pressbook also suggested that local merchants be given pictures of Wayne's scowling visage in order to promote various products. For instance, "WOMEN'S WEAR: Things to Attract Your Conqueror! COSMETICS: The Lipstick That 'Conquers' All Day Long! DANCING SCHOOLS: Conquer the Most Difficult Steps! APPLIANCE STORES: The Conquerors of their field!" etc., etc.

A large number of asinine products were "inspired" by this film. Sea Nymph Swimsuits developed a gold-shot cotton "Conqueror Swimsuit." Wilson Brothers, a leading men's clothing manufacturer, came out with a new tie introduced as "THE CONQUEROR—By Special Appointment of RKO Radio Pictures." It sold for $2.50 and featured a design of Genghis Khan's warriors available in twelve different colors. Meanwhile, hair stylist Gabriel Garland introduced the "Conqueror Coiffure." This style consisted of three pigtails protruding from the back of a girl's head. The triple braids were "reined in by strands of pearls to achieve an effect that many Paris beauties copied."

Domestically, *The Conqueror* grossed only $4.5 million of its original $6 million cost, but its successful foreign run turned in a tidy profit. None of this mattered in the last analysis since Howard Hughes fell personally in love with his film. On lonely evenings, the eccentric billionaire showed the film over and over again, most often viewing it in glorious solitude. He felt such a strong personal attachment to this favorite project that he eventually shelled out some $12 million to buy up every existing print of the film. He refused to allow his masterpiece to be shown on television. For seventeen years, no one in the world was allowed to see the film except Hughes himself, until 1974, when Paramount secured rights to reissue it. At that time, *The Conqueror* played on a double bill with another Hughes-Wayne collaboration, *Jet Pilot*.

SPECIAL AWARD

The Joseph Goebbels Big Lie Award goes to Terry Turner, the PR genius at RKO Radio Pictures who devised most of the advertising for *The Conqueror*. RKO spent the staggering sum of $1.3 million to foist this turkey on an unwilling public, and the greater the popular resistance to the hard sell, the more hysterical the advertising campaign became. With few favorable notices to quote from, the RKO advertising men made up their own rave reviews. "MIGHTY IN SCOPE," proclaimed one of the ads. "When GREAT pictures are talked about, this one is mentioned first." "MIGHTY IN SPECTACLE," read another tag line, "Surpasses *anything* ever filmed." In case cynics out there still had doubts about the quality of Hughes's product, the RKO ad mill proudly announced, "SPECTACULAR as its barbaric passions and savage conquests. . . . One of the truly GREAT motion pictures of the past 20 years." Caught up in the fervor of his own hyperbole, Mr. Turner went on to award his producer and boss with a still greater accolade: "*The Conqueror* is probably the finest action picture ever made in Hollywood." Anyone who was naïve enough to take seriously these ludicrous pieces of RKO self-congratulation deserved the experience of watching this picture.

DAUGHTER OF THE JUNGLE (1949)

Directed by: GEORGE BLAIR
Written by: WILLIAM LIVELY from an original
story by SOL SHOR
Produced by: FRANKLIN ADREON
Featuring: LOIS HALL, JAMES CARDWELL,
SHELDON LEONARD, JIM NOLAN, and WIL-
LIAM WRIGHT

Republic Pictures

The Critics Rave

". . . the plot is preposterous, bolstered by some dialogue that might better have been reduced to monosyllables. Even the kids will hoot at this. The production is a shoddy piece of merchandise and the direction no better than uninspired. . . ."

—*The Hollywood Reporter*

". . . leaps broadly outside the realm of logic."
—*Variety*

"The amazing adventures of a female Tarzan."
—*The Monthly Film Bulletin*

Plot Summary

A small airplane runs out of gas over Africa and crash-lands in the "uncharted" jungle. Inside are two policemen transporting a Chicago-style gangster named Dalton Kraik (Sheldon Leonard) and his accomplice, Lamser. The cop in charge gets his chest crushed in the smashup, so his assistant, Paul Cooper (James Cardwell), a devilishly handsome fellow in a clean white sport shirt, takes charge of the mobsters. Suddenly the group is set upon by ferocious natives. But just as the situation looks grim for the white men, a familiar "ah-ee-ah-ee-ah-ee-ah-ee-ah" is heard. But that's

Police officer Paul Cooper (James Cardwell) struggles to bring law and order to darkest Africa in Daughter of the Jungle.

odd, Tarzan was no soprano—could it be that the apeman has had surgery in Denmark? Nosirree, this is the Daughter of the Jungle, Irene, called Takoora by the natives (Lois Hall). With pleated miniskirt, shaved legs, and fashionably coiffed hairdo, she swings down to the stranded foursome and saves them from the fierce (ha!) savages. Then she takes the grateful gang of cops and robbers back to her camp, where she lives with her father, Vincent Walker, a multimillionaire long believed to be dead, and his secretary, Carl Easton. The three have lived in the jungle for the past ten years. They too arrived by plane crash (it's the only way to fly), and are revered as gods (naturally) by the natives who have never seen a white man die. Walker is eager to keep that myth alive, and is none too happy when Takoora arrives with a dying policeman in her retinue. As soon as the cop pops off, Walker has him plowed under before the natives know the difference.

Mr. Walker, besides having an aversion to the non-living, has left a will back in the States stipulating that if his daughter doesn't claim her inheritance by the time she turns twenty-one, the entire Walker fortune goes to charity. And wouldn't you know it, Takoora is going to be twenty-one in only one month. Heavens to Murgatroyd. Paul, a red-blooded American boy, decides that it's a shame to let all that money go to charity, and cooks up a rescue plan. He figures that if he can get to the Ketobe River he can sail downstream for help.

But Dalton Kraik has other ideas. He approaches the secretary, who has spent the entire ten years making liquor out of leaves. The gangster has a plan to eliminate the rest of the group and show up in New York with a bogus Takoora to claim the Walker fortune.

And now for the native news. It seems that there are two warring factions in the wilds of the jungle. Liongo, the chief of the local tribe (Kiwanis can be found farther inland), has proclaimed Vincent Walker a wizard because he practices "good magic" ("He means the magic of boiled water and sanitation," explains Walker). But Chief Liongo is opposed by the old-fashioned voodoo-practicing witch doctor, Mahorib, who would do anything to prove that the white man is mortal, even kill him (if that doesn't prove it, nothing will).

So the whole merry group, with Takoora and Lamser (who has decided to go straight) in the lead, sets off in search of the Ketobe. Walker, too old for the journey, stays behind to await rescue. As the small safari jingles through the jungle they are set upon by a man in a gorilla suit, a lion, and an alligator, and when these don't work, Mahorib sets upon them with good old-fashioned bows and arrows. But somehow, all the bad guys are killed off (because the good guys have all the guns), and Paul, in unsoiled sport shirt, and Takoora, in equally unsoiled miniskirt, arrive together at the Ketobe. At this point the director apparently ran out of film, because "The End" abruptly appears on the screen.

Unforgettable Performances

Since all the natives in this film are protrayed by white actors, the viewer may be tempted to ask, "If all the actors are white, how do we tell the difference between the natives and the Americans?" Easy. All the "Africans" sport Elliott Gould style curls on their heads, a few bones around their necks, and finger-paint stripes on their noses. And for that touch of authenticity, they speak in a language somewhere between "ga-ga, goo-goo" and "ooga-booga." Check with your neighborhood anthropologist on that one.

As for the heroes: James Cardwell and Lois Hall appear to have recently swung out of the land of graham crackers and milk (low-fat). Swinging nimbly through the trees on vines (which hang out of every tree in this picture, including eucalyptus), Miss Hall takes as many opportunities as she can to unleash good old-fashioned bloodcurdling screams whenever anything, including her hair, is amiss. And Mr. Cardwell seems to be either bored or simply mentally retarded. He expresses no grave concern for his predicament, and seems preoccupied with keeping his shirt clean for Wednesday night bowling.

Immortal Dialogue

LIONGO: The great bird come, bwana!
WALKER: Yeah, we know, Liongo.

Takoora, the "Daughter of the Jungle," threatens Sheldon Leonard in the 1949 Republic Pictures saga. Leonard portrays Dalton Kraik, a vicious Chicago-style mobster, who ends up in the "uncharted" African jungle thanks to a timely plane crash.

❈   ❈   ❈

TAKOORA: Mahorib! Stop this. What will Liongo think?

MAHORIB: Ogah yogo magia.

TAKOORA: Harango!

MAHORIB: Hanama!

TAKOORA: Penagullem!

MAHORIB: No. White devils kill.

TAKOORA: You attacked them when they were in trouble.

MAHORIB: Mahorib kill. Great bird bring evil.

TAKOORA: A great bird brought my father. Dare you say to chief Liongo that Bwana Walker is evil? Order your warriors to stop the attack. Now!

❈   ❈   ❈

LAMSER: What kind of jungle is this?

KRAIK: I don't know, but I could learn to like it.

(Eats fruit of a wild bush.) These things are looscious.

LAMSER: Looscious—you mean they're deluscious.

KRAIK: What's the difference? Either way they're tasty.

❈   ❈   ❈

LIONGO: That white man still alive.

MAHORIB: Mahorib make voodoo. Death spirit come soon.

LIONGO: Liongo say no. He say white man god. White man no die.

MAHORIB: Liongo lie!

❈   ❈   ❈

TAKOORA: Oh, but now tell me of . . . tell me of home. About the things I've always dreamed of.

PAUL: Well, that's a pretty tough assignment.

TAKOORA: Oh, let's see. When we left, my favorite singer was Bing Crosby, and . . . and his song that I liked best was "Love in Bloom."

PAUL: Well, Bing's still king with lots of people.

TAKOORA: And then there was Shirley Temple, and . . . and ice skating in the park, and circuses, and . . . and new clothes every Easter. . . .

      ❖   ❖   ❖

Final Scene:

PAUL: Well, here we are at the Ketobe!

TAKOORA: The rest of the way should be easy for you, Paul. I'll go back and wait with Dad.

PAUL: Oh no you're not. I wouldn't let you go back through that jungle alone. You're goin' with me. We'll keep that date with your dad . . . together.

(Music swells—fade-out.)

      ❖   ❖   ❖

The Story Behind the Film

1949, when *Daughter of the Jungle* was made, was a big year for jungle pictures. Johnny Weissmuller gave up Tarzan to become Jungle Jim, Johnny Sheffield made his first appearance as Bomba the Jungle Boy, and Bud Abbott and Lou Costello made *Africa Screams*. As well, not one, but two jungle documentaries appeared, *Savage Splendor* and *Black Shadows*. And so, said *The Hollywood Reporter*, "It was inevitable that the current epidemic of jungle fever should spread to Republic." Republic Pictures, the studio that tried to strike it big with Orson Welles's *Macbeth*, was also responsible for quite a few low-budget Westerns.

A considerable amount of collaboration went into the picture, but from viewing it one gets the feeling that the collaborators were not exactly on speaking terms. The original story was conceived by Sol Shor, and the screenplay was "written" by William Lively, whose name is a prime example of false advertising. There were even two special-effects men—Howard and Theodore Lydecker. Their contributions to this film are not immediately apparent, unless they were responsible for giving permanents to the natives and draping vines from all the eucalyptus trees.

The Balance Sheet

"ACTION! ADVENTURE! JUNGLE EXCITEMENT AT FEVER PITCH!" screamed the ad lines for this cookie. The enthusiastic ad campaigns helped make the movie what it is today—one of those wonderful features that appear on television weeknights at four-thirty in the morning.

While most of the members of the cast are unknowns (and rightfully so), *Daughter of the Jungle* does boast one familiar face—Sheldon Leonard. Familiar to most motion picture and television audiences as a gangster a la Al Capone who spews snide remarks out of the corner of his mouth while chomping a cigar, Mr. Leonard has become one of the top producers in the television industry, with shows like "*I Spy*," "*The Dick Van Dyke Show*," and "*Gomer Pyle, USMC*" to his credit (?).

On the old "*Jack Benny Program*," he was the thug who sidled up to Benny at the racetrack to whisper, "Hey, bud." And he was Harry the Horse in the film version of *Guys and Dolls*, with Marlon Brando. *Los Angeles Times* reporter Don Page characterized Mr. Leonard as "so realistic that legitimate gangsters started emulating him. He became the pin-up boy of the Mafia." How did such a respectable actor wind up in *Daughter of the Jungle*? Leonard, a Phi Beta Kappa graduate of Syracuse University, explains, "I stepped right into the Depression when I got out of college. I was whirling like a log roller, trying to keep from drowning. Luckily, I got a job as a theater manager in '31 and did reasonably well. After that it was acting on Broadway until '39 when production dropped about 25 per cent. Staying one step ahead, I came to Hollywood when pictures were booming and did a lot of films." We were anxious to talk to him about the production secrets of *Daughter of the Jungle*, but he declined an interview. This might lead one to believe that he has forgotten having made the film, or wishes that he could.

DICK TRACY VERSUS CUEBALL
(1946)

Gripping suspense in Dick Tracy Versus Cueball. *As the super-sleuth surmises, "Well, it's quite obviously death by strangulation."*

Directed by: GORDON M. DOUGLAS
Written by: DANE LUSSIER and ROBERT E. KENT
Based on the comic strip by: CHESTER GOULD
Featuring: MORGAN CONWAY, ANNE JEF-FREYS, DICK WESSEL, LYLE LATELL, IAN KEITH, ESTHER HOWARD, RITA CORDAY, DOUGLAS WALTON, JOSEPH CREHAN, BYRON FOULGER, JIMMY CRANE, SKELTON KNAGGS

RKO Radio Pictures

The Critics Rave

"Two-dimensional police blotter nightmare. What was that about childish tastes for blood and gore?"

—*The Hollywood Reporter*

"Lurid . . . frankly quick."

—*Variety*

" . . . an assortment of grotesque killings."
—*Independent Film Journal*

"Cueball is always strangling somebody with a leather hatband and leaving corpses all over the place."

—*Film Daily*

"The estimable sleuth and his amiable side-kick, Pat Patton, had better go back where they belong if they don't want to lose a lot of friends."
—Thomas M. Pryor, *New York Times*

"Clues are handed to Dick Tracy on a plate and it would be difficult not to solve the crimes. The story is poorly constructed and full of flaws;

71

the acting is amateurish in the extreme and even Cueball's sinister appearance and behavior are soulless."

—*Monthly Film Bulletin*

Plot Summary

Cueball (Dick Wessel), a short little baldie in a smelly leather jacket, steals aboard a just-docked ocean liner and seeks out the stateroom of a messenger carrying $300,000 in diamonds. With as much insidiousness as he can muster, Cueball forces his way inside and says, "Gimme them diamonds. Gimme 'em. Hurry up!" The hapless go-between tries to call for help, Cueball whips off his hatband, and with nothing more than a muffled gurgle, his victim is strangled.

Hmm. This sounds like a job for Sherlock

The dashing detective Dick Tracy (Morgan Conway) relaxes with his sweetie, Tess Trueheart (Anne Jeffreys). "By a strange quirk," the star's press agent announced, "Conway's earliest ambition had been to be a member of the FBI."

Holmes and Dr. Watson—but this is a low-budget film, so we must settle for Dick Tracy (Morgan Conway), who bears a striking resemblance to Robert Young in "Father Knows Best," and Pat Patton (Lyle Latell), who's just plain embarrassing. Together they go through great pains to do wretched impersonations of the famed British duo.

Tracy is called from his own birthday celebration to investigate the murder. He zooms to the scene, carefully examines the corpse, and somberly pronounces, "Well, it's quite obviously death by strangulation." Master of deduction, this Dick Tracy.

Tracy and Patton take off for the offices of Jules Sparkle, the jeweler (with a name like that what else could he be?). Meanwhile, Cueball heads for his favorite night spot—the Dripping Dagger Saloon. There he meets Filthy Flora (Esther Howard), the owner, and tells her repeatedly, "I gotta have a place. I gotta have a place," sounding more and more like a recent college graduate talking to his parents. Flora offers him her Roman catacomb-like basement for $500 a night.

Cueball meets with a fence named—now get this—Percival Priceless in his room at the Dripping Dagger. Cueball happens to glance out the door and see Dick Tracy, who has trailed Priceless to the saloon. Cueball accuses Priceless of calling the cops, the hatband comes off—exit Percival Priceless.

Poor Flora finds the diamonds in Cueball's room and tucks them into her (ahem) bosom—but who should be looking in through the window but Cueball himself. He enters the room with a sinister expression: she reaches for her bosom, he reaches for his hatband—exit Filthy Flora. Tracy and Patton burst onto the scene, find the hatband next to Flora's body, and give chase to Cueball. Patton is driving and they, of course, end up in an accident. The car jumps the curb at sixty miles an hour and collides head on with a light pole. But this is the movies, and no one is injured. Cueball escapes into the night, luminating the darkness with his light-bulb-like pate. Tracy runs for a telephone, and Patton is arrested for drunk driving. Impersonating an actor would have been a more just charge.

Now the Dashing Dick is stumped. Who is that bald man, he wonders, and just why is he leaving his hatbands all over the place. At that moment,

one of Junior Tracy's little friends, Butch, bounds into the room in a cowboy outfit, shouting, "Stick 'em up, podner," Tracy notices the hatband on the little boy's hat. "Let me see that hatband, son!" he commands. "Oh that," says Junior, a little kid with a big mouth who says "Holy Smoke!" a lot. "All the kids have 'em." He shows Tracy an ad in a comic book for a genuine Indian leather hatband. The address is traced to a prison, and it turns out that the kids have been buying their hatbands from Cueball, who made them in the prison shop.

With this new information, the Daring Dick has an idea. He dresses up his wife, Tess Trueheart, as a woman of high society on the market for some very unusual diamonds, and hopes she'll connect with the culprit. Tess gets into a cab and, sure enough, guess who's driving—why, it's Cueball. He grabs her purse away from her to get the $300,-000 he thinks she has in her wallet (smart one, this guy), but finds a framed picture of her and Tracy instead. "Why you dirty double crosser," he grumbles, and goes for his hatband. But by now Tracy and Patton are wondering what's taking Tess so long, and take off to find her. They give chase, once again, to the elusive oddball. This chase is on foot—they jump from bridges onto trains, and then smack into the heart of a train yard. A gun battle ensues, and Cueball makes a break for it across the tracks, but his foot gets caught in the crossties, and just as the audience thinks to itself, "Don't tell me he's going to get mowed down by a train," he gets mowed down by a train. Case solved, or dismissed, or something. Thank goodness.

Unforgettable Performances

This is a low-budget film with even lower-budget actors. Dick Wessel, as Cueball, wears a bald wig that looks like an oversized bathing cap, and attempts to look tough with grimaces and sneers that would be more appropriate on a baby food jar. He speaks in monotoned, staccato spurts, and tries to dominate the other characters with lines like "All right, quit stalling. Let's have the dough" and "Why the dirty cheap double crosser." Wessel, listed in the actors' directory as a comedian, was the star of the "Riverboat" television series.

The only thing Morgan Conway has in common with Dick Tracy is his two-dimensionality. His screen presence is so pallid that he would have been better cast as the lead in *The Invisible Man*. It may seem impossible to be consistently upstaged by the likes of Dick Wessel, Lyle Latell, et al., but Conway shows that it can be done after all. His other screen triumphs include *Nurse from Brooklyn, Sinners in Paradise, Crime Ring*, and *Charlie Chan in Reno*.

Immortal Dialogue

DICK TRACY: Where have you been?
PAT PATTON: If I told you, you wouldn't believe me.
TRACY: Well, don't tell me.
PATTON: I'll tell you anyway.

*   *   *

PATTON: I called Sparkle's house. . . .
TRACY: Did you say who you were?
PATTON: No! You think I'm dumb?
TRACY: Well, we won't go into that!

*   *   *

LITTLE: Why you . . . you fool! You big, stupid, blundering fool!
CUEBALL: Shaddup!
LITTLE: You killed him . . . you murdered Abbott! Why did you kill him? Why? Why?
CUEBALL: 'Cause he was gonna plug me. Okay. I got the diamonds, where's my dough?
LITTLE: Keep the diamonds, go to the chair with them. I won't touch them.
CUEBALL: You rat!

*   *   *

The Story Behind the Film

Dick Tracy versus Cueball, based on characters from the comic strip by Chester Gould, was second in a series of four thrilling and chilling Dick Tracy feature films. The first film, also made in 1945 and also starring Morgan Conway, was titled *Dick Tracy—Detective*. In this immortal saga, the wonder sleuth tracks down the evil Splitface, a crazy fella on a murder rampage. *Cueball* was followed by *Dick Tracy Meets Gruesome*. Conway was replaced by Ralph Byrd (who looked quite a bit more like the cartoon character, which may or may not be a compliment), and Boris Karloff appeared as the maleficent Gruesome. In this film Detective Dick goes chasing after a quartet of robbers who utilize a new kind of paralyzing gas. That's probably the only way they could keep the audience from leaving their seats. The last film of the lot, *Dick Tracy's Dilemma*, again featured Ralph Byrd, and co-starred Lyle Latell (gosh, that man just doesn't give up).

For release of *Dick Tracy versus Cueball* the producers planned an ingenious promotional campaign. Ads appeared with headlines such as "Dick the Dauntless Dares Death to Deliver Diamonds!" and "Meet the Man You Love to Hate" (presumably the second headline refers to Cueball, not Dick Tracy). The filmmakers suggested that theater owners promote the film in conjunction with jewelers (put diamonds in the showcases surrounded by production stills) and barbers ("Don't be like Cueball—let us treat your hair!").

The Balance Sheet

For actor Morgan Conway, his starring role in *Dick Tracy versus Cueball* was a remarkable break. His agent proposed to make the most of his opportunity by issuing a lengthy press release that concentrated on Conway's personal qualities rather than his acting ability—for obvious reasons. "By a strange quirk, Conway's earliest ambition had been to be a member of the FBI. He read everything concerning the service and studies every FBI case whose history he could find. . . . He likes to attend prize fights. His favorite meal is rare roast beef, baked potatoes and fresh peas. He loves horses and dogs and can't stand people who pretend to be what they are not. Good, old-fashioned people are his favorite. . . . He is very friendly and has a large circle of friends. He prefers house parties to those in night spots, and thinks a Christmas Eve party with all the family present is the height of entertainment. . . . He dislikes too much make-up on a woman. He loves children and gets along famously with them. If he ever is wealthy he intends to finance orphan-

Mr. Conway has attained this worthy goal, but ages." History has not recorded whether or not the fact that *Cueball* achieved only a modest success, and that Conway was soon dropped from the series, can only leave us pessimistic.

SPECIAL AWARD

Skelton Knaggs, possibly one of the ugliest men in motion pictures, practically steals the film away with his brief appearance as Rudolph, an assistant baddy. His hair drips with oil, and he wears eyeglasses with lenses that appear to be made out of the bottoms of soda-pop bottles. His head is deformed, and his face is sadly corroded. A close-up of one of his cheeks might serve a low-budget producer as a facsimile of a telescopic photograph of the lunar surface. Yes, there is a resemblance to (melted) green cheese. His presence in this and many other films is convincing testimony to the fact that the glass used for camera lenses is indeed unbreakable. Few people have ever noticed the details of Mr. Knaggs' performance because viewers instinctively cover their faces whenever he appears on the screen. Billed in the actors' directory as a veteran of the British stage and screen, he has appeared in such other unforgettable films as *Chamber of Horrors*, *Island of the Dead*, and *Ghost Ship*.

For their generous use of Skelton Knaggs in *Dick Tracy Versus Cueball*, we present director Gordon M. Douglas and RKO Radio Pictures with the Hire the Handicapped—Good Citizenship Award.

The sadistic Cueball (Dick Wessel) prepares to strangle another victim: "Okay. I got the diamonds, where's my dough?"

DONDI (1961)

Directed by: ALBERT ZUGSMITH
Written by: ALBERT ZUGSMITH and GUS EDSON
Based on the comic strip by: GUS EDSON and IRWIN HASEN
Produced by: ALBERT ZUGSMITH and GUS EDSON
Music by: TOMMY MORGAN
Featuring: DAVID JANSSEN, PATTI PAGE, DAVID KORY, WALTER WINCHELL, ARNOLD STANG, ROBERT STRAUSS, GALE GORDON, MICKEY SHAUGHNESSY, LOUIS QUINN, DICK PATTERSON, SUSAN KELLY, JOHN MELFI, BONNIE SCOTT, WILLIAM WELLMAN, JR.

Allied Artists

The Critics Rave

"Insipid. . . . Dondi is played by one of the most untalented child performers ever to appear on the screen."
—Steven H. Scheuer, *Movies on TV*

". . . Trite and maudlin."
—James Powers, *The Hollywood Reporter*

"Intolerably sweet . . . syrupy . . . the lovableness bit simply grows intolerable."
—*Variety*

"So saccharinely cute that adults in the audience will be embarrassed before the film's half over . . . even the kiddies get restless. I'm not sure for whom Dondi was made."
—Phillip T. Hartung, *Commonweal*

Dondi, a wandering orphan boy, is shocked when he reads the newspaper and learns of his own disappearance. Concerning the outfit he is wearing—given to him by his "buddies" in the U.S. Army—the insufferable little bugger commented, "Maybe is too big—yes?"

"David Kory as 'Dondi' will steal your heart away in this once-in-a-lifetime picture."
—David Janssen in the preview trailer for *Dondi.*

"Watch this film and you'll know why Janssen became a fugitive! . . . Bomb: Lowest rating!"
—Leonard Maltin, *TV Movies*

Plot Summary

Christmas Eve. An Army meteorological station in Italy. Somewhere a radio is playing a jazzed-up version of "Jingle Bells" sung by (as billed in the promotional ads) "everybody's favorite girlfriend, the singing rage, Patti Page."

Inside the barracks, Peewee (Arnold Stang) is trimming a Christmas tree. Dealey (David Janssen) enters and announces his plans to hit the town. He tells Peewee, "While you're trimming your tree-sa/I'll be out dancing with Theresa!" Hoo-boy.

Meanwhile, a five-year-old boy stands outside looking through the window. Supposedly he is attracted by the sight of the Christmas tree. Dealey sees the kid and promptly accuses him of trying to steal some of the Army equipment left outside in the snow. The boy mumbles, "Not stealing—honest! Looking pretty tree. No okay looking at pretty tree, Mr. GI?" With those unforgettable lines, David Kory makes his screen debut, making each successive line equally unintelligible and fatuous. The boy approaches Peewee and asks permission to look at the Christmas tree. "Is looking tree is okay—no?" he asks. Peewee tells him that it's all right and asks him if he would like to help decorate the tree. "Oh goshers!" the boy enthusiastically exclaims ("P.U.!" the audience enthusiastically replies). Explaining why he is not at home in bed, the kid tells his heartrending life story, in prose of the same mushy consistency. He has no parents or relatives. He doesn't have a home; he takes care of himself and sleeps outside in the cold. He has no name and no decent clothes, and (horrors!) doesn't even know who Santa Claus is. Even worse, as it is later revealed in the film, he has never seen himself, except for

one time when he saw his reflection in a mud puddle.

The soldiers promise that he can sleep in the barracks. They obligingly give him cookies to eat while he exclaims with his mouth full, "Thanks, buddies!" Nothing like a little kid displaying masticated food to make an audience chuckle. The boy starts to eat with a cookie in each hand, taking a bite from one, and then the other. "Hey! He eats like there's no tomorrow!" remarks a soldier. Another soldier adds, "Yeah, looks like there wasn't much yesterdays, either!" Witty fellas, these soldiers.

A tough Army sergeant comes to the barracks and the soldiers try to hide the boy. They toss the waif around the room as the boy remarks, "Is swell ride—like airplane!" After the sergeant leaves, the soldiers try to get the kid some decent clothes. They outfit him in a GI uniform and cap, but the tot asks, "Maybe is too big—yes?" The soldiers don't know if he means the uniform or his mouth. Then they realize that they don't even have a name for the little fella. He adopts the name "Dondi" from a soldier's mispronunciation of "dandy" when he describes the boy as a "dandy kid." (What he probably meant was "*damned* kid.")

The soldiers are called back to America. The only problem is that they can't take Dondi with them. After a tearful parting, the soldiers board their ship only to find that "cute little Dondi" has stowed away. When the ship arrives in New York, the GI's lose Dondi in a crowd welcoming them back. While being pushed around in the crowd, Dondi whimpers, "Buddies! Where you are?! Is me—*Dondi!*" Having spent the entire boat ride with the little wretch, the soldiers know better than to reply. After he has lost his buddies, we see Dondi stumbling symbolically down a long, empty dock.

For the rest of the picture Dondi bumbles around New York. He wanders into Macy's and sees a television on display. He watches for a minute, and all of a sudden, there's a woman on the screen. It's Patti Page! Hmm, what a coincidence.

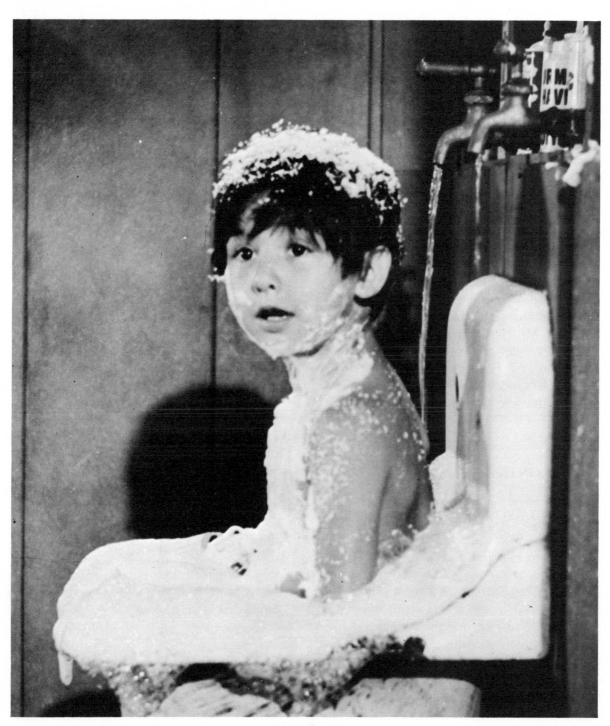

*Dondi (David Kory)
wanders into an army
barracks on Christmas
Eve and kindhearted
GI's give him a bath in a
sink. As the delighted
tyke is led to observe:
"Them soaps sure make
big bubbles!"*

While Dondi is busy with his wild adventures in Macy's, Dealey (remember?) and his girl friend are organizing a compaign to adopt Dondi as an American citizen. At the moment he is an illegal alien. But wait a second. Who is that woman playing Dealey's girl friend? Why, it's Patti Page again, kiddies! Together Dealey and his girlie inform the country of Dondi's fight for freedom. Dealey has printed up 500,000 stickers saying, "Save Dondi—Write Your Congressman!" He also has organized a "Dondi rally" at the Waldorf-Astoria. The headline on the *New York Daily News* reads DONDI MISSING. Walter Winchell makes a plea over the radio to Congress, asking that it adopt this courageous youngster. Explaining the big fuss, Dealey's girl friend states, "He's only five and we just can't afford a perceptive citizen like this get away from us!" [sic].

Dondi is then seen bumming the streets of New York with a dog (of the animal variety). They're both eventually spotted and taken to jail, where Dealey's girl friend visits him frequently. At long last, Congress grants Dondi his citizenship. Dealey and his tootsie pie decide to marry and adopt Dondi as their child.

"Come on, kid, we're taking you home," Dealey tels Dondi in jail. "Mr. Dog, too? Yes?" asks Dondi. "Yes, Mr. Dog, too," answers Dealey. Dondi yells "Yippie" and puts his arms around Dealey and his girl friend, hugging one, then the other, just as he munched the cookies the soldiers gave him. Dealey and his girl friend get the worst part of the bargain. They would have done better to leave the kid and take the dog.

Unforgettable Performances

The trouble with David Kory as Dondi is not so much that he is an inexperienced five-year-old making his "acting" debut, but that he is directed by a man with a five-year-old's maturity. Kory does, however, contribute his own share of nausea. His nasal voice makes him sound as though he has a bad cold, and the audience is forever wanting to blow its collective nose. With his puffed-up cheeks, large guilty eyes, and repulsive use of the English language, one can easily understand who no one has bothered to take care of the five-year-old orphan.

As Dealey's girl friend, Patti Page (the singing rage) floats through the film as if she accidentally wandered off the set of a Pepsodent commercial. Since her silly grin communicates so few emotions, the producer has let her sing three songs that express her deepest self: "Jingle Bells," "There's a Meadow in the Sky," and the heart-warming "Dondi, Little Dondi." (See IMMORTAL DIALOGUE.)

Even though *Dondi* is an adaptation of a comic strip, there's no excuse for Arnold Stang to be a cartoon character. Stang, as Peewee, incessantly looks pop-eyed and refers to his mama. He decorates Christmas trees, and seems to be the only one who really understands Dondi. The reason is obvious: their aptitudes are equal. In all fairness, though, Stang doesn't drool over his shirt, nor is he seen playing with a rattle in the film.

Immortal Dialogue

PATTI PAGE (talking to Louella Parsons about Dondi): How many people do you know can cross the Atlantic with only a hunk of Salami as luggage?

❋   ❋   ❋

(Peewee is trimming his Christmas tree on Christmas Eve.)
DEALEY (to Peewee): What do you say we stop all this tree-trimming jazz and hit the road to town?
PEEWEE: Oh now, Dealey, you know how I promised Mama about Christmas. You see, while she's trimming her tree in Peoria, I'm trimming mine right here. It's almost as if we're together!

❋   ❋   ❋

DONDI (seeing Dealey eating dinner): Goshers! Chow! Is sure smelling good, Mr. Dealey-Buddy! Is tasting good too?

❋   ❋   ❋

(The soldiers discuss Dondi's sad and sorry plight.)
PERKY (a soldier): The kid needs a mother. Ev-

ery kid needs a mother. Somebody to take his troubles to, or somebody to hear his prayers.

PEEWEE: Well, he could always bring his troubles to me. I'd be glad to hear his prayers. I like prayers.

SAMMYBOY (another soldier): You can't be no mother, Peewee! Mothers is female!

✺   ✺   ✺

Song: "Dondi, Little Dondi" (sung by Patti Page)

Dondi, oh Dondi,
Think of birds in the sky
Or a rainbow up high,
That's Dondi, little Dondi. . . .

His smile can chase the clouds
And brighten skies above
And every empty heart
Will fill up with love.

"Dealey-Buddy" (David Janssen), Dondi (David Kory), Patti Page, and "Mr. Dog-Buddy" are happily united in the heartwarming conclusion to Dondi. *As one critic observed, "Watch this film and you'll know why Janssen became a fugitive."*

81

DONDI (kneeling in prayer to God): I wish you make them let me stay in America, Mr. Big-Buddy, please.

PATTI PAGE (with tears in her eyes): Dondi's talking to the most influential friend of all!

The Story Behind the Film

Albert Zugsmith, the director, co-producer, and co-writer of *Dondi*, started his career with some respectable projects, and at one time even produced an Orson Welles film—*Touch of Evil*. Zugsmith went on to directing and producing sex and drug exploitation moves such as *High School Confidential, L.S.D., I Hate You, The Private Lives of Adam and Eve, The Incredible Sex Revolution*, and *The Rapist!* One of his masterpieces underwent an interesting series of title changes: from *Teacher Versus Sexpot* to *Sexpot Goes to College* to *Teacher Was a Sexpot* to *Sex Kittens Go to College*. Asked why he made these films Zugsmith said, "I wanted to change, but every time I'd suggest a property like *Gulliver's Travels*, the front office would say, 'Naw, make another picture like your last one—it made money.'" With *Dondi*, Zugsmith planned "wholesome movie entertainment the way it used to be when the big stars in movie town were the kids and Will Rogers."

In making *Dondi*, the biggest problem was finding someone to play the title role. A contest was advertised in all the newspapers that carried the comic strip, asking boys to send in their photographs to see who looked most like Dondi. More than 100,000 contestants applied. The pool was narrowed down to two: David Kory and Damon Lanza, the son of singer-actor Mario Lanza. David Kory was judged to look most like a cartoon and was given the part. Kory is the son of Diane Kory, an ex-Rockette. Young David was spotted playing in the street by a census taker and was brought to Zugsmith. The census taker was rewarded with the job of dialogue director for the film (honest). "Is making nice talky movie, maybe yes, Mr. Director-buddy?"

The Balance Sheet

Dondi was released in August of 1961 and producer Zugsmith thoughtfully arranged special screenings for theater managers and their children. A national magazine advertising campaign followed the film's release. Toy makers were induced to manufacture seventeen different Dondi-related items, ranging from Dondi paints and pencil sets to Dondi dolls and squeeze toys. With all this promotion, the film began showing a tidy profit and the ambitious producers dreamed of a sequel, again with David Kory, entitled *Dondi Goes Native in Brooklyn*. There was even talk of developing a Dondi television series. Fortunately, the entire Dondi epidemic came under control just in time, and the grandiose plans for profitable spin-offs never materialized.

SPECIAL AWARD

A slightly used monophonic recording of the Melachrino strings playing "Turkey in the Straw" goes to Tommy Morgan, composer of the film score. Morgan, a veteran mouth organist, composed and played the entire background score for *Dondi* on a single harmonica. *Variety* reported that this was "the first time harmonica has been used for a complete dramatic score." This innovation no doubt saved money for the artful producers, since a solo mouth organist can be hired at considerably less expense than a regular studio orchestra. Demonstrating unparalleled harmonica virtuosity, Morgan makes his instrument laugh, cry, gurgle, snicker, and cough at appropriate moments in the film. At each new twist of the plot, the harmonica expressively trembles "Wuh-oh," or with an explosion of cuteness from Dondi the instrument chortles, "Nya-nya-nya." Morgan's background score, in short, seems perfectly matched to the quality of the entertainment taking place on screen.

Beauty and the Beast: Marilyn Manning and Richard Kiel in a dramatic highlight from Eegah!

EEGAH! (1962)

Directed by NICHOLAS MERRIWETHER (ARCH W. HALL, SR.)
Written by: NICHOLAS MERRIWETHER and BOB WEHLING
Produced by: NICHOLAS MERRIWETHER
Music supplied by: ARCH W. HALL, JR., and THE ARCHERS
Featuring: ARCH W. HALL, JR., RICHARD KIEL, MARILYN MANNING, WILLIAM WATTERS (ARCH W. HALL, SR.), RAY STECKLER

Fairway-International

The Critics Rave

"Lowest rating. . . . Ridiculous thriller."
—Steven H. Scheuer, *Movies on TV*

"Home-movie time."
—Ed Naha, *Horrors from Screen to Scream*

"Humorous in spite of itself."
—Judith Crist, *TV Guide*

Plot Summary

Roxy Miller, the teen queen of Palm Springs, is driving across the desert one night when the headlights of her yellow sports car illuminate a prehistoric giant in the road. The car screeches to a halt and Roxy screams hysterically—but without the sound track her scream could be mistaken for a yawn, which would have been the appropriate response. The giant is dressed in a fasionable velour loincloth that also extends over one shoulder.

His scraggly fiber glass beard seems in imminent danger of falling off. As he raises his massive plastic club, Roxy manages to escape, running off to tell her father and her boy friend what she has seen. Her father, a noted writer of adventure books, decides to investigate for himself. The very next day he sets off to follow a trail of suspicious footprints. He is dressed in his best Captain Spaulding outfit, complete with pith helmet, safari shorts, camera, and canteen. As he pauses to photograph a smoking campfire, two hairy legs in a pair of cute black booties suddenly appear in his viewfinder. The adventurer screams; the caveman raises his club and prepares to make mincemeat of him; and the suspense is unbearable as both actors glance around uneasily, waiting for the scene to end.

We cut jerkily to a swimming pool back in Palm Springs in what must surely be the worst editing job of the century. Roxy is splashing around in the pool, displaying her breasts, while her boy friend, Tommy, serenades her from poolside, displaying his gap-toothed smile. After this musical-aquatic interlude, the two fun-loving youngsters suddenly become worried about Roxy's father. They ride out in Tommy's dune buggy to find dear old dad. We are treated to at least four different shots of the dune buggy going up the same hill while the sound track throbs with vintage '62 surfing music. Unable to locate Roxy's father, they spread out their sleeping bags (at least twenty feet apart—remember, this is a family picture) and bed down for the night. The caveman creeps up and drools for a while over the sleeping Roxy, but he is scared away when Tommy rolls over in his sleep and accidentally turns on his transistor radio. Next day, while Tommy is out exploring with shotgun in hand, our prehistoric friend takes advantage of the situation, grabs Roxy, and carries her off (after she conveniently faints). When she arrives in the "cave" (a backdrop of black rubber sheets decorated with Neolithic sketches) she is delighted to find her father there. His arm is in a sling, and she asks what happened. "I think I broke my collarbone," he answers, rubbing his elbow. Meanwhile, the troublesome giant is falling all over himself to be a gracious host. He brings Roxy a meaty bone and a drink from a sulfur spring that bubbles in the center of the set. Mr. Miller answers the question that is by now surely on everyone's mind: "It must be the sulfur in the walls of his cave that have kept this creature alive for all these years." Meanwhile, their host is rubbing his nose along Roxy's arm, sniffing her perfume, while keeping up a constant stream of gibberish and grunting, strongly suggestive of a demented cow. Roxy and her father deduce that their friend's name must be Eegah, since that is the word he pronounces most often.

For lack of anything better to do, Roxy has decided to give her father a shave and Eegah demands the same treatment. After a few swipes of the razor, his beard magically falls away, and he turns out to resemble a young Russ Tamblyn with acne. In fact, the monster is considerably more attractive than the male lead. He may be the only caveman in history with neatly parted, Brylcreemed hair. Through trickery, Roxy lures Eegah outside the cave. Tommy, who has been tramping around the desert, sees them from below and calls her name. Eegah responds by ripping off the top of Roxy's dress (revealing a blacklace camisole), which really sparks Tommy. In the ensuing fistfight, our plucky teen-ager miraculously defeats the prehistoric giant. Tommy, Roxy, and Mr. Miller then scramble for the dune buggy and take off. As they zoom into the desert, Roxy keeps her eyes transfixed on her primitive admirer: she can hardly control her emotions. Needless to say, Eegah is lovesick also and returns, limping, to his cave. Picking up the blue perfume-scented scarf Roxy has left behind, he raises it to his face and runs off tearfully in the direction of the city of Palm Springs as the camera goes into a melancholy and dramatic soft focus.

From here to the end of the film, Eegah follows the well-worn path originally blazed by *King Kong*, with the love-struck monster stumbling off to the big city in pursuit of his light-of-love. Eegah comes to a Palm Springs dinner club called The Cocktail Lounge, smashes through the back window, and storms down the hall. He ambles on to the dining room, which is filled with about twenty extras, many of whom have difficulty keeping straight faces. Half of them hardly look up from their plates and continue eating. Even Richard Kiel, the actor who plays Eegah, looks embarrassed as he grabs a juicy hunk of prime rib away from the chef and proceeds to devour it, caveman style.

The titanic struggle between the lovesick caveman, Eegah (Richard Kiel), and our youthful protagonist, Arch Hall, Jr.

We cut to a party, where Tommy's popular combo is entertaining Roxy, Mr. Miller, and about a dozen others. Tommy warns us about his group, "Man, do they swing!" They do indeed: dressed in tight dinner jackets they swing from side to side, up and down, backward and forward behind their twirling guitars as they provide an unforgettable musical experience entitled "Nobody Lives on the Brownsville Road."

As the music dies down, Eegah comes climbing over the fence behind the swimming pool to liven up the party. The police follow closely behind. Roxy screams, "Don't shoot—he doesn't understand!" But alas, it is too late. A policeman fires his revolver, and Eegah collapses into the pool with an enormous splash. "Poor devil!" sobs Roxy, as the crowd gathers around the floating body. People begin whispering to one another, "Where'd he come from?" "Was he real?" Mr. Miller's voice is heard over the fade-out saying, "Yes, he was

real. It says so in the Bible, the Book of Genesis, Chapter 4, Verse 32: 'In those days, giants walked the earth!'"

We checked the Book of Genesis for the accuracy of the quote. Chapter 4 has only twenty-six verses—there is no Chapter 4, Verse 32. This last bit of gratuitous stupidity provides the perfect ending for an astonishing film.

Unforgettable Performances

Promotional material on Richard Kiel, who plays the title role in *Eegah!*, tells us that he is 7′2″ and weighs over three hundred pounds. At first glance, you might wonder why a man with these formidable assets isn't playing professional basketball rather than acting in Grade "Z" movies. But after seeing *Eegah!* you will understand: Mr. Kiel is far too uncoordinated to succeed at any sport. To say that he walks through his role would be too generous; he actually staggers through it. We will, however, give credit where credit is due: assigning Kiel the role of a prehistoric giant is an example of excellent casting.

The real star of the film, however, is Arch W. Hall, Jr., whose performance as Tommy marks one of the low points in the history of American cinema. In all fairness to Mr. Hall, we should mention that he was only sixteen at the time the film was made, and that he comes to his role with serious physical handicaps: he has a face that only a mother could love, and his body and mannerisms suggest nothing so much as a walking gingerbread man, or, to be more precise, the little white Pillsbury dough boy. His upturned nose with flaring nostrils, his beady green eyes, his blond greasy hair combed out over his forehead like a visor to protect his face from the sun—these images will remain imprinted on the mind of the viewer long after the film's less disturbing visions have faded from memory. The script gives Mr. Hall every change to make a fool of himself, and the young actor makes the most of each opportunity. On three different occasions he bursts into song, twanging away at the two guitar chords he knows while an unseen chorus of feminine voices "doo-wahs" in the background. The makers of this film may have entertained the notion that

Arch W. Hall would someday win public acceptance as a rock 'n' roll singing/acting sensation a la Elvis Presley, or at least Ricky Nelson. Yet in pursuing these aspirations Mr. Hall is not helped by his own song lyrics, For example:

If I had a thousand paintings
In a marble gallery
Every single picture
Would be of Valerie.
Vitamins are good, they say,
And so's a calorie
But I feel like a tiger
On one kiss from Valerie . . .

Mr. Hall tries hard to project a sense of innocence, freshness, and bumbling but lovable naïveté, so that all the fourteen-year-old girls in his audience will coo, "Isn't he *cute*!!!" His attempts, however, fall so far from success that at his best moments he is only pitiable, and at his worst he is downright nauseating.

Immortal Dialogue

TOMMY (when Roxy first tells him of her encounter with Eegah): Honest, Roxy! I believe you! I swear on my Elvis Presley LP!

° ° °

ROXY (staring down at the desert sands): What is that?
MR. MILLER: I don't know. It looks like a footprint.
ROXY: It is a footprint! There's the heel and there's the toe.

° ° °

MR. MILLER: He's offering you a drink of sulfur water.
ROXY: A prehistoric gentleman, huh?

° ° °

TOMMY: I can drive, Mr. Miller. I got my dad's wheels tonight.
MR. MILLER: Really? Do they fit on your car?
TOMMY: You're funny, Mr. Miller . . . real funny!

° ° °

(Roxy is too depressed to enjoy herself at the party.)
MR. MILLER: You know, I think she's still worried about Eegah.
TOMMY: Oh sure. A girl like Roxy don't get over a thing like that right away.

° ° °

(At the party, Roxy is still concerned about Eegah.)
ROXY: Dad, I can't describe it, but I know something has happened to him. He's a creature—why, you just have to look at him to see that! But I know, whatever he is, he's a human being.
MR. MILLER (understandingly): You just can't get him out of your mind, huh?

° ° °

The Story Behind the Film

One of the most obvious questions about *Eegah!* is why, even in a film of this caliber, an actor with the talents of Arch W. Hall, Jr., was ever allowed on the set. The answer is easy to come by: the official roster of Fairway-International, producer of *Eegah!*, tells us that the president of the firm was Mr. Arch W. Hall, Sr. Further investigation revealed that in addition to producing this classic, the elder Mr. Hall also directed it (under the pseudonym "Nicholas Merriwether") and co-starred in it (as Mr. Miller) under the stage name "William Watters."

We arranged to meet Mr. Hall for lunch one afternoon at Bob's Big Boy hamburger stand in beautiful downtown Burbank. We found him to be a tall, elegantly dressed gentleman with a gray beard, sparkling blue eyes, and a delightful sense of humor. "The story for *Eegah!*? I concocted it real quick," he told us. "At the time that I first met Dick [Richard Kiel] he was a kind of a bouncer for a Western nightclub. He was looking for a place to stay, so he came over. I got one look at this man—he filled a whole doorway. So right away I had the idea to use him in a picture. The different ingredients came together to make the story.

"Marilyn Manning—who played Roxy—was a receptionist for a chiropractor who had rented an office from me. After *Eegah!*, I used her in two or three other pictures.

"My son had been in one of my pictures before. He always used to say, 'Gee, Pop, I can't sing.' But I told him that a lot of people had done well who didn't know how to sing. In *Eegah!*, he worked for peanuts. He was only sixteen. After the film came out, I bought him a car later on.

"I had to sell my own car, borrow money, make exchanges, offer pay-you-laters to finance the thing. When I think of all the special deals—it was just Mickey Mouse all the way through. It ended up costing about fifteen thousand dollars, not counting the lab costs.

"We loaded the equipment into trucks and drove out to the desert. We used every device we

Arch Hall, Jr., and one of the "Archers" entertain their fellow teen-agers with an unforgettable rendition of "Nobody Lives on the Brownsville Road." As producer-director Arch Hall, Sr., told us about his smash hit Eegah!: *"It was always sort of a subject of laughter that the darned thing did so well."*

could possibly think of to make that picture. We actually had a lot of fun. I ended up having to direct, which I didn't want to do. I was also the cook, and the runner-after-things. At first it was dreadful, just dreadful. It was terribly hot, around a hundred and fifteen degrees. Whenever we saw something, we'd just shoot. We'd wander around, and some of the fellows almost got sunstroke. We shot a lot of film, and some of it didn't work out at all. We actually got sand in some of it. We also lost a lot of the sound. The sound man had told us that everything was okay, but in a lot of the scenes he turned on "Playback" instead of "Record" by mistake. So an awful lot of the dialogue was dubbed. The actors had been ad-libbing all over the place, and we couldn't even remember what they said. It was murder. Really murder. For the voice of Eegah, I did a lot of the dubbing myself—grunting, incoherent noises, speaking some words in Sioux Indian, whatever....

"By hook or by crook, in desperation, I made that picture. It was my last hope for paying my debts from the project before."

The Balance Sheet

Eegah! opened at a drive-in theatre in Omaha, Nebraska, and in its first run did about $15,000 in business. It went on to other triumphal engagements in Cincinnati and Louisville, and then began to catch fire nationwide. Arch W. Hall, Sr., gleefully fanned the flames: "We went out on tour to promote the picture, and the personal appearances were very successful. My son would strum out the *Eegah!* theme on his guitar, and then the lights would go down low. All of a sudden, Dick would come out with his suit on and his club. People went wild. They just loved that giant. Sometimes they mobbed him, and they'd almost rip his clothes off. I never saw anything like it."

According to Mr. Hall, his film has by now grossed well over a million dollars—not a bad return on an initial investment of $15,000. The film has even been dubbed into Spanish, Japanese, Portuguese, and other languages. It has established itself as a special favorite on the Late Late Shows—where it appears as a filler between used car commercials—and has become something of a cult film among chronic insomniacs. We asked Mr. Hall how he would explain his film's astonishing and durable appeal.

"I think it's the idea of a lost, lovesick giant. You know, the idea of a Bigfoot, the unknown. I think those things have a lot of appeal to the imagination. At the time the film was made, the dune buggy was just coming in, and that had appeal too. Maybe the idea of a boy and his guitar, and his singing. Also, the title probably had something to do with it. It's a very unique title. To tell you the truth, I used to get teased about it quite a lot. It was always sort of a subject of laughter that the darned thing did so well."

Encouraged by *Eegah!*'s success, Mr. Hall went on to make other films with his son—including an unheralded classic entitled *The Nasty Rabbit* concerning a group of Russian spies disguised as cowboys who land in America with an infected rabbit, which they plan to let loose to destroy the country.

In more recent years, the elder Mr. Hall has concentrated his energy on the production of documentary films, while his son has found his true career as a pilot for a small California airline.

The smog monster (Hedorah) enjoys a snack of matchbox cars while in training for his featured bout with Godzilla.

GODZILLA VERSUS THE SMOG MONSTER (1972)

(Original Title: GOJIRA TAI HEDORA)

Directed by: YOSHIMITU BANNO
Written by: KAORU MABUCHI and YOSHIM-
ITU BANNO
Produced by: TOMAKOYUKI TANAKA
Music by: RIICHIRRO MANABE
Featuring: GODZILLA, THE SMOG MON-
STER, AKIRA YAMAUCHI, HIROYUKI KA-
WASE, TOSHIE KIMURA, TOSHIO SHIBAKI,
KEIKO MARI

American International Pictures

The Critics Rave

"There isn't any attempt at acting unless you count Godzilla's. Twenty minutes could be edited out of the picture at no loss to anyone, and we are treated to the same tedious shots of the polluted bay over and over again. . . ."
—Anitra Earle, *San Francisco Chronicle*

"Godzilla freelances as a do-gooder. . . . Dubbed and daffy."
—Leonard Maltin, *TV Movies*

"One of the worst monster films ever . . . an idiotic kiddie show! . . . The theme song can drive you right up a ceiling."
—Jason Thomas and Joe Kane,
The Monster Times

Plot Summary

A dead black tadpole-shaped animal is found in polluted Suruga Bay, near Tokyo. Dr. Yano exam-

A wild teen-age party on a mountaintop near Tokyo is rudely interrupted by two uninvited guests: Godzilla and the smog monster. The two biggies proceed to do battle, with the future of the human race hanging in the balance.

ines it as his small son Ken gleefully exclaims, "Wow! A monster tadpole!" After conducting experiments, Dr. Yano discovers that particles of the tadpole become alive in polluted water. The doctor decides to investigate further and goes skin diving in a muddy bay. While he explores, an ambulatory mass of sludge moves over the water's surface. It's the smog monster!! which looks like nothing so much as a four-hundred-foot high melted candle with burning red eyes. It brushes up against Dr. Yano and then ventures to another part of the sea. The doctor emerges from the bay with acid burns on his face.

At his house, Dr. Yano is lying on his bed. Blue glaze is painted on one half of his face, which apparently is supposed to represent acid burns. A television news cameraman is filming Dr. Yano, showing the effect of having a smog monster brush up against you. Meanwhile, the smog monster has grown larger and plunges into a harbor. It capsizes two Japanese ships in a scene that looks as if it may well have been filmed in a bathtub.

Ken, Dr. Yano's son, dreams of Godzilla coming to save Japan from the smog monster. Godzilla, a two-hundred-foot-high fire-breathing dinosaur, is presumably well-known to all aficionados of Japanese monster movies. The next morning, the tot announces to his father, "Papa—Godzilla's going to come."

The boy also conceives a name for the smog monster: Hedorah. As he explains, "They come out of mud, that's why I call 'em Hedorah." (*Hedorah* is the Japanese word for "pollution.")

Hedorah has been attacking all over the city. It creeps into a far-out discotheque where Japanese teen-agers are dancing to right-on songs about ecology. The monster also learns to assume a different shape and make itself fly. It flies over a building in construction and reduces several construction workers to piles of clothes, hard hats, and skeletons.

The teen-agers from the discotheque decide that hedonism is better than Hedorah. The leader of the group (who is also Ken's older brother) suggests, "We'll get all the hep kids we know and stage a party on Mount Fuji." The teen-agers all cheer the idea. On the night of the party, the long hairs set a large campfire on Mount Fuji. The music is provided by teen-agers playing sax-

ophones, guitars, drums, a Moog synthesizer, and other instruments. Even little Ken Yano is invited to the party and he snaps his fingers to the big beat while the be-boppers continue to rock out. Suddenly the party is interrupted by—who else— the smog monster. The teen-agers throw flaming torches onto the monster but this only makes it mad. Hedorah starts to emit smut on the teen-agers and it looks as if all is doomed, until—(yay!) Godzilla comes to save the day.

The two monsters are now in the spotlight and they display the best acting in the film. Godzilla stabs his paw into Hedorah's side and Hedorah spurts mud out of its stomach. Hedorah gets back at Godzilla and throws him into a deep canyon. Hedorah then proceeds to give off a quantity of soft mud (resembling excrement) and covers the canyon with it.

During the war of the monsters, Dr. Yano has designed a machine that can dehydrate living things. It is made of two huge electrodes that can be operated at the doctor's command. The two monsters stumble in between the two electrodes. The rays are turned on and Hedorah is reduced to dried mud. Godzilla jabs his fist into the dried mud and flings out assorted refuse that was contained in the monster. Godzilla finally pulls out the monster's two eyeballs. However, a miniature Hedorah has grown out of the refuse. Godzilla stamps it to death with his feet and with the help of some rays from the electrodes. Godzilla, his mission accomplished, leaves Tokyo until the next time an invader threatens to overthrow the world. Ken waves and yells to him, "Godzilla! Thanks a lot!"

Unforgettable Performances

Godzilla has long been a favorite Japanese leading man. His riveting performance in *Godzilla Versus the Smog Monster* ranks among his best. To register anger he throws his arms about, wiggles his hips, stomps his feet, and makes obscene hand gestures to the smog monster. In addition to his natural charm, Godzilla has the advantage of a jazzy nightclub band that plays his theme music. He gains much sympathy from the audience in the sensitive last sequence, when, after destroying the smog monster, Godzilla must return to his lower depths. Hats off to the Big Boy for a masterful bravura performance!

The smog monster (a.k.a. Hedorah) is a promising newcomer with a fresh young face. He (it?) is composed of equal parts of rubber tentacles, teriyaki, melted caramel, chicken skin, goulash, and two big red eyes, and is decorated with muddy seaweed. He turns in the best performance by a mass of sludge we've seen this year. When he is attacked by the electrodes he tries again and again to get up, looking slightly intoxicated. Most of the time he is content with getting nourishment by sucking on smokestacks.

Immortal Dialogue

Title Song: "Save the Earth" (repeated twice during the film)
> We have cobalt,
> it's full of mercury.
> Too many fumes in our oxygen.
> And the smog now
> is choking you and me.
> Good lord, where is it gonna end? . . .
>
> It's up to us
> to make a choice.
>
> Save the earth!
> CHORUS: Save the earth!
>   Save the earth!

    *   *   *

BROTHER: Oh, you like Godzilla, right?
KEN: Superman beats them all!

    *   *   *

BROTHER (after seeing Ken motioning several punches to the sky): You're pretending you're Godzilla, right?

    *   *   *

(Ken composes a poem about ecology and reads it to the audience.)
> Atomic bombs, hydrogen bombs,
>   and radioactive fallout
> Fall into the sea.

> Godzilla would rage,
> If he could see.
> He'd turn the page
> And clear it for you and me.

    *   *   *

DR. YANO: Do you know what a meteor is?
KEN: Sure, it's a falling star that falls to the earth.
DR. YANO: Well, Hedorah attached itself to one of those stars.

    *   *   *

Another Enlightening Conversation:
DR. YANO: In each creature a weakness exists.
KEN: Hedorah's only sludge—he can be dried.

    *   *   *

(Godzilla battles it out with Hedorah on top of Mount Fuji.)
KEN (watching them): C'mon, Godzilla!

The Story Behind the Film

In his spectacular career, Godzilla has made more than thirteen films. In the past, he has taken on such weighty competition as Mothra (a gargantuan moth), Rodan (a gigantic pterodactyl), Ghidrah (a fire-breathing, three-headed monster), Ebirah (a tremendous crab), and even King Kong. His joust with the smog monster was filmed in 1971, but did not reach America until 1973. The special effects were supervised by Eiji Tsuburuya. Godzilla was actualized by having a man in a dragon suit walk around a miniature set. Apparently the smog monster was created in the same way. A man dressed up in a sludge suit for the part. The two men wrestled and tossed each other around as the cameras began to roll. Godzilla is popular all over Japan. Plastic Godzilla dolls are sold in battery-operated models. Other popular items include Godzilla T-shirts and Godzilla lunch boxes.

The Balance Sheet

According to the film pressbook, Godzilla in *this*

Little Ken and his mother stand aside and root for Godzilla during the climax of the ecological epic God-zilla Versus the Smog Monster.

film is "a mighty benefactor to mankind, a towering fighter battling to save the world from destruction . . . and a true friend to little boys and girls." The advertising campaign for the film included such lines as "The Greatest Duels—the Deadliest—A slithering slimy horror spawned from the poisons of pollution" and "Creature of Slime and Sludge Spawned by Pollution's Poison Threatens to Destroy the Earth." The pressbook also suggested that the symbol of Godzilla as a fighter of pollution "might be promoted just as Smokey the Bear symbolizes the campaign against forest fires. An anti-pollution drive could be set up with the backing of local Boy and Girl Scout headquarter officials and 4-H clubs, rallying their membership to clean up streets and alleys, and deliver bottles and cans to recycling centers." (!) It was also suggested that theater managers talk to their local bartenders to concoct a mixed drink named "the Godzilla Cocktail." It would be advertised with the description "It clears that five o'clock smog from your brain." Another suggestion to the theater manager was to record the screams of Godzilla and the smog monster with a tape recorder, then place a speaker on the sidewalk near the theater. The screams would be blasted at peaceful passersby in order to call attention to the movie.

Godzilla Versus the Smog Monster was immensely popular in Japan. In the United States, however, despite its ingenious promotional campaign, the film received a somewhat shorter run.

In Los Angeles the movie ran for all of two days. Even worse, it only had matinees for these two days.

The film was greeted with similar, well-deserved treatment in other cities. American International Pictures, the film's American distributor, did not give up all hope. Several months after the film's initial release AIP introduced a packet of horror films intended to be shown on the same bill. The packet was entitled *Monsterama*, and consisted of *Godzilla Versus the Smog Monster* and three other monster films. They were: *The Incredible Two-Headed Transplant, Destroy All Monsters,* and *Yog, Monster from Space* (a.k.a. *Space Amoeba*).

The Toho Films Corporation plans a sequel to *Godzilla Versus the Smog Monster,* which will actually be a sequel to a sequel. Hedorah will not be in this feature, but it will involve an all-new monster bred from pollution. However, plans for making the new movie have not been carried out since they were originally announced four years ago.

SPECIAL AWARD

A year's supply of LSD or any other hallucinogen goes to the Japanese monster film industry—and in particular Toho Corporation for the fertile imagination that has brought us a continuing parade of stars. To ensure consistent quality, each of these new creations was presented with atrocious acting, sloppy direction, farfetched scripts, execrable music, amateurish photography, laughable sets, and last but certainly not least, ludicrous monsters.

Among distinguished titles in this seemingly endless series are *Matango the Fungus of Terror* (retitled *Attack of the Mushroom People*), about a group of voyagers who slowly turn into mushrooms; *Gamera the Invincible,* a giant fire-breathing turtle that flies; *Varan the Unbelievable,* about an unbelievably huge bat; *The Green Slime,* featuring slithery blobs that invade a space station; *Dagora the Space Monster,* concerning a gang of criminals that is thwarted by an enormous jellyfish; *Gyaos,* a titanic flying fox with fangs. *The Evil Brain from Outer Space* is self-explanatory. *Majin the Monster of Terror* is about a mammoth statue that walks. We anxiously await future offerings.

THE GOLDWYN FOLLIES (1938)

Directed by: GEORGE MARSHALL
Written by: BEN HECHT
Produced by: SAMUEL GOLDWYN
Music by: GEORGE GERSHWIN
Lyrics by: IRA GERSHWIN
Music for ballets and "Spring Again" by: VERNON DUKE Ballets conceived and staged by: GEORGE BALANCHINE
Featuring: ADOLPHE MENJOU, THE RITZ BROTHERS, VERA ZORINA, KENNY BAKER, ANDREA LEEDS, PHIL BAKER, THE AMERICAN BALLET of the METROPOLITAN OPERA, THE GORGEOUS GOLDWYN GIRLS, and introducing EDGAR BERGEN and "CHARLIE McCARTHY"

United Artists

The Critics Rave

"Lacking flash and glitter...."

—Variety

"Dreadful hodgepodge."
—Leonard Maltin, *TV Movies*

"The bizarre in musical pretentiousness."
—James P. Cunningham, *Commonweal*

"Absurd farce; drags...."
—Daughters of the American Revolution

"A certain nightmarish quality. . . . On the evidence it appears that Mr. Goldwyn tossed the story out to make room for his cast. . . . I stayed awake with an effort."
—Frank S. Nugent, *New York Times*

"Too many personalities and their not always successful routines crammed into the film's two hours."

—Newsweek

Kenny Baker and Andrea Leeds (lower left) provide romantic uplift, Adolphe Menjou (extreme right) plays a producer of bad films, while the Ritz Brothers (second row) offer intelligent facial expressions. This dreadful 1938 mishmash was called The Goldwyn Follies.

"Dull. . . . A choppy extravaganza with many features to suit all tastes and not enough of any of them to suit anybody's."

—*Time*

Plot Summary

Oliver Merlin (Adolphe Menjou) is a producer of bad movies (how prophetic!). Every time he releases a new film the audiences roar with laughter, particularly in the death scenes. One day, while filming his latest flop on location in a small town, Oliver encounters a young lady named Hazel Dawes (Andrea Leeds), sipping a soda and explaining to a friend why movies are so bad. Oliver is smitten with the girl's honesty and insight (and her shapeliness, though he doesn't say that). He offers to whisk her away to Hollywood where she will serve as his adviser. Oliver explains that she is the voice of 200 million Americans who "only know what they like" and want to see real life and honesty in the cinema. Olivers dubs Hazel "Miss Humanity" and installs her at the studio.

Despite her new position, Merlin wants his Miss Humanity to remain untouched by any Hollywood types, for fear she will lose her endearing simplicity (not to mention her virginity), so he smuggles her in and out of the studio under a blanket. Lord knows what she does under there. He buys her a small house, where she resides with a chaperone, an unnamed actress who does imitations of retarded children. At this cozy retreat, Oliver visits Hazel and reads screenplays to her, asking her advice. One of the projects she helps to shape is Oliver's film of *Romeo and Juliet*. Hazel insists that the ending be changed to allow the lovers to live happily ever after—as it is, it's too sad. Merlin immediately complies with her suggestion.

Merlin's major project, however, is a large-scale non-Shakespearean production. He must devise a script that will incorporate various diverse talents, including: a god-awful Russian actress named Olga (Vera Zorina) who walks around the set accompanied by a background orchestra playing "The Volga Boatman"; a trio of third-rate comics (The Ritz Brothers) who perform one bad imitation of the Marx Brothers after another; and finally, a severely untalented accordionist (Phil Baker) who is cast and recast as a gigolo, door-

man, French customs officer, and Russian impresario. Edgar Bergen and Charlie McCarthy provide the only real humor in the film and they never get into the masterpiece Merlin is making.

After conferring with his Miss Humanity time and again, Merlin comes up with a script that goes something like this: the untalented accordionist runs away from the god-awful Russian actress, and then the god-awful actress takes up with a gondolier. Right in the middle of these goings-on is some sort of Water Nymph Ballet, where the god-awful actress pops out of a reflecting pool, dances away with a man in evening clothes, climbs around an enormous equestrian statue (you don't have to be Freud to figure that one out), and then jumps back into her pond. At this point the Ritz Brothers pop up out of a Venetian canal and sing a serenade to a fish, and finally an operatic soprano appears from nowhere to sing some arias from *La Traviata*. Well, Miss Humanity said this is what America wants to see.

Merlin's only problem is to find some innocent lad to play the gondolier who comforts the Russian actress after she's ditched by the accordionist. Hazel Dawes, once again, solves that problem. She strolls into a hamburger stand one evening while the short-order cook is singing George Gershwin's "Love Walked In" (accompanied by full orchestra) at the same time he prepares the 1937 equivalent of a Big Mac. Hazel and the young chef, Kenny Baker, strike up quite a friendship (woo hoo!) and before long Miss Humanity has landed him the part of the gondolier in the new Oliver Merlin flopperoo.

Well, it looks as though our young hero is on the way to fame and fortune, so he and Hazel make plans to settle down and make babies. Producer Merlin, however, has fallen in love with the girl himself (surprise!) and tells Hazel that if she marries Kenny, the little gondolier will be kicked out of the picture. In the film's climactic scene (at a cocktail party, no less) Kenny walks up to Merlin and tells him he is ready to quit on his own if he can't have the woman he loves. Merlin admires the boy's courage, has a change of heart, and gives the singing chef a five-year contract. Just like real life. And so the entire cast gathers around the piano for another rendition of "Love Walked In." The scene fades from the screen, and hopefully from our memories as well. We never do find out if the gondolier epic was a success or not, which might tell us whether *The Goldwyn Follies* was a satire or not. Whatever the answer, this film is certainly more than a folly—it is a travesty.

Unforgettable Performances

If Andrea Leeds (as Hazel Dawes) were representing 200 million Americans, most of us would have defected by now. She sits around with glazed-eyed innocence, and speaks her lines with all the conviction of a miraculously healed cripple being interviewed by the late evangelist Katherine Kuhlman.

Kenny Baker has a nice voice, and at least he's talented enough to be able to sing and flip a hamburger at the same time. But he romances Miss Leeds as if he were a pre-pubescent junior-high-school student who can't stop fidgeting. When he plays the Venetian gondolier in the film within the film, he sports a set of sideburns that are the same shape as the paisley on his pajama bottoms.

The ballets in this film were intended to add a touch of culture, but instead add a touch of indigestion. It seems that Sam Goldwyn hired the American Ballet of the Metropolitan Opera and choreographer George Balanchine, and felt obliged to use them wherever he could, particularly where they are irrelevant. The abysmal Water Nymph Ballet is accompanied by a Vernon Duke score that's about as graceful as a Polish mazurka danced in the mud. The dancers wobble around with facial expressions that indicate they are having their innards squeezed out by tutus that are much too tight.

Immortal Dialogue

(Producer Oliver Merlin meets Hazel Dawes in a small-town soda shop.)

OLIVER: I'm a producer of movies. I get my wagonloads of poets and dramatists, but I can't buy common sense—I cannot buy humanity!

HAZEL: Well, I don't know why, Mr. Merlin, there's an awful lot of it.

OLIVER: Yes, I know, but the moment I buy it, it turns into something else, usually genius, and it isn't worth a dime. Now, if you could stay just as simple as you are, you'd be invaluable to me. . . . I'll put you on my staff. . . . I'll give you

a title: "Miss Humanity." Don't rush, you can finish your ice cream soda.

      ❖   ❖   ❖

Chorus to Ritz Brothers' Song
Here pussy pussy pussy pussy pussy pussy pussy
Here pussy pussy pussy pussy pussy pussy pussy
Here pussy pussy pussy pussy pussy pussy pussy
Here pussy pussy pussy pussy pussy pussy pussy
Here pussy pussy pussy pussy pussy pussy pussy
Where is the dog-gone cat?

      ❖   ❖   ❖

Love Scene (first heat):
KENNY BAKER: You live near here?
HAZEL: Just down the street.
KENNY: Oh, that's too bad. I was hoping it would be a long walk. But maybe you'd like to go exploring? I heard there's an ocean near here and we could sit on the beach and get sunburned.
HAZEL: Tonight?
KENNY: I'm sorry. With you, it seems like the sun *is* shining.

      ❖   ❖   ❖

OLIVER (cuddling up to Hazel): You look so beautiful tonight, forgive me if I hold your hand and admire you, more than I've ever admired any young lady in the world!

      ❖   ❖   ❖

Love Scene (second heat):
KENNY: Gee, I love you more every time I see ya.
HAZEL: Oh, and I love you! Isn't it wonderful the way everything has turned out for you?
KENNY: Yes. Fame, fortune, and the girl I love. All because you got hungry for a hamburger one night.
HAZEL: I love hamburgers.

The Story Behind the Film

For years, producer Samuel Goldwyn had dreamed of using the tried-and-true Broadway formula of the *Ziegfeld Follies* as the basis for a Hollywood triumph. He used part of the Ziegfeld formula in his 1930 success *Whoopee*, and in 1937 he was ready to mount a large-scale, full-color, music-dance-comedy-high culture extravaganza. The result was *The Goldwyn Follies*, a film intended to establish its producer, once and for all, as the "Ziegfeld of Hollywood."

To accomplish this grand design, Goldwyn first hired the great George and Ira Gershwin to write music and lyrics, and brought out to Hollywood the celebrated George Balanchine and his American Ballet of the Metropolitan Opera. This company of sixty dancers included Balanchine's wife, the ballerina Vera Zorina, who eventually appeared as the god-awful Russian actress in the completed film. For some reason, Goldwyn also hired the Ritz Brothers—a knockabout comedy team with a dubious track record. Even sympathetic critic Leonard Maltin admits that "since 1925 the Ritz Brothers have been receiving strongly divided responses from critics and audiences alike." Perhaps to salve his conscience after stooping to contract the Ritz Brothers, Goldwyn secured the services of Helen Jepson, a well-known operatic star. It was her job to sing excerpts from *La Traviata* while wearing a bright red dress that would show up well in the "glorious new color technique" employed in this film. With all this emphasis on fabulous color, Goldwyn inexplicably hired camera artist Gregg Toland, a man noted for his achievements in black and white, who had never before photographed a color film. When criticized for this move, Goldwyn shrugged his shoulders and said, "Toland always photographs color; it just comes out black and white."

The biggest problem for Goldwyn, as for producer Oliver Merlin within the film, was to develop a script that would tie together all the diverse elements he was intent on using. For this purpose Goldwyn hired nine (count 'em—nine!) of Hollywood's most gifted writers, including such luminaries as Dorothy Parker and Anita Loos. Various treatments, scripts, and rewrites were prepared and then rejected over a two-year period, until just weeks before shooting was due to begin, Goldwyn still had no workable script. At the last moment, Ben Hecht (who won Academy Awards for *Underworld* and *The Scoundrel* and also co-authored the Broadway hit *The Front Page*) was brought in to pick up the pieces. Hecht wrote a final script in just two weeks, and the time pressures he encountered may help to excuse the total inanity of the finished product.

All along, Goldwyn understood that his film's major asset was its George Gershwin score, but then, before finishing his work, Gershwin was inconsiderate enough to die suddenly at the age of thirty-eight. In the midst of production, Goldwyn cast about desperately for some solution to save his film: Gershwin had not yet prepared any usable music for the crucial ballet sequences in the script. The late composer's brother Ira suggested that Gershwin's beautiful tone poem *An American in Paris* be adapted for the ballet; Ira even prepared a suitable scenario which delighted Balanchine, who immediately began working on it with his company. Several weeks later, however, Goldwyn summoned Balanchine and Ira Gershwin to his office. The "Ziegfeld of Hollywood" then announced that he had decided that *An American in Paris* was simply too "highbrow" for a mass audience. "What would the miners of Harrisburg, Pennsylvania, think of it?" he asked. Balanchine

answered immediately, "Mr. Goldwyn, I am not President Roosevelt and I am not interested in what the miners of Harrisburg think." He might also have mentioned that in a film which already included operatic excerpts from *Traviata*, the inclusion of *An American in Paris* could hardly be seen as an unsettling highbrow element. Nevertheless, Sam Goldwyn, perhaps having consulted his own real-life equivalent of Miss Humanity, had already decided that Gershwin's gorgeous masterpiece could not be used in his film. Instead, he hired hack composer Vernon Duke, who provided a score so banal and heavy-handed that it makes for some of the film's most ludicrous moments, including (heaven help us!) the unspeakable Water Nymph Ballet.

The Balance Sheet

When the final $2 million epic opened in New York's Rivoli Theatre on February 20, 1938, *The Goldwyn Follies* left both reviewers and audiences somewhat bewildered. Critics seemed genuinely astonished that Goldwyn could bring together the talent involved here and still come up with such an atrocious piece of entertainment. They were also amazed at the film's lackluster and "strangely de-saturated" Technicolor. Not surprisingly, *The Goldwyn Follies* did sluggish business across the country, and Goldwyn quietly dropped his plans for a sequel.

George Marshall, who received the dubious credit for having directed this turkey, went on to other triumphs in his checkered career. A quarter of a century after completing *The Goldwyn Follies*, Marshall was responsible for another all-time clinker, *Boy, Did I Get a Wrong Number!* (q.v.). Some artists just seem to have that magic touch.

Unaware of the bloodcurdling terror that awaits them, the golden youth in The Horror of Party Beach *live it up in the fresh air and sunshine. This 1964 production is so laughably awful that it has attracted a devoted cult following in recent years.*

Publicity material for the film. Need we say more?

THE HORROR OF PARTY BEACH
(1964)

Directed by: DEL TENNEY
Written by: RICHARD L. HILLIARD
Produced by: DEL TENNEY
Music by: BILL HOLMES
Featuring: JOHN SCOTT, ALICE LYON, AL-
LEN LAUREL, EULABELLE MOORE, MARI-
LYN CLARK, AGUSTIN MAYER, and THE
DEL-AIRES (Ronny Linares, Bob Osborne, Garry
Jones, John Becker)

Twentieth Century-Fox

The Critics Rave

"There have been some comical monsters in
previous horrific B pictures, but nothing quite so
hilariously ridiculous as this assembly of sea-born
brutes. Their rig-out is so phoney as to become almost fascinating, particularly a cluster of what
looks like sausages in their mouths. The standard
of acting is incredibly weak—including the most
expressionless and inanimate heroine of all time—"
—*Monthly Film Bulletin*

"A radio-active vampire-zombie-sex-maniac
would be disturbing enough, but musical numbers
like "The Zombie Stomp" by the Del-Aires push
this Twentieth Century-Fox release over the bottom as the worst movie of the last twelve
months...."

—*Newsweek*

"The question in *The Horror of Party Beach* is,
which is more horrible—the monsters or the rock
'n' roll? The most curious aspect . . . is why,

WEIRD ATOMIC BEASTS...
WHO LIVE OFF HUMAN BLOOD!

THE FIRST
HORROR
MONSTER
MUSICAL!
Hear the big-
beat sound of
the Del-Aires
swingin' with the
beach party set!

THE
HORROR
OF PARTY
BEACH

FANTASTIC!!!
The big-beat sound of the
Del-Aires swingin' out
with 6 rockin' hits!

HORRIFYING!!!
Teen-age slumber party
ravaged by demons
from the dead!

WEIRD!!!
Ghoulish atomic beasts who
live off warm, human blood!

AN ISELIN-TENNEY Production

after the first couple of homicides, the rest of the victims linger around the disaster area, waiting for the worst. Audiences lured into the theater may ask themselves the same thing."
—Eugene Archer, *New York Times*

"A dozen of the most ridiculous-looking 'monsters' we've ever seen . . . unbelievably amateurish acting and direction. . . ."
Bob Salmaggi, *New York Herald Tribune*

"I've never seen such a bandy-legged monster in my life . . . boredom is abject and total . . . 72 minutes (which felt to me like 72 centuries) . . . not only dreary but half-witted."
—Raymond Durgnat, *Films and Filming*

"One of the WORST movies of that or any other year, managing . . . to merge bad rock 'n' roll with atrocious acting, inept direction, and ludicrous fish monsters . . . a movie that will long be remembered by monster fans of a masochistic bent."
—Jason Thomas, *The Monster Times*

Plot Summary

Radioactive waste is carelessly dumped into the sea near New York City. Lying on the ocean floor are the skeletons of dead sailors. By a chemical phenomenon well known to sci-fi movie buffs, the radioactive chemicals and the human remains come together to form a flock of scaly sea monsters. These freaks walk upright on their hind legs in a manner suggesting an All-American broken-field runner showing the effects of LSD. Their bodies are covered with scales resembling massive artichoke leaves. Dorsal fins protrude from the top of their heads. Knowing in advance that they will not win acceptance in any neighborhood inhabited by normal human beings, they make their way toward Party Beach.

Party Beach is apparently the "hot spot" of Long Island (though for inexplicable reasons the film was shot in Stamford, Connecticut). This miserable stretch of seashore is infested by hundreds of swinging happy-go-lucky teen-agers, sporting daring 1960 swimsuits, white T-shirts,

and dark glasses. The lovable youngsters spend day after day in orgiastic ecstasy, wiggling to the music of a bosso rock group called the Del-Aires. The lively lyrics to their songs include lines such as "Everybody's doin' it, doin' it, doin' it, doin' it!" and "Shake it, shake it, shake it, shake it, shake it!" In the midst of these revels, one of the "hot chicks" decides she wants to go swimming (presumably to cool off). At that point, to no one's surprise, a monster strolls in from the sea as the music on the sound track plays a chilling "boing." Rather than asking for the next dance, the monster happily slices our pretty little filly into neat chunks of meat with its fingernails.

The next day, the news of the murder is announced. A newspaper's banner headline spells out in huge letters, SEA MONSTER KILLS GIRL! Next to this, a small headline reads, "Panic in New York; Menagerie Breaks Loose." Throughout the film, several newspapers will be flashed on the screen with large banner headlines. However, the small headline "Panic in New York; Menagerie Breaks Loose" remains, for some odd reason, on every new copy of the up-to-the-minute newspapers.

Some more of the sea creatures decide to hit the town and they shred several more people to pieces. The suspense is unbearable. Dr. Gavin, a local scientist, and officials from all over the United States rack their brains in order to figure out a way to kill the monstrous party-poopers. They finally discover that when sodium is applied to a radioactive monster, it ignites, and the creature becomes a flaming inferno. (Ask your chemistry prof about that one.) Dr. Gavin is then informed that his courageous daughter (Alice Lyon) has gone out into the woods alone so that she can say peekaboo to the mysterious monsters. One can hardly blame her since the scaly creatures are the most interesting and attractive males in this film. Dr. Gavin and the police arrive just in time to save his daughter from the ubiquitous weirdos. Gavin and the police throw tons of sodium onto the creatures as they turn into walking forest fires and slowly disappear. These actors throw the sodium with so little élan that the scene looks like some sort of a monster multiple wedding in which Dr. Gavin and the police are the bridesmaids throwing rice at the happy cou-

The terrifying sea monster (an unexpected by-product of atomic radiation) prepares to ravage the fun-loving beboppers at Party Beach. Since he could not get a date, he is going stag to crash the festivities.

ples. At last the freaks (the monsters, that is) disappear and the teen-agers are free once more to ride the waves at Party Beach and to rock out to the keeno songs by the Del-Aires. Like crazy, man!

Unforgettable Performances

Alice Lyon plays Elaine, Dr. Gavin's teen-age daughter. Her reactions seem remarkably slow until one understands that she is probably having trouble remembering her lines. At the end of the film when the monsters burst into flames, she is required to scream. She does so, in the polite, obliging way that a parent might scream after seeing his or her child in a Halloween costume.

Eulabelle (that's right, Eulabelle) Moore plays Eulabelle, Dr. Gavin's black maid. She is a fat woman, a voodoo worshiper, and carries a voodoo doll. She believes that the monsters were caused by the mystical powers of voodoo. She also constantly makes cretinous grammatical errors in her speech. She delivers such deathless lines as "It's the voodoo, Dr. Gavin! It's the voodoo, I tells ya!" She also shuffles her feet and booms out, "Yassuh, yassuh" at periodic intervals. Those who thought that this racist stereotype had long before died out will be relieved to know that Aunt Jemima is alive and well and living at Party Beach.

The Del-Aires are a rock 'n' roll group composed of Ronny Linares, Bob Osborne, Garry Jones, and John Becker. What a cool ensemble! Man, they play songs about dancing zombies and about applying for a driver's license. (See IMMORTAL DIALOGUE.) Their featured number is entitled "The Zombie Stomp" and tells us that a zombie pounds his feet into the ground when he jitterbugs. There is also a moving "protest song" complaining that the current speed limit does not let one drive at ninety miles per hour.

Immortal Dialogue

(A teen-age couple embrace on the sands of Party Beach.)
GIRL: Johnny, I never let anyone kiss me like this before!
BOY: My name's not Johnny!
GIRL: Well, what is it?
BOY: Irving!

GIRL: Irving?! (She chuckles and then resumes her passionate voice.) What's in a name?

*   *   *

Song: "The Zombie Stomp" (sung by the Del-Aires)

Oh everybody do the zombie stomp!
Doo-doo-doo-doop.
Just land your foot down with an awful bump!
Doo-doo-doo-doop.

Baby, baby, don't you care?
Something here looking kinda weird.
Honey, I'm no Frankenstein.
Oh yeah, baby, really I feel fine.

*   *   *

(Another couple on Party Beach.)
GIRL: Do you believe that kissing is unhealthy?
BOY: I don't know. I've never been—
GIRL: (interrupting): You've never been kissed?
BOY: No, I've never been sick.

*   *   *

Dr. Gavin Makes a Scientific Discovery
DR. GAVIN: Of course! This creature needs the ordinary necessities of human life. Proteins, fats, sugars and so forth. But since his organs are so decomposed it needs the only food which can keep it alive.
ASSISTANT: Blood?
DR. GAVIN: Human blood. If a human body—a drowned person—were attacked by tiny sea plants which became parasites and completely infiltrated that human body before it had a chance to decompose, would the body be considered dead or alive?
ASSISTANT: Dead?
DR. GAVIN: No—it's still alive. But it's changed into a—well, is it a plant or an animal?
ASSISTANT: It's both?
DR. GAVIN: It's a giant protozoa!
(By George, we think he's got it!)

*   *   *

The Story Behind the Film

The Horror of Party Beach, directed by Del Tenney, was shot in Stamford, Connecticut—not exactly a sun-drenched, exclusive resort, but what do you want on this sort of budget? Del Tenney had a background in television and stage work, and this film was his first big break as a movie director. Later he went on to other triumphs such as *The Curse of the Living Corpse*.

Alan V. Iselin, who helped produce the film, just happened to own a chain of drive-in theaters, where *The Horror of Party Beach* was to be shown. He owned three drive-ins in Albany, three in Florida, and one in Poughkeepsie. Somehow, these gentlemen persuaded Twentieth Century-Fox to involve itself with the project, which was originally titled *Invasion of the Zombies*. It may seem incredible that a major studio product would offer the sort of production values seen here but this is science fiction, remember, and anything is possible.

The Balance Sheet

The Horror of Party Beach was released at the end of spring 1964. In most cases, it was released on a double bill with that other gem from Del Tenney, *The Curse of the Living Corpse*. One exploitation suggestion to theater managers included getting a local teen-age rock 'n' roll group "to serenade incoming patrons in the lobby opening night. Send the same bunch out on an open truck for several days suitably bannered." One gimmick that most theaters used was a "fright release." The "fright release" cleared the management of "all responsibility for death by fright," but they forgot to mention the far greater threat of death by boredom. The film was also billed as "The First Horror Monster Musical!" and advertised with lines like "Hear the Big-Beat Sound of the Del-Aires, Swingin' with the Beach Party Set!" and "Weird Atomic Beasts—Living off Human Blood!" Horror of horrors, the *Horror* has shown a considerable profit, and emerged as a major cult object in the late sixties.

HURRY SUNDOWN (1967)

Directed by: OTTO PREMINGER
Written by: THOMAS C. RYAN and HORTON FOOTE
Produced by: OTTO PREMINGER
Based on the novel by: K. B. GILDEN
Music by: HUGO MONTENEGRO
Featuring: MICHAEL CAINE, JANE FONDA, JOHN PHILIP LAW, DIAHANN CARROLL, ROBERT HOOKS, FAYE DUNAWAY, BURGESS MEREDITH, ROBERT REED, GEORGE KENNEDY, FRANK CONVERSE, LORING SMITH, BEAH RICHARDS, MADELEINE SHERWOOD, REX INGRAM, JIM BACKUS

Paramount Pictures

The Critics Rave

". . . an execrable film. Indeed, it is very possibly the worst major production to come out of Hollywood in the 1960s. This statement takes in a lot of territory, but there is a special kind of unredeemed awfulness about the movie that narrows the competition to a very few films. . . . Reduction of difficult issues to a discussional level approximating that which obtains in *Rex Morgan, M.D.* . . . Much sexual activity presented with such determined bad taste and insensate boorishness that one does not know whether to avert one's eyes or join the adolescent hooting emanating from the balcony."

—Richard Schickel, *Life*

"A terrible movie . . . meretricious nonsense from start to finish."

—Brendan Gill, *The New Yorker*

"Crummy . . . monumentally tasteless saga. . . . Unfortunately, Otto Preminger apparently was

George Kennedy as the bigoted sheriff and John Philip Law as the poor-but-honest white trash meet head to head in Otto Preminger's Hurry Sundown. *As critic Richard Schickel observed concerning this 1967 film: ". . . it is very possibly the worst major production to come out of Hollywood in the 1960s."*

out of town when the civil-rights movement started and still hasn't checked back in. Nobody told him t'..t the old prewar collection of pickaninnies, Uncle Toms, Uncle Remuses and Little Black Sambos just doesn't stand up any more as a sociological cross section of the black community in the South."

—Paul D. Zimmerman, *Newsweek*

"A gigantic masquerade in which the participants put on two things: a Southern accent and the audience. . . . Two hours of such cinematic clichés make the viewer intolerant of everyone in the film, regardless of race, creed or color."

—*Time*

"Two hour and 22 minute monstrosity . . . *Hurry Sundown* is sheer pulp fiction. . . . It is a massive mishmash of stereotyped Southern characters and hackneyed melodramatic incidents. . . . Totally flimsy in texture and dramatically beyond belief. . . . Stereotypes are lifted from the bottom of the Southern cracker barrel. . . . An offense to intelligence."

—Bosley Crowther, *New York Times*

"To criticize it would be like tripping a dwarf. . . . So low has the South fallen that Otto Preminger hasn't even bothered to get the accents straight."

—Wilfrid Sheed, *Esquire*

"It is Otto Preminger's worst, a hopelessly corny, clichéd soap opera. . . . Preminger's taste is atrocious. His idea of erotic symbolism is Jane Fonda caressing Michael Caine's saxophone. Like the film, the scene is decidedly off-key."

—William Wolf, *Cue*

"I'm sure that Mr. Preminger didn't aim at boring viewers or making them laugh at the wrong times, but he's doing just that. . . . Dreary, old-fashioned script. . . . I doubt if even the scenes in bad taste and those relying on sex symbols to make their point will hold the restless audience."

—Philip T. Hartung, *Commonweal*

"Disaster . . . to say that *Hurry Sundown* is the worst film of the still-young year is to belittle it. It stands with the worst films of any number of years. Otto Preminger has provided us not only with soap-opera plotting that gives *Peyton Place* Dostoievskian stature but also with cartoon characters and patronage of Negroes that are incredible in 1967. The whole melange would be offensive were it not simply ludicrous."

—Judith Crist,
New York World Journal Tribune

Plot Summary

Henry Warren (Michael Caine) is a ruthless speculator who combines all the worst features of Simon Legree and Sammy Glick. He is buying up real estate right and left, and only two parcels of land stand between him and his dreams of an enormous killing. One of the pieces of land belongs to a family of humble-but-hard-working poor blacks, while the other belongs to a family of hard-working-but-humble poor whites. Our anti-hero sends his conniving wife, Julie (Jane Fonda), to the black family to try to talk them out of their homestead. Conveniently enough, the matriarch of this tribe also served as Julie's ol' black mammy once upon a time. When Julie asks Mammy to part with her land, however, the old lady registers her surprise and indignation by collapsing on the floor in one of the most ludicrous heart-attack scenes in motion picture history.

After Mammy dies, leaving not a dry eye in the house, her strong, handsome young son Reeve (Robert Hooks) takes over the family farm. When Reeve also refuses to sell out to Henry Warren, this unspeakable baddie tries to ensnare the young buck in the toils of the law. He brings a complaint charging that Reeve lacks proper title to his land, but despite the efforts of a bigoted judge (Burgess Meredith) goodness prevails in the courtroom. Having tried everything else—except chasing Little Eva across the ice—Warren plays his trump card: a good ol' South'n-fried lynch mob. The mob marches over to the humble-but-hard working black farm, where they see all God's chillun enjoying an innocent, old-fashioned hoedown. They are eating fried chicken (what else?), guzzling watermelon juice (every detail is realistic, yassuh!), and singing (you guessed it!) Negro spirituals in perfect harmony. The lynch mob is so touched by the fact that some folks still care enough to honor all the old clichés that they leave the blacks alone and go

Beah Richards as the suffering mammy and Robert Hooks as her son Reeve: "I don' know nothin' 'bout radar, but I know when somethin's plaguin' ma chile." These two stars help make Hurry Sundown *the most realistic drama about life in the South since* Uncle Tom's Cabin.

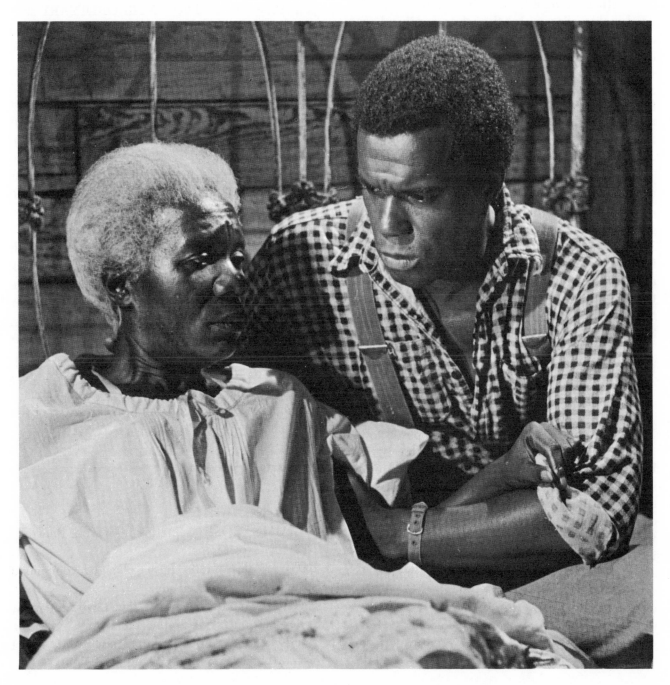

home to listen to their Stephen Foster records.

Frustrated in his tireless attempts to cheat the blacks, Henry meets similar failure in his dealings with the humble-but-hard-working poor whites who also happen to be his cousins. At this point, Henry decides that the only way to save his plans (and to arouse the audience) is to explode several tons of dynamite. He manages to blow up the local dam, causing a flood that is supposed to render the coveted land worthless and force the stubborn-but-humble-and-hard-working farmers to part with it. Whoosh! goes the water as the big flood makes all gone for the white family's house and land, but somehow, through heroic exertions, the blacks preserve their home. ("They endured," says William Faulkner in his famous note to *The Sound and the Fury*.) As everyone dries off, the blacks generously offer to help their neighbors rebuild the ruined farms. All is tranquillity and brotherhood reigns as the sun sinks slowly in the west.

As Richard Schickel has eloquently written, Otto Preminger "has made a movie about the relationship between the races in which men of good will—and even men of bad will—North and South, white and black, can come together and form a mighty chorus of agreement. Unfortunately, this agreement will be in the realm of aesthetics rather than morality and, more unfortunately still, it will have to be that *Hurry Sundown* is an execrable film."

Unforgettable Performances

Michael Caine as Henry Warren is supposed to be the heavy in this film, but instead of inspiring our hatred he provokes only pity for his losing struggle to reproduce a Southern accent. According to studio publicity, Caine learned the accent from a tape recorder while in Britain working on a film. We suggest that he begin looking for a better tape recorder. He generally sounds more Cockney than Southern, though occasionally he does manage to suggest the clipped diction of one of the Oxford-educated East Indian diplomats. Sorry, Michael, wrong colonies.

In *Hurry Sundown*, Burgess Meredith gets one of those roles he craves, in which his well-developed penchant for overacting can be indulged to its fullest. As a racist judge he wheezes and snarls and growls, suggesting a mad dog—complete with foam around the lips. Bored viewers can also entertain themselves by observing Meredith's pointless tendency to emphasize every third word or so of his speech—an endearing foible that surely must rank with Eric Sevareid's constantly blinking eyelids on the evening news. When Meredith addresses a lawyer defending a black, for instance, he delivers his lines as follows: "Are you AWARE, sir, how EXTRAORDINARY it is for a WHITE man to come into MY court and represent a BLACK boy?"

Beah Richards gives us "Aunt Rose"—Julie Warren's former mammy. She wears a stringy wig which seems to have been decorated with silver spray paint. Her performance is strictly Aunt Jemima, until her big moment, when she is supposed to have a heart attack. One can imagine Ms. Richards spending months in preparation for this scene—her big break in motion pictures. The result is a sequence that inevitably provokes hysterical laughter from film audiences. Perhaps some medical adviser should have explained to Beah Richards the difference between a heart attack and an epileptic seizure. She stumbles from side to side with her hands clutching the air and her eyes nearly popping out of her kindly old face. She gags and says, "Hwaargwhaaauceeick!" At long last she falls from view and we hear a booming thud on the floor. Jane Fonda, who is standing there to witness the "tragedy," seems to have a difficult time keeping a straight face. She's not the only one.

Immortal Dialogue

"MAMMY" ROSE: Sometin's ailin' you, Reeve.

REEVE: No, Mama.

ROSE: Well, sometin' hasn't changed your mood since breakfast. Tell me.

REEVE: Mama, you better dan anyo' dat radar dey had out in de Souf Pacific!

ROSE: I don' know nothin' 'bout radar, but I know when somethin's plaguin' ma chile.

110

(Rose is expecting Julie Warren to pay her a visit.)

ROSE (hearing people outside): Lor' Almighty, there she is!

(A black friend enters with her grandfather.)

REEVE: Shucks! An' we thought it was white folks!

* * *

(Rose and Julie carry on a conversation while Julie's child rests in Rose's arms.)

JULIE: Ah declare, Rose, Ah never saw him take to anyone like he does to you!

ROSE: Chillun' know who loves 'em.

JULIE: Oh, somtimes, Rose, Ah think you just about invented love. . . . Mind if Ah crochet while we talk?

* * *

(The bigoted judge gives a white lawyer a tongue-lashing for his help to the Negro defendant.)

JUDGE (steaming): Don't you RATTLE your skeleton in MY court!!! Your being here at ALL constitutes a TREACHERY to the ENTIRE white community that's too COLOSSAL to be believed!!!

The Story Behind the Film

When Otto Preminger began work on *Hurry Sundown*, he described the film as his "most important project." He had acquired the rights to the best-selling novel by K. B. Gilden and budgeted $4 million for production. Preminger always prefers to shoot his films on location, but rather than filming in Georgia, where the book was set, he moved his crew to Baton Rouge, Louisiana. From the start, a number of production complications marred the solemn, do-gooder aura surrounding the film. Several members of the crew had to be discharged because they outraged the Louisiana natives one hot day by sunbathing on (gasp!) a Confederate flag.

Among its other distinctions, *Hurry Sundown* was the first film with black actors in starring roles to be shot totally in the South. During produc-

Jane Fonda playing Michael Caine's saxophone in Hurry Sundown. *Could this scene be intended symbolically?*

tion, the company was greeted with much antagonism. Town scenes were filmed in St. Francisville, which happened to be the center of Ku Klux Klan activities in Louisiana. Many of the black actors were unable to receive service in the village's restaurants. Threatening telephone calls were made to other members of the cast and crew. The motel that sheltered the outcast company was protected by armed state troopers every minute of their stay. Many of the crew's cars ended up with slashed tires. All this excitement concerning a film that proved so fatuous and backward in its racial outlook thoroughly demonstrates the demented nature of the racist mentality. Diahann Carroll, who plays a young black schoolteacher in the film, commented, "You can cut the hostility here with a knife. I'm not a fighter. I usually smile and then go into my room and cry my eyes out. But down here the terror has killed my taste for going anywhere."

The Balance Sheet

Hurry Sundown received its New York premiere at a gala occasion under the honorary chairmanship of Mayor and Mrs. John V. Lindsay. Lindsay's special relationship with Preminger later payed off when the retired politician played the part of a U.S. senator in another Preminger turkey, *Rosebud*.

In promoting *Hurry Sundown,* Preminger used one of the most sanctimonious ad campaigns in Hollywood history. The tag line that most frequently appeared was "Will the South Overcome the Bigotry of the Hate-Laden White Aristocrats?" Preminger obviously hoped to set up a situation in which anyone who criticized his awful film was taking the side of the "hate-laden white aristocrats"—heaven forbid! The promotional strategy fell on its face, however, and the film was widely attacked for its hoary and two-dimensional stereotypes. Preminger responded by insisting, "This is not a *Defiant Ones* or the Sammy Davis show. It is a very fair picture that shows the problems of all people."

The National Catholic Office of Motion Pictures added to the swelling chorus of criticism by giving the film a "C"—or "condemned"—rating. A representative of that agency reported, "Superficial and patronizing in its treatment of racial attitudes and tensions, this melodramatic depiction of life in a small Southern town during the 1940s is also frequently prurient and demeaning in its approach to sex." In reply, Preminger could only comment weakly, "I'm sorry they didn't like my film."

Despite all the controversy surrounding it, *Hurry Sundown* grossed a limp $4.05 million—producing only a very modest return on the initial investment. Preminger received no honors from the film industry for his achievement, but he did receive a badge as "honorary sheriff" of Baton Rouge, Louisiana, one of the cities in which the film was made. Perhaps the townspeople felt he deserved the award because of his striking resemblance to the bumbling, slow-witted sheriff in the film.

Nikolai Cherkassov, going through his interminable death throes in Ivan the Terrible. *As one viewer called out in the French premiere audience:* "Alors, mon vieux, *kick the bucket and we'll all go home!*"

IVAN THE TERRIBLE (1943–1946)

PARTS I AND II

Directed by: SERGEI EISENSTEIN
Written by: SERGEI EISENSTEIN
Produced by: SERGEI EISENSTEIN
Music by: SERGEI PROKOFIEV
Featuring: NIKOLAI CHERKASSOV, SERA-
PHIMA BIRMAN, LUDMILA TSELIKOV-
SKAYA, PAVEL KADOCHNIKOV, MIKHAIL
NAZVANOV, ANDREI ABRIKOSOV, VSEVO-
LOD PUDOVKIN

Mosfilm

The Critics Rave

". . . a motionless motion picture. In some
scenes only the slow movement of the eyeballs
gives evidence of life."
  —Virginia Wright, *Los Angeles Daily News*

". . . over-long and ponderous."

—*Variety*

". . . a series of dramatic tableaux with
rather choppy continuity and a minimum of subtlety in the characterization."

—*Newsweek*

". . . demoded, primitive acting that combines the weighty drama of early opera with the
first rushes of *The Great Train Robbery*."
  —Shirley O'Hara, *The New Republic*

"... slow-paced to the point of discomfort. . . . The film appears to be more a curiosity than anything else, filled with plots rather than plot, done in a style that is supposedly monumental, and containing much rolling of eyes by leading Soviet actors."

—*Saturday Review*

"I've missed my chance, I didn't die at the right time. What a monument you would have raised in my memory if I had died straight after *The Battleship Potemkin*! I've made a mess of my own biography!"

—Sergei Eisenstein, director of the film.

Plot Summary

Young Ivan is crowned Czar of Russia but the nobles (the Boyars) refuse to accept his authority. In the interminable coronation scene, the costumes and make-up appear to have been designed by Dr. Seuss, and we are treated to at least ten different species of "suspicious leers." Apparently, all of this is enough to make Ivan sick, for he is soon lying on his deathbed. The Boyars impatiently await his demise, and Ivan builds up their hopes—and the hopes of the audience—by proclaiming, "The end is near. . . . I bid the world farewell. Swear allegiance to my legitimate heir—Dmitri." Dmitri is Ivan's infant son, but since most of the nobles have long hated Ivan, they all look in different directions pretending that they haven't heard anything. Even in his death throes, Ivan somehow notices that they are not paying attention, and so staggers out of bed, extends his arms, yells their names desperately. They uncomfortably turn their heads from him and face the wall or look up at the ceiling as if waiting for a train. Ivan scrambles around the floor on his hands and knees, bellowing again and again, "Swear allegiance to my son!" At long last he struggles to his feet and cries, "You will all be cursed forever!" as he melodramatically stumbles around the room with one arm thrown over his forehead, looking like an intoxicated go-go dancer.

To everyone's disappointment, Ivan survives.

His resurrection, in fact, is one of the most remarkable ever filmed: within ten minutes of straight time sequence he proceeds from his deathbed to complete recovery, at the cost of only two extra inches of make-up.

Particularly hard hit by Ivan's recovery is the ambitious Prince Kurbsky, commander of the Imperial Army. While Ivan was sick, Kurbsky had been lasciviously eyeing the pretty young Empress, but now he has to limit himself to raising one eyebrow suggestively in her direction. With his wavy blond hair, watery sheep's eyes, and chronic indecisiveness, Kurbsky in this film resembles Gene Wilder clowning his way through a Mel Brooks comedy. In fact, the way Eisenstein handles his actors throughout the film recalls Brooks more strongly than it does any other director. The key distinction between the two is that *Ivan the Terrible* was not *intended* as parody.

Ivan's chief enemy is another figure from stock comedy: the sinister, menacing, battle-ax aunt, complete with heavy eyebrows and tight-lipped frown. One evening when Ivan's wife requests a glass of water before going beddy-bye, this aunt, slinking around the palace as is her wont, puts a goblet of poison on the bed table. Ivan, not noticing the overweight, threatening figure two feet behind him, takes the poison cup and passes it on. The Empress dies and Ivan swears vengeance on his unknown enemies. Eventually he accumulates a significant bundle of dead bodies at his feet, but he proclaims, "That is not enough!" The audience may well be inclined to disagree with him.

Part II of this seemingly endless epic is highlighted by the attempts of Ivan's aunt to destroy the Czar and to place her own retarded son on the throne. At one point she admits to the audience that her boy "is worse than a child—he is moronic." This line is perhaps the only aspect of the entire film that is understated.

During a drunken banquet, Ivan has a burst of conspiratorial genius. He dresses his imbecile cousin in the imperial robe and crown, and the assassin hired by the Boyars kills the moron instead of Ivan. When Ivan's aunt realizes that it is her own son, not Ivan, who has been killed, she bursts into spasmodic screams. The assassin meanwhile yells, "Torture me! Execute me! You'll never make me speak!" Ivan's aunt finally holds her dead son in her arms and sings him a lullaby about a beaver. The triumphant closing music plays as Ivan delivers his inspiring lines: "The internal enemies of Russia's unity have been vanquished. Now my hands are free!"

Unforgettable Performances

Nikolai Cherkassov, who plays the title role, is a magnetic screen presence. He was undeniably great in Eisenstein's masterpiece *Alexander Nevsky,* but here, like the rest of the cast, his acting sinks to the level of absurd burlesque. He registers every emotion by opening his eyes as wide as he possibly can, twisting his mouth into a grimace, and thrusting his bearded chin toward the heavens. A former ballet dancer, Cherkassov's performance is as stilted and stylized as that of a mask dancer in a Kabuki drama. He also demonstrates his balletic skills by pirouetting around his bedchamber several times in the laughable death scene. He prided himself on his make-up for this role—going through sixteen make-up changes during the course of the picture. But for all that trouble he could only manage a long, scraggly black beard that recalls Richard Kiel's caveman in the horror classic *Eegah!* (q.v.). In a desperate attempt to make Ivan into a heroic figure, Eisenstein apparently ordered Cherkassov to bellow all his lines like a moose during mating season. The result is particularly entertaining whenever the other performers attempt to outshout him.

Cherkassov is most notably upstaged by one Seraphima Birman, who plays Ivan's wicked aunt with all the subtlety and complexity one might expect from the evil witch in a *Hansel and Gretel* children's pageant. Her range of dramatic expression is limited to two distinct facial expressions: a menacing frown, or a tight-lipped grin denoting vicious glee. She doesn't so much bellow her lines as bleat them, and like all the actors in this film, she rolls her eyes endlessly.

The only performer who seems entirely at home in his role is Pavel Kadochnikov, who plays Ivan's retarded cousin. With his gigantic child-like eyes and moppy hair, he looks like Harpo Marx on tranquilizers.

Immortal Dialogue

KURBSKY: Anastasia . . . if you will be mine, we will rule Russia together! (She tries to run

Czar Ivan the Terrible (Nikolai Cherkassov) with his Queen, Ludmila Tselikovskaya. In Cherkassov's performance, he registers every emotion by opening his eyes as wide as possible, twisting his mouth into a grimace, and thrusting his bearded chin toward the heavens.

away, but he holds her back.) Without you, my life has no meaning! With you, the throne or the scaffold—it's all the same. (He moves closer to her.) My Czarina of Moscow!

ANASTASIA: Prince, one does not bury a man before he is dead.

KURBSKY (astonished): You mean—Ivan isn't dead?!

ANASTASIA: God will be your judge! (She hurries out.)

KURBSKY (whispering to himself): Ivan is not dead!

*   *   *

IVAN: I hold great power. But I have no close friends. God refuses me the sweet consolations of friendship. On whose shoulders can I rest my head? With whom can I share my joys and sorrows? I am alone, abandoned.

*   *   *

MALYUTA: Why give the bishop such power over you? Why let yourself be humiliated by an ignorant priest?

IVAN: None of your business, dog!

MALYUTA: I know I am a dog . . . but a faithful dog. You are wrong, Czar, to prefer a priest to a dog.

*   *   *

IVAN: Henceforth, I will be as you call me—terrible!

*   *   *

The Story Behind the Film

Ivan the Terrible was originally commissioned by Stalin as a means of building support for the political persecutions and mass murders of his regime. In Part I, the view of Ivan struggling heroically against "internal enemies" in order to achieve "Russian unity" was specifically designed to please the Maximum Leader, and Eisenstein was rewarded with the Stalin Prize First Class. Part II, however, with its emphasis on the bloody and demented aspects of Ivan's rule, made Stalin uncomfortable. In 1946, the Party Central Committee duly announced that production on Eisenstein's projected Part III would be halted. *Ivan, Part II* was officially banned in Russia until 1956—three years after Stalin's death.

Nearly all of this epic was shot in Alma-Ata in Central Asia. .Filming of the interior scenes was done at night, since the area was plagued by fuel shortages ånd electricity was unavailable in the daytime. The entire film was made without benefit of a shooting script: the only basis for this monumental project was informal notes and drawings made by Eisenstein. This procedure may help to account for the thousand meaningless silent interchanges that mar the film: the characters are constantly making idiotic faces at one another as if they can think of nothing better to do.

The music for this production was provided by no less a man than Sergei Prokofiev, one of the major figures in twentieth-century music. Prokofiev had previously proved his genius as a film composer with his unforgettable score for Eisenstein's *Alexander Nevsky*. Yet for *Ivan*, Prokofiev's heart was obviously not in his work. The score oscillates between banality and hysteria—much of the time Prokofiev's main purpose appears to be to generate enough noise to keep the audience awake during the film's many somnolent sequences.

The Balance Sheet

The western premiere of *Ivan, Part I* came at the Normandie Theater on Paris's Champs Elysées. The over-flow crowd was so outraged and disappointed by the film that a minor riot ensued. As *Time* Magazine reported, the French sophisticates booed and stomped and hissed at Eisenstein's ludicrous excesses. "When Ivan's enemies mugged fear, Frenchmen cheerfully shouted, 'Cowards!' When the sound track jammed as Ivan received a chess set from Queen Elizabeth, someone in the balcony yelped: 'Speech!' In the long scene where Ivan almost dies, the theater rustled with smothered laughter and one strident voice speared up from the dark: '*Alors, mon vieux*, kick the bucket and we'll all go home!' " In the United States, the film opened to an equally noisy and frustrated crowd.

Yet in the thirty years since its premiere *Ivan* has risen consistently in critical estimation until it now enjoys the status of an enshrined "classic." This unmerited acclaim is not hard to understand: many critics are moved by respect for Eisenstein's previous great achievements, others are operating on the theory that any film so painful and tedious to watch must count as some sort of classic. Inspired by the solemn hosannas of this critical elite, thousands upon thousands of viewers have subjected themselves to this cinematic torture over the years, and come away shaking their heads. The average filmgoer should trust his own instincts in reacting to a film like this—the fact that a movie is overwrought and boring does not mean that it is somehow edifying or "good for you." We hope that by including this film on our list we will be striking a blow for oppressed viewers everywhere, and pointing out that in *Ivan's* case, at least, this much-heralded Russian Emperor is wearing no clothes.

116

JAMAICA INN (1939)

Directed by: ALFRED HITCHCOCK
Written by: SIDNEY GILLIAT, JOAN HAR-
RISON, ALMA REVILLE, J. B. PRIESTLEY
Produced by: ERICH POMMER and CHARLES
LAUGHTON
Music by: ERIC FENBY
Featuring: CHARLES LAUGHTON, MAUREEN
O'HARA, LESLIE BANKS, ROBERT NEWTON,
EMLYN WILLIAMS, MARIE NEY, WYLIE
WATSON, MORLAND GRAHAM, EDWIN
GREENWOOD, MERVYN JOHNS, STEPHEN
HAGGARD, HORACE HODGES, HAY PETRIE

Mayflower Productions/Paramount Pictures

The Critics Rave

"Doubly disappointing . . . misfired period
melodrama of smugglers and wreckers . . . one
of the problems of the film was that there really
was no mystery."
　　　　　　　　—William K. Everson, *Take One*

"If Hitchcock's ennui isn't so apparent on the
screen, the phlegmatic acting of Charles
Laughton is . . . bombastic gesticulations and
schticks, all of which made the story drag."
　　—Robert A. Harris and Michael S. Lasky, *The
Films of Alfred Hitchcock*

"A dully boisterous smuggling adventure. . . ."
　　　　　　　　—Lindsay Anderson, *Sequence*

"Mr. Laughton's Laughtonism has slowed
things down . . . overplaying unashamedly
. . . it doesn't seem like Hitchcock."
　　　　　　　—Frank S. Nugent, *New York Times*

"Undistinguished and creaky . . . there is a
marked lack of enthusiasm in all this early nine-

teenth-century nonsense. . . . The film was grotesquely overshadowed by the extravagant performance of Charles Laughton . . . dreary improbability."

—George Perry, *Hitchcock*

"One of the 25 Worst Films on TV . . . incredibly dull. How could you, Alfred?"

—Leonard Maltin, *Esquire*

Plot Summary

In England of the 1800s, a band of smugglers comes up with a "brilliant" idea. They black out warning signals to ships during storms, thereby causing the ships to crash on the nearby rocks. At first, we see an inexpensive toy boat tossed back and forth in a viciously churning bathtub, while the sound track goes wild with howling and thunderclaps. This dinky Revel model eventually tips over and the ruthless smugglers kill off all the sailors who wash ashore. The head of this motley collection of no-goodniks is a distinguished squire named Sir Humphrey Pengallon (Charles Laughton). The feeble plot, such as it is, actually commences when a sweet young orphan, Mary (Maureen O'Hara), goes to visit her uncle, Joss Merlyn (Leslie Banks), at a creepy hostelry known as Jamaica Inn. Little does she know that her uncle is actually one of the smugglers (oh horror!).

Lloyd's of London begins to wonder why so many ships just happen to crash off the Cornish coast near Jamaica Inn, and why there are never any survivors of the shipwrecks. They send one of their sturdiest men, Mr. Jem Trahearne (Robert Newton), to investigate. Trahearne checks in at the unsavory Jamaica Inn; the smugglers soon catch on to him and try to hang him. Sweet Mary, however (remember her?), cuts him loose and saves his life. This forms an emotional bond between them, and together they hide from the smugglers, the smugglers hide from them, and everyone hides from everyone else. In fact, the whole film resembles a colossal game of hide-and-go-seek; in every scene, someone is dodging just out of the way of someone else. People look through windows and then cower away just before being noticed. Others creep beneath staircases while their opponents go up or down. In one scene, Mary lurks suspiciously behind a pillar as Sir Humphrey Pengallon talks to one of his colleagues. She stands only two feet away from him, and Charles Laughton as Pengallon must exert all his acting abilities to pretend not to notice her.

The fun and games at Jamaica Inn eventually drive Sir Humphrey mad, and the viewer can certainly sympathize with him. He seems as desperate for genuine action as we are, and so kidnaps Mary, gags her, dresses her in a concealing black robe, and tosses her over his shoulder. Losing interest in this caper, he scrambles up to the crow's nest (cuckoo's nest?) of a ship and theatrically demonstrates his insanity by yelling to the townspeople gathered at the dock, "What are you all wating for? A spectacle? You shall have it! . . . Make way for Pengallon!" He then proceeds to jump, and leaves a predictably tremendous hole in the ship's deck. Once the big bad wolf has done himself in, the rest of the cast is free to live happily ever after, to the surprise of absolutely no one.

Robert Newton (left), as the heroic insurance investigator Jem Trahearne, confronts the sly criminal, Leslie Banks, in Jamaica Inn. *Charles Laughton, as arch-fiend Sir Humphrey Pengallon, looks on in abject terror.*

You may think that Maureen O'Hara is helping Leslie Banks adjust his contact lens. Wrong again. She's actually comforting her smuggler uncle in Alfred Hitchcock's Jamaica Inn.

Unforgettable Performances

Charles Laughton plays Sir Humphrey Pengallon, the obese smuggler king. In order to demonstrate the fact that he is a cultured aristocrat he wears a white ruffled shirt and black vested suit. (He does not, however, wear a Pen-gallon hat.) Actually, he resembles Sir Humphrey Dumpty more than Sir Humphrey Pengallon. His giant dark eyebrows seem to have been painted on with shoe polish. His plump, blubbery cheeks and ripe prune mouth suggest the happy baby on the label of Gerber's baby food jars. When he registers emotion—fear, lust, greed, anything—he simply wrinkles his face and takes on a resemblance to that same baby with a disturbing case of colic. In nearly all his roles Laughton has a tendency toward overacting, but when a director can hold that tendency in check the result can be a riveting, electrifying performance. Here, Laughton is allowed to run wild, stumbling through his role with self-indulgent mannerisms, shameless upstaging, and an obvious desire to caricature rather than to characterize. The worst of it is that with the flat texture of the direction and the lifeless dimensions of the plot, the result of all his bluster and gooniness isn't even vaguely amusing.

This film marked Maureen O'Hara's screen debut. She was eighteen years old at the time the film was made and her tender years, as well as her quite astonishing beauty, should help us to forget her abysmal performance. Perhaps Miss O'Hara was misinformed about her role, and told that she was supposed to play the part of a suffering consumptive: every sentence is punctuated with a half-dozen extra breaths, and for moments of genuinely high drama she manages to register a gasp.

Leslie Banks is Joss Merlyn, Mary's smuggler uncle. For this role, Mr. Banks sports a furry frock resembling the jacket usually worn by Frankenstein's monster. He even walks with a stiff, heavy-footed stride that further suggests that he has just emerged from a laboratory table. His sporadic "fits of anger" provide the film with some of its few entertaining moments, as he shouts and twists and rolls his eyes, lifting his eyebrows menacingly up to his forehead. It is the sort of vivid, clownish overacting that one would expect at the monkey house in the zoo, though in this film it is Mr. Banks's only hope to win some attention away from the overwhelming Mr. Laughton.

Immortal Dialogue

(A stagecoach passes by eerie Jamaica Inn.)

STAGECOACH DRIVER: That place—Jamaica Inn. It's got a bad name. It's not healthy, that's why. There's queer things goes on there.
WOMAN: Eh?
STAGECOACH DRIVER: *Queer* things. I once slept there and not a sheet was on my double bed.

* * *

(Sir Humphrey Pengallon admires one of his figurines.)
SIR HUMPHREY: What a rare beauty.
LADY: But it's not alive!
SIR HUMPHREY: More alive than half the people here.

(Hear! Hear!)

* * *

(Mary and Aunt Patience are finally reunited.)
AUNT PATIENCE: Mary! Mary! My sweet, sweet Mary! (Suddenly looking at Mary's clothes.) Mary, you're in black!
MARY: Yes— (looking down at the ground)— Mother died three weeks ago.
AUNT PATIENCE (sympathetically): How did it happen?
MARY: She hadn't been well. . . .You know how Mother was.

* * *

(One of the smugglers' prisoners is afraid of death.)
PRISONER: I don't want to die! I don't want to die! Not yet! I'm only a boy! . . . You can't hang me! You mustn't! You can't!

* * *

The Story Behind the Film

No one who sees this film could doubt that the self-indulgent star, and not the director, was in control, and a glance at the credits confirms that impression. Producer of this epic was Mayflower Productions—Charles Laughton's very own company. Previously, Mayflower had offered the public two less-than-choice appetizers: *Vessel of Wrath* (a.k.a. *The Beachcomber*) and *St. Martin's Lane* (a.k.a. *The Sidewalks of London*). Unfortunately, Laughton's struggling enterprise began going bankrupt and needed a hit to help retire its growing debts. In desperation, they hoped to persuade the famed Alfred Hitchcock—who had just enjoyed international success with his great film *The Lady Vanishes*—to apply his magic touch to Mayflower's failing fortunes. Hitchcock, who was preoccupied with the arrangements for his move to America and a contract with David O. Selznick, carelessly agreed to direct an adaptation of Daphne du Maurier's novel *Jamaica Inn*. He hardly knew what he was getting into.

On the sets, the quarrels between Hitchcock and Laughton reached legendary dimensions. Producer-star Laughton usually got his way, much to the detriment of the film. He wasted precious time while the entire crew stood by as he experimented for hours with various walks for his characterization of Sir Humphey Pengallon. He also demanded to wear a putty nose for the role, in order to make the squire seem even fatter. Seeing that the film would become burlesque whether he wanted it that way or not, Hitchcock proceeded to dash it off in perfunctory style, while he packed his bags and looked forward to America. *Jamaica Inn* would prove to be his last British film until *Stage Fright* (1950).

The Balance Sheet

By the time *Jamaica Inn* was released in 1939, Hitchcock had already established such a great name for himself that audiences crowded into the theater expecting to see a taut, fascinating mystery. The film broke records at London's Regal Theatre with its five-week run. When the word got out about the actual content and quality of this sloppy, dismal melodrama public interest began to taper off. Though the film ultimately showed a profit, it was not enough to prevent Mayflower Productions from sinking. The production company folded shortly after the film's release, while Hitchcock, Laughton, O'Hara, et al. went on to projects more worthy of their talents.

JET ATTACK (1958)

Directed by: EDWARD L. CAHN
Written by: ORVILLE HAMPTON
Produced by: ALEX GORDON
Story by: MARK HANNA
Music by: RONALD STEIN
Featuring: JOHN AGAR, AUDREY TOTTER, GREGORY WALCOTT, JAMES DOBSON, LEONARD STRONG, NICKY BLAIR, JOE HAMILTON, ROBERT CARRICART, GEORGE CISAR

American International Pictures

The Critics Rave

Gregory Walcott, James Dobson, and John Agar await a new assignment in Jet Attack—*an inspiring patriotic film about America's triumphal role in Korea.*

"After specializing so long in rock and roll epics and little etudes of assorted teenage monstrosities, American International has finally discovered that war is box office. Which helps explain the arrival of *Jet Attack*. . . . Scriptwise, the film crawls with clichés. . . . There is also an improbable ease of movement and concealment behind 'enemy' lines, but then, when Korea looks so much like Chatsworth, we suppose anything is possible."
                                    —*Los Angeles Times*

"Badly written, poorly directed and acted. The photography ranges from good to bad with a considerable amount of the air footage very grainy and probably coming from the files."
                                    —*Motion Picture Exhibitor*

"BOMB (lowest rating). . . . Sloppy Korean War programmer about rescue of U.S. scientist caught behind North Korean lines."
                                    —Leonard Maltin, *TV Movies*

Plot Summary

As brass and timpani play a heroic fanfare, an American jet squadron is suddenly attacked by airborne North Koreans. The Americans are testing out a new radio device, and wouldn't you know it, the jet carrying the scientist who invented the gizmo, Dean Olmstead, is shot down.

When the leader of the American squad, Captain Tom Arnette (John Agar), returns to the air base, he is informed by his commanding officer, Colonel Catlett (George Cisar), that the experiment was an enormous success, except for the unfortunate loss of Dr. Olmstead: "We can appreciate what we've lost," says the colonel. Suddenly a Korean peasant appears with news of an old man's being taken prisoner after a jet crash in the vicinity where Olmstead's plane was downed. Could it be? Well, let's see now. Judging by what we saw of Olmstead's crash, only the Bionic Man (with a St. Christopher medal) could survive such a smashup. But Colonel Catlett decides it's worth the risk of sending in some soldiers to investigate. With thinking like that, no wonder we did so well in Korea.

Captain Arnette is ordered to head the mission. Assigned to accompany him are Bill Clayborne (Gregory Walcott), a hillbilly navigator who likes to shoot people, and a beatnik communications officer named Chick, a sort of poor man's Maynard G. Krebs.

The team parachutes into North Korea, where they are to meet some indigenous friendlies who will provide background support. All the while the studio orchestra is providing background support of its own. The heroic fanfare by this time has been repeated about 840 times, and the film is only a quarter of the way over.

As our three heroes float gracefully down to earth, they are greeted by enemy gunfire. "Reds! Hit the dirt!" shouts Captain Tom. A battle ensues, but the Americans are hopelessly outnumbered. "Looks like we've had it!" shouts Clayborne, with his gun blazing. "At least we gave it a good try!" answers Tom. But, lo and behold, bursting out of the bush come the friendly guerrillas. They kill off the naughty Reds and whisk our heroes to their cave hideaway.

In the romantic cavern, Tom makes a rendezvous with Tanya (Audrey Totter), a Russian medical aide who had saved Tom's life a year before when he plunged down behind enemy lines. Tanya's willingness to collaborate with the American is explained by the fact that she is a White Russian. To make certain that the film avoids racism, we also are offered an alternative explanation: she's in love with Tom. When she enters the cave, the music changes from heroic fanfare to gypsy violin. That's so you know Tanya's Russian. Her accent would lead you to believe that she's mongoloid. Tanya promises that she'll do everything she can to find out whether Olmstead is still alive. She returns to her medical station and attempts to pry some information out of her commanding officer, Dr. Kuban (Robert Carricart). Her snooping arouses the suspicion of a Korean officer, Major Wan (Leonard Strong), who is "inscrutable" in the best Fu Manchu tradition. When he enters, the music changes to the "Fang Yang Song." It's reassuring to know that Hollywood has put Wagner's concept of *leitmotif* to good use.

Tanya discovers Olmstead in a hospital bed, uninjured. Actually, this man's powers of invulnerability are far more important than his radio device. Tanya reports back to Tom and company, and they disguise themselves as Russian doctors (which isn't very difficult—all you need is a uniform and a silly accent). Under cover from the Korean guerrillas, Tom, Clayborne, and Tanya, escape with Olmstead, but Chick the bongo boy is captured.

With Olmstead safe but hungry they arrive at the appointed rendezvous spot and await a helicopter. The Reds are hot on their trail. As the chopper lands, the pilot is shot and slumps, like a corpse, on the seat. Clayborne makes a dash for the whirlybird, nudges the pilot, and says, "C'mon, you're all right." And sure enough, the pilot gets up, jumps out of the helicopter, and runs for cover. There are more miracles in this film than in *Solomon and Sheba* (q.v.). However, Clayborne is shot down before he's able to melt the enemy's guns into plowshares. Tom, Tanya, Olmstead, and Sandy the helicopter pilot jump into a truck and take off down a nearby road. In hot pursuit are two truckloads of North Korean soldiers, firing at our heroes. Tanya is nicked in the arm but manages to drive the truck to a Red airbase. The others jump out of the truck, and Tom carries Tanya to a rock where she dies of her nick, while the violin plays romantically in the background, with just a subtle hint of gypsy strains.

Now the Reds are coming fast. Tom and Sandy spy two idle MIGs at the end of the airstrip. "Ever have a ride in a MIG?" asks Captain Tom. "You ever flown one before?" asks Dr. Olmstead. "Always wanted to try," says the daring captain. "Well, I guess if . . . you can get it off the ground, I . . . I can sit in it," says Olmstead heartily. Sandy jumps into one of the Russian planes, while Tom and Olmstead (the latter still in his nightshirt) pile into the other. The two planes make perfect takeoffs. Suddenly the North Koreans arrive, blasting away in their own MIGs. Tom and Olmstead make it away safely, but Sandy can't seem to find the button that fires the machine gun (apparently the only difference between American and Russian jet fighters is the location of the machine gun trigger). Sandy is so busy looking for the button that he takes his eyes off the road and flies smack dab into a Korean jet. Tom, watching the fiery collision, says, his voice hushed in somber sincerity, "He did it . . . to save us." No, folks, he didn't—he just couldn't find the darned button. Tom and Olmstead make a perfect landing in the Russian MIG (who says foreign makes are hard to drive?). Colonel Catlett meets them on the ground and says proudly, "Nice work, Captain." Tom replies, "Thanks to the boys up there." He looks heavenward. The heroic fanfare swells, and a triangle formation of jets passes overhead.

Unforgettable Performances

It seems that Audrey Totter wasn't quite sure of which accent to use as the Russian Tanya. At different points in the film she could be either English, American, German, Russian, Japanese, Italian, or Cretin. She wears a black beret that looks like an enormous sock, and her lipstick is pure Crayola.

As Dr. Kuban, Robert Carricart misunderstood the director and thought that the name of his character also signified his nationality. He was made up to look like Desi Arnaz. His accent is more exaggerated than the one Fred Astaire used

in *Shall We Dance*, when the nimble dancer pretended to be Russian and ran around yelling, "Orchichornia!" Carricart's accent is so thick he distorts his face to speak such simple phrases as "Yes, yes, yes. That is best. Go!" He gesticulates so wildly that it would seem he is cuing deaf viewers in on the dialogue.

George Cisar, as Colonel Catlett, orders his soldiers around with the authority of Wally Cox coaching a pro football team. When his men steal the MIG, he practically stamps his foot as if to say, "Oh, those boys . . . just what mischief will they get into in their next exciting adventure?"

Although John Agar gets top billing in *Jet Attack*, all the other characters and performances are so much more bizarre than his that he seems to disappear. At best he looks dopey. Director Edward L. Cahn seems to have given Agar the direction, "Look handsome, and feel patriotic." Unfortunately, Agar seems unable to perform both actions at the same time.

Immortal Dialogue

CATLETT: If Olmstead is alive there is a chance the enemy may find ways to make him talk!
TOM: The old brainwash!
CATLETT: Exactly.

* * *

CATLETT: Tanya Nikova . . . you knew her quite well. . . .
TOM: A little more than casually, sir. I owe her my life.
CATLETT: And uh . . . she can be trusted?

* * *

BILL: You see? Such is life in Uncle Sam's air force!
CHICK: With wings you swing. Without a pair you're nowhere.
BILL: Y'know, I think I understand that!

* * *

123

Love Scene:

TANYA: Eef eet had not been for ze var, I vould not haf met you, und ve vould not be here now.

TOM: Yeah, I guess you're right. But there's . . . something better that the war can do for us.

TANYA: Vat's dat?

TOM: End.

TANYA: Oh, Tom. I hope ve both live to zee zat.

*   *   *

(The baddies torture Chick to try to make him talk.)

CHICK: Your whole caper's a boodle of bad jive. You're comin' strictly from Squaresville. Ha ha. What a gas!

WAN: (smacking him): Where are the others? How did you get here? Where are they taking the prisoner?

CHICK: Crazy.

WAN: We will stay here until he answers . . . in words I understand.

*   *   *

BILL: I'd feel a lot better if I knew what happened to Chick and the others.

TOM: Why think about it? We all know what happened to him.

BILL: He was a real offbeat character. But you couldn't help likin' the little schmo.

*   *   *

The Story Behind the Film

Jet Attack experienced several title changes before it claimed its current catchy cognomen. It was originally called *Jet Pilot*, but Howard Hughes objected because he had made a film of the same name with John Wayne. So *Jet Attack* producer Alex Gordon changed the title of his movie to *Jet Alert*. That apparently didn't sit right either, and the title was again changed, this time to *Jet Command*, and then finally to *Jet Attack*. The most appropriate title of all, *Jet Bomb*, never occurred to them.

The Korean War hit Hollywood at the wrong time. World War II, and the wealth of films it engendered, had just about depleted the public's interest in war movies. As the United Nations' forces battled away in Korea, Joe McCarthy and the House committee on Un-American Activities captured the public interest at home. And when the Committee pointed its finger at Hollywood itself, movieland quickly countered with films like *My Son John,* which (among other things) tells of a mother's reactions when she learns that her son is a member of the Communist Party. In the meantime, the Korean War was relegated to the "B" grade studios, and it was not until 1970 that Hollywood, via Robert Altman's *M*A*S*H*, discovered that black comedy was the only appropriate way of dealing with the Korean War.

The Balance Sheet

This film was budgeted at $100,000, which probably explains the number of stock shots used of jets flying around and crashing. Yet even this minimal investment proved misguided when the film was released.

Jet Attack was billed with *Suicide Battalion,* another winner from the same production company (American International Pictures), and by the same director, Edward L. Cahn. This film starred Mike Connors (see *Swamp Women*), who later became famous for his television portrayal of the detective Mannix. Director Cahn, however, became infamous for films such as *Experiment Alcatraz, The Creature with the Atom Brain, Girls in Prison, Curse of the Faceless Man, Guns, Girls and Gangsters, It, the Terror from Beyond Space,* and *Riot in a Juvenile Prison.*

Jet Attack and *Suicide Battalion* opened at three theaters in Los Angeles. Their first-run combined box-office receipts hit a record low of $14,000.

The stirring combat sequences from Jet Attack *will keep you on the edge of your chair.*

JONATHAN LIVINGSTON SEAGULL (1973)

Directed by: HALL BARTLETT
Written by: RICHARD BACH and HALL BART-LETT
Produced by: HALL BARTLETT
Music by: NEIL DIAMOND
Featuring the voices of: JAMES FRANCISCUS, JULIET MILLS, HAL HOLBROOK, RICHARD CRENNA, DOROTHY McGUIRE

Paramount Pictures

The Critics Rave

"No, I have not read *Jonathan Livingston Seagull*, but, oh, my God, did I ever see the movie! Seagulls, as the film stresses, subsist on garbage, and, I guess, you are what you eat. . . . As if this were not nauseating enough in itself, Neil Diamond composed and sings an ear-splitting and stomach-turning score, its platitudes and decibels running abreast and amuck. Jack Couffer's color cinematography looks like a morganatic marriage between the *National Geographic* and *Vogue*. . . . The dialogue—for the birds—is supplied by uncredited voices that speak in tones usually reserved for biblical epics and heartwarming B movies about boys and their pet hamsters. . . ."

—John Simon, *Esquire*

"Bird droppings. . . . If one must spend the better part of two hours following the adventures of a bird, far better that the hero be Daffy Duck than Johnathan Livingston Seagull . . . vomitous theosophy. . . ."

—Jay Cocks, *Time*

"A seemingly endless soppy stream of scenery, seagulls, and religiosity that flooded the screen for nearly two hours. . . . It's the sort of garbage only a seagull could love."

—Judith Crist, *New York*

"Strictly for the birds."

—Frank Rich, *New Times*

"Teeny-bopper psychedelics, facile moralizing. . . . The sort of slippery, equivocal goo found on weighing machine cards, fortune cookies and dime astrology guides. Interminable."

—Art Murphy, *Variety*

"These screen droppings add up to one laughable absurdity. . . . Here we have gulls who talk, seemingly endlessly, like adult idiots, and music by Neil Diamond that defies the ear, fine-feathered or human. Debit the direction to Hall Bartlett, and the screenplay to both Bartlett and author Richard Bach. This film is strictly for the gullible."

—William Wolf, *Cue*

Plot Summary

A flock of seagulls is seen surrounding a boat that is dumping fish heads into a harbor. The birds fight each other for the fish heads and from nowhere we hear voices on the sound track. Apparently these voices are supposed to represent the seagulls communicating with each other, but we do not see their beaks move. One of the seagulls, Jonathan Livingston (played by the voice of James Franciscus), doesn't like his current life of eating garbage. He wants to fly high up in the sky and see what there is to see of other parts of the earth. For his non-conformist views (hey man, I can *relate!*) Jonathan is commanded by the eldest member of the flock to depart and never return.

Jonathan takes a little vacation around the world and apparently dies. He goes up to the big aviary in the sky, where he meets a nice gull named Maureen Seagull (Juliet Mills). He is also taught that there are things seagulls can do other than eat garbage. Doing daredevil flying stunts, for instance. That's always good for a couple of kicks. He returns to his flock and brings the great news.

At first, the other seagulls scorn him. However, he soon shows *them* up. Jonathan plays faith healer as he makes the injured Fletcher Seagull fly loop-the-loops in the air. But Fletcher gets a little carried away and makes a crash landing. That's the end of Fletcher, but Jonathan still has a few tricks up his wing. He miraculously brings Fletcher back from the dead. Just in case anyone misses the religious significance, the producers provide a triumphant choral "Kyrie" on the sound track. The entire flock comments that he must be "the Son of the Great Gull" and everyone now loves little Jonny. They ask him to stay awhile, but Jonathan tells them that he has plenty more good deeds to do and that he must go—sailing off into the sunset to answer the summons wherever a seagulls calls out for help and cries for truth, justice, and the American way. Amen.

Jonathan Livingston Seagull (right) and Maureen Seagull (left) generate steamy sensuality in their love scene from the Hall Bartlett film.

128

Unforgettable Performances

The part of Jonathan was considered so demanding that two different seagulls and one dubbed voice (human) were used to fill the role. Thanks to skilled cinematography, the seagulls fared somewhat better than the human actor, James Franciscus, who was forced to mouth a series of "inspiring" clichés. Franciscus rises to the occasion by proving as earnest and forceful as an announcer on TV aspirin commercials. When he tries to show deepest emotion, Franciscus sounds as if he has a raw fish caught in his mouth.

Hal Holbrook was so anxious to finish his work on this film that he decided to dispense with any attempt at acting and simply shouted his way through his role as the Elder in the flock.

As for the other actors whose voices were used in the film: what can you say about a bunch of full-grown adults who are earning their living by providing speech for seagulls? At least they had the good sense to prevent their names from appearing on the formal credits of the film, though the studio graciously informed reviewers of the true identities of the guilty parties. They included Richard Crenna, Dorothy McGuire, and Juliet Mills.

Immortal Dialogue

(Jonathan explains his non-conformist ideals.)
JONATHAN: I want to fly where no seagull has flown before! . . . I want to know what there is to know of this life!

❖   ❖   ❖

JONATHAN'S PARENTS (Dorothy McGuire and Richard Crenna): Son, this may not be the best life, but it's all we know.
JONATHAN: There's got to be more to life than fighting for fish heads!

❖   ❖   ❖

(The Elder (Hal Holbrook) dismisses Jonathan from the flock.)
ELDER: You are henceforth and forever outcast!

❖   ❖   ❖

(Jonathan returns excitedly to his flock, bringing good news.)
JONATHAN: *Listen, everybody*! There's no limit to how high we can fly! We can dive for fish and never have to live on garbage again!

❖   ❖   ❖

The Story Behind the Film

Hall Bartlett, in the true *auteur* fashion, produced, directed, and wrote *Jonathan Livingston Seagull* and so must accept full responsibility. He

129

also made lesser-known films such as *All the Young Men, Navajo,* and *The Caretakers.* His first connection with the material for this film came when "the woman I loved" presented him with a copy of Richard Bach's smash best seller. Bartlett said, "I've been through about ten years of hell, up until very, very recently, where everything went wrong. I couldn't make a right move. The fear was on me that I would never make a picture again . . . then came a woman with such love to share, and then Jonathan, and suddenly everything was right." (Little did he know. . . .) Bartlett made the film independently at a budget of $1.5 million and on a production schedule of ten months. He sank as much of his own money into the film as possible. He mortgaged his home and put the money into the film's budget. He took most of his savings and invested them in the film. Several warnings from the gods were issued, trying to stop Bartlett from making the film. Most of the film was shot on the sunny California coast, but the crew suffered the coldest winter in fifty-two years. They persevered through temperatures as low as 28 degrees and six inches of rain. At one time, the crew was damned with an actual snowstorm. Another time, a gigantic wave came close to drowning part of the crew. One of the gulls attacked director of photography Jack Couffer and Bartlett was forced to give most of the workers baseball catcher's masks. Five of the ma-

jor seagulls used in filming became sick. With all these misfortunes, Bartlett unfortunately persevered, explaining, "I was born to make this movie."

The Balance Sheet

Before the film was even released, Bartlett had a flock of delightful lawsuits on his hands. Filmmaker Ovady Julber claimed the film had copied scenes from his 1936 film *La Mer,* and sued, but the case was dismissed. Neil Diamond sued, claiming that five minutes of his score was cut from the film without his personal approval and that twelve minutes of other music was inserted into the final print. Richard Bach sued, claiming that he was never given a copy of the final screenplay and insisting that the film had distorted the book. He wanted another forty minutes added to the already overlong product. The only folks who missed their chance to sue were the members of the Seagull Anti-Defamation League. Finally, Bartlett gave in to Neil Diamond's requests; but instead of adding the forty minutes that Bach demanded, he cut an additional seventeen minutes from the final version. It didn't help.

A study guide was prepared especially for students and teachers in hope that they would

study the film. The guide's introduction read, "Obviously, young people really dig—in every sense of the word—*Jonathan Livingston Seagull*. They look under its surface, and discover a clarification of their personal values. In the myth of a seagull who sought perfection, they find a focus for their quest for a life-style."

Attempting to cash in on the anticipated seagull bandwagon, several manufacturers created new products relating to the film. These articles all bore the name and official insignia of the famed seagull. The equipment included leisure footwear, bedsheets, autographed pillows, blankets, ready-made draperies, tablecloths, T-shirts, sweatshirts, tank tops, iron-on patches, handcrafted copper enamel pins, handcrafted yarn, punch needle rug kits, stuffed toys, greeting cards, plaques, posters, key chains, puzzles, and a game devised by Mattel, Inc.

The film was awarded the Blue Ribbon by the National Screen Council as "Best Picture of the Month for the Whole Family." It also happened to be one of the few G-rated films that month. The film was advertised as "Everyone's Book Is Now Everyone's Motion Picture." Well, not exactly everyone. The critics tore the film apart and it seems that the audiences weren't too attracted to it either. Despite the expensive promotional campaign and all the publicity, the film grossed only $1.6 million. Since Paramount had pur-

chased distribution rights from Bartlett for $2.1 million—not counting the enormous advertising expenses—the project was recorded as a major bomb.

SPECIAL AWARD

A collection of official *Jonathan Livingston Seagull* ready-made draperies, tablecloths, and punch needle rug kits goes to the Holiday Inn motel in Carmel, California. In the motel's room number 336, the most important seagulls for the film were kept. They were taken up to their motel room through the regular elevator after each day's work. Hotel guests would constantly get in the same elevator with these birds and think they were hallucinating—but no such luck. Ten sheets were placed around room 336 to protect the carpet. These sheets were changed each day. There were over twenty sea-gulls in the room. A ritual gag was to assign a new maid to change the sheets in room 336. She would open the door and walk right into a room full of birds. The only problem with the seagulls was that guests constantly complained about the noise: sometimes the birds could be heard as far down as the lobby. Things began to get a little bit violent as the gulls began to knock over the telephones and lamps. At the end, the entire motel room had been completely ruined . . . but what a worthy sacrifice for the cause of a great art.

KING RICHARD AND THE CRUSADERS (1954)

Directed by: DAVID BUTLER
Written by: JOHN TWIST
Produced by: HENRY BLANKE
Music by: MAX STEINER
Featuring: REX HARRISON, VIRGINIA MAYO, GEORGE SANDERS, LAURENCE HARVEY, ROBERT DOUGLAS, MICHAEL PATE, PAULA RAYMOND, NICK CRAVAT

Warner Brothers

The Critics Rave

"Director David Butler shows us why the Crusades never really amounted to much."
—*Time*

"With all the sound and fury and show of pageantry, the actor in the epic who steals the scene, for my money, is a Great Dane dog."
—Erskine Johnson, *Los Angeles Daily News*

"Richard conducts himself with a stupidity so immense as to be truly royal. . . . Laurence Harvey plays a Scottish knight who demonstrates his manly qualities by bellowing every speech, including his professions of love, at the very top of the decibel range. . . ."
—Lee Rogow, *Saturday Review*

". . . A Massive Hunk of Celluloid. . . . A hundred and fourteen minutes of *King Richard and the Crusaders* got me exactly nowhere. Don't ask me what it was all about. . . . There is continuous trouble, a fight a minute, and the sands of the Holy Land are stirred into thick clouds. . . . There is also a girl aboard—I think she's old Richard's cousin—who keeps calling him Dick Plantagenet. Tell

George Sanders (left) and Laurence Harvey joust furiously in the action-packed adventure King Richard and the Crusaders.

133

your children to try *that* one on their history teacher."

—Philip Hamburger, *The New Yorker*

"No doubt this film will make a tremendous contribution to the education of people throughout the nation."

—Dr. Frank Baxter,
University of Southern California.

Plot Summary

Richard the Lionhearted and his allies have hardly set foot in the Holy Land on the Third Crusade when a group of treacherous nobles plans to kill Richard and take command of the whole operation. They sneak up to his tent one night with a hired bowman. "Strike deep!" he is urged, "this is no ordinary man!" Instead of hitting his heart, the arrow lands in his stomach, which, in this film, is a difficult target to miss.

Nevertheless, the nobles all assume that Richard has gone on to his reward, and a council is held for the purpose of choosing a new leader. In the middle of the voting, the King makes his entrance. The trumpets sound and the drum roll begins as he is carried in on a carpet lifted by his obedient servants. George Sanders, as Richard, is grossly overweight. Dressed in his white nightie,

Virginia Mayo begs her fellow Christians to be tolerant of the Sultan Saladin (Rex Harrison): "He's a creature of conditions. It's this strange land, I think. This land is so different from our own."

riding on his carpet, he looks for all the world like a helpless oaf about to have his stomach pumped. As he enters, the extras enthusiastically wave their clenched fists in the air and shout, "God save the King! Hoo-ray!" King Richard then addresses his subjects with, "Dear traitors—it is still my odious pleasure to command you." To which the extras loudly respond: "Not traitors, sire! No! No!" It should be noted that throughout this film, the extras are always a peculiar sight. They wear laughable gray costumes (it is hard to tell the court jester from the others) and have gray bowls strapped over their heads. In fact, all the principal actors wear gray or brown bowls, except for George Sanders: he wears a silver pot. Whenever a nobleman or newly appointed officer walks on screen, these extras go wild. They jump up and down, raise their fists, and flap their arms enthusiastically as if preparing for takeoff. Oddly enough, it is only during the battle scenes that they seem lifeless and subdued.

In any event, in the midst of this interminable council scene Sir Kenneth (Laurence Harvey) first makes his appearance. He is a noble Scotsman, the only knight who is truly loyal to Richard. To make sure that we remember at all times that he is a Scot, Max Steiner's overblown score swells into a lively Highland fling whenever Harvey appears on screen. Sir Kenneth warns Richard about the traitors in his midst, and rides off to find evidence against them. Lady Edith (Virginia Mayo), Richard's cousin, is hopelessly in love with Sir Kenneth, but she can't marry him until he proves himself. Saladin (Rex Harrison), the wily Sultan, comes riding into camp disguised as a humble physician: he helps Richard recover from his wound, because without Dick Plantagenet to play with, all the fun would go out of their battles. The key element in his cure is a mystic song, full of the wisdom of the East, which Harrison croons to Richard while strumming a hand-held harp:

> "Dream, dream
> When paradise is in the heart
> There is no room for death."

All things considered, this serenade outdoes Harrison's later performance in *Doctor Dolittle* as the most embarrassing moment of his career. It is not enough, however, to deter the developing love

George Sanders (left) as Richard the Lionhearted, Rex Harrison (center) as Saladin, and Laurence Harvey as Sir Kenneth seem puzzled by the script of King Richard and the Crusaders.

interest between Saladin and Lady Edith. As a result, the Saracen continues to hang around, helps Sir Kenneth get the better of the traitors, and after innumerable chases, maces, jousts, and battles, the bad guys get what they deserve and Saladin and Richard can go back to the noble and enjoyable business of trying to kill one another. Sir Kenneth, however, as well as the viewer, has had more than enough: he decides to go home to Scotland with his lady love, where he will be free to play merrily on his pipes. (What else can a fun-loving Scottish knight do in his spare time?) In the last scene of the film, Richard tries in vain to persuade Sir Kenneth to re-enlist for another war in England. But pert Virginia Mayo gets the better of the argument with one deathless line: "War! War! That's all you think of, Dick Plantagenet! You burner! You pillager!" After this there is little more to say, and the lovers sail off together into the sunset.

Unforgettable Performances

Poor Rex Harrison! As Saladin, his ridiculous accent and hissing delivery make it seem as if he has just stumbled, by accident, off the set of *The Mikado*. The script calls for him to speak in quaint parables, as if each line were preceded by the two words "Confucius say." The director has obviously suggested that Harrison play the Saracen Sultan as "inscrutable," and the result is a lame imitation of Charlie Chan. Understandably, Harrison has done his best to disguise himself beyond the point of recognition. He is dressed in flowing Arab robes, with a blue towel piled on his head as if he just had his hair shampooed, and his skin is stained a dark brown like an imitation mahogany table. In the course of the film, Virginia Mayo defends Harrison and delivers her own powerful plea for racial understanding: "You must remember—he's a creature of conditions. He's not at fault for the sorry state of his soul. . . . It's this strange land, I think. This land is so different from our own."

Paula Raymond has only a small part in this film, but she takes advantage of every brief moment before the camera to make herself utterly ridiculous. She plays Queen Berengaria, Richard's wife, and her big scene comes as she is sobbing over her husband's wounded hulk. She is without question one of the worst sobbers in motion picture history. No tears come forth from her eyes, but a lot of bellowing comes forth from her mouth. Instead of holding a handkerchief to her eyes to wipe away the tears, she holds a handkerchief to her lips to wipe away the saliva. Her performance in *King Richard* put an end to her cinema career for about ten years, but her daughter has recently turned up as a star for Fairway-International, makers of the classic *Eegah!* (q.v.).

Laurence Harvey, described by one critic as "a promising young English newcomer," determinedly makes the most of the fact that *King Richard* was one of the first major film productions to use stereophonic sound. It is easy to imagine the unfortunate audio engineers covering their ears every time Harvey enters a scene. Sporting flowing blond locks and an obviously bogus blond beard, Harvey attacks his role with the raucous, panting enthusiasm of a high school yell-leader in the last five minutes of the Big Game. His love scenes with Virginia Mayo (there are four of them!) are particularly ludicrous. He is obviously unable to look at her and keep a straight face, and so he invariably stares directly into the camera.

Immortal Dialogue

Love Scene:

SIR KENNETH (Laurence Harvey): Oh, Edith! (He tries to sneak a kiss.)
LADY EDITH (Virginia Mayo): No, no, my dearly betrothed! Richard would set the headsman on your neck; he has said as much!
KENNETH: Then kiss me quickly, my bonnie, while these lips are still warm!
EDITH: No, no! (They kiss—music swells to a climax.) Ah . . . this is a pleasant madness!
KENNETH: A lunacy with which I would love to be afflicted—to the end of my life. If Richard would take my life, I must kiss softly.

     ❖   ❖   ❖

SALADIN: May the Seven Doves rest on your shoulders.
KENNETH: Doves or vultures, you slippery infidel?
SALADIN: Come, I invite you to share the waters of the oasis with me.

     ❖   ❖   ❖

EDITH (to Kenneth): I'm a Plantagenet—yet somehow I feel less proud. I'm beginning to despise war. The dread, the wondering each time you ride away if you'll come back among the living.

     ❖   ❖   ❖

The Story Behind the Film

King Richard and the Crusaders is very loosely based on Sir Walter Scott's romantic novel *The Talisman*. Whole generations of junior high school students have complained about being forced to read this book, yet they still might prefer that onerous task to 114 minutes spent in watching this film. The press book for *King Richard* boasts that Warners used 600 persons, 400 horses, 2 camels, a pair of falcons, goats, sheep, cattle, pigs, and dogs in this production. The studio also employed the greatest number of weapons used in a single film up to that time. These included 10,000 arrows, 400 shields and swords, 200 bows, 100 crossbows, as well as several hundred spears, lances, pikes, maces, battle-axes, flails, and daggers. The effectiveness of these props is seriously compromised by the ineptitude of the direction. In one memorable scene a flock of arrows floats limply through the air before falling to earth: it is clear that the stagehands have simply tossed them skyward and allowed them to settle to the ground like so many pick-up sticks. In addition to this film, the hapless director, David Butler, has a whole string of other triumphs to his credit, including four Bob Hope and seven Doris Day vehicles.

The Balance Sheet

It cost more than $3 million to produce this film, but to date, some twenty years after its premiere, it has grossed only $2.1 million. Though *King Richard* opened to an "enthusiastic crowd" at its Hollywood premiere in 1954, it closed after only three weeks. All was not lost, however: a colorful children's comic book was based directly on the film, and it has achieved a wide distribution.

Domestic tension between dying movie wrangler Dennis Hopper and his prostitute mistress Stella Garcia: just part of the fun in The Last Movie.

THE LAST MOVIE (1971)

Directed by: DENNIS HOPPER
Written by: STEWART STERN
Produced by: PAUL LEWIS
Music by: KRIS KRISTOFFERSON, JOHN BUCK WILKIN, CHABUCA GRANDA, SEVERN DARDEN, and THE VILLAGERS OF CHINCHERO, PERU
Featuring: DENNIS HOPPER, STELLA GARCIA, JULIE ADAMS, TOMAS MILIAN, DON GORDON, ROY ENGEL, DONNA BACCALA

Universal Pictures

The Critics Rave

"A hateful experience. . . ."
　　　—Andrew Sarris, *The Village Voice*

"Pure fiasco. . . ."
　　　　　　—Judith Crist, *New York*

"Inept and pretentious. . . ."
　　　—Bruce Williamson, *Playboy*

"An artistic disaster. . . ."
　　　　　　—William Wolf, *Cue*

"A wasteland of cinematic wreckage . . . the drug culture's *Around the World in Eighty Days* . . . just plain pitiful."
　　　—Robert Ebert, *Chicago Sun-Times*

"Gaseous and overblown mess. . . . I hope that *The Last Movie* fails very badly and that it's difficult for Dennis Hopper to get another picture. . . ."
　　　—Stanley Kauffmann, *New Republic*

"Inchoate, amateurish, self-indulgent, tedious, superficial, unfocused . . . dismally disappointing and depressing."

—Charles Champlin, *Los Angeles Times*

"Puerile . . . it is narcissistic but not introspective, psycho but not analytic—a shotgun wedding of R. D. Laing and 'The Late Show.'"

—Stefan Kanfer, *Time*

"Lowest rating . . . a prime example of the kind of self-gratification that is destroying the film industry."

—Kathleen Carroll, *New York Daily News*

"Everywhere we sniff Hopper's overwhelming egotism. . . ."

—Paul D. Zimmerman, *Newsweek*

"This movie performs the astounding feat of dying on the screen in the first few minutes, before the credits come on. One would have to be playing Judas to the public to advise *anyone* to go see *The Last Movie*."

—Pauline Kael, *The New Yorker*

"An extravagant mess . . . my mind had a good deal of trouble tolerating the inflated pretensions of Dennis Hopper, who, it's now apparent, is gifted with all the insights of a weekend mystic who drives to and from his retreat in a Jaguar. . . ."

—Vincent Canby, *New York Times*

"An embarrassment . . . an endless, chaotic, suffocating, acid-soaked movie."

—David Denby, *Atlantic Monthly*

"The work of a kid playing with a toy. . . ."

—Joseph Gelmis, *Newsday*

"*The Last Movie* is claimed to be an allegory 'concerning the destruction of innocence.' Just what or whose innocence is being destroyed in this sorry cinematic melange is impossible to determine; my own guess is that the reference is to whoever allocated the million or more dollars required to mount what we might loosely call the production."

—Hollis Alpert, *Saturday Review*

Plot Summary

A company of Hollywood filmmakers shoots a Western in a remote mountain village in Peru. When the production is completed, the company goes back to Hollywood. A young stunt man named Kansas (Dennis Hopper—who also happens to be the film's director) decides to stay behind in order to live with a resident whore named Maria (Stella Garcia). At first, we see an irrelevant flash forward of Kansas being crucified by the villagers. Ten minutes later, a superimposed title reads, "A Film by Dennis Hopper." Fifteen minutes or so after that, another title reads "The Last Movie" and the members of the audience finally find out the title of the film they have been watching for a half hour or so.

The Peruvian natives, after watching the filming of a Hollywood production, decide that they want to make their own movie. They construct bamboo make-believe movie cameras, bamboo microphones, and other wooden film equipment—none of which actually works. They substitute real killings and violence for the faked Hollywood violence they had seen. All hell breaks loose. The local priest (played by Tomas Milian, a veteran of several spaghetti Westerns) is horrified by the violence and blames Kansas for introducing it to the villagers. The priest concludes that movies are the root of all evil—and if all films were as bad as this one, he might have a point. The villagers eventually grab Kansas and in an orgy of savagery begin to brutalize him. We are treated to shots of Kansas wobbling around the Peruvian countryside, holding his bleeding shoulder, while we hear sounds of soldiers marching, babies crying, animals growling, and eerie voices moaning "Woo-ooo-ooo!" Kansas then begins writhing in the dirt, exclaiming, "I'm dying! I'm dying! I'm dying! I'm dying!" and we quickly cut to a baby nursing at its mother's breast. A long series of "heavy" but unrelated images compounds our confusion. In one of them, Kansas is running down a dirt road, when he suddenly collapses. This shot is repeated. And repeated. Finally, we see a number of out-takes from the actual production of this "film," in which Dennis Hopper attempts to direct Tomas Milian and his other friends. In one of them, Hopper shouts, "Hey, you guys, I want to get this thing over with. I got a lot of things I want to do." Eventually, we see a few clips with the words "The End" sloppily scratched onto the surface of the film. Since Dennis Hopper had so many things to do, he apparently didn't have time to edit his film. We suggest that Hopper's first priority on his list of things to do should be to go out and search for a job that has nothing to do with making films.

Unforgettable Performances

As reviewer Stefan Kanfer reports in *Time* magazine, the director of this film (Dennis Hopper) "presents a gallery of his favorite art works: 'Waterfall with a Distant View of Dennis'; 'Effect of Dennis Through Peruvian Haze'; 'Ruins of Dennis by Twilight'; and his favorite: 'Dennis as the Universal Infant.'" This last title adequately summarizes Hopper's ridiculous performance as the star of his own film. Portraying the stunt man Kansas, he continually blinks his baby blue eyes bewilderedly at his surroundings and expresses all the utter stupefaction of a newly born 180-pound baby. Occasionally he runs his hands over his face, massages his neck with his fingers, or mumbles lines of inane dialogue (which he wrote himself, naturally), but for the most part he simply toddles around the set with no apparent purpose. In one sequence, he throws back his head, opens his mouth as wide as he can, and bawls out loud for no reason at all. Mr. Hopper appears to be under the influence of something stronger than a cocktail, and his incoherent directing reflects the same influence. After he is beaten by the villagers, Hopper clutches his left shoulder with his right hand—and that hand remains there, practically immobile, for the remainder of the film.

Stella Garcia plays Maria, the village prostitute who becomes Hopper's room-mate. She speaks surprisingly good English for someone who's spent all her life in a remote Andean village, and she uses her command of the language to nag Kansas mercilessly about wanting a swimming pool, a General Electric refrigerator, and a fur coat. Ms. Garcia is supposed to serve as a symbol of capitalism's corruption of the poor innocent natives, and so she delivers her lines with all the raw emotional power of the lady in TV commercials worrying about the shine on her kitchen floor.

Noted director Samuel Fuller, actors Kris Kristofferson, Sylvia Miles, Peter Fonda, Rod Cameron, Dean Stockwell, Michelle Philips, John Phillip Law, and Russ Tamblyn all put in cameo appearances in the course of the film. For these jolly adventurers *The Last Movie* no doubt provided a convenient excuse for a visit to Peru to play with their far-out buddy Dennis the Menace. On screen, these visiting stars portray filmmakers or businessmen, and some of of them appear for only a few seconds. They look like the walk-on relatives in a home movie who are intent on drawing attention to themselves. Sylvia Miles, as a script girl, conducts herself in a particularly asinine manner. She gives orders into thin air, waves her pencil, and shouts, "That's not in the script!" She's probably right, but in this disjointed film does it really matter?

Immortal Dialogue

KANSAS: Hmm—it's *muy frío* tonight, ain't it?
MARIA: (Agreeing): Um.
KANSAS: You cold?
MARIA: Um. My feet are cold.
KANSAS: Yeah?
MARIA: Yeah.
KANSAS (his hand reaching under her skirt): Hey, hey, I know something that's hot and—uh, heh, heh!! Yes sir!
MARIA: Hee, hee.

* * *

(The priest is worried about the actual violence created by the villagers, and about a leading villager assuming the role of director.)
PRIEST: I'm scared.
KANSAS: You're scared, padre? Uh, what are you—what are you—uh—scared about?
PRIEST (refering to the general commotion): Listen to that, listen to that. That man is teaching them to make movies....
KANSAS: Yeah, it's pretty weird, all right!

* * *

(Kansas tells Mrs. Anderson, a rich American woman [Julie Adams], about how he beat Maria.)

MRS. ANDERSON: You beat Maria up? (Teasingly.) Why, you bad boy, you!

KANSAS: Yeah, well—

MRS. ANDERSON: How'd you do it?

KANSAS: Oh—slugged her—

MRS. ANDERSON: Did you hit her with your fist?

KANSAS: No—I—I slapped her—hard. You see, I—er—look, listen to me for one—

MRS. ANDERSON: You know, I had fantasies like that, about being beat up. Did you ever have a fantasy about women beating you? Or don't cowboys have fantasies?

◦   ◦   ◦

The Story Behind the Film

In order to learn how an organization like Universal happened to sponsor a self-indulgent cult project like *The Last Movie*, we chatted with a young man who was an associate producer at the studio at the time of the production. At his request, his name has been withheld—after all, he does not want to terminate his career in Hollywood.

"It all came out of *Easy Rider*," our informant told us, referring to the "road film" Dennis Hopper made in 1969 with his buddy Peter Fonda. "Along comes this crappy little picture which no one will even give distribution to and it makes a fortune. The critics fall all over themselves in praising it. Nobody at the studios understood it— Hopper was just a funny-looking guy sitting around smoking dope. But a lot of the studio moguls got it into their minds that there must be a trend emerging—a trend which they couldn't fathom themselves—the trend of the drug-oriented, experimental, youth-market picture. Since that trend seemed to be there, the people at Universal decided to clean up on it. They went to Dennis Hopper and told him to make a picture—anything he wanted—and they would bankroll it. What they were saying is, 'Dennis, you're a genius. We didn't understand what made *Easy Rider* work so we're in no position to evaluate your next project. You've got the magic touch, and so we'll give you a totally free hand. No interference. No advice. We're

not young; we don't understand the cult of youth. But it's there and we know if we hire a young hip person who's got long hair and looks a little weird, then we can make a successful motion picture.'

"They gave Hopper a bundle of money to play with. Like a million bucks, cash; which was far in excess of anything he had spent on *Easy Rider*. Hopper decided to go down to Peru with all his friends to try to get a movie together. The rumor in the studio was that the real reason he went to Peru was that he had heard about some particular kind of mushroom down there, and he wanted to try it."

Press accounts of Hopper's adventures in South America seem to lend credence to our friend's story. It was reported that on the flight to Peru members of Hopper's crew tried to "turn on" the stewardesses—thereby causing a minor scandal. The use of drugs on the set was so frequent that the U.S. government began to fear an international incident, and eventually put the production under surveillance by the CIA. During his shooting schedule in Cuzco, Hopper was quoted in the press as saying, "Oh man, it's all real! It's like, you know, we're using real life, real motion, real light, so many levels. You know?"

The Balance Sheet

According to our friend at Universal, "Hopper spent just a ridiculous amount of time down in Peru. Finally, he took all these miles and miles of film back to Taos, New Mexico, where he had set up his own place for editing and dubbing the film and all the rest.

"It took him months. Just months! It was endless. Everybody would walk around the studio saying, 'When is *The Last Movie* going to be ready?' But the big studio brass just kept saying, 'Relax. Don't try to understand them. Hopper and his friends just don't work the same way we do. But everything's going to be okay.'

"Eventually, Hopper's film was ready, and there was a screening for the bigger executives, or so the story goes. They couldn't believe what they were seeing. We spent more than a million dollars—for this? They decided they must be missing something. After all, they never understood *Easy Rider* either. So they called in the next echelon of

140

studio executives, who still couldn't understand it. What finally happened was that they said, 'Well, let's get some of the young people from around here. Maybe they can tell us that this is really a great picture. Maybe the young people will understand it. It could be great.'

"So one day a bunch of us got called up and herded together and they just said, 'You gotta see a picture.' It was four in the afternoon. There were about ten of us from different areas of the company—all under thirty. So we sat down to watch this film—and it was terrible! Just pitiful. We couldn't make heads or tails of it. But we couldn't say that because the big brass had made a decision that we were supposed to like it because we were under thirty. They had made a decision that there was value in having young people around who had a perception that older people didn't have. Now, if we told them that we didn't have that perception, that we hated this film just as much as they did, they might say, 'Great, we don't need any young people and let's forget the whole thing and this film is a piece of shit!' Even though we couldn't be up front about putting the film down, it was pretty clear that our enthusiasm was under control. Just looking at our faces I think they got the idea that they had a turkey on their hands."

None of this seemed to discourage the indomitable Dennis Hopper, who remained convinced that he had produced a masterpiece. He wanted to have his film exhibited at the New York Film Festival, but Universal refused. Hopper attacked the studio for its "greed" and told the press, "My producers are afraid that my film is a bomb." Universal did, however, agree to give the film its premiere at the 31st International Venice Film Festival. Astonishingly enough, the film received a special unofficial award. According to critic Andre Sarris in *The Village Voice*, Hopper's masterpiece "was lionized in Venice simply because Europeans get orgasms from the thought that Americans are prepared to commit suicide en masse."

We don't know of any suicides at Universal concerning this film, but there was certainly intense depression. The producers tried to release the film to "art houses," but even that desperation play fell on its face. The project proved a major financial disaster, though the studio has kept the embarrassing details and statistics very much to itself.

Delphine Seyrig emoting in Alain Resnais's Last Year at Marienbad. *"Everyone wants to think of me as a dedicated intellectual," says Resnais, "but truthfully, I don't really like making films. If I didn't have to earn a living, I wouldn't work at all."*

LAST YEAR AT MARIENBAD (1962)

Directed by: ALAIN RESNAIS
Written by: ALAIN ROBBE-GRILLET
Produced by: ALAIN RESNAIS
Featuring: DELPHINE SEYRIG, GIORGIO AL-BERTAZZI, SACHA PITOEFF, WILHELM VON DEEK, JEAN LANIER, GERARD LORIN

Astor Films

The Critics Rave

"A truly extraordinary French film . . . an experience full of beauty and mood."
—Bosley Crowther, *New York Times*

"A work of art."
—Dwight MacDonald, *Esquire*

"Marvelously fascinating . . . a ritualized, almost lifeless experience."
—Hollis Alpert, *Saturday Review*

"*Marienbad* is both brilliant and banal, soaringly poetic and tiresomely talky, mature and sophomoric, photographically lovely as a symphony in celluloid, but dramatically as dizzying and monotonously repetitious as a carousel. Its murky, shallow, 'ultra-civilized' love-story-triangle has been devitalized to the point of dramatic anemia. . . .The snail-like pace of the film's emotions—vicariously felt, dialoguishly dissected and almost yak-yakked to death—becomes altogether exhausting."
—Jesse Zunser, *Cue*

"Resnais has created a spectacle that is elaborate, ponderous and meaningless."
—*Newsweek*

"So basically sterile and emotionally frustrating that interest drains long before France's young New Wave director concludes his camera explorations. . . .There are interminable views of ornate halls and formal gardens. People in elegant dinner dress stand frozen into stylized patterns against the baroque trappings. . . . Repetitious and meaningless."

—Margaret Harford, *Los Angeles Times*

"I got one clear impression from *Last Year at Marienbad,* and that was of Resnais and Robbe-Grillet grinning wickedly at each other above the heads of a trustful public that was flagging its poor little brain into some notion of what in hell the picture is all about."

—Robert Hatch, *The Nation*

"So repetitious, slow-moving and difficult to understand that it made me drowsy. This film is really the oddest thing ever shown on the screen. . . . I think it's a lot of pseudo-artistic HOOEY."

—Hazel Flynn, *Hollywood Citizen-News*

"Historians of the future who are concerned with the Decline of the West would do well to glance at this so-called motion picture, and to ponder the reasons for the fatuous things that are currently being said in its praise. . . .The narration is nothing but adolescently grandiloquent gabble. . . . Resnais, and his publicity-agented claque, have uttered the usual rationalizations for the ineptitudes and incompetence of the film. If you approach *Last Year at Marienbad* rationally, they say, you are stupid. . . . if you won't admit *Last Year at Marienbad* is a 'refraction' of the eternal triangle you are a Philistine, etc., etc., etc. . . . The simple truth about *Last Year at Marienbad* is that a not untalented young filmmaker (Resnais) has forsworn the hard work artistic creation entails and has allowed his immature and meaningless fumbling to be promoted by those who wish to convert Western culture into an irrational confusion."

—Louise Corbin, *Films in Review*

Plot Summary

A man by the name of "X" (Giorgio Albertazzi) takes a stroll in a baroque spa, mumbling interminably about the different features in the place. He meets a woman named "A" (Delphine Seyrig), whom "X" claims to have met there last year. Or perhaps it was Marienbad? On second thought it could have been Frederiksbad. Of course, there's a possibility that it was in Karlstadt. But then again, maybe it was Baden-Salsa? At any rate, "A" tells "X" that she doesn't have the faintest idea what he is talking about, and neither does the audience for that matter. She urges him to pester someone else.

"A" is married to a man named "M" (played by Sacha Pitoeff, or maybe it was Jean Lanier?), who might get a little suspicious. He might not really be her husband, though. Perhaps he's her suitor? Or her bodyguard? Or a curious bystander who happened to walk in front of the meandering camera? "A" begins to remember some of the past occurrences that "X" mentions. Is he a hypnotist? Is she going insane? Is the audience leaving the theater? "A" finally succumbs to "X" and agrees to elope with him. At least it *looks* as if she is going to elope. Does she or doesn't she? Only her hairdresser knows for sure. At the finish, they leave the spa. Or was it a spa? Was it a hotel? Was it a palace? Was it a morgue? Was it a wax museum? Does anyone care?

Unforgettable Performances

In *Last Year at Marienbad,* the three stars compete with one another to see who can do the best imitation of a talking corpse. Sacha Pitoeff (as "M") wins hands down because he looks like a corpse to begin with. His sunken cheeks appear to have been chewed every day and it seems that his glassy eyes would shatter if he accidentally tripped and fell on his face. He delivers few lines, and the viewer is genuinely shocked when we first see his lips move.

Giogio Albertazzi (as "X") does most of the talking. He rattles off a list of objects in the ele-

Giorgio Albertazzi and Delphine Seyrig limp through the overpraised "art film" Last Year at Marienbad. Newsweek *called it "elaborate, ponderous and meaningless." It is also the most painfully boring spectacle we have ever witnessed.*

gant hotel, ranging from the thick carpets down to the stucco on the walls. He sounds as if he were the builder of the place and is taking a final inventory before presenting it to the new owners. But he doesn't have a very good memory, so he repeats the same inventory four or five times much to the agony of the audience. His whispery "sensitive" voice has all the animation of a forgetful parrot endlessly repeating the few words it knows.

Delphine Seyrig (as "A") shows her acting ability by standing motionless for several minutes with her arms rigidly at her sides—she seems to be playing a game of freeze tag with herself. In terms of her facial expressions, she is easily more wooden than Charlie McCarthy. She would seem to be more at home in a storefront window than in a motion picture.

Immortal Dialogue

(We hear the voice of "X," murmuring softly over the sound of "ghostly" atonal organ music as the camera wanders through the ancient hotel.)
"X": I walk on, once again, down these corridors, through these halls, these galleries, in this structure—of another century, this enormous, luxurious, baroque, lugubrious hotel—where corridors succeed endless corridors—silent deserted corridors overloaded with a dim, cold ornamentation of woodwork, stucco, moldings, marble, black mirrors, dark paintings, columns, heavy hangings, sculptured doorframes, series of doorways,

galleries, transverse corridors that open in turn on empty salons, rooms overloaded with an ornamentation from another century, silent halls where the sound of advancing footsteps is absorbed by carpets so thick and heavy that nothing can be heard, as if the ear of the man walking on once again, down these corridors, through these halls, these galleries, in this structure of another century, this enormous, luxurious, baroque, lugubrious hotel . . . etc., etc.

(We overhear the conversation of a sophisticated couple.)
MAN: You are still the same. It is as if I had left you yesterday. What's become of you in all this time?
WOMAN: Nothing, as you see, since I'm still the same.
MAN: You haven't gotten married?
WOMAN: Oh, no!
MAN: You're mistaken. It's a lot of fun.
WOMAN: I like my freedom.
MAN: Here, for instance?
WOMAN: Why not here?
MAN: It's a strange spot.

        ❃   ❃   ❃

"X": I must have you alive. Alive, as you have already been every evening, for weeks, for months—
"A": I have never stayed so long anywhere.
"X": Yes, I know. I don't care. For days, and days. Why don't you still want to remember anything?
"A": You're raving! I'm tired; let me alone!

        ❃   ❃   ❃

("X" once again mumbles his way through the "endless corridors" of the hotel while the unfortunate viewer covers his ears and buries his head in his lap.)
"X": Empty salons. Corridors. Salons. Doors. Doors. Salons. Empty chairs, deep armchairs, thick carpets. Heavy hangings. Stairs, steps. Steps, one after the other. Glass objects, objects still intact, empty glasses. A glass that falls, three, two, one, zero. Glass partition, letters (and so forth).

145

The Story Behind the Film

Last Year at Marienbad was the brainchild of French avant-garde novelist Alain Robbe-Grillet, who prepared an amazingly detailed script, including shot-by-shot descriptions. Alain Resnais, the director, was then responsible for transcribing this concept onto celluloid. Resnais's chief contribution, it seems, was to add his own distinctive touch of ennui to the final result. The film was shot at three different German locations: the palaces and gardens of Nymphenburg, Schleissheim, and Oranienburg.

It is no accident that the characters in *Marienbad* often seem as static and formalized as the figures in comic strips. Director Resnais admits to a special passion for "the funnies" that began when he was a child. At age ten, he began making home movies using the storytelling techniques he found in the comics. He also claims that his "mature" films have developed the same techniques. In *Marienbad* the only active presence in the film is the camera, like the eye of a reader moving from frame to frame of "Doonesbury." For the record, Resnais has revealed that he has his favorite comic strip, "Dick Tracy," sent to him every day by special arrangement from New York. (see *Dick Tracy Versus Cueball*).

In candid interviews, M. Resnais has cleared away any possible doubts about his "higher intentions" as a filmmaker. "Everyone wants to think of me as a dedicated intellectual," he once said, "but truthfully, I don't really like making films. If I didn't have to earn a living, I wouldn't work at all." About *Marienbad* itself he has been equally frank. "It's possible that the entire action of *Marienbad* takes place within one minute. It could be simply: 'I've come to get you.' 'I don't know you.' 'Come with me.' 'Yes, perhaps I will go with you.'"

The Balance Sheet

Despite such breezy disclaimers from its creator, the public persisted in taking *Marienbad* with the utmost seriousness. At the 22nd Venice Film Festival it won the top prize, the Golden Lion of St. Mark. It shared the André Bazin Gold Medal (with Michelangelo Antonioni's *La Notte*), given by the International Federation of Film Critics. It won the French film critics' Melies Award as the best picture of the year. With such critical hosannas to greet its arrival, the film did sensational business in France and broke an all-time box-office record at one Champs-Elysées movie house. Cynthia Grénier in *The New York Times* wrote, "Parisians have been lining up in record-breaking queues from two o'clock in the afternoon on the brightest Indian summer days, as well as under the coldest drizzles." In the United States, the film also proved highly profitable, though it failed to achieve genuine popularity outside of New York City. Many patrons left the film convinced that they had been "put on" by this "artistic" spectacle, and wrote angry letters to magazines and newspapers. One of the most amusing of these was produced by Miss Frances Monson of Brooklyn Heights, who sent *Esquire* a protest of this "vapid, boring, pointless and infuriating film." In her letter, she included a complete parody of the film, entitled *Last Year at Grand Central*, which featured such lines as "The dirty marble floors, the ticketbooths, the wan smell of indiscretions reminiscent of yesterday, concentric conundrum of fate, the dirty marble floors, the fake heavens on the ceiling in this place where there is no heaven, concentric conundrum of fate, the Hershey machines, the Kodak exhibit, frozen people looking down on a frozen world, the ladies' room, the benches for waiting, the frozen people on a frozen wall looking down on a frozen world, concentric conundrum of fate, the dirty marble floors . . ." Resnais and Robbe-Grillet could hardly have done better.

After its release, the film launched several fads that enjoyed brief moments of glory. First there was "the Marienbad game" (a game played with matchsticks in the film by Sacha Pitoeff). Then came "the Marienbad haircut," based on the style worn by Delphine Seyrig in the film. Fortunately, the public did not imitate the film's characters in every detail, and for the most part people continued to speak in coherent sentences, to register facial expressions, and even to move their bodies every once in a while.

LOST HORIZON (1973)

Directed by: CHARLES JARROTT
Written by: LARRY KRAMER
Based on a novel by: JAMES HILTON
Produced by: ROSS HUNTER
Music by: BURT BACHARACH
Featuring: PETER FINCH, LIV ULLMANN, SALLY KELLERMAN, GEORGE KENNEDY, MICHAEL YORK, OLIVIA HUSSEY, BOBBY VAN, JAMES SHIGETA, CHARLES BOYER, SIR JOHN GIELGUD

Columbia Pictures

The Critics Rave

"Worst Movie of the Year."

—Esquire

"Totally unmemorable. . . . Without redeeming feature in either its direction, scenario, acting, sets, music, choreography, or photography, it can't even be enjoyed as camp. . . ."
—Joy Gould Boyum, *The Wall Street Journal*

"Atrocious . . . lame-brained. . . . Some $6 million was spent on this worst-of-worst remake. . . ."
—William Wolf, *Cue*

"As uplifting as a whalebone bra—and just as dated. There are . . . a dozen songs by Burt Bacharach and Hal David, which are so pitifully pedestrian it's doubtful that they'd sound good even if the actors could sing, which they can't. One lavish production number, 'Living Together, Growing Together,' may indeed be the silliest choreography ever put on film. The set for Shangri-La resembles the valley of the Jolly Green Giant—a fitting showcase for a film that is so much spinach."

—Arthur Cooper, *Newsweek*

"Awful Burt Bacharach-Hal David songs. 'Lost' is right."

—Leonard Maltin, *TV Movies*

"Cartoonlike self-parody."

—Steven H. Scheuer, *Movies on TV*

"Fatuous and tasteless . . . could stand (or leap) as a concise definition of camp. . . ."

—Jay Cocks, *Time*

"Trash . . . an empty, wooden-headed musical . . . that should be frozen, like a chow mein TV dinner. I have never understood why anyone would want to improve old movies by remaking them. The result is almost always disastrous, and in this case, it's even worse than that. . . . The dance numbers ·are like half-time at the Super Bowl. The songs are dreadful. . . . The dialogue is dumbfoundedly simple-minded. The costumes would embarrass Yvonne De Carlo. The photography would be laughed off the screen at a campfire briefing for the National Forestry Service convention at Knott's Berry Farm."

—Rex Reed, *New York Daily News*

"It's entirely possible that to the nostalgic viewers Ross Hunter is aiming at, this torpor will be soothing. They may like to doze from time to time without fear of missing anything . . . banal . . . wan . . . flatulent. . . ."

—Pauline Kael, *The New Yorker*

"Mawkish songs . . . costuming that could kindly be called comic . . . a vision of Shangri-La . . . that would embarrass a junior high film class . . . the simplemindedness of *Lost Horizon* suggests that only Ross Hunter would remake a 1937 movie into a 1932 one."

—Judith Crist, *New York*

"Any Ten Worst list would have to start with Columbia's *Lost Horizon*."

—John Barbour, *Los Angeles*

"Dreadfully old-fashioned in the rigid handling of song and dance routines. . . . One major trouble is that few of this cast can sing, and the songs have lyrics of awful banality and tunes to match. . . ."

—Patrick Gibbs, *London Daily Telegraph*

Immensely silly . . . simple-minded. . . . There's also a dancing chorus, picking up the beat of something that might as well be called Shangri-rock . . . merely a high-camp compendium of all the Hollywood clichés ever visited upon an unsuspecting public, with or without the music."

—Bruce Williamson, *Playboy*

"Cumbersome, unlyrical and tedious . . . a flat-footed disappointment."

—Charles Champlin, *Los Angeles Times*

. . . AND hats off to Julian Fox of *Films and Filming*, who had the courage to take this lonely stand:

"Total delight . . . this really is a marvelous film. It's entertaining . . . awe-inspiring. . . . Rarely have I experienced such an abundance of actual pleasure in an actor's performance (Peter Finch's). Here is a film with something for everyone. Even the most hard-hearted cynic who steadfastly refused to melt at *The Sound of Music* had better stock up plentifully with Kleenex before venturing forth this time . . . a beautiful film full of beautiful moments. Who said that remakes are only shadows?"

Plot Summary

When a revolution begins in a small town in southern Asia, a party of five English-speaking people escape the uprising by flying off in a small airplane. As they take off, several extras wave their fists angrily in the air. On the plane, the escapees introduce themselves. They are Richard Conway (Peter Finch), an eminent British diplomat; George Conway (Michael York), Richard's short-tempered brother; Sally Hughes (Sally Kellerman), a nervous *Newsweek* correspondent; Sam Cornelius (George Kennedy), an American businessman; and Harry Lovett (Bobby Van), an immature nightclub comic whose sophistication rivals the film's. As they reach a high altitude Sally comments, "I feel like I'm heading for outer space!" Later, the passengers realize that their Mongolian pilot has hijacked them. Eventually the plane runs out of fuel and crashes into a snowbank, instantly killing the scheming pilot but miraculously leaving the passengers unscathed (unfortunately).

The next day they are rescued by an Oriental named Chang (Sir John Gielgud) and his porters. Explaining his astoundingly fluent English, Chang tells the survivors, "I was an undergraduate of Oxford in my young days." Chang outfits them in woolly clothes and they begin to climb up the snowbank. They eventually reach a secluded lamasery called the Valley of the Blue Moon, better known as Shangri-La. As heavenly golden voices ring out, Chang exclaims, "Welcome to Shangri-La." In Shangri-La, we are told, the sun always shines, the air is blue, children frolic gaily in the green meadows, and there are no taxes to pay. In short, it's a combination of Camelot and Palm Springs conveniently set in the remote Himalayas. All that is missing in this vacation hacienda is an Olympic-size swimming pool.

However, we may assume that it's going to be installed next week. Chang calls the situation "a strange phenomenon for which we are very grateful." (After all, this "strange situation" has provided jobs for a dozen stars and hundreds of extras.) On a tour of Shangri-La, the group is introduced to Catherine (Liv Ullmann), a French teacher, and Maria (Olivia Hussey), a ballerina who dances like a disabled war veteran. After witnessing one of Maria's dance recitals, George tells her with a straight face, "You know, in the outside world you'd be a knockout! I bet people would fight to see you dance!"

Almost everyone is content to stay in Shangri-La for the rest of their lives—even the room service is satisfactory. Harry tells Chang, "I know I speak for all of us when I say that this place is terrific!" The only problem is that George wants to get back to America and also wants to take his new sweetie, Maria, with him. Richard, not able to discipline his kid brother George, asks advice from the High-Lama (Charles Boyer), Shangri-La's "leader," who is apparently a graduate of the Charlie Chan school of inscrutable acting. The Lama reveals many tales. He tells Richard that he himself caused the hijacking of the plane. He also tells Richard that Maria is actually one hundred years old, but that she keeps her youthful complexion by staying in Shangri-La.

Richard decides that the High Lama is a fibber and abandons Shangri-La with his brother George and Maria. While climbing down a snowbank, Maria begins to show her age—her face turns into a ripe prune. George is so enraged by this turn of events that he yells his head off, which just happens to cause an avalanche that kills him. This is convincingly depicted by having some prop men roll an underweight dummy off a precipice. If this sounds farfetched in print, you can imagine how it looks on the screen. Richard continues the journey alone, but finally drops from exhaustion. He wakes up in a hospital, but because his nurse isn't as pretty as Liv Ullmann he quickly recovers and runs back to the snowcapped mountains and Shangri-La. Everyone smiles in relief at his return, and the film ends with the self-congratulatory tone of a ten-year reunion of a class at Tibet Tech.

Unforgettable Performances

Peter Finch, as Richard Conway, looks like a man about to receive a big, juicy paycheck and so prepares to endure the inevitable brickbats from the public and film critics. Finch appears particularly perturbed at those moments when the character he portrays reveals his most intimate thoughts in song. We don't see him singing and his lips don't move; we just hear him singing on the sound track. It's as if we were to overhear his heart of hearts, whispering secret dreams to his brain of brains. The songs themselves, and their groaning presentation, inevitably suggest a milk of magnesia ad.

Liv Ullmann can't sing any better than Peter Finch, but at least most of her songs are cheerful. In production, these numbers involve groups of repulsive children who kick, dance, and sing out of synchronization. The idea was to offer Liv Ullmann as a successor to Julie Andrews in *The Sound of Music*. Good try. Liv teaches the kiddies French and they later join her in a song and dance called, "The World Is a Circle," staged in the same format as the "Do-Re-Mi" number in

The Sound of Music. Ms. Ullmann, however, is so halfhearted that she could not even convince a five-year-old that a "Doe is a deer/a female deer . . ."

Sally Kellerman, the poor man's Barbra Streisand, plays Sally Hughes, a photographer from *Newsweek*. Ms. Kellerman is perfectly cast as a neurotic female—however, like everyone else in this film, she is at her most neurotic when she sings and dances. She is assigned very peculiar places to dance. In one scene, she jiggles her arms and shoulders and wiggles her hips while dancing on a large rock. In another, she dances in a library while swinging from research ladders and stomping on desks. Her acting consists of a series of blinks, smiles, and a few hand gestures. Halfway through the film she ponders committing suicide, but Chang beneficently changes her mind. Chang, you idiot!

Immortal Dialogue

SAM: Are you an American?
SALLY: No—Mongolian.
SAM: You'll have to teach me the language sometime.

*   *   *

SAM (explaining why the plane might have been hijacked): For good measure, they've got two journalists and—by his own account—a famous comedian.
HARRY (the comedian): Very funny. But what about you, Cornelius? Maybe they want you? Who are you!?
SAM: I'm somebody flying in a strange plane to a strange place with a lunatic pilot and I'm trying to find out why, that's who I am!!!

*   *   *

CHANG (seeing Sally Hughes about to jump out the window): Miss Hughes! (She turns around.) You are in the midst of life. Do not seek death, it will find you. But choose the road that makes death a fulfillment.

*   *   *

Peter Finch, as an eminent British diplomat, bids a fond farewell to an unnamed South Asian country in the midst of a revolution. The response of the "natives" in the film was friendly compared to the reaction of the critics after Lost Horizon *was released.*

LOVE SCENE:

GEORGE: You are more beautiful than the women of Thailand. More feminine than the women of France. More pliable than the women of Japan. More—

MARIA: Stop, stop. I don't want to hear about all these other women. What I want to hear is that you won't leave me.

GEORGE: Oh, I adore you!

         ❂   ❂   ❂

Song: "Reflections"

SALLY (sings while dancing on a rock):
Doing something for someone else
Isn't really for someone else
It does twice as much for you as
Something you do
Just for yourself.

         ❂   ❂   ❂

The Story Behind the Film

This film is a remake of the 1937 Frank Capra classic of the same name, based on the novel by James Hilton. The present producer, Ross Hunter, is a firm believer in good clean family entertainment. His big claim to fame was the highly popular triumph *Airport.*

The budget for *Lost Horizon* was over $6 million. The sets were built on Columbia's back lot in Burbank, on an area of four acres and at a cost of $500,000. The scenes in the beginning of the film, those taking place at a South Asian airport, were filmed in Tucson, Arizona. The aerial views of snowy mountains were shot at Mount Hood, Oregon, and in the Cascades in Washington. Footage of actors trekking through snow and ice was shot at Bronson Canyon, the same locale used for the desert sequences in the horror classic *Eegah!* (q.v.). To convert this dry, sandy canyon into the snowy Himalayas, Columbia used tons of artificial snow, but failed to fool anyone over the age of five.

During the filming of *Lost Horizon*, the producers were publicly chastised by the Japanese-

American Citizens League. They protested the casting of John Gielgud as Chang (right on) and other Occidentals in Oriental roles. Hunter apologetically replied that he originally offered the role of Chang to Toshiro Mifune, samurai star of scores of excellent Japanese films, but Mifune had the good sense to turn it down.

The Balance Sheet

The promotional lines for *Lost Horizon* were nearly as poetic as the lyrics in the film. For instance: "The Adventure That Will Live Forever Has Been Transformed into Spectacular Musical Drama." The world premiere of the film was held at the National Theater in Westwood, California. James Bacon of the *Los Angeles Herald-Examiner* called it "probably the biggest premiere in recent Hollywood memory." Included on the guest list were California governor Ronald Reagan (also one helluva actor; see *That Hagen Girl*), Dean Martin, Doris Day, Liza Minnelli, Lucille Ball, Carol Burnett, Jane Wyman, Irene Dunne, Milton Berle, Dorothy Lamour, Rosalind Russell, Gregory Peck, Susan Hayward, Greer Garson, Red Buttons, Ann Miller, Binnie Barnes, Dionne Warwicke, and loads of other Hollywood celebrities. Liv Ullmann came all the way from Norway just to attend the premiere. Besides the film itself, the only other disaster of the evening involved the weather. It rained incessantly that night and several minks and tuxes were ruined. An omen of things to come, no doubt.

Before the word got out about this turkey, the film had been chosen for a Command Performance before Queen Elizabeth (and people wonder why the British Empire has gone into decline!). *Lost Horizon* was the first American film in seventeen years to receive this honor. Chances are that it will be a long, long time before Her Majesty picks an American film again.

Despite this royal intercession, the critical response to the film was an overwhelming Bronx cheer, in unison. (See THE CRITICS RAVE.) Nor could even the most ambitious advertising compaign pull the producer's chestnuts out of the fire (or out of the snow, or whatever). Today, *Lost Horizon* is known in the motion picture industry as "Lost Investment." The backers of the

Sir John Gielgud as Chang demonstrates old-fashioned hospitality in Ross Hunter's 1973 musical remake of Lost Horizon.

film lost nearly half of their more than $6 million investment, and considering the quality of their product, they got off cheaply.

SPECIAL AWARD

One dancing bear goes to choreographer Hermes Pan (that's right, Hermes Pan) and a tin-ear forked-tongue charm bracelet is presented to the song-writing team of Bacharach and David.

Never before was the choreography in a major film provoked such extensive and widespread discussion—and nearly all of it critical. Mr. Pan, who also staged the ostentatious pomp in the monumental flop *Cleopatra*, treats us to such antics as children accidentally bopping heads while they sway back and forth in line. The fault lies partly with the children themselves, who seem to have been recruited from a home for the handicapped, but the more experienced dancers are hardly any better. In the "Living Together, Growing Together" number (obviously intended as a showstopper) Oriental men walk in a slow procession with pendulating teapots dangling from strings, and the entire scene resembles a Duncan Yo Yo tournament convened in San Francisco's Chinatown. Originally there also was a "fertility dance" which featured bikini-clad musclemen dancing in circles "ring-around-the-rosy" style. This dance, however, was cut from the final print because of the hysterical laughter it aroused from all preview audiences.

In the past, Burt Bacharach and Hal David have come together to create innumerable hits, but here they offer only hopeless inanity. One of the few questions left for the audience to settle during this dreary film is which is worse, Bacharach's music or David's lyrics? The melodies here are so insistent, tedious, and monochromatic that they sound like tape recordings used to torture prisoners of war into revealing their secrets. Hal David's lyrics, meanwhile, suggest a chronic stutterer suffering from a bad overdose of barbiturates. For example:

> The world is a circle without a beginning
> And nobody knows where it really ends
> Everything depends on where you are.
> In the circle that never begins
> Nobody knows where the circle ends.

and:

> The chance to live forever
> Is really no illusion
> Why can't I make myself believe it?
> Can I accept what I see around me?
> Have I found Shangri-La or has it found me?

> *Why can't we make ourselves believe it?*
> *Have we found nausea or has it found we?*

*Rex Reed dancing
with his trans-
sexual twin Raquel
Welch in Myra
Breckinridge: "...
about as funny as
a child molester."*

154

MYRA BRECKINRIDGE (1970)

Directed by: MICHAEL SARNE
Written by: MICHAEL SARNE and DAVID GILER
Based on the novel by: GORE VIDAL
Produced by: ROBERT FRYER and GORE VIDAL
Featuring: RAQUEL WELCH, JOHN HUSTON, MAE WEST, REX REED, FARRAH FAWCETT, ROGER HERREN, CALVIN LOCKHART, JOHN CARRADINE, JIM BACKUS, GEORGE FURTH, ROGER C. CARMEL, B. S. PULLY, GRADY SUTTON, ANDY DEVINE

Twentieth Century-Fox

The Critics Rave

"Lowest rating! (BOMB) . . . As bad as any movie ever made. . . ."

—Leonard Maltin, *TV Movies*

"So tasteless that it represents some sort of nadir in American cinema. . . . *Myra Breckinridge* is about as funny as a child molester. It is an insult to intelligence, an affront to sensibility and an abomination to the eye. . . ."

—*Time*

"I still can't believe I saw this freak show, a self-consciously mod, disjointed patchwork of leers, vulgarity, and general ineptness."

—William Wolf, *Cue*

"The most flamboyant elaboration ever of the silliest, most meandering and sickest of nocturnal, sex-sprung fantasies . . . repulsively neurotic. . . ."

—Winfred Blevins,
Los Angeles Herald-Examiner

Mae West, a ghastly self-parody in Myra Breckinridge: *"Never mind about the six feet. Let's talk about the seven inches."*

"A horrifying movie . . . an entirely incompetent, impotent attempt at exploitation by an industry that knew once, at the very least, how to make a dishonest buck . . . unprecedented unpleasantness. . . ."

—Joseph Morgenstern, *Newsweek*

". . . a single monument to sterile fantasies and pathetic impotence."

—John J. O'Connor, *The Wall Street Journal*

"One long, relatively meaningless bore. . . ."

—Hollis Alpert, *Saturday Review*

"The only redeeming thought is that *Myra* is evidently aimed at the jaded and spent over-35's. Someone may have judged that a younger generation is happy to leave this sort of putrescence to their elders. I hope so."

—Charles Champlin, *Los Angeles Times*

"A junk film. . . . Satirizes nothing except, perhaps, the desperate lengths to which today's moviemakers will go to try to be different and dirty . . . unpleasant . . . dumb . . . inane . . ."

—Vincent Canby, *New York Times*

"*Myra Breckinridge* collapses like a tired, smirking elephant with no place to go. . . ."

—Howard Thompson, *New York Times*

". . . muddled and boringly smutty. . . . Stay home!"

—Francis Russell, *National Review*

"The structure is a mess . . . the film applies great violence to no visible object for violence. Something is being ridiculed . . . —the people who swallow the picture perhaps."

—Penelope Gilliatt, *The New Yorker*

"The film looks like an abandoned battlefield after a lot of studio forces tussled and nobody won. . . . *Myra* isn't even good opportunism."

—Stanley Kauffmann, *New Republic*

"A new low in amateur squalor. . . ."

—Gene Shalit, *Look*

"The bad taste is beyond belief."

—*Variety*

"I don't want subtlety. I want vulgarity in this film."

—Michael Sarne,
director and co-writer of *Myra Breckinridge*

Plot Summary

Myron Breckinridge (Rex Reed) is waiting for his sex-change operation while a stoned surgeon stumbles into the operating room. Before the drugged doctor (played embarrassingly by John Carradine) begins Myron's operation, he counsels him, and asks, "What about circumcision? It's cheaper, you know." Myron persists and the doctor goes through with the operation. An enthusiastic audience observing the operation applauds the medical achievement and rises in a standing ovation. The movie audience rises in disgust.

After the operation, Myron arrives in Hollywood as Myra. The Myra part is played by Raquel Welch, while in the rest of the film Rex Reed shows up as Myra's alter ego. Myra goes to an acting academy owned by her uncle, Buck Loner (John Huston), a former cowboy star. Attending an acting academy is quite understandable—as Myra Breckinridge, Raquel Welch proves that she could use more than a few acting lessons. The real reason for Myra's arrival is to claim her half of Uncle Buck's estate, which she says she's entitled to, God knows why. Buck Loner stalls by giving her a job teaching the history of motion pictures.

Buck Loner has several friends. One of them is Letitia Van Allen (Mae West), an ancient Hollywood talent scout. The sex-starved septuagenarian runs an acting agency "for leading men only." When introduced to a 6' 7" cowboy she lasciviously remarks to him, "Never mind about the six feet. Let's talk about the seven inches." Somehow, this line becomes even more revolting when delivered by a woman who is close to eighty years old. "I've seen things, Buck, that would turn your stomach!" another friend comments. If we've gone this far into the film, so have we all.

The rest of the film dedicates itself to being as offensive as possible. Four-letter words are frequently uttered, a judge smokes marijuana, and

Myra performs fellatio on Myron—a fantasy Myron has while he masturbates. However, the low point occurs when Myra straps a dildo around her waist and commits sodomy with a brawny young man. "My goal is the destruction of the last vestigial traces of traditional manhood from the race," she comments.

At the end of this heartwarming film, it is suggested that Myron Breckinridge was actually the victim of an auto accident, and this movie was only Myron's homosexual fantasy during his stay at the hospital. How imaginative.

Unforgettable Performances

Raquel Welch has yet to produce something resembling a performance and this film is no exception. The only thing that might save her would be a nude scene.

Mae West, close to eighty, resembles nothing less than a dressed-up corpse. There is a touch of necrophilia in having potent young men lining up to see her. It seems that rigor mortis will set in at any moment. In all fairness, the make-up department does its best to disguise Miss West in a plastic face and a blond wig. She wails two songs in the film and blinks her eyelids every now and then to assure the audience that she is still alive. Had *Myra Breckinridge* been intended to be a horror film Miss West's performance might have been successful.

John Huston, as Buck Loner, is massaged frequently in the film, which gives him numerous opportunities to smack his lips and leer. At one point, he turns his head to the masseuse to say, "Oh, dat feeuhls real good, hunny!" He also brays, snorts, and bellows. In point of fact, Huston displays all the lovable idiosyncrasies of Francis the Talking Mule.

Film critic Rex Reed makes his "acting" debut as Myron. He manages to carry considerable enthusiasm into his masturbation sequence.

A newcomer named Farrah Fawcett (yes, that's *the* Farrah Fawcett) made her screen debut in this film. The highlight of her performance is a lesbian love scene, played under the covers with Raquel Welch. By auctioning off those sheets today, Twentieth Century-Fox might recoup some of their losses from this picture.

Immortal Dialogue

SURGEON (preparing to perform Myron's sex-change operation): You realize that once we cut it off, it won't grow back.
MYRON: What do you think I am?—stupid?

*   *   *

LETITIA VAN ALLEN (Mae West) (pulled over to the side of the road by a policeman): Don't forget to remind me about the policeman's balls—I mean the policeman's ball!

*   *   *

MYRA: How should a man act?
MALE STUDENT: He should ball chicks, that's how.

*   *   *

(An Italian man expresses his feelings to Letitia Van Allen.)
ITALIAN PARAMOUR: In my country to wait for love is like to burn by inches.
LETITIA: You're the best salesman since Columbus.
ITALIAN PARAMOUR: He was good lover too?
LETITIA: Yeah, he raised hell-a with Isabella!

*   *   *

MYRA (to Buck Loner, furiously): You unmitigated piece of shit!

*   *   *

MYRON (waking up in the hospital room): Where are my tits?! Where are my tits?!

*   *   *

The Story Behind the Film

The problems that occurred on the set of *Myra Breckinridge* are legendary. Jack Hamilton, in *Look* magazine, wrote that the film had "more disagreements among cast, writer, director and producer than any other movie I can remember."

157

The film was based on the novel by Gore Vidal, with ten scripts written before the final draft emerged. Robert Fryer (the producer of *Mame*, *Travels with My Aunt*, and *The Boston Strangler*) was producer. He quit three times but came back each time. Bud Yorkin (who, with Norman Lear, later created TV shows "All in the Family," "Maude," and "Sanford and Son") was originally hired as director, but quit in disgust and was replaced by a young British filmmaker named Michael Sarne, the co-writer of the final script. The only other feature film he had directed was *Joanna*.

Sarne quickly gained notoriety. As Rex Reed summed it up: "Everyone hates him." Reed also said that Sarne looked like "a wolf with rabies." Producer Fryer said, "He's unprepared. He comes in not knowing what to do. We're so disorganized we're casting on weekends. And then there's this anti-American thing he has. He dresses all the baddies in red, white, and blue. God, I hate him. I don't know what to do." David Giler, co-writer of the final script, remarked, "I don't understand it. Bobby Kennedy and John Kennedy, they were assassinated. But no one touches Sarne. Sarne's script for *Myra* should be hermetically sealed." Giler then posted in his office all the negative reviews (including Rex Reed's) of Sarne's other film *Joanna*. Gore Vidal, who was supposed to serve as co-producer, ran off to Italy after Sarne interjected some "new" ideas into the script. Discussing the disagreements between Sarne and the crew, co-producer James Cresson explained, "It's simply a matter of humor, casting, costumes, and camera angles. I hope to God we'll get rid of Sarne next week." Unfortunately, Sarne stayed on to finish the film.

Before Raquel Welch was cast as Myra, Sarne considered using a transvestite for the dual roles of Myra and Myron. He tested six transvestites for the part, but later decided that casting just wouldn't work out. Sarne yelled constantly at Miss Welch, and mentioned that she was "useful only because she's a joke." After Sarne's tirades, Raquel would burst into tears, lock herself in her dressing room, and go home with tremendous headaches. As a result, she lost ten pounds. Ms. Welch commented, "I cried until my stomach would feel as if it were dropping out. I felt I was going to faint dead away."

Mae West received $350,000 for her small role and demanded and received top billing. She also got to write her own dialogue, making eight script changes. It was her first film role in twenty-six years.

The Balance Sheet

The film was advertised with the lines "The Book That Couldn't Be Written Is Now a Movie That Couldn't Be Filmed" and "Everything You've Heard About *Myra Breckinridge* Is True!" The film was unanimously panned by critics, and the $5 million project grossed only $4.3 million. During production, Michael Sarne remarked, "I would never consciously do anything bad. I can't afford at this stage of my career to make a bad film." He couldn't be more correct; he couldn't afford it. Outraged by the critical, financial, and personal fiasco of *Myra Breckinridge*, the Hollywood film industry dropped Michael Sarne like a hot potato. We can only hope that the producers stick to their guns and keep him away from important responsibilities on major studio productions.

SPECIAL AWARD

The Hooray for Hollywood Award of a free pass to the Hollywood Wax Museum goes to Michael Sarne. Realizing that his story was completely empty, he decided to throw in some film clips of past movie stars from old Twentieth Century-Fox films. The clips ravage the Hollywood film stars or satirize *Myra Breckinridge* itself. During the sodomy sequence, we see Alice Faye singing "America, I Love You" and a shot of Marilyn Monroe emerging from a pool. Other film stars trampled upon include Loretta Young, Laurel and Hardy, Shirley Temple, Gary Cooper, Ronald Colman, Marlene Dietrich, Tyrone Power, Judy Garland, and Peter Lorre. There are also several scenes of audiences clapping, atomic bombs exploding, and fires breaking loose. There is one film clip, however, that is used perceptively to analyze all that has gone before. The clip is taken from a Twentieth Century-Fox war movie in which an offended Army Sergeant exclaims, "That's what I call disgusting!" Who says all Army sergeants are dumb?

NEW MOON (1940)

Directed by: ROBERT Z. LEONARD
Written by: JACQUES DEVAL and ROBERT ARTHUR
Based on the operetta *New Moon*
Book and lyrics by: OSCAR HAMMERSTEIN II, FRANK MANDEL, and LAWRENCE SCHWAB
Produced by: ROBERT Z. LEONARD
Music by: SIGMUND ROMBERG
Featuring: JEANETTE MacDONALD, NELSON EDDY, MARY BOLAND, GEORGE ZUCCO, H.B. WARNER, GRANT MITCHELL, STANLEY FIELDS

Metro-Goldwyn-Mayer

The Critics Rave

"Pretentious . . . little substance . . . too long. Twenty minutes can be clipped from stagey passages that try to unfold a story in which to interweave the necessary songs. . . . Miss MacDonald overemphasizes the coyness of her characterization which could better have been eliminated."

—*Variety*

"The habit of breaking into song at the slightest excuse becomes exasperating. . . . Nelson Eddy is especially ineffective."

—*Monthly Film Bulletin*

"Between one kiss and another, there is too much palling palaver, too much time to observe that the Eddy figure is becoming almost as operatic as the Eddy acting."

—*Time*

"The script, provided by Jacques Deval and Robert Arthur, is meager in lively details, and what there is of it seems to flow rather sluggishly under Robert Z. Leonard's direction. . . . With the tears welling in our eyes (sniff, sniff), we rather sadly suspect that this sort of sugar-coated musical fiction has seen its better days."

—Bosley Crowther, *New York Times*

Plot Summary

Charles Henri (Nelson Eddy) is a French nobleman who gets himself in trouble because of his revolutionary sympathies. In order to escape the long arm of the King, he disguises himself as a bondsman sailing to New Orleans to be sold at auction. On the very same ship (imagine that!) is a noblewoman sailing to the New World, Marianne de Beaumanoir (Jeanette MacDonald).

While Charles is groveling in the hold with a hundred other bonded slaves, Marianne is up on deck singing to entertain the gentry. The servants in the hold join in, and the captain sends some sailors to silence the rabble with the squirt of a fire hose—yes, a fire hose (pay no attention to the anachronisms which abound like the plague). Later Charles serves as representative of the bondsmen and goes to see the captain. But while he is waiting for the captain to appear, who should walk in but Marianne. Not wishing to have the little lady embarrassed by the sight of his sweat-stained armpits, he grabs for a jacket (which just happens to belong to the captain), and tells Marianne that he's an officer. So smitten by the sight of the dashing young seafarer she can do nothing but make goo-goo eyes at him, Marianne falls head over heals in love with Charles (what do you expect from Nelson Eddy and Jeanette MacDonald?).

After arriving in Louisiana, Charles is conveniently assigned as a footman in Marianne's entourage. He apologizes for misleading her. Too smitten to be angry, Marianne decides to keep him in her service. When she throws a bash for the nobility of New Orleans, and entertains them with another song, Charles embarrasses her by sighing and drooling in her direction. Losing her temper, she storms off into the night and plops herself down in front of "De Trubble Tree," where the black slaves are performing some sort of mysterious voodoo ritual that looks like the hokey-pokey. When Charles comes bounding after her, the two meet in front of this picturesque background, one thing leads to another, and, well—they sing a song, "Wanting You."

Charles now becomes familiar with his amour, calling her Marianne (which is better because he pronounced "Mademoiselle" dreadfully). But then, the governor of the colony arrives to report that one of the bonded servants recently sold at auction is really an escaped nobleman. Wonder who that is. In an effort to protect Charles's secret identity, Marianne hastily sells him to another woman without explanation, and he leaves in a huff.

Instead of going to meet the other woman, Charles meets with the other bondsmen. They conspire to take over a nearby ship, the *New Moon*. He tries to convince his cohorts that they can easily overpower the French sailors guarding the ship. "Friends! What have we to lose but a life of starvation and servitude?" Charles shouts. "But without guns we haven't a chance!" they reply. "We have a chance," Charles boasts proudly. Yes, they do have a chance. They can sing. Joining arms and plowing through marshes, fields, and bogs, the servants belt out "Stout Hearted Men." Singing all the while they take over the ship with much waving of swords and beating of chests. Except for the inferior music, this could be *The Pirates of Penzance*.

Meanwhile, back at the plantation, news comes to Marianne that Charles has overpowered the French sailors. She decides that New Orleans has brought her nothing but unhappiness, and makes plans to go back to Paris. She boards a ship, whose other passengers are sixty brides bound for mail-order husbands in Martinique. But no sooner does the ship pull out to sea than it is captured by pirates, with none other than the nobleman turned servant turned swashbuckler as captain.

A storm strikes. The boat practically turns over, but hardly anyone gets hurt, or even wet. Movie

160

magic, we suppose. The ship is dashed to pieces on the rocks, but everyone makes it to an island, where a democratic colony is established. Why, there are sixty brides, and at least that many sailors, and there's even a priest to perform the ceremonies that will placate the censors, so Nelson Eddy proclaims that "Soon, very soon, we must count and figure by families." Naturally, all the men want to marry Jeanette MacDonald. Flocks of these anxious hopefuls serenade her nightly with a song entitled "Oh We Only Want to Love You." Not with a song like that you don't. Poor Marianne is nearly driven berserk by the serenading, and Charles offers to marry her to save her from the lustful songsters. She agrees.

This is a family movie, however, so Charles provides her with a separate room. The boom of a cannon is heard. Charles rushes off to investigate,

and Marianne, overcome with emotion (or possibly malaria), sings "Lover, Come Back to Me." Charles stops at the seashore and sings back his response, "Near or Far Where'er You Are I'm Coming Back to You." And sure enough, Charles returns with a corps of French soldiers. That was no attack—it was a salute. The Revolution has overthrown the monarchy, and all live happily ever after. At least as long as Charles and Marianne don't sing.

Unforgettable Performances

This film is about as French as *The Courtship of Andy Hardy*. The studio orchestra in period dress looks like a group of jazz musicians in drag. Sigmund Romberg's music is lovely, but having it in this film is a pathetic waste.

Nelson Eddy seems uncomfortable with all the dialogue and speaks as though he were in a daze. In one of the many pointless numbers, he sings to the shoes he is polishing while his wig is falling off. While he sings, the black slaves sit and listen, probably glad that they're not polishing shoes this time.

Most of the songs have nothing to do with the story, and since there are so many songs and so little dialogue in between them, the plot advances at the pace of a Wagnerian opera. Theaters could do good popcorn business on this film.

Jeanette MacDonald, in a hairdo that appears to be adorned with toilet paper rolls, makes a lot of faces, which may have been intended to be funny, but would probably make Skeleton Knaggs (see *Dick Tracy versus Cueball*) cringe. And every time she finishes a song she follows the same odd routine: first she looks heavenward, then tears pour out of her eyes, and lastly, she buries her head in her arms. Once, maybe twice, okay. But just what does she have buried in her arms that she can't keep her head out of them?

Immortal Dialogue

Love Scene (at "De Trubble Tree"):
CHARLES: It's a strange ritual, mademoiselle.

161

Nelson Eddy and Jeanette MacDonald gaze lovingly at one another in the wedding scene from the saccharine 1940 musical New Moon. *Even fans of* Rose Marie *and* Naughty Marietta *blush at this one.*

MARIANNE: You're a strange servant, Charles. Look, they're going to the "Trouble Tree."

CHARLES: The "Trouble Tree"?

MARIANNE: Yes. It's an old jungle superstition. The magnolia is an enchanted tree. Look! One by one now they'll stroke the trunk, each one chanting his trouble. The tree is supposed to take away their sorrows . . . grant their longings . . . bring back their loved ones.

CHARLES: We have a legend at home, too. . . . The story of a humble shepherd who loved a lady of high rank. Hardly daring to hope, he sang his longing.

MARIANNE: Did she hear him?

CHARLES: She answered his song.

MARIANNE: I seem to recall that legend . . .

162

and the song, too.

CHARLES: Remember the words: My heart is aching for someone . . . ♪♫♪ ♩♪!

＊   ＊   ＊

CHARLES: Anger makes you very charming, mademoiselle.

MARIANNE: Patronizing makes you very boring, monsieur.

＊   ＊   ＊

Nelson Eddy's Unforgettable Serenade to the Shoes:

Shoes to shine, shoes to shine.
Prancing shoes for dancing new romances to,
Shoes for morning, noon, and night,
Every shade from black to white.
Every type from boot to pump,
Suddenly my heart goes "bump." . . .

The Story Behind the Film

New Moon is based on the operetta by lyricist Oscar Hammerstein II and composer Sigmund Romberg. It was first filmed in 1930 with Grace Moore and Lawrence Tibbett in the leading roles.

The producer-director, Robert Z. Leonard, was also director of such Eddy/MacDonald unforgettables as *Maytime* and *The Girl of the Golden West*. He directed *Broadway Serenade* with Miss MacDonald, and *The Great Ziegfeld, Escapade,* and Eugene O'Neill's *Strange Interlude*. Finding his dual role of producer/director of *New Moon* a bit time-consuming, he called in veteran filmmaker W.S. Van Dyke II to take over on the set. Van Dyke had scored well with *Naughty Marietta, Rose Marie,* and *Sweethearts,* all starring Nelson Eddy and Jeanette MacDonald. Pre-production publicity reported that comic genius Buster Keaton would make a guest appearance in *New Moon,* but someone must have wised up the

Great Stone Face, as he is nowhere to be seen in the finished product.

The film's appeal is slanted toward aging matrons in love with Nelson Eddy, who don't mind the interminable dialogue, ridiculous plot, and heavy-handed moralizing, and could just sit back and watch the fancy costumes for hours. A press release reported that Jeanette MacDonald "will have sixteen changes in all, a little matter that involves eighty petticoats, or an average of five petticoats to a costume. Her most elaborate gown of emerald green [this is a black-and-white film, remember] tips the scales at thirty-five pounds." No wonder she is grimacing on camera so much of the time.

The Balance Sheet

Nelson Eddy and Jeanette MacDonald first appeared together in the film *Naughty Marietta* in 1935, and after seven successive films became known as America's "Singing Sweethearts." By 1940, Nelson Eddy was recognized as the highest-paid singer in the world.

New Moon was a moderate success, but it fell far short of the public acclaim to which the stars were accustomed. Despite its many embarrassing moments, *New Moon* did no permanent damage to Eddy's and MacDonald's careers, and the Singing Sweethearts went on to other triumphs such as *Bittersweet* and *I Married an Angel.*

Contrary to popular belief, and to the fervent wishes of Ms. MacDonald's *two* national fan clubs, Nelson and Jeanette were never married. In fact, rumor had it that they really hated each other. After *New Moon,* they may have properly turned their resentment toward the screenwriters, costume designer, choreographer, cinematographers, key-grips, gaffers, and all others connected with this lumbering vehicle. Intended as a piece of fluffy French pastry, it is nonetheless difficult to digest, and gas was reported as a common symptom in many viewers.

Robert Preston, betrayed, curses his former lover Paulette Goddard: "You crawling black scum! . . . You sneaking she-wolf!" (from North West Mounted Police).

Square shooter Dusty Rivers (Gary Cooper) has little tolerance for the flirtatious wiles of the half-breed Louvette (Paulette Goddard). They are both part of Cecil B. De-Mille's "historical" drama, which promised its viewers "1,000 Unforgettable Thrills."

NORTH WEST MOUNTED POLICE (1940)

Directed by: CECIL B. DeMILLE
Written by: ALAN LeMAY, JESSE LASKY, JR., and C. GARDNER SULLIVAN
Produced by: CECIL B. DeMILLE
Music by: VICTOR YOUNG
Featuring: GARY COOPER, MADELEINE CARROLL, PAULETTE GODDARD, PRESTON FOSTER, ROBERT PRESTON, CHIEF BIG TREE, CHIEF YOWLACHIE, CHIEF THUNDERBIRD, CHIEF THUNDERCLOUD

Paramount Pictures

The Critics Rave

". . . as usual in Mr. DeMille's pictures, the story is a heavy accumulation of dramatic clichés . . . it is overplayed . . . [a] big, sprawling, sometimes tedious picture in which the note of heroism is beaten like a drum to the accompanying clash of color symbols."
—Bosley Crowther, *New York Times*

"Veteran cinema addicts will not be fooled into forgetting its parentage by either sound or Technicolor when they hear the halfbreed Louvette (Paulette Goddard) woo the heroine's wayward brother (Robert Preston) with such primitive verbal caresses as: 'I eat your heart out,' or 'My heart sings lack a bird.'"
—*Time*

"DeMille at his most ridiculous . . . much of outdoor action filmed on obviously indoor sets."
—Leonard Maltin, *TV Movies*

". . . a loosely-written script drags in two handfuls of characters with individual stories

165

wandering all over the lot, and an equal number of Hollywood stars glittering so brightly that they detract from each other. . . . tedious. . . . stereotyped plot and comic horseplay."

—Philip T. Hartung, *Commonweal*

". . . Frankly claptrap . . . neither affair of the heart contributes very much to the total entertainment, and DeMille and his cast are at their best when amour makes way for armaments."

—*Newsweek*

Plot Summary

Dusty Rivers (Gary Cooper), a lone Texas Ranger, makes his way to a fort of the Royal Canadian Mounted Police in Saskatchewan. He asks the Mounties for permission to hunt down Jacques Corbeau (George Bancroft), a wanted killer and whiskey runner. But the Mounties want Corbeau for themselves. It seems that this all-purpose villain is working with revolutionary Louis Riel, inciting the Indians and half-breeds of Saskatchewan to rebel against the British. Corbeau has stolen a Gatling gun, and this impresses the Indians so much that they agree to do everything Corbeau says—after all, what else can you do when there's a Gatling gun pointed at you?

The half-breeds are distinguishable not by any physical characteristics but by their accents. They talk in dialects so thick that it would seem that English is their fourth language and Bulgarian their native tongue. The Indians run around in leather swimsuits, and some of them wear cake make-up thick enough to resemble the living dead. They leap around and shout "Hi-o-hey, hoy-o-hey," sounding more like the sailors in Wagner's *Flying Dutchman* than savages. Not to be outdone, however, the Mounties have costumes that are also attention-getters. Their uniforms are bright red, which serves as terrific camouflage, particularly in forest fires. They also sport little fur caps with a leather flap hanging over the side. Viewed from above, these fuzzy *chapeaux* look like open mouths with large floppy tongues.

While waiting for permission to hunt for Corbeau, Dusty meets his competition: Sergeant James Brett (Preston Foster), also looking for Corbeau. Brett is in love with April Logan (Madeleine Carroll), a nurse, but she won't marry him because everyone knows that two career people in one family never work out. Dusty takes an immediate liking to this liberated Florence Nightingale, and a two-barreled rivalry takes shape. Both Brett and Dusty are after the same man (Corbeau, in case you've forgotten) and the same woman. Sounds like a rustic version of *Sunday, Bloody Sunday*.

Tired of waiting around at the fort looking for beavers, Dusty takes off to look for Corbeau. He trails him to an Indian Camp, but when our hero enters an Indian bigwig wigwam, he finds himself face to face with the Gatling gun, with Corbeau on the trigger side. No fool, Dusty hightails it back to the fort.

Corbeau and his rebels prepare to ambush a Mountie outpost. There are fifty Mounties, and thousands of Indians and half-breeds. To make up for the disparity, many of the Mounties can be seen to be killed twice. The Gatling gun becomes the real star of the show, and we watch transfixed as the Mounties get shot in the eyes, groin, and hands.

While the battle rages outside, April tends the wounded men. As the enemy moves in for the massacre, she escapes in a canoe with Dusty, who has spent the entire battle firing an occasional round with his six-shooter. As they float down the river, Dusty is seized by thoughts of love and passion (how can one think of anything else with bodies dropping dead right and left?). He asks April to come to Texas with him. She agrees. "Texas must be heaven," she coos. "It will be when you get there," says Dusty.

On the way to Texas, Dusty goes to rescue a captured Mountie, who also happens to be April's brother. But wouldn't you know it, in the process, he bumbles into the Gatling gun, which after all is the real star of the show. Dusty fights off the half-breeds guarding the weapon, ties the gun to his horse, and gallops down a mountain angled at eighty degrees. The horse does a triple sommersault with Dusty on it, and the Gatling gun spills into a river, gone forever. Dusty and his horse get up as if nothing happened and continue on their merry way. And just think, Gene Autry could only get his horse to jump onto a moving truck (see *Twilight on the Rio Grande*).

Eventually Dusty finds April's brother, but as they make their escape, this poor sibling is shot down by a half-breed sniper. Dusty throws the body over his horse and away they ride, back to the fort. When they arrive, Dusty dramatically throws the limp corpse down on a table where the commanding officer is sitting, and announces that the young man was a hero, and had single-handedly destroyed the Gatling gun. Nobody ever said the Texas Rangers were honest.

In the meantime, Brett has found the half-breeds and Corbeau an easy conquest without their beloved Gatling gun. That's right, the Mounties always get their man. The Rangers have a different maxim—they always get their woman. A cowboy's a cowboy, and Dusty prepares to ride home with his beloved April. Brett re-evaluates the situation, then says, "I'll trade ya," and Dusty swaps Corbeau for April. Only Cecil B. DeMille would trade human beings around as if they were baseball cards.

With Brett and April reunited, Dusty heads back to Texas. He doesn't have a woman any more, but he's got Jacques Corbeau on a horse with his hands tied. And we all know those stories about cowboys out on the prairie.

Unforgettable Performances

Dusty Rivers might be more aptly called Muddy Waters, for that is where this role seems to have been conceived. Gary Cooper's face rivals Buster Keaton's in immobility, although Cooper does curl his lip every now and then. Actually, he looks as though he wishes he were somewhere else. In one poignant scene, in the canoe with Miss Carroll, he looks heavenward as if to say, "Help! Lemme outa this movie, Mr. DeMille! I'll do anything—I'll even play Pharaoh!" No such luck. Cooper does, however, have a marvelous gift for keeping his cowboy suit clean—and he has certainly managed to pack quite a few of those outfits into his tiny little saddlebag.

Paulette Goddard, as a mischievous little half-breed, tries to repeat the impishness of her performance in Chaplin's *Modern Times*. But it appears that here director DeMille neglected to tell her that *North West* was a talkie. She wanders around in leather with feathers dangling from her hair, and has an accent thicker than Audrey Tot-

ter's in *Jet Attack* (q.v.). She calls herself a half-breed—one wonders what sorts of animals went into the mixture.

Preston Foster does nothing to dispel the common belief that the ordinary Canadian Mountie has the same stature and intelligence as Dudley Doright. Lon Chaney, Jr., makes a brief appearance in this movie, as a half-breed named Shorty. In one scene he runs inside a medical station and exclaims, "A boy . . . hey look . . . out of zee way . . . I just have baby boy!" When he holds the child he says, "She not very big. How you make sure dat boy?" He seems to be doing a repeat of his performance as Lenny in *Of Mice and Men*.

Lynne Overman provides comic relief as a red-haired Scottish scout who guides Gary Cooper on the trail. You can tell he's a Scotsman because the strains of a bagpipe accompany him whenever he appears on screen. He wears a tam-o'-shanter and sports muttonchops that look like shag-carpet samples pasted on his cheeks.

Immortal Dialogue

DUROC: We don' fail! Corbeau's got somezin' you never see no gun lahk that . . . she squirt lead lahk . . . lahk ze hurricane.
RIEL (slow and ominous): Blood will run like water.
CORBEAU: Blood—you won't notice it much. The Mounted Police wear read coats.

❊   ❊   ❊

LOVESICK MOUNTIE (Robert Preston): Listen, you little wildcat, you're the only real thing that's ever happened to me. And nobody, nothing could ever make me let you go.
HALF-BREED GIRL: (Paulette Goddard) I love you so terrible bad I feel good.

❊   ❊   ❊

DUSTY: You know, I . . . I kinda gotta feelin' that I could make things easier for ya . . . if you'd let me.
APRIL: You're a grand person, Dusty. But there ain't anything anyone can do for me.
DUSTY: Sure there is. Come to Texas with

me. . . . You're the loveliest and gentlest lady I've ever known.

* * *

(Meanwhile, passion mounts between the lovesick Mountie (Robert Preston) and his half-breed femme fatale (Paulette Goddard).)

MOUNTIE: You're the sweetest poison that ever got into a man's blood! I love you! I *want* you!

* * *

(Dusty and April enjoy romantic banter.)

APRIL: Oh, Dusty! You're an angel in leather!

DUSTY: Heh, heh—I'd look funny with leather wings.

* * *

(The half-breed vixen betrays her Mountie lover.)

MOUNTIE: You crawling black scum! . . . You sneaking she-wolf!! . . . You dirty squaw!!! I'll kill you when I get loose!

The Story Behind the Film

It was reported that Cecil B. DeMille, that grand monarch of Hollywood megalomania, long believed that the resemblances between Canada's celebrated Mounted Police and their movieland counterparts stopped with the uniforms. He said that he never liked the "mythical Mounted," as he called the Hollywood variety, but was convinced that there was good material in there somewhere. In this, the sixty-fourth film of his career, he proved himself wrong.

Taking down his trusty World Book Encyclopedia, DeMille researched the famous Riel rebellion of 1885, when Canadian half-breeds and Indians rebelled against the British in the Canadian northwest. He decided that with a little juicing up the incident would make a terrific epic, or debacle, or whatever he was prone to call his movies. Paramount was a little edgy about making such a big film, what with war having broken out in Europe and all. DeMille saved his project by pointing out that a stirring picture of life in the British commonwealth was exactly what the world needed—his gospel proved so moving that the studio went along with it.

DeMille hired Alan LeMay, Commodore Frank Wead, Jesse Lasky, Jr., and Jeanie Macpherson to write the script. After weeks of collaboration, they came up with nothing more than a straggly series of disconnected incidents. DeMille decided that this was good enough and shot the script anyway.

The filming was originally set for Canada, but at the last minute the studio decided not to authorize the extra expense but to save $62,000. This didn't faze DeMille in the least. He said himself: "The trouble with filming the real thing is that on the screen it looks sham. Overmuch confidence in Nature won't do." So with that profound thought, Saskatchewan was re-created on the back lot of Paramount Studios. Three hundred pine trees were planted. A ranger was hired to patrol the mini-forest; it is reported that he found it easy to stop persons from smoking, but spent a lot of time chasing seagulls from the branches to prevent them from appearing on camera.

Joel McCrea was originally cast as Dusty Rivers, but he dropped out at the last moment due to prior commitments. Or at least that's what he said. He probably sat down and read the script, and figured he'd better get out while he still could. The real casting dilemma was finding an actress to play the half-breed heartbreaker Louvette. The problem was solved when Paulette Goddard walked into DeMille's office, dressed in leather and feathers, and propped her leg up on the director's desk. He gave her the part in a minute.

For the Indian multitudes, a studio press release reported that DeMille had employed about two hundred savages, "full bloods, mixed, and ersatz." All Indian players were decorated with the same shade of make-up stick. They were given the Blackfoot hue, which was between copper and mahogany. "Each player has a stick, it costs fifteen cents, and lasts a week. The total cost is $300 a month." And fifteen days in jail if you're caught wearing that slop out on the street. For Walter Hampden, who played Chief Big Bear in the film, a more extensive make-up job was required, including a $500 pair of primitive contact lenses made to fit under the eyelids and change the color of his eyes. One elderly Navajo, who saw Hampden's eyes brown when they had been blue ten minutes before, looked quizzically at him,

Gary Cooper and Madeleine Carroll in North West Mounted Police.
HE: "You're the loveliest and gentlest lady I've ever known."
SHE: "Oh, Dusty! You're an angel in leather!"

then shuffled away, not to return for three days.

The film boasted several Indian chiefs in its cast lineup, including Chief Big Tree, Chief Yowlachie, Chief Thunderbird, and Chief Thundercloud. Don't try to find them in the picture, because they switch roles so many times it's impossible to tell them apart. One young Navajo warrior, Tom Hightree, became known on the set for his war whoops. A university graduate and football cheerleader, Hightree had been taught the traditional battle cries by his grandfather, who thought they might come in handy someday. During the filming of one scene, after a spate of chilling yells, director DeMille found it necessary to restrain the Indian yodeler: "Mr. Hightree, please—if you could just moderate a little. It's too harrowing. After all, this is only a massacre."

DeMille saved quite a bit on technical assistants by hiding sixteen loudspeakers among the rocks and branches, so that his slightest whispered command to cast and crew would roll thunderously through the foliage. He liked this setup so much that he decided playing God was his true calling, as reflected in his subsequent film *The Ten Commandments*.

The Balance Sheet

North West Mounted Police was billed as "An Historical Drama in Technicolor." It proved to be an historical drama in bad taste. It was heralded as the "Mightiest Adventure-Romance Ever," with "1,000 Unforgettable Thrills." The only way this latter claim could have been made good was by placing a "whoopee" cushion beneath all the seats of the movie house.

The title of the film experienced several changes. It was originally titled *The Royal Canadian Mounted*, but that sounded like an incomplete obscene sentence, so a change was made to *The Scarlet Riders*. This title called to mind prostitutes on parade, and Paramount finally decided on the present title.

World War II had just begun, and the American public seemed to enjoy any diversion it could get its claws on. With *Gone with the Wind, Boom Town, Rebecca, The Fighting 69th*, and *Strike Up the Band, North West Mounted Police* was one of the top six box-office grossers of 1940.

*Gregory Peck and David Warner,
gravely troubled in* The Omen.

*Lee Remick, clutching her
troubled baby in* The Omen:
*"Remember . . . You Have Been
Warned."*

THE OMEN (1976)

Directed by: RICHARD DONNER
Written by: DAVID SELTZER
Produced by: HARVEY BERNHARD
Music by: JERY GOLDSMITH
Featuring: GREGORY PECK, LEE REMICK, BILLIE WHITELAW, DAVID WARNER, HARVEY STEPHENS, LEO McKERN, PATRICK TROUGHTON, MARTIN BENSON, HOLLY PALANCE

Twentieth Century-Fox

The Critics Rave

"A dreadfully silly film. . . . Its horrors are not horrible, its terrors are not terrifying, its violence is ludicrous."

—Richard Eder, *New York Times*

"Contrivance is self-evident in *The Omen,* wherein Scripture is quoted endlessly to warn us that the Antichrist is upon us. . . . The resultant idiocy offers more laughs than the average comedy."

—Judith Crist, *Saturday Review*

"Trash. . . .When a producer spends as much money on ads and commercials for a movie as he spends on making the movie itself, perhaps audiences have a right to suspect that they are being sucked into seeing a piece of junk. And that junk is called *The Omen.*"

—Gene Shalit, *Ladies' Home Journal*

"Quite a number of silly scares . . . starring a very sonorous and vapid Gregory Peck."

—Penelope Gilliat, *The New Yorker*

"*The Omen* is certainly all dog from snout to tail. . . . Nowhere can you glimpse a hint of subtlety or credibility."

—John Simon, *New York*

"A dumb and largely dull movie. . . . The latest serving of deviled ham."

—Jack Kroll, *Newsweek*

"Crude, derivative, heavy-handed. . . . There is something sleazy about the whole enterprise partly because of its cold commercial calculation, and partly because of its reliance on excessively gory shock effects. . . . The climax of *The Omen* is particularly unsavory."

—Stephen Farber, *New West*

"Although *The Omen* is pretty beastly, its treatment of The Beast is superficial and silly. . . . A pathetic attempt to sound ominous."

—James M. Martin, *Coast*

"A package of nonsense. . . . Not to be taken seriously. . . . Stick a pin in this nonsensical balloon at any point and the story will deflate."

—William Wolf, *Cue*

"I did it strictly for the money. I was flat broke. . . . I do find it horrifying to find how many people actually believe all this silliness."

—David Seltzer, author of the original screenplay for *The Omen*

Plot Summary

Robert Thorn (Gregory Peck) is an American millionaire living in Europe. One dreary night in Rome his wife (Lee Remick) gives birth to a stillborn child. When he arrives at the hospital, Thorn learns that the Mrs. has not yet been told the tragic news, and a sleazy priest comes up with an interesting proposition. In that same hospital is a healthy baby whose mother has just died, leaving it an orphan. Why not substitute this precious bundle for the Thorns' dead child? No one—not even Mrs. Thorn—need know the difference.

Thorn agrees to this sneaky switcheroo, and shortly thereafter his high moral standards are appropriately rewarded as he wins appointment as United States Ambassador to Great Britain. He and wifey and baby all live happily ever after in a great big house—except that the child turns out a wee bit strange. His nanny mysteriously hangs herself. He nearly claws his mother's eyes out when the good woman tries to take him to church. When the little bugger visits a zoo, all the animals become hysterically afraid. On another occasion sweet little Damien (that's his name, all right) deliberately runs his mommy down with a tricycle, thereby pushing her off a second-story landing and nearly killing her. The child's only friend is a growling black dog with fiery eyes who drifts mysteriously in and out of the film.

None of this seems to alarm the proud papa, until a demented priest appears on the scene to warn Thorn about the diabolical little mischief-maker. This is one clerical role that even Bing Crosby wouldn't touch. The prophetic padre sobs, sweats, growls, and howls, but never seems to get to the point. Clearly, he is trying to say something about little Damien being the Antichrist—Satan's only begotten son. After one of his inconclusive meetings with Thorn, a storm suddenly comes up and lightning begins flashing all around the pathetic priest. Will he be struck by a bolt of lightning? No, that would be a cliché. Instead, a gigantic bolt strikes the lightning rod of a church and the pole comes hurtling down to impale the old man through the heart. Now *that's* entertainment!

Yet no sooner does one buttinsky die than another one appears. This time it's a curious photographer (David Warner) whose main interest in the case is that whenever he is around Damien, mysterious demonic rays appear in his photographs. These rays apparently indicate who is due to be zapped next. The photographer persuades Ambassador Thorn that the whole business is worth investigation, and so they leave together for Italy in search of the priest who had orchestrated the original baby trade at the hospital. When they finally find him they learn that he has been punished for his sins by suffering through a ghastly fire, not to mention one of the most ludicrous make-up jobs in Hollywood history. The right side of his face seems to be composed of equal parts of dried mud and pepperoni pizza. His numerous lumps and pustulating sores are complemented by a bloodshot eye twisted toward his forehead. Actually, the poor man bears a startling resemblance to the "atomic monster" in *The Horror of Party Beach* (q.v.). This colorful relic sends Thorn and the faithful photographer to a remote Italian cemetery. There they dig up the casket of Damien's real mother and find that it contains not a human skeleton, but the bones of a dog. This, apparently, is to prove to us that Damien is really a son of a bitch. A herd of snarling, bloodthirsty hounds suddenly appears out of nowhere, and our heroes barely escape the cemetery with their lives. Ambassador Thorn is still recuperating from this shock when he learns that his wife back home finally bit the dust. Damien's new zombie-nanny sweetly pushed the mistress out the window of the hospital room where the poor lady was recovering from her previous fall.

This does not sit well with the Ambassador, who heads for Jerusalem to consult the world's leading expert on the Antichrist. Naturally, this well-informed mystic (Leo McKern) lives in a cave and tells Thorn he must kill his adopted son on the altar of a church. He gives the American a bundle of holy daggers for this purpose—nothing else will do. The good Ambassador remains somewhat dubious about this novel proposal until his photographer sidekick, while walking the streets of Jerusalem, is hideously decapitated by a huge sheet of glass that slides off the back of a flatbed truck. Nothing like raw, convincing realism to give the audiences who patronize Satanic pictures exactly what they're paying for.

At long last, Thorn jets back to London and grabs his little bundle of joy; he wants to use Damien as a pincushion for the holy daggers. Before he can finish the job he must tediously battle barking black dogs and the diabolical nanny, but finally he carries Damien, kicking and screaming, into a church. He is about to slaughter the child when the police suddenly appear at the church door and order the Ambassador to stop. Thorn ignores them and the officers fire. We see a lovely fat bullet emerging in slow motion out of the barrel of a gun and wait in bearable suspense to see what happens. Do they kill Thorn? Do they plug Damien? Does the Ambassador succeed in puncturing the little bugger before he eats the bullet?

These questions are answered with a quick cut to the final scene, in which Ambassador Thorn's flag-draped casket is being lowered into the

Gregory Peck suffers an unfortunate altercation with man's best friend. In this and all other scenes of The Omen, *Mr. Peck expresses his emotions by raising his elegantly arched left eyebrow.*

ground back in the U.S.A. As the camera pulls away from the grave, we see little Damien, as adorable as ever, watching the proceedings approvingly. The child is now in the company of the President of the United States, who has adopted the orphan as a tribute to the unfortunate Ambassador who ran amok.

At the very close, Damien smiles sweetly into the camera. And why shouldn't he smile? According to our statistics, he is the very first Antichrist in American history to win his way into the White House by the age of five.

Unforgettable Performances

Gregory Peck, as Ambassador Thorn, often sinks to the level of pompous self-parody that characterized actor Adam West in the old "Batman" TV series. His delivery is punctuated by so many lengthy and "dramatic" pauses that at times we are left to wonder whether the great actor has fallen asleep. In this role, Mr. Peck expresses every emotion simply by raising his left eyebrow. It is a silken and elegantly arched eyebrow indeed, and it surely must have benefited from the workout it received in this film. Is Mr. Peck shocked at the antics of his adopted son? Up goes the eyebrow. Is he pained at the loss of his wife? Up goes the eyebrow. Is he pursuing Damien in a murderous rage? Keep that eyebrow up there. Since the canine theme runs so prominently throughout this film, the analogy is inescapable: his left eyebrow plays the same expressive role for Mr. Peck as a wagging tail does for man's best friend.

Lee Remick, on the other hand, shows enormous range in registering fright and horror in this film: she even goes to the extent of allowing her mascara to be occasionally smeared. At moments of extreme dramatic tension—such as her own death scene—she mechanically opens her mouth as if preparing to swallow a butterfly.

Billie Whitelaw, as Mrs. Baylock, Damien's demonic nanny, is a rigid, tight-lipped robot. David Warner as the worried photographer looks like a hemorrhoid sufferer from a TV commercial. And little Harvey Stephens, as the adorable Damien, apparently manifested far more interesting behavior off the screen than anything we see in this film. According to publicity releases about the production, he regularly kicked and scratched at cameramen and other technicians, and on one occasion even took a sock at director Richard Donner, splitting the poor man's lip. Right on, Harvey, and please hit him again for us.

Immortal Dialogue

(Ambassador Thorn and his wife look for a new home in England.)

THORN (surveying a mansion): It's a bit much.
KATHERINE: No, nothing's too much for the wife of the future President of the United States!
THORN: You know—you're pushy. . . . (He embraces her.)
KATHERINE: Something in mind, Mr. Ambassador?
THORN (leeringly): Oh, I might have a little look upstairs. . . .
KATHERINE: Well, there's no furniture up there either.
THORN: Awww! You know, you may be too sexy for the White House!

❖   ❖   ❖

(Ambassador Thorn, in his office, has a fiery conversation with a priest.)

THORN: What do you know about my son?
PRIEST: Everything.
THORN: And what is that?
PRIEST: I saw its mother.

THORN: Its what!
PRIEST: I saw its mother.
THORN (archly): You are referring to my wife!
PRIEST: *Its* mother, Mr. Thorn!
THORN: If this is blackmail, come out and say it! What is it you're trying to say?!
PRIEST: *Its mother was a—*
(The priest is interrupted as the door bursts open violently.)
SECURITY GUARD (to Thorn): Everything all right, sir?
THORN'S SECRETARY: You sounded strange. The door was locked.

❖   ❖   ❖

(As the plot thickens . . .)
THORN (to his wife): If there were anything wrong, you'd tell me, wouldn't you?
KATHERINE: Wrong? What could be wrong with our child, Robert? We're beautiful people, aren't we?

❖   ❖   ❖

The Story Behind the Film

The Omen marked the feature-film debut of director Richard Donner. Previous to making the film Donner had worked as an actor, a director of TV commercials, and finally a director of assorted television series. The real evil genius behind the film, however, was David Seltzer, author of both the original screenplay and a best-selling novelization based on the film. Seltzer recently admitted, "I did it strictly for money. . . . It's very pleasant not having to worry for the first time in my life about the grocery bills. I just wish I'd had this kind of success with something I personally found more meaningful. . . . I was warned by a religious adviser that Satan would sabotage the movie. But I ask you, how powerful can the devil be when *The Omen* is grossing one million dollars a day?"

The film was made for a total production cost of $2.8 million and most of the shooting was done in England. Three weeks of filming were spent at Pyford Court, a thousand-acre estate near Ripley. The sixty-room mansion at Pyford Court was used as Ambassador Thorn's country home—conveniently ignoring the fact that the U.S.

Ambassador to England actually has an official residence he is required to occupy.

In one of the most transparent and tasteless publicity campaigns in Hollywood history, the studio attempted to communicate the idea that the devil actually did try to interfere with the production. Press releases boasted about the sudden fits of violence on the part of five-year-old child star Harvey Stephens. The fourteen Rottweiler attack dogs used in the graveyard sequence also began acting up and several stunt men were severely bitten as a result. And there were several omen-ous incidents involving airplanes. Writer David Seltzer and star Gregory Peck took separate flights to London, but both planes were struck by lightning. This sounds fairly impressive until you talk to a pilot and learn that such occurrences are fairly routine and hardly dangerous. Publicity also claimed that the crew "almost" chartered another jet which later crashed and killed six people. As the fun continued, director Richard Donner was hit by an automobile just two days after landing in London. Three other members of the production company narrowly avoided injury in terrorist bombings in the British capital. Then, when little Harvey Stephens visited the London Safari Park, a tiger escaped and killed its trainer, proving conclusively that it's better not to allow tigers to escape. When the producer of the film Harvey Bernhard (no relation to Harvey Stephens) went to Rome to help supervise the Italian scenes, lightning struck the top of Hadrian's Gate across from his hotel. To studio publicists and to gullible zombies, these occurrences may all suggest a diabolical pattern, but it is worth noting that, to the best of our knowledge, no one in the crew was impaled by a toppling lightning rod or decapitated by a sliding sheet of plate glass. Better luck next time.

The Balance Sheet

The advertising campaign for *The Omen* not only cost far more than the production itself, but showed a good deal more imagination. Dramatic, stark black and white ads appeared everywhere, proclaiming: "Good Morning. You Are One Day Closer to the End of the World" or "If Something Frightening Happens to You Today, Think About It. It May Be *The Omen*" or, most notably, "Remember . . . You Have Been Warned."

Critics and major religious organizations also did their best to warn people—not about the Antichrist himself, but about the atrocious film that purported to deal with the subject. The United States Catholic Conference proclaimed the film "one of the most distasteful" ever put out by a major studio and called it "an essentially trashy horror show." None of the warnings served to diminish the crowds who flocked to see this film in unprecedented numbers. The film was released in the summer of 1976, and in its first three days at 516 theaters in 321 cities, it grossed an astounding $4,273,000. By the first week of September, the film had returned more than $22 million in domestic rentals alone. To date, Twentieth Century-Fox claims that the film is heading for a projected $160 million to $200 million worldwide gross. Not bad for a project that cost $2.8 million to produce.

Nearly as astonishing as the success of the film was the triumph of David Seltzer's spin-off novelization—which for several months was the nation's number one best-selling paperback. All of this popular enthusiasm has naturally and inevitably provoked plans for several sequels. In *The Omen II*, Damien will be eleven years old. In *The Omen III*, Damien will be a teen-ager. Finally, in *The Omen IV*, Damien will be about thirty-five years old and will commence Armageddon and the destruction of the world, thereby preventing any further sequels. Meanwhile, director Richard Donner is developing a screenplay entitled *The Day the Bluegills Died*, concerning an enraged citizen wreaking revenge on the industries that pollute our water and air. No comment is planned on the industries that pollute our movie screens and our minds. Perhaps Mr. Donner sees such a socially responsible project as a means of atonement for the pernicious nonsense presented in *The Omen*. Certainly the people responsible for this film, as well as some of the millions who paid to see it, must feel a sense of contamination or at least embarrassment for their association with this garbage. If so, because of the film's subject matter they can at least offer a glib excuse, and claim simply, "The devil made me do it."

176

PARNELL (1937)

Directed by: JOHN M. STAHL
Written by: JOHN VAN DRUTEN and S. N. BEHRMAN
Adapted from the play by: ELSIE T. SCHAUF-FLER
Produced by: JOHN M. STAHL
Music by: DR. WILLIAM AXT
Featuring: CLARK GABLE, MYRNA LOY, EDNA MAY OLIVER, EDMUND GWENN, ALAN MARSHAL, DONALD CRISP, BILLIE BURKE, BERTON CHURCHILL, DONALD MEEK, MONTAGU LOVE, BYRON RUSSELL, BRANDON TYNAN, PHYLLIS COGHLAN, NEIL FITZGERALD, GEORGE ZUCCO

Metro-Goldwyn-Mayer

The Critics Rave

"Disastrous. . . . Probably the worst biopic ever made."
>—David Shipman, *The Great Movie Stars— The Golden Years*

"A singularly pallid, tedious and unconvincing drama. . . . Mr. Gable's speeches ring with insincerity. His half-smile, which frequently develops into a full smirk, gives the lie to every other sentence he utters."
>—Frank S. Nugent, *New York Times*

"Sluggish."
>—James P. Cunningham, *Commonweal*

"As history, it ranks low. . . . Myrna Loy behaves as though she missed *The Thin Man*, and

Clark Gable and Myrna Loy strike a tragic pose in M-G-M's 1937 disaster Parnell. *One cinema historian described the film as "probably the worst biopic ever made."*

not even mutton chop whiskers and a turret-top collar can make Clark Gable look, sound or act like the uncrowned King of Ireland . . . ."

—*Time*

"Parnell? No! Clark Gable, in his worst miscasting. He looks like a steel-union organizer gone Park Avenue and walks through his part with the heavy tread of the Golem. Nor is Myrna Loy any help to him, for she is equally stodgy and unbending . . ."

—Rob Wagner, *Script*

"If Parnell was as woozy a goof as Gable portrayed him in that picture, Ireland still wouldn't be free."

—Carole Lombard (Mrs. Clark Gable)

Plot Summary

This film is about Ireland and Irish politics and so, with impeccable Hollywood logic, the action begins in America. Charles Stewart Parnell (Clark Gable), a member of Parliament and "the uncrowned King of Ireland," is touring the States to raise money for his drive to win Irish home rule. Upon his return home, our hero attends the opera to take his mind off his troubles, and there he catches a glimpse of a beautiful, mysterious stranger. The only detail missing from this heart-stopping soap-opera sequence is cupids fluttering at the edges of the screen. Later, Parnell meets this beauty once again and learns that she is Katie O'Shea (Myrna Loy), the wife of one of his political opponents. At the first opportunity, Parnell-Gable breathlessly confesses that he is in love with her, and, what's more, "I knew the moment that I saw you."

As their love affair develops, Parnell devotes his free time to campaigning for Irish home rule. Unfortunately, there are many meanies who try to stop him. One of them forges a letter in Parnell's name showing the great leader to be a murderer. At the trial, however, the forger conveniently shoots himself and everyone is happy again. Charles and Katie now have the time to do "romantic" things together, like getting lost in the fog or eating hot potatoes from a street vendor. Little do they suspect that Katie's husband, who has always been a brute to his wife anyway, is planning to blackmail them. The heartless cad demands a government job, and when Parnell refuses to give it to him he finds himself named as "the other man" in a highly publicized divorce suit. To his Roman Catholic supporters, this makes Parnell about as appetizing as a slab of roast beef on Friday afternoon. Our hero's political career quickly goes down the sewer, along with his good health. Though he lies near death, Katie gamely remains at his side, while a crowd of humble working folk gathers around the house offering up their prayers. (Ah! The touching simplicity of those good Irish working folk!) With his last ounce of strength he tells Katie that he will get better and someday they will get married. It matters very little that in real life Charles Parnell married Katie O'Shea and then died a year later. Isn't Ireland the home of the blarney stone, after all? On screen, Katie holds his brave little hand, and promises she'll never leave him, while Parnell passes on to his reward. As the music swells we have hints of a choir of unseen angels, and the promise that the two lovers will soon be dancing a jig together in the shamrock fields up in the sky.

Unforgettable Performances

How did the M-G-M executives first hit upon the brilliant idea of casting Clark Gable as Charles Stewart Parnell? In 1936, Gable was named "King of Hollywood" in an Ed Sullivan poll and this must have seemed a sound enough reason for him to portray "the uncrowned King of Ireland." It didn't matter that the only thing Gable had in common with Parnell was a moustache. Even this natural asset had to be supplemented by a pair of absurd muttonchop sidewhiskers as Gable prepared for his role. In rallying support for the home rule cause, Gable bears a closer resemblance to a Tammany ward boss than to a brilliant parliamentary leader. His occasional, feeble attempts to inject an Irish lilt into his delivery only make matters worse: he sounds drunk instead of Gaelic. The dramatic high point of the film is of course the excruciating death scene. Gable turns his moist eyes heavenward and lies back on a solid mound of pillows. His words grow steadily softer, and we wait for wings to sprout on his back as wires pull him up to the ceiling.

It's easy to understand why Myrna Loy was

contracted to play Katie O'Shea: the same poll
that showed Gable as Hollywood's King named
her as the film industry's reigning female star. It
made no difference that this luscious young
woman was asked to play a matron who was according to all accounts graced with a plain face
and bulky figure. The most absorbing dramatic
tension in the film is provided by Miss Loy's brave
efforts to avoid giggling as she views the pathetic
antics of her unhappy co-star.

Immortal Dialogue

(Parnell, while visiting America, gives some char-
ity to a poverty-stricken family.)
POOR MAN (watching him ride off): It's little
wonder that they call him King of Ireland.
SHERIFF (correcting him): The *uncrowned*
King.
POOR WOMAN: He'll get his crown in heaven.

❀   ❀   ❀

(Parnell tries to convince Katie of his love.)
PARNELL (to Katie): Have you never felt there
might be someone, somewhere—who, if you
could meet them, was the person that you'd
been always meant to meet? Have you never
felt that?

❀   ❀   ❀

(Parnell and Katie predict that their love story
might someday become a great film (or something).)
PARNELL: Ours could be a great love story, Katie.
KATIE: Great love stories are always unhappy
ones.
PARNELL: Then I hope ours *won't* be great.

❀   ❀   ❀

(Parnell is dying in his bed with Katie at his
side.)
PARNELL: Where shall we be married?
KATIE: Darling, I don't know.
PARNELL: Do you think I'll make a good hus-
band?
KATIE: The best, darling. The best.
PARNELL: You'll have to teach me all the things
that are expected of me. It'll be strange to say
'My wife.' I'll have to practice. (His voice be-
comes weaker.) Only, you mustn't go away
from me.
KATIE: Darling, I won't.
PARNELL (giving her a look of assurance): I
know you won't. (His speech begins to fade.)
One's destiny can't—ever—go—away from—one—
(Parnell takes his last breath and dies.)
KATIE (screaming): Charles! Charles! Charles,
speak to me!

The Story Behind the Film

Parnell was based on the Broadway play of the
same name by Elsie T. Schauffler. Metro-

Goldwyn-Mayer provided a production budget of $750,000—a reasonably generous sum for those days. The part of Katie O'Shea was originally offered to Joan Crawford, who wisely turned it down. The director for the project was John M. Stahl, who was already an old hand at tearjerkers, including the original *Imitation of Life* and *Magnificent Obsession*. In order to lend a note of realism to this historical drama, a replica of the lobby and the chamber of the House of Commons was built on a sound stage three months before filming. An entire Irish village was also constructed on a five-hundred-acre chunk of land in Chatsworth, California. Some fifteen hundred extras worked on the film, and a ton and a half of crepe hair was bought to provide them with sideburns, moustaches, and other hirsute ornaments. Gable's facial hair, however, was entirely his own. He let his sideburns and moustache grow especially for the film. Originally he was supposed to have a curly moustache, but the make-up man used a curling iron that was too hot, and the cherished curls broke off and fell into ashes. Gable did not enjoy acting in this film; he frequently complained of discomfort in his stiff costume, and that discomfort is highly visible on screen. During the deathbed scene, Gable seemed so distracted that director John Stahl ordered that funeral music be played on a record player in order to put his unhappy star in the proper frame of mind.

For the crew, the most difficult scene was the sequence in which Parnell and Katie devour hot potatoes while lost in the fog. In the first take, a horse offstage was heard coughing. The horse continued to cough during subsequent takes, and it was only on the nineteenth try that the two stars succeeded in consuming their potatoes in peace. By that time, neither Gable nor Loy ever wanted to see another potato as long as they lived. One studio wag, however, thoughtfully called ahead to the homes of the two stars and when they arrived for dinner they both were greeted with meals consisting entirely of baked potatoes.

The Balance Sheet

How can you possibly hope to sell a ludicrous product without thinking up some ludicrous ad lines? For *Parnell*, the studio marketing geniuses designed a number of riveting headlines: "As Though Torn from Life's Pages!", "It Teems with Reality—That's Why It Is So Powerful!" M-G-M had high hopes for the film: another advertisement in a trade paper featured a photograph of a pair of boxing gloves with huge lettering underneath that read "Sock Coming!" The only sock M-G-M ultimately received was a kick in the posterior. *Parnell* proved to be Gable's biggest financial disaster, and the studio was flooded with hostile comments from the public and the critics. One "fan letter" read, "Let others portray historical figures. Gable is cut out for roles where he gets tough with women. That's what he's good at, and that's what I'll pay to see." After this flop, Gable told friends that he would never again be talked into playing a historical character in a period film. "I know my limitations," he said, "and I really am at my best in an open shirt, blue jeans, and boots." Because of his failure in *Parnell*, Gable required a good deal of persuading before he finally agreed to portray Rhett Butler in *Gone with the Wind*.

Gable's wife, Carole Lombard, loved to tease him about this wretched film. She often aggravated him by placing *Parnell* publicity stickers behind his clothing or books, or under food that he was eating. Once when Gable bragged about his reputation as a great actor, Lombard had leaflets printed that read "If you think Gable is the world's greatest actor, see him in *Parnell*. You'll never forget it." She wanted to drop the leaflets from an airplane over the M-G-M studio, but had to settle for a less spectacular means of distribution. She hired a couple of small-time actors to stand in front of the studio's entrance and hand the leaflets to passersby.

Faye Dunaway and Marcello Mastroianni in a romantic interlude from A Place for Lovers. *Miss Dunaway is dying of a mysterious but incurable disease, as her facial expression seems to imply.*

A PLACE FOR LOVERS (1969)

Directed by: VITTORIO DE SICA
Written by: PETER BALDWIN, ENNIO DE CONCINI, TONINO GUERRA, JULIAN HALEVY, and CESARE ZAVATTINI
Based on the play *Gli Amanti* by: BRUNELLO RONDI and RENALDO CABIERI
Produced by: CARLO PONTI and ARTHUR COHN
Music by: MANUEL DE SICA
Featuring: FAYE DUNAWAY, MARCELLO MASTROIANNI, CAROLINE MORTIMER, KARIN ENGH, ESMERALDA RUSPOLI, ENRICO SIMONETTI, MIRELLA PAMPHILI

Metro-Goldwyn-Mayer

The Critics Rave

"The most godawful piece of pseudo-romantic slop I've ever seen! . . . Even a director who had made no movies would have a hard time making one as bad as this."
—Roger Ebert, *Chicago Sun-Times*

"It gives me no pleasure whatever to report that Vittorio De Sica's *A Place for Lovers* is the worst movie I have seen all year and possibly since 1926. It is endlessly, interminably, paralyzingly, stupefyingly bad. . . . I found myself resenting having to commit two hours of my life to this posturing and phony piece of derivative melodramatics. It isn't even an interesting failure. . . ."
—Charles Champlin, *Los Angeles Times*

"Woefully inept . . . Marcello Mastroianni displays all the zest of a man summoned up for tax evasion. The five scriptwriters who supposedly worked on the film must have spent enough time at the water-cooler to flood a camel. The only smidgen of plot is that Dunaway makes a late abortive attempt at suicide, something the film successfully achieves after about ten minutes."
—*Time*

"The one distinction this sickly melodrama has is that it succeeds in making not only Miss Dunaway but Marcello Mastroianni appear to be the worst actress and actor ever to darken the silver screen . . . about as exciting to watch as a game of tiddly-winks."
—Kathleen Carroll, *New York Daily News*

"A pretentious and overwrought tale . . . unfailingly boring. . . . Mastroianni stumbles over his English, and everyone stumbles over the dialogue . . . a hundred or more violins play the ever-present background score with great panache."
—Stanley Newman, *Cue*

"Trashy soap opera. . . . It's a disaster for all concerned, including the gifted director Vittorio De Sica."
—Steven H. Scheuer, *Movies on TV*

"Poor: Lowest rating! . . . Intermingling of the love-and-death theme with the more staple clichés of the women's magazine. . . . Glutinous tearjerker . . . singularly unaffecting."
—*Monthly Film Bulletin*

"*A Place for Lovers* fails in all major categories . . . no more than a fierce screen test for two emotionless creatures. . . ."
—James Robert Parish, *Motion Picture Herald*

"Bomb: . . . marks career low points for Dunaway, Mastroianni, De Sica."
—Leonard Maltin, *TV Movies*

"Interminable. . . . Apparently, De Sica lacked footage so the viewers are subjected to a tour of the villa's interior. . . . It's impossible to be moved by a performance that suggests a headache rather than a terminal illness."
—Dean Holzapple, *Hollywood Citizen-News*

"A dismal mess . . . schmaltz. . . . *A Place for Lovers* involves Faye Dunaway, Marcello Mastroianni and Vittorio De Sica in what I sincerely hope will be the worst movie of their respective careers. . . . On the assumption that the movie was not honestly meant to be funny, I must conclude that all the comedy is unintentional."
—Roger Greenspun, *New York Times*

Plot Summary

Julia (Faye Dunaway), a divorced American fashion designer, is dying of a tragic, incurable disease in the best Hollywood tradition. With only ten days to live, she spends her time vacationing in an Italian villa and watching television—apparently she is preparing for the boredom of the grave. She is awakened from her TV trance by an interview with an Italian engineer, Valerio (Marcello Mastroianni), who designs plastic air bags to protect passengers in automobile collisions. She is stunned as she stares at his face. Can it be? Can he possibly be the one? Sure enough, she has met him before, by pure chance at an airport. On that occasion, Valerio, true to

Marcello Mastroianni can scarcely conceal his embarrassment at one of his touching scenes with Faye Dunaway in Vittorio De Sica's putrid tearjerker A Place for Lovers.

his Italian heritage, made a pass at our heroine, dropping a suggestive remark along with his business card. She apparently decides that even this sort of oily charm is better than the Italian equivalent of "Dialing for Dollars," so she reaches for the telephone, dials Valerio's number, and begins whispering vulgar things into the receiver. Obscene phone calls must turn him on, because he races over to her villa. He knows nothing of her tragic disease, and they decide to spend the next several days together, making love.

The course of true lust never did run smooth, and this complex love story is soon made even more complicated by the addition of a few "old friends" who stop by the villa to say hello. The ensuing party soon develops into a wild orgy and

Julia, who has begun to find Valerio as exciting as an inflatable air bag, joins the frolic with enthusiasm. Remember, she has only ten days left to live, so even the Legion of Decency can't really object to her perversions. Valerio, however, finds his male vanity wounded and storms out of the house. The suspense is unbearable until the star-crossed lovers kiss, make up, and jet away to another scenic locale—this time an isolated Alpine chalet. While they show how much they love life by embracing and crying interminably, our disgust is heightened by the ridiculous musical score, which consists of a huge formal orchestra wailing and groaning in what must be one of the world's largest echo chambers. It should be noted that the composer of this kitsch was Manuel De Sica, son of the film's director Vittorio De Sica, who seems perfectly in tune with his old man's heavy-handed direction. At key moments, however, the younger De Sica appears to let his mind and musicians wander. During peaceful scenes of quiet countryside, for instance, we hear blaring trumpets, bleating saxophones, and a massive brass choir working itself into a lather over nothing at all.

The entire romantic interlude is interrupted when Julia meets her old friend Maggie (Caroline Mortimer), who reveals that Julia is actually an escapee from the hospital where she was being treated for her mysterious disease. Maggie urges Julia to return to the hospital, where she can die a painless death. Julia ignores her and returns to the chalet and the arms of her lover. Maggie then tattles on her old friend by phoning Valerio and telling him about Julia's condition. Though he realizes now that not even his inflatable air bags can save her, Valerio is willing to stay for the duration—which is more than can be said for the audience. Julia, however, is so upset by the fact that her lover knows her secret that she runs to a nearby mountaintop with the intention of committing suicide. Valerio catches up with her in the nick of time and talks her out of it. On the way back down the mountain Julia is still mad at the world and she drives their jeep recklessly and at a suicidal speed. After a few yawn-raising close calls, she screeches to a halt, and changes places with Valerio, giving him the driver's seat. The conclusion is profound: that life is better than death, and even more exciting than sitting back at a villa watching Italian TV.

Unforgettable Performances

Faye Dunaway is supposed to portray a character at death's door, so apparently she contracted an embalmer to do her make-up. Her appearance and facial expressions suggest the masks of Japanese No drama while her idiotic high-fashion posturing would embarrass even a wooden manikin. To help disguise her monochromatic performance, director De Sica gives Ms. Dunaway a change of wardrobe every three minutes, but this does nothing to change the look of bored discomfort on her face. Later in the film, in order to suggest that our heroine is closer to death's door, the surrealistic image she presents intensifies even further. Her complexion is such a thick, caked yellow that it looks as if she has had her head dunked into a vat of lemon custard.

As Charles Champlin reported, "Marcello Mastroianni looks embarrassed and befuddled, also a bit puffy, as if he had his nap interrupted or had tarried too long at the pasta." Perhaps one of the reasons for Champlin's conclusion is that Mastroianni daydreams so noticeably between his lines. He also fumbles with the English dialogue and looks aside much of the time, as if pretending that he were actually somewhere else. He seems totally uninterested in Ms. Dunaway (for one thing, he can hardly see her under her make-up) and when he embraces her, their clutches have all the enthusiasm of rival Mafia dons hugging one another to end their feud.

Immortal Dialogue

(Julia comments to Valerio on his profession as an engineer.)
JULIA: I see you like experiments. How would you like to experiment by staying with me for two days?

∘   ∘   ∘

(Later, Valerio wonders about her decision.)
VALERIO: Why did you ask me for only two days? (Julia blinks her eyes and offers a cutie-pie look.)
JULIA: So you can ask me for the next eight.

∘   ∘   ∘

(Julia, in tears, explains to Maggie why she is staying with Valerio rather than returning to the hospital.)

JULIA: I'm . . . in love . . . for the first time in my life! (Suddenly the violins in the orchestra swell on the sound track.)

The Story Behind the Film

A Place for Lovers was adapted from the stage play Gli Amanti (The Lovers). The brilliant Italian director Vittorio De Sica had displayed elements of sentimentality in many of his greatest films (The Bicycle Thief, Miracle in Milan), and the emotional, romantic material in the play naturally appealed to him. From the very beginning, however, he seemed to run into trouble in adapting the play to the screen. Five scriptwriters were credited in the project: Cesare Zavattini, co-author of most of De Sica's classics; Tonino Guerra, co-author of Zabriskie Point (q.v.); Julian Halevy; Peter Baldwin; and Ennio de Concini. There is an old adage that too many cooks spoil the broth, and since the soup of A Place for Lovers was decidedly thin to begin with, the net result of all these screenwriters was a horribly rancid pot. Even before the film's production had been completed, A. J. Langguth in The Saturday Evening Post commented on its "truly bad script." After visiting the set, he described how contemptuously the production crew itself viewed the inane plot about a young woman with a mysterious illness. "Each day during working hours everyone connected with the production pretended to take the situation seriously. But among the lower ranks the second drink of the evening set off a barrage of sick jokes about doomed, desperate ladies."

Additional difficulties on the set involved Mastroianni's struggle with the English language. Scenes constantly had to be reshot because of his comical mispronunciation. The word "toothbrush," for instance, apparently presented the star with a nearly insurmountable obstacle: he continually rendered it "Brooshtup" before the camera.

Hoping to salvage something worthwhile from this brewing disaster, De Sica employed five credited film editors—perhaps to try to undo the work of the five screenwriters. The result, however, was only further confusion, and De Sica could hardly have anticipated the film's opening with anything other than palpable dread.

The Balance Sheet

When the film was released, the critical response soon realized everyone's worst fears. The tidal wave of disgust for this project was nearly unprecedented. *Filmfacts,* a magazine devoted to the critical record of current films, reported their "Critical Consensus" for *A Place for Lovers* as "Favorable: O; Mixed: O; Negative: 10." Even vintage turkeys like *Che!* (q.v.) had managed to garner some "mixed" reviews.

Despite this disheartening news, the publicity men moved bravely forward with their limp promotional campaign. "Wherever They Meet They Make It A PLACE FOR LOVERS" read one tag line. Getting desperate, they tried to lure audiences with a promise of titillation, using the line "They Do It in the Name of Love."

One of the few factors working in the movie's favor was the real-life romance that had blossomed between its two stars. Early in their affair, Ms. Dunaway commented, "I've fallen in love with him as an actor—he is *simpático.* I think his chief strength is his intuitiveness. I don't think he spends a minute thinking." Certainly, anyone who has seen this film would agree with her conclusion.

As the Dunaway-Mastroianni romance intensified, it began to gather international headlines. In a semi-public forum, Ms. Dunaway asked her beau to "give her a child." Mastroianni politely declined, pointing out that he was already married and had children of his own. Eventually the leading lady flew into a rage and the affair ended in what was described as a "screaming match" in the room they shared at a fancy Italian hotel. It was, no doubt, all for the best. After watching their tepid, awkward love scenes in the film it was clear that they were physically incompatible anyway.

Lee Van Cleef, star of innumerable spaghetti Westerns, doing his thing in Return of Sabata: "Being born with a beady-eyed sneer was the luckiest thing that ever happened to me."

RETURN OF SABATA (1972)

(Original Title: É TORNATO SABATA . . .
HAI CHIUSO UN'ALTRA VOLTA)

Directed by: FRANK KRAMER (Gianfranco Parolini)
Written by: RENATO IZZO and GIANFRANCO PAROLINI
Produced by: ALBERTO GRIMALDI
Music by: MARCELLO GIOMBINI
Featuring: LEE VAN CLEEF, REINER SCHONE, GIAMPIERO ALBERTINI, ANNABELLA INCONTRERA, GIANNI RIZZO, JACQUELINE ALEXANDRE, IGNAZIO SPALLA, ALDO CANTI

United Artists

The Critics Rave

"There is comic irony in an Italian-made Western in which the villains are an Irish family who act like the Mafia and are headed by a redhead 'pater familias' played by an actor named Giampiero Albertini. This latest Lee Van Cleef film (this week's Van Cleef film) is so muddled and plodding on the screen, that I noticed not only members of the audience sleeping, but one reviewer as well. I envied them!"
—Donald J. Mayerson, *Cue*

"Italian western heroes never die, but, oh, how one wishes they would fade away. . . . *Return of Sabata* looks like all the leftovers of the previous *Sabata* films, scrambled together. . . . It makes little or no sense. Lee Van Cleef simply does his thing which consists of moving his right nostril (the rest of his face remains as immovable as stone)."
—Kathleen Carroll, *New York Daily News*

"Gianfranco Parolini, alias Frank Kramer, has now made three Lee Van Cleef *Sabata* movies; and in doing so he has established an approach to directing the Italian Western in which he seems sometimes to be mounting grand opera, sometimes to be interpreting Kafka and sometimes to be decorating a Christmas tree. . . . *Return of Sabata* shows the style at a very low ebb. . . . There is simply no pleasure in almost two hours of watching a man admit that he is making a fool of himself."

—Roger Greenspun, *New York Times*

"Lowest rating! Insanity out West, junk on the screen. . . . Van Cleef shoots up most of the population of a town, apparently for no good reason."

—Steven H. Scheuer, *Movies on TV*

"Extremely puzzling. . . . The whole exercise remains thoroughly mechanical."

—Alistair Whyte, *Monthly Film Bulletin*

"All downhill and much confused. . . . 19th century James Bond, replete with weapons. . . . The film is below average even for spaghetti westerns."

—*Boxoffice*

Plot Summary

Sabata, a rat-faced Confederate soldier returning from the Civil War, comes to the town of Hobsonville, Texas. An Irish Bible-thumper runs the town and has been heavily taxing the inhabitants, claiming that the money will go toward construction needs. Actually, the Irishman keeps the money for himself. Sabata launches his own subtle form of taxpayers' revolt: he goes around town killing everybody in sight until he finds the Irishman. The townspeople, with their cherubic faces and wavy hair, seem to have just emerged from Fellini's *Amarcord*. As they are shot, they sloppily fall to the ground and give forth great geysers of horrendously fake blood that more closely resembles spaghetti sauce. All this is accompanied by happy-go-lucky music that would have been more appropriate for the "Yogi Bear" television series. Eventually, we find out that Sabata has more on his vicious little mind than merely killing

the Irishman: he also wants to seduce his wife and steal his gold. When an innocent bystander asks Sabata why he bothered to come to town in the first place, "This rotten town suits me just fine," he wittily replies. More killing is done and is all duly photographed with unbelievably absurd camera angles. Whenever someone is punched or shoved, we see a fist plunging into the camera lens. If a woman is about to scream, the camera zooms directly into her mouth. If Sabata is hiding a gun under a card table, a hand-held camera glides upside down, turns sharply to the right, and then finally ducks beneath the table to show the audience his gun.

Sabata finally saves the day, rescues the town, and awakens the viewers by shooting the Irishman. He finds the pilfered gold stuffed in a chimney, and as it pours down into the fireplace an echo of Handel's "Hallelujah Chorus" is heard on the sound track. Sabata then rides off into the sunset until the next time his sadistic desires—or his producer's greed—demand fulfillment. At the film's conclusion, a freeze frame is held on Sabata's sneering face for twenty seconds while we hear his theme song played in its entirety for the second time. It bears the catchy title "Sabata Is the Most Invincible Man in the Countryside." The words "The End" at long last appear across Sabata's face, which is positioned dead center on the screen like a target. Viewers who wish to attend this epic fully prepared are advised to bring their darts.

Unforgettable Performances

Lee Van Cleef once commented, "Being born with a beady-eyed sneer was the luckiest thing that ever happened to me." Having congratulated himself on this good fortune, he apparently concluded that any exertions in the direction of acting were entirely superfluous. In *Return of Sabata* we are treated to so many views of his intense and totally frozen physiognomy that we can only conclude that the producers are trying to give us nightmares. Van Cleef bears a stunning resemblance to a six-foot-tall rodent with a moustache: the pointed nose, menacing, piercing eyes, and grim little mouth are there—all that is missing is whiskers. Every once in a great while, the star demonstrates his versatility by smiling or turning his head, but in general the only signs of life are the repeated twitching movements with which he reaches for his guns to shoot people.

Giampiero Albertini plays the corrupt Irishman, with endless growls and much clenching of teeth and knitting of eyebrows. His Chianti-red hair looks somewhat less than authentic, and his interpretation of the Irish national character has an oddly anthropological character—as if he were presenting the peculiarities of some remote, bizarre, heretofore undiscovered culture. Actually, his crude impersonation of a leprechaun brings to mind the pathetic confusion of those nineteenth-century Japanese artists who portrayed the first Westerners to visit their country.

The other actors in this film have all the animation of the mechanically moving tin cutouts in a shooting gallery: their primary function is to absorb the bullets that pour out of Sabata's guns. They die in the best operatic style, staggering around clutching their chests, or collapsing in quivering, jerking heaps. One might think that the victims in this film were trying to pioneer a new dance craze. We wish them luck.

Immortal Dialogue

Theme Song:

> Bum-ba, bum-ba, bum, bum, bum.
> Bum-ba, bum-ba, bum, bum, bum.
> Sabata, Sabata—
> Fastest gun in the West.
> Fastest gun in the West . . .
> Bum-ba, bum-ba, bum, bum, bum.
> Bum-ba, bum-ba, bum bum, bum. (and so forth, ad nauseam)

°   °   °

A FRIEND: I give you my word.
SABATA: It's pretty difficult to cash that!

°   °   °

(Sabata enters a room where a girl is waiting for him.)
GIRL (her first words): When are you going to begin making love?

°   °   °

SABATA (to the Irishman): You're not very hospitable for an Irishman!

The Story Behind the Film

In the early 1960s, a number of savvy European producers began noticing a curious phenomenon: American Westerns which did mediocre business in the United States were often smash hits in Europe. They began to ask the question, why not make Western movies in Europe in the first place, especially since the production costs were much lower than in America? Any distribution of such films to the United States would be pure gravy.

The result of this brainstorm was the "sauerkraut Western" (German), the "Made in Japan Western," and, most notable and durable of all, the ever popular "spaghetti Western."

The first major Italian horse opera was an epic entitled *A Fistful of Dollars (Per un Pergunia di Dollari)*, which featured a rising young TV actor named Clint Eastwood. The film was directed by spaghetti Western pioneer Sergio Leone and cost slightly more than $245,000. To date, it has grossed over $5 million. This spectacular success launched a seemingly endless stream of Italian-made shoot-'em-ups, generally featuring an American star (Eastwood, Van Cleef, even Ernest Borgnine or James Coburn) with Italian actors in the supporting roles. Michael Parkinson in *A Pictorial History of the Western* describes these Italian products as "black, violent, amoral, surrealistic, noisy, naïve, pretentious, ridiculed, revered, and astonishingly popular and lucrative pastiches of the hallowed American Westerns."

Next to the "immortal" Eastwood, Lee Van Cleef—antihero of the Sabata series—is the greatest star in the brief history of the spaghetti Western. In the mid-'60s, Van Cleef, suffering from an injured leg, was living on television residuals, unemployment compensation, and the salary that his wife brought home as a secretary at IBM. Then Sergio Leone asked him if he wanted a part in *For a Few Dollars More*. Van Cleef jumped at the chance. His first starring role came in *The Big Gundown* (1967)—a film that grossed over $2 million in America. Van Cleef soon emerged as one of the five leading actors in Italy according to a national popularity poll. The moral of this success story is obvious: take heart, misfits—your "beady-eyed sneer" may yet make you a leading man.

The director of the Sabata series is "Frank Kramer," whose real name is Gianfranco Parolini. Where Kramer/Parolini derived his knowledge and affection for the Old West is not known. Before turning his hand to cowboy epics, he worked as an assistant to the great Italian director Roberto Rossellini—a man who put out his films without using an alias.

The Balance Sheet

Return of Sabata was preceded by two other classics along the same lines, *Sabata* and *Adios, Sabata*. The third piece in the trilogy seemed to require more than a good bottle of Chianti for the public to wash it down: *Variety* reported its business in New York as "plodding" and indicated that in its first week "it did $12,000 in opener, which doesn't even pay the house nut." A desperate advertising campaign soon followed, featuring the lines "He's Judge . . . Jury . . . Executioner!" and "The Man with the Gunsight Eyes Is Back!" Finally, after its national release, the film barely managed to gain back its small cost.

SPECIAL AWARD

A lead-plated thinking cap goes to those geniuses, whoever they are, who dream up the titles for spaghetti Westerns. *Return of Sabata* seems beautifully literary and sensitive in comparison to some of the names that have recently graced the screen, such as: *Jesse and Lester, Two Brothers in a Place Called Trinity; They Call Me Trinity; Trinity Is Still My Name; My Name Is Nobody;*

My Name Is Pecos; The Dirty Story of the West; The Most Vicious Bandit in the West; Ringo the Texan; The Return of Ringo; Ringo and His Golden Pistol; $1,000 for Ringo; $10,000 Blood Money; For a Dollar in the Teeth; For a Few Bullets More; Bullets Don't Argue; Shoot First, Laugh Last; Adios Gringo; Today It's Me—Tomorrow You!; Poker with Pistols; Bury Them Deep; Deaf Smith and Johnny Ears; Drop Them or I'll Shoot; He Who Shoots First; Alive Is Better Than Dead; A Man Called Sledge; John the Bastard; I Want Him Dead!; I Go, I See, I Shoot; I'll Go, I'll Kill Him and Come Back; For a Fist in the Eye; Ranch of the Ruthless; The Pitiless Colt of the Gringo; Django Kill!; Django Shoots First; A Man Called Apocalypse Joe; A Man Called Shanghai Joe; Ah Well, That's Providence; Life's Tough, Isn't It?; God Forgives—I Don't; Kill Them All and Come Back Alone; and last, but hardly least, the unforgettable Heads You Die, Tails I Kill You.

Giampiero Albertini as "the Irishman" (foreground) and three of his henchmen are up to no good in Return of Sabata. These are mean, tough hombres, as you will notice from their menacing postures.

191

192

ROBOT MONSTER (1953)

Directed by: PHIL TUCKER
Written by: WYOTT ORDUNG
Produced by: PHIL TUCKER
Music by: ELMER BERNSTEIN
Featuring: GEORGE NADER, CLAUDIA BAR-
RETT, JOHN MYLONG, SELENA ROYLE,
GREGORY MOFFETT, PAMELA PAULSON,
GEORGE BARROWS, and the voice of JOHN
BROWN

Astor Films

The Critics Rave

"Incredibly bad. . . . Ranks right up there
with *Fire Maidens from Outer Space;* or should I
have said 'right down there'. . . . The story
had something to do with ridiculous-looking creatures from the moon that looked like gorillas with
deep sea diving helmets."
— Jerry Neely, *Famous Monsters of Filmland*

"Ancient and hackneyed. . . . Incredible. . . . Dialogue is strictly for the birds. The audience is
asked to accept some rather far-fetched situations,
even for a fantasy.
— *Hollywood Citizen-News*

"Scripting and majority of performances rarely
rise to a professional level. . . . of the principals, the less said the better. . . . Phil
Tucker's direction (he also draws producer
credit) is off."
— *Variety*

"A crazy, mixed-up movie. . . . The seven
man cast has to keep pretty busy, especially the
not-too-threatening robot, who resembles a gorilla

*George Nader and Claudia
Barrett, two of the last six
human beings on earth,
get down to work on
creating a new generation
in the sci-fi thriller* Robot
Monster. *That is supposed
to be blood, not ear wax,
trickling down Nader's
cheek.*

from the neck down. . . . Even children may be a little bored by it all."

—*Los Angeles Times*

"On the comic book level. . . . Loaded with inconsistencies."

—*Hollywood Reporter*

"Poor! Lowest rating!!! . . . Science fiction on the now familiar comic strip level, containing a sequence of prehistoric monsters."

—*Monthly Film Bulletin*

Plot Summary

Six people wander through a barren California canyon on a Sunday outing. They are an old German scientist ("the Professor"), his wife, three children, and his handsome young research assistant, Roy. The youngest member of the group, adorable little Johnny, falls asleep after their picnic. He wakes up a short while later to find all the others asleep, and so he runs off to frolic in a nearby cave. Imagine his surprise when out of that cave stalks the awesome monster Ro-Man. This creature is surely the most laughable monster ever to appear on screen. Ro-Man (interplanetary slang for "Robot Man") is dressed in a furry black gorilla suit, the kind used at masquerade parties. Over his face he wears a nylon stocking mask, and on top of that is a plastic deep-sea-diving helmet. Ro-Man also comes fully equipped with two wiggly antennae protruding from the top of his helmet. He walks with a flat-footed rolling clomp and occasionally waves clenched fists in the air. The only frightening thing about him is his huge, bloated stomach, which is sure to alarm all of us in the audience with a tendency to overeat.

Ro-Man reaches the Professor's family via tele-viewer screen and informs them that he has just destroyed everyone on earth. His "calcinator death ray" has done the job thoroughly, though he never explains how these six somehow managed to survive. To prove his accomplishments, Ro-Man shows footage on his televiewer of the earth blowing up. We are treated to stock World War II footage of bombed cities and crumbling buildings, complete with planes circling overhead.

Mmm, perhaps Ro-Man's "calcinator death ray" is just a code name for the good old B-25. Ro-Man also shows the humans (he pronounces it "hu-mans" as opposed to "Ro-Mans") a rocketship containing human passengers in outer space. This special effect is created by manipulating a toy spacecraft through a black room, with a black-gloved hand holding the ship and appearing unintentionally in one corner of the screen. Ro-Man activates his death ray and the ship explodes in a puff of talcum powder. Menacingly, the furry robots warns the surviving hu-mans that they are next in line.

To get his plans straight, Ro-Man reports back to his boss, who is referred to as "the Great One" (no, it is not Jackie Gleason, even though the body build is the same). The Great One wears the same gorilla-helmet costume as Ro-Man—his only mark of distinction is the violin bow he holds (apparently a badge of authority) and the electric light bulb on his desk. He refers to his employee as "Earth Ro-Man" and he gives his commands from the televiewer screen. We also get a view of the televiewer's "master control panel"—a complicated collection of dials and levers that inexplicably blows soap bubbles whenever it is in operation.

After conferring with his chief, the Earth Ro-Man discovers that the six hu-mans have all taken a special serum to protect them from the dreaded "calcinator death ray." Faced with this challenge, Ro-Man demonstrates his command of a superior technology. "I will calculate the spectrum dust in the calcinator death ray to counteract this antibiotic," he explains. Nonetheless, he becomes impatient with this sophisticated approach and soon resorts to tactics more appropriate to his simian appearance. He strangles the professor's little daughter, Carla; punches his research assistant, Roy, to death; and kidnaps the voluptuous older daughter, Alice. For poor Alice, the furry fiend has reserved a fate worse than death: yup, you guessed it, he may be a robot, but there is hot monkey blood in his veins. He rips open her blouse, but before his fumbling paws can move further, he is interrupted by the televiewer. The remaining humans are broadcasting their offer to surrender. Instead of accepting their offer he angrily grunts, "Why do you call me at this time?" and resumes his business with Alice. Suddenly, he receives another call on the televiewer—this time from the head Ro-Man. The Great One curses him for having disobeyed orders: he was supposed to accept the surrender and he was also supposed to *kill* the girl. At this point the Earth Ro-Man gamely admits that he's bored with his job because there's never any time for relaxation. He'd rather be like a hu-man, he says, with a lusty glance at the irresistible Alice. This only makes the Great One more furious and he comments, "You wish to be a hu-man? Good! You can *die* a hu-man!"

With this witty line, the Great One extends a menacing index finger and points it at the viewer. His finger magically emits "cosmic U-rays"—which resemble anemic lightning bolts. Meanwhile, the sound track is all snap, crackle, and pop, as if someone had sprinkled cracker crumbs on the grooves of an already worn record. Suddenly, as the sound of the static and the view of the electrical beams dancing off the Great One's index finger have become absolutely intolerable, we cut to some totally irrelevant footage of playful dinosaurs. For about fifteen minutes we watch dinosaurs crawling through jungle underbrush, battling each other for survival, or growling at the camera. Interspersed between these scenes of prehistoric monsters are views of bison running downhill, woolly mammoths stampeding, and even a volcano erupting. When it is all over, the Professor and his family are huddling together in a cave. They have just found Johnny, who has bumped his head and passed out. It turns out that all the action in the film was only a nightmare—and that all the characters are still alive. Johnny shakes his head in disbelief and remarks, "Boy! Was that a dream—or was it?" His sister Alice replies, "Really, Johnny, you're overdoing the space man act. There simply are no such thing as monsters!" The entire cast walks off the screen, and we think the film is over. But director Phil Tucker has not yet offered his subtle statement about artistic ambiguity, or the inherently dreamlike quality of all dramatic entertainment. Suddenly Ro-Man walks out of a cave and heads straight into the camera. Believe it or not, this same shot is repeated twice more—we see Ro-Man approaching the camera lens three different times, raising his hairy arms in a gesture that is supposed to be frightening. Finally we see the words "The End"

as bells chime out the last chords of the overorchestrated score. Perhaps only Shakespeare could have said it better than Phil Tucker:

> If we shadows have offended
> Think but this and all is mended:
> That you have but slumbered here,
> While these visions did appear.

Unforgettable Performances

John Mylong as the Professor sports a German accent so outrageously bogus that it couldn't even qualify for "Hogan's Heroes." At times, he sounds like a small Schnauzer trying to imitate human speech through barking. Like everyone else in the film, he spends most of his time staring straight into the camera and awaiting direction that never seems to come. Unlike the others, however, he does register some emotion: whenever he hears bad news he shows how sad he is by smashing his fist into a brick wall. This gesture is repeated so often that one would guess it was the only move Mylong ever learned in acting school.

Pamela Paulson, a giggly, curly-headed little girl, plays Johnny's cutesie-wootsie playmate Carla. Through most of the film she appears on the verge of wetting her pants: she wiggles and squirms so incessantly that John Mylong often has to hold her in place to prevent the child star from running off camera. We are denied a comprehensive view of her acting ability by the limited nature of her role. Her part consists principally of one line, repeated over and over again, ad nauseam: "Can I play house now?" she says to whoever will listen. One of the film's most poignant moments comes after the little girl has been killed by Ro-Man, and Johnny, musing over the riddle of mortality, soberly remarks, "I should have played house with her more often when she wanted to."

The film's "romantic lead" is George Nader, as the Professor's research assistant, Roy. He goes through the entire movie in an undershirt that has been carefully torn to provide provocative glimpses of the star's manly physique. Another purpose for the holes in the shirt is to prove to the audience that Mr. Nader is not wearing a back brace: his posture is so stiff and awkward that we might otherwise be confused. Mr. Nader's nervous delivery suggests that the director asked him to take a deep breath before the filming began, but forgot to tell him it was all right to exhale.

The true star of the film, of course, is George Barrows, who demonstrates his astounding versatility by portraying both Earth Ro-Man and the Great One. To his credit, Mr. Barrows does try to make himself as frightening as possible. He continually waves his arms menacingly at nothing in particular, and thereby manages to suggest that he is suffocating inside his gorilla suit and desperately calling for help. In one memorable scene, we see the furry, roly-poly monster ambling down a hillside when he comes upon some bushes blocking his path. He struggles violently for a moment to show his brutish nature, then clears the obstacle and continues on his way. Apparently these sequences placed such heavy demands on the talents of Mr. Barrows that another actor had to be called in to dub most of the lines. The voices of Ro-Man and the Great One were provided by John Brown, a character actor with a slight British accent. Since the monsters' faces are covered with stockings and diving helmets there were no problems with coordinating lines to lip movements, yet the entire dubbing process nonetheless failed miserably. At one point, Ro-Man claps his hands and points a furry finger to his chest while the voice on the sound track declares, "You will all be destroyed!"

Immortal Dialogue

GREAT ONE: Have you made the correction?

RO-MAN: I need guidance, Great One. For the first time in my life, I am not sure.

GREAT ONE: You sound like a hu-man, not a Ro-Man. Can you not verify a fact?

RO-MAN: I meshed my LPI with the view-screen auditor, and picked up a count of five.

GREAT ONE (waving his arms furiously as a buzzer sounds): Error! Error! There are eight!

RO-MAN: Then the other three still elude me. Is it possible they have a counterpower?

❄   ❄   ❄

(Ro-Man and Carla meet on a hillside.)

RO-MAN: What are you doing here alone, girl-child?

CARLA: My daddy won't let you hurt me.

RO-MAN (picking her up in his arms as she kicks in protest): We'll see!

❄   ❄   ❄

RO-MAN: Great Guidance, I have a favorable report. I have already eliminated one of them.

GREAT-ONE: Good.

RO-MAN: Force was necessary. It was a simple matter of strangulation. That leaves four.

GREAT ONE (as buzzer sounds): Error! Again! Five!

RO-MAN (correcting himself): Four—and one more on whom I have made an estimate in relation to our strategic reserve. The plan should include one living human [and guess which one he'll choose] for reference in case of unforeseen contingencies.

❄   ❄   ❄

(Beauty and the beast—Alice and Ro-Man alone in a cave.)

RO-MAN: I am ordered to kill you. I must do it with my hands.

ALICE (enticingly): How is it you're so strong, Ro-Man? It seems impossible.

RO-MAN: We Ro-Mans obtain our strength from the planet Ro-Man, relayed from individual energizers.

❄   ❄   ❄

GREAT ONE: Earth Ro-Man, you violate the laws of plans. . . . To think for yourself is to be like the hu-man.

RO-MAN (delivering an impassioned plea for individual liberty): Yes!—to be like the hu-man! To laugh! Feel! Want! Why are these things not in the plan?

GREAT ONE: You are an extension of the Ro-Man, and a Ro-Man you will remain. Now, I set you into motion. One: destroy the girl. Two: destroy the family. Fail, and I will destroy *you*!

The pressbook accompanying this poster promised viewers they would "SEE . . . Robots from Space in All Their Glory!" and billed the film as "The Most Sensational Screen Offering of the Decade."

(The Great One signs off, and Ro-Man soliloquizes for the audience.)

RO-MAN: I cannot—yet I must. How do you calculate that? At what point on the graph do 'must' and 'cannot' meet? Yet I must—but I cannot!

The Story Behind the Film

Robot Monster was the brainchild of a 26 year old filmmaker named Phil Tucker, who served as both producer and director of the project. Judging from the quality of his work, we felt sure that Mr. Tucker was an unusual personality—to say the least. When we managed to track him down and arrange an interview, we were not disappointed.

Phil Tucker today is a tall, gaunt Westerner who might have played the villain in a Grade B horse opera of an earlier era. He reminisced in a rich, melodious voice about his past and the strange genesis of *Robot Monster*.

Before arriving in Hollywood, Tucker served in the Marine Corps, worked as a dish washer, wrote short stories for Sci Fi pulp magazines and showed "low budget 'strip' pictures" at a theatre in Fairbanks, Alaska. Then, with the aid of a few good-natured buddies, he landed a job directing cheapjack sexploitation movies. "I did what they called the 'After Midnight' series—*Tiajuana After Midnight, Hollywood After Midnight, Paris After Midnight* . . . I directed and produced about twenty-five or thirty of them."

With these satisfying experiences under his belt, Tucker was ready to tackle the magnum opus that will always be associated with his name. "When I set out to make *Robot Monster*, I was accomplished and knew the tools of directing," he recalls. "Whether or not I was able to use them well is a different matter. I did not use them properly." *Robot Monster* was shot in a mere four days, utilizing no sets: all the action was filmed out of doors in and around Bronson Canyon in the desert East of Los Angeles. All scenes of dinosaurs, volcanoes and woolly mammoths were adopted from stock footage taken from Hal Roach's 1940 caveman epic, *One Million, B.C.* The human actors received minimal pay but the two child stars were the only ones who made trouble. We had a lot of problems with them," Tucker confessed. "Selena Royle (who played the Professor's wife in the film) always had to hold them in front of the camera so they wouldn't wiggle away. At least as it turned out, you could see them."

Tucker claims personal credit for conceiving the unforgettable costumes seen in the film. "Well, I originally envisioned the monster as a kind of robot," he recalls. "I talked to several people that I knew who had robot suits, but it was just out-of-the-way, money wise. I thought, 'Okay, I know George Barrows.' George's occupation was gorilla suit man. When they needed a gorilla in a picture they called George, because he owned his own suit and got like forty bucks a day. I thought, 'I know George will work for me for nothing. I'll get a diving helmet, put it on him, and it'll work!' And that's how it came to be."

When the film was released, *Variety* reported that it had been "brought in for somewhere under $50,000". Even this was an inflated estimate, since the true cost was only $16,000 plus lab rentals. Tucker remembers "a conversation that took place between Ed Mosk, Al Zimbalist and myself, relative to revealing the cost of the picture. They felt that it would damage the film if people knew how cheaply it had been made, and I agreed. But also I felt that we couldn't quote a high price because people would look at that and say, 'Jesus, what a terrible picture they made, spending that much money on that piece of shit!' I remember vaguely agreeing that when people asked, we would all say somewhere under $50,000."

Despite its pathetically low budget, *Robot Monster* boasts a musical score by the highly talented Elmer Bernstein. His work in this film is a far cry from later triumphs such as *The Ten Commandments, The Magnificent Seven, To Kill a Mockingbird,* and *True Grit.* For *Robot Monster*—one of his first scores—Bernstein offers a single heroic theme repeated over and over again by a loud brass section, piano, xylophone, and glockenspiel. These ruffles and flourishes seem more appropriate for some widescreen biblical spectacle than for the shabby antics in Bronson Canyon.

The Balance Sheet

The distributors of *Robot Monster* felt certain they had acquired a "hot property", but seemed hopelessly confused in trying to package it. An early title for the film was *Monster from Mars*, while a later TV release handle was *Monsters from the Moon*. Since they were apparently unable to decide just where the creature came from, the title *Robot Monster* may have represented a happy, noncommittal compromise.

The press book on *Robot Monster* modestly described it with adjectives such as "brilliant", "spectacular", "thrill-packed", "overwhelming", "terrifying", "gripping", "tremendously vivid and suspenseful". The press book also announced that the film had been "hailed as the most sensational screen offering of the decade". *Robot Monster* was originally presented in both 3-D and glorious black and white. It also had the distinction of being the first science fiction film with stereophonic sound.

According to Mr. Tucker, the novelty of 3-D and stereo allowed his masterpiece to emerge as a resounding financial success. He claims that "the film did considerably over a million" though his shady business partners "soaked up all the film's profits" and left him without a penny. "They personally made money on that picture by stealing from me. I didn't get anything from that picture. At one time, I was going to sue but I couldn't find a lawyer who would help."

Tucker's feelings toward *Robot Monster* hover paradoxically between pride and self-abasement. At one point he will dismiss it as "a piece of shit", but then a few minutes later he insists that, "to this day I still believe that not a soul alive could have done as well for as little money as I was able to do." After a moment of silence, he reveals, with quiet intensity, that, "for the budget, and for the time, I felt I had achieved greatness . . . Among low budget films, it was the most outstanding picture of the year, in my opinion."

Despite his sense of accomplishment, the twenty-six-year-old Tucker was frustrated by the hostile critical response and the continuing financial hassles concerning the film. His depression became so severe that he was finally admitted to the psychopathic ward of Veterans Administration Hospital in West Los Angeles. After a few weeks of medical attention, he was released temporarily and checked into a nearby hotel. While alone in his room he composed a rambling, pathetic letter to a local newspaper. He complained that his film had not received the recognition that it deserved. Because of quarrels with his business associates, theater owners had received strict orders not to let Tucker see his own picture unless he paid admission. Eventually Tucker found himself unable to secure Hollywood employment of any kind. "When I was refused a job—even as an usher," he wrote, "I finally realized that my future in the film industry was bleak." At the end of his letter, Tucker promised the press and public that he would kill himself. The newspaper took him seriously enough to rush a reporter over to his hotel room and, sure enough, the director lay unconscious on the floor from an overdose of sleeping pills, with the pass from his psychiatrist in his pocket. Tucker was rushed to an emergency hospital and then returned to the V.A. psychopathic ward where his condition was listed as "fair". Everyone involved with Tucker's unfortunate situation expressed sympathy, though theater men, according to the *Los Angeles Times*, could not resist describing *Robot Monster* as "one of the top turkeys of the year".

In the years following his suicide attempt, Tucker won few directorial assignments. He did turn out a drag-strip saga called *Pachuco* (his self-proclaimed "Masterpiece" and "greatest achievement") as well as *Dance Hall Racket*, which starred a young nightclub comic and friend of Tucker's named Lenny Bruce.

In 1960, Tucker returned to the format he had used with such memorable results in *Robot Monster* and created another science fiction treat known as *Cape Canaveral Monsters*. This time, Phil was entirely back in form, with a "plot" concerning zombies from outer space, one of whom has the ability to grow back his arm after ferocious dogs chew it off. Hollywood rumors suggest that this new film was financed, at least in part, by a group of kindly psychiatrists at the Veterans Administration Hospital in an attempt to rehabilitate their one-time patient.

Considering his checkered career, Tucker has proven himself a remarkably durable figure on the Hollywood scene. During the 1960s he served as an associate producer for T.V. shows and documentaries, and today works as a post-production supervisor for one of the world's leading motion picture corporations.

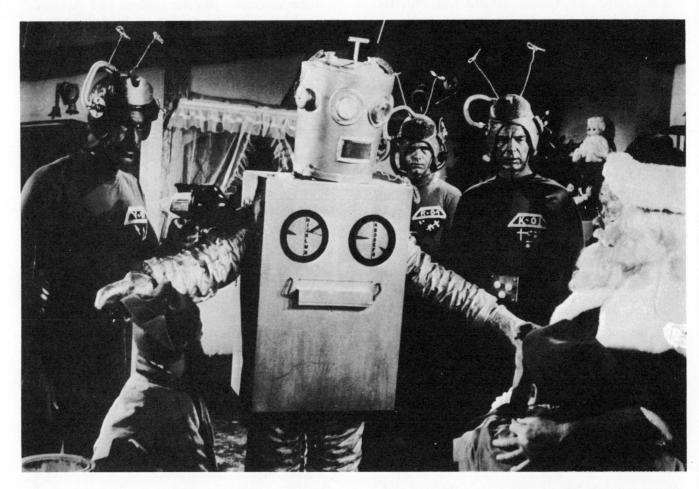

The chilling kidnap scene from
Santa Claus Conquers the
Martians. *Interplanetary invaders,
supported by an awesome product
of their superior technology, storm
the North Pole workshop of
You-Know-Who. The costumes and
special effects in this film helped
earn it a nomination as "absolutely
the worst science-fiction flick ever
made, bar none!"*

*Santa Claus (John Call)
nostalgically describes the joys
of an earthly Christmas feast to
the skeptical Martian leader Kimar
(Leonard Hicks). Music for this
Joseph E. Levine presentation,
including the hit song "Hooray for
Santa Claus," was provided by
Milton DeLugg and the Little
Eskimos.*

SANTA CLAUS CONQUERS THE MARTIANS (1964)

A Joseph E. Levine Presentation
Directed by: NICHOLAS WEBSTER
Written by: GLENVILLE MARETH
Produced by: PAUL JACOBSON
Featuring: JOHN CALL,. LEONARD HICKS, VINCENT BECK, VICTOR STILES, DONNA CONFORTI, BILL McCUTCHEON, LEILA MARTIN

Embassy Pictures

The Critics Rave

"Absolutely the worst science-fiction flick ever made, bar none! . . ."
> —Jason Thomas and Joe Kane,
> *The Monster Times*

"Overly saccharine and nonsensical. . . . A lobby sign with 'No One Admitted OVER 16 Years of Age' might be appropriate. . . ."
> —*Boxoffice*

"Joseph E. Levine offers a blend of sentiment and science fiction that involves a pipe-smoking, hen-pecked Santa as the victim of a Martian kidnap plot. . . . Youngsters who are old hands at science fiction may notice the limited use of special effects. . . . It could have benefitted from the interjection of a little more humor."
> —Ronald Gold, *Motion Picture Herald*

"The story itself runs along stereotyped lines. . . . Yields little in the way of substance. . . ."
> —Mandel Herbstman, *Film Daily*

"Absurd fantasy; low-budget film."
> —Leonard Maltin, *TV Movies*

"Obvious and square cut as cheese. . . . Like a children's television show enlarged on movie house screens. . . . Supplies humor not quite attuned to this planet, anyway."
—Howard Thompson, *New York Times*

Plot Summary

The children of Mars never have any fun. All they do is sit around like zombies, casting longing eyes on TV programs about Santa Claus which they receive from earth. The leaders of the Red Planet call a planetary council to discuss this troubling situation, and they consult an eight-hundred-year-old wise man who lives (where else?) in a cave. The perceptive geezer suggests that the only way to save the younger generation is to kidnap Santa Claus and install him on Mars.

A raiding party boards a spaceship and heads for earth. The U. S. Air Force is alerted to the invasion, and we enjoy several minutes of early '60s footage of the American strategic arsenal in action, as we see airmen scrambling, jets taking off, missiles rising into place, and even a B-52 refueling in midair. None of this succeeds in deterring the Martians, however, who cleverly throw up a "radar screen" and land without incident. They were not clever· enough, however, to find out where on earth they can find Santa Claus, so they approach two earth children. Drawing their ray guns (which bear a marked resemblance to that popular toy, the Whamo Air Blaster) they ask Billy and Betty where Santa Claus lives. The savvy kids, amazed at the ignorance of these visitors from outer space, reveal that the fat one lives at the North Pole. The Martians are so impressed that they kidnap the children and take them along as resident Santa Claus experts.

After a brief scuffle in which Mrs. Claus and a few elves are paralyzed by Martian "freeze rays," St. Nick is loaded onto the Martian spacecraft, a prisoner of the green-skinned fiends. On the journey back to the Red Planet, however, we discover woeful divisions in the Martian ranks. Volgar, a dyed-in-the-wool meanie with a drooping moustache, actually resists the whole idea of bringing Santa to Mars: at every opportunity, he tries to murder Claus and the earth children. Dropo, on the other hand, is a squirmy, rubber-faced Martian who immediately identifies with the eight-year-old kids and develops a crush on the old man in the red suit. He helps our heroes foil every vicious plot against them.

After a safe landing, Santa meets the troubled Martian children, who immediately burst into laughter. (Who wouldn't?) The adult Martians are delighted that the kids are finally happy, and they furnish Santa with a marvelously automated toy workshop to provide all of Mars with toys. Without protest from Elves' Local 1019, Santa sets to work with his machines and the cooperation of the children. Dropo wants to play with the toys and make the kids laugh, so he dresses up in one of Santa's extra outfits and dances around town. He is mistaken for the real Santa Claus by the unspeakable Volgar, who takes him hostage and demands ransom from Mars's head man, Kimar, who bears a certain resemblance to Charlton Heston. Kimar claims that the real Santa is safe in his workshop, so Volgar walks into the Santa-torium and discovers he has kidnapped an imposter. Suddenly, dozens of kids emerge from the corners of the workshop and bombard meanie Volgar with ping-pong balls, paper airplanes, soap bubbles, toy tanks, and anything else the brats can get their hands on. Volgar stands in the middle of the assault, crying, without trying to fight back or even reaching for his Whamo Air Blaster.

After this climactic scene the Martian authorities arrive to arrest the renegade. They also allow Santa to return to earth, where it is almost Christmas. It turns out the Martians don't need him any more, since Dropo, dressed in his Santa suit, beating his chest, and yelling, "Ho! Ho! Ho! Everybody!" does a perfectly acceptable job of keeping the children happy. Finally, as we see Santa's rocket leaving Mars, we hear the title song one more time: "Hooray for Santy Claus." The producers of the film were so proud of their moronic lyrics that they flash them on the screen as we are urged to sing along. The final image we see is a greeting card illustration of Santa with the words "Merry Christmas" imprinted across his face. Bah, humbug! Where is Ebenezer Scrooge when you really need him?

Unforgettable Performances

The acting in this film has to be seen to be believed: it would embarrass even the players in a sixth-grade Christmas pageant. The tendency toward overstatement is so prevalent that we wonder whether the director was specifically hoping for an audience of children with defective hearing and poor eyesight. John Call, as Santa Claus, is the "star." His jolly presence throughout the film suggests that he prepared for his role by consuming seven double martinis or ingesting a blast of laughing gas. He manages to make Santa's "Ho! Ho! Ho!" seem like a lewd chuckle, while his wet, lecherous stares make one wonder whether Kris Kringle was in reality a child molester.

Vincent Beck "portrays" Volgar, the villain of this passion play. His long black moustache and scowling countenance make one think of a Martian Frank Zappa. In the climax, in which the children bombard him with toys, his performance reaches its peak. Beck lifts his legs up and down in order to dodge their playthings, and as the scene ends the camera zooms in for a full close-up of the tears streaming down his face. In Beck's approach to this demanding moment, there is more than a hint of the whimpering Stan Laurel at his worst (see *The Big Noise*).

Bill McCutcheon is Dropo, whose character bears a strong resemblance to Arnold Stang's in *Dondi* (q.v.). There are also hints of Danny Kaye, or a poor man's Pinky Lee. The idea is that Dropo should win the hearts of children in the audience, who will point their chubby little fingers toward the screen and say, "Aw, looky, he's so *silly*!" Instead, any child with the gift of speech will simply point and comment, "Aw, he's so disgusting!" and then go home to play with a Whamo Air Blaster.

Immortal Dialogue

Title Song: "Hooray for Santy Claus" (sung to the swingin' strains of a mid-'60s "twist")

You spell it S-a-n-t-a C-l-a-u-s,
Hooray for Santy Claus!
Hooray for Santy Claus!
Yeah, yeah, for Santy Claus!

He's fat and round, but jumping jiminy,
He can climb down any chimiey.
Why do we hear sleigh bells ring?
Our hearts go ding-a-ling!

❋   ❋   ❋

(A TV interviewer tours Santa's workshop, while the Martian children watch the program in silence.)

INTERVIEWER: What is this strange little creature over here?

SANTA CLAUS: Oh, Winky made that. That's his idea of a Martian.

INTERVIEWER: A Martian!? Wow-wee—wow! I'd hate to meet a creature like that on a dark night!

❋   ❋   ❋

(Kimar wakes up the sleeping Dropo.)

KIMAR (scolding him): Dropo, you are the laziest man on Mars. Why are you sleeping during working hours?

DROPO: I wasn't sleeping, chief. It's just that I haven't been able to sleep these last few months. I forgot how. So I was just practicing.

❋   ❋   ❋

(Volgar doesn't think that it's worth it to bring Santa Claus to Mars.)

VOLGAR (grumbling): All this trouble over a fat little man in a red suit!

❋   ❋   ❋

(Kimar and fellow Martians meet two earth children, Billy and Betty.)

BILLY: Who are you?

KIMAR: We're from Mars. Don't be afraid, we have children just like you on Mars.

BETTY: What are those funny things sticking out of your head?

KIMAR: Those are our antennae.

BETTY: Are you a television set?

❋   ❋   ❋

The Story Behind The Film

In 1964 a production note in the *Los Angeles Times* read: "*Santa Claus Conquers the Martians*! Don't laugh. Somebody is making a movie with that title." That somebody was one Paul Jacobson, whose previous distinction in life had been his work as onetime unit manager for the Howdy Doody television show. To produce *Santa Claus*, Jacobson organized Jalor Productions and rented a converted airport hangar at Roosevelt Field on Long Island to serve as his studio. The total budget for the production was $200,000—not bad, considering the fact that the action of the film moves back and forth between two planets, but still far more than was budgeted for other classic turkeys like *Eegah!* and *Robot Monster*.

Jacobson himself conceived the idea of *Santa Claus* and went on to write the original story. A "screenwriter," one Glenville Mareth, was then hired to "polish" the material for final production. Most of the film's budget was financed by private investors, who assumed that anything with the name Santa Claus on it was sure to show a profit. The crew for the film was "handpicked" by Arnold Leeds, who served as both associate producer and production manager. This crew was composed chiefly of veteran TV technicians, and this may explain the fact that the TV broadcast monitored on Mars is so much more convincing than the rest of this ridiculous film. Producer Jacobson, who called his film "a Yuletide science-fiction fantasy," commented, "The people working on a film make or break a picture budget-wise. Everyone knew from the very beginning we had a low-budget film and that they would have to be satisfied with scale payments and no overtime. . . . At this particular studio, with a group of wonderfully cooperative technicians, we've been able to get a lot of production value [sic] from our low budget. We're also shooting in color to get full, picturesque effects with our toy factories and Martian and North Pole backgrounds. . . . There was not a single problem created by my crews."

He neglected to mention the problems created by the cast, who seemed to go wild when they stepped before the cameras. Their lack of motion-picture experience can hardly excuse these ludicrous performances. John Call, the hapless Santa Claus, was recruited from the Broadway production of *Oliver!*, in which he played the minor part of the doctor. Victor Stiles, who played the earth child Billy, had played a pickpocket in the same Broadway musical. Donna Conforti, who portrayed the little girl Betty, was "discovered" by Jacobson as a Dutch child in *Here's Love*, a current "Broadway musical Christmas frolic."

The Balance Sheet

Paul Jacobson once explained that the real reason for making *Santa Claus Conquers the Martians* was a sort of altruism. "There is a great void when it comes to a Christmas film for children," he observed. "Except for the Disneys, there's very little in film houses during the season that the kids can recognize and claim as their own." Mr. Jacobson nobly set out to fill that void, and apparently saw himself in a role comparable to Santa's, bringing joy and gimmicks to the fun-starved children of Mars.

For his Christmas crusade, Jacobson soon enlisted the aid of that other well-known philanthropist, Joseph E. Levine. Levine's Embassy Pictures (later to be known as Avco-Embassy Pictures) acquired worldwide distribution rights to the film. *Santa Claus* premiered in some one hundred theaters in the Chicago and Milwaukee areas in November 1964. For the most part, it showed only for Saturday and Sunday matinees. After all, such a realistic film might have been too frightening for children if shown in the dark of night. The film received a large promotion and a zippy recording of the unforgettable "Hooray for Santa Claus" was made and released. The film was advertised with the lively lines "Santa Claus Goes to Mars to Entertain the Children of Another Planet" and "A Holiday Funfest for Young and old" (??!!!!). One gimmick connected with the promotion included giving away balloons or space-related gadgets at the matinees. This was probably an attempt to stop the kids from getting restless and fidgeting unnecessarily in their seats during the film's interminable eighty-two minutes.

Jacobson's theory about the commercial viability of anything concerning Santa Claus proved largely correct. The film has been released annually every Christmas by Avco-Embassy and has turned in a handsome profit. We anxiously await some sequels. How about *Santa Claus Versus*

Frankenstein's Brother-in-law, or *Jesse James Meets Santa Claus.* If neither of these work, we can approach the Japanese and perhaps soon enjoy *Santa Claus Battles Godzilla,* in which all the children of Tokyo are given cheap little toys, made in the U.S.A.

Santa Claus, Dropo (center), and Kimar can hardly contain their euphoria at the triumphal conclusion of Santa Claus Conquers the Martians. *The children of two planets look on approvingly as it is decided that Dropo will serve as the Santa for Mars, thereby freeing the real Kris Kringle to return to his pressing duties on earth.*

Bob Wagner, a heel who undergoes
a miraculous reformation, marries
up-and-coming dancer Debbie
Reynolds in Say One for Me. Bing
Crosby (Father Conroy) presides.

Bing Crosby plays his most dismal
clerical role as Father Conroy
("sort of a Milton Berle with
candles") in Say One for Me.

SAY ONE FOR ME (1959)

Directed by: FRANK TASHLIN
Written by: ROBERT O'BRIEN
Produced by: FRANK TASHLIN
Music by: LIONEL NEWMAN
Featuring: BING CROSBY, DEBBIE REY-
NOLDS, ROBERT WAGNER, RAY WALSTON,
LES TREMAYNE, CONNIE GILCHRIST,
FRANK McHUGH, JOE BESSER, JUDY HAR-
RIET, STELLA STEVENS, SEBASTIAN CABOT

Twentieth Century-Fox

The Critics Rave

"About as simple and uncerebral as it can get
without coming to a dead stop."
—Paul V. Beckley,
New York Herald Tribune

"Makes an aggressive attempt to combine religion and vaudeville . . . offends both propriety
and common sense . . . trying to prove that
God is on the side of the biggest production numbers. . . ."

—*Time*

"Poor: Lowest Rating! It offers a seduction
scene, a drunk scene and a couple of disturbingly
tasteless cabaret numbers—all angled, of course,
with the cause of virtue uppermost. . . . Sets,
some old-fashioned and mediocre songs, the
unimpressive story and even the credit titles are
all in equivocal taste. . . ."

—*Monthly Film Bulletin*

"Mawkish business. . . . Bing Crosby plays
another of his cheerful singing priests, who uses
song more than prayer to uplift his parishioners. . . . By the time Bing has straightened out
their affairs, one feels him to be a sentimental,

meddling cluck, whose ways of doing good seem faintly specious. . . . The songs by Sammy Cahn and James Van Heusen, as well as the dances by Miss Reynolds, only added to my clammy state of irritation."

—Hollis Alpert, *Saturday Review*

"Writer-producer-director Frank Tashlin, who frequently confuses soap with celluloid, has done it again. His latest drama-detergent is a tasteless mixture of sloppy sentimentality slapped into a compote of unappetizing romance—with a heel made whole, a drunk made sober, gaudily theatricalized religion, and with the film's unpleasant key-romance concluding on a Christmas TV spectacular."

—Jesse Zunser, *Cue*

"Pass the clichés . . . a bland blend of religion, sentiment, and song. . . ."

—*Newsweek*

"Schmaltz decorated with song-and-dance numbers . . . some in quite dubious taste. . . . *Say One for Me* is very, very tired."

—Philip T. Hartung, *Commonweal*

"Coarse-grained and insensitive . . . an uneasy two hours. . . . Crosby himself wears a pained expression a lot of the time. . . ."

—Philip K. Scheuer, *Los Angeles Times*

"An obvious attempt to remake *Going My Way* with a different plot. . . . The film as a whole is overlong, and there is much needless dialogue and dull scenes. . . ."

—*Hollywood Citizen-News*

"Terribly contrived; no memorable songs."
—Leonard Maltin, *TV Movies*

"Tasteless and disturbing . . . the entertainment values are short of impressive."

—*Variety*

Plot Summary

Because his church is located in the heart of New York's theater district, Father Conroy (Bing Crosby) ministers almost exclusively to a flock of colorful Broadway folk. The good father has adjusted his own personality accordingly: he reads *Variety*, describes his 2 A.M. mass as "the late late show" and refers to his sermons as his "monologues." He is, as one of his parishioners describes him, "sort of a Milton Berle with candles."

Into the midst of this delightful, heartwarming show business maelstrom comes pretty Holly, an innocent college drop-out who wants to become a star. Since she is played by Debbie Reynolds, Holly, naturally, has no selfish reasons for her lust for show business success: she wants to earn money to pay for a necessary operation for her ailing daddy. As it turns out, Daddy is an old friend of Father's (Father Conroy, that is), and the pandering priest agrees to look after Holly's interests.

Unfortunately, Holly gets a job as a dancer at a night spot called The Black Garter, which is run by a heel named Tony (Robert Wagner). Tony realizes that Holly is "some dame" and resolves to take advantage of her. It is Father Conroy's job to see to it that Tony keeps his hands to himself. If heaven won't protect the working girl, at least Bing Crosby will.

This stirring drama reaches its climax at (ho, ho, ho!) Christmastime. Father Conroy's show business abilities have finally been recognized, and he has become producer of a gala television charity benefit. He manages to enlist the services of a Presbyterian minister and a rabbi (something for everybody in this film!) and he also attracts some of the biggest names in show business (after all, God's got plenty of connections). In the midst of the frantic preparations, Tony the Heel comes to Father Bing and asks to appear on the show. Before the priest can turn him down, our antihero pulls out his ace in the hole: he has turned his slimy charm on Holly, and Holly now wants to marry him. Knowing that Debbie Reynolds has just divorced Eddie Fisher, Father Conroy figures she's already suffered enough. He agrees to let Tony appear on the show if he promises to leave Holly alone and back out of his plans to marry her.

The grand finale is the Christmas charity benefit itself. Here Bing gets to trot out his ol' ba-ba-boo in such forgettable numbers as "The Secret of Christmas." To cover all bases, we even see a teen-age overnight sensation singing "The Night Rock 'n' Roll Died." This number is actually performed by Judy Harriet, a former Mouseketeer making her feature-film debut. When it comes Tony's turn to perform, he gets on stage, bursts into tears, and undergoes a remarkable conversion (after all, it's Christmas). He admits he's been a louse all his life, but explains to the nationwide TV audience that it's only because of his unhappy childhood. Father Conroy is so moved by this explanation that he gives the suddenly reformed Tony approval to marry Holly. In fact, Bing even performs the wedding. The two lovebirds go off to Florida for their honeymoon and the concluding title superimposed on the screen inspiringly reads "The Beginning." Apparently, a sadistic projectionist is going to show the film again.

Unforgettable Performances

Cast once again as a lovable priest, Bing Crosby hoped to repeat the successes he had enjoyed in *Going My Way* and *The Bells of St. Mary's*. Many Hollywood observers wondered if it weren't time for the old crooner to take holy orders in earnest. Crosby admitted, "I'm tough to cast these days. I'm too old to get the girl and too mean to let her go." As if to prove his point, in his portrayal of Father Conroy he seems more interested in Debbie Reynolds' legs than in the glory of God's holy church. There is the strong suggestion of a dirty old man who takes out his personal frustrations by meddling in other people's affairs. In exasperation, Debbie and her beau might have turned to the good father with the immortal words of that celebrated and lamented clown, former Agriculture Secretary Earl Butz: "You no play-a de game, you no make-a de rules." With his puffy, sagging cheeks, melting blue eyes, and occasional mellifluous howling, Crosby suggests a faithful old hound, slightly off the scent on one of his last hunts. Even those who get their goose bumps from the hallowed strains of "White Christmas" will only blush at the "entertainment" Bing provides us here.

Debbie Reynolds stumbles through another absurd role as a lovely, naïve adolescent. Instead of convincing us of her youth, she transmits a sense of absolutely ageless stupidity. In this film, she is supposed to realize that great American male fantasy of the innocent, childlike fairy who nonetheless possesses a fiery, explosive sexual drive. In *Say One for Me*, the erotic side of Ms. Reynolds' performance is no more convincing than her impersonation of an adolescent. We're sorry, Debbie, but you have failed miserably in your cheerleader tryout.

Father Bing, reforming hopeless drunk Ray Walston: "Give it a try! Stop bending your elbow and start bending your knee!"

Immortal Dialogue

(Holly rehearses some of her new dance steps with Father Conroy coaching her.)
HOLLY: Every time I think of an audience out there I start getting butterflies.
FATHER: *All* performers get butterflies.
HOLLY: But mine feel like they're wearing Army shoes, Father!

      ✿   ✿   ✿

(Holly auditions for a part in Tony's show at The Black Garter.)
TONY (ogling her legs): If you ever decide to swim the Channel, I'd like to handle the grease job!

      ✿   ✿   ✿

(Tony declares his plans to go on to bigger and brighter things.)

TONY'S AGENT: Hey, maybe we are moving up in the world.

TONY (predicting): I'm going so high it'll make your nose bleed!

*　　*　　*

(Father Conroy tries to reform a drunkard, Phil (Ray Walston).)

PHIL: I'm a little too old to still believe in Santa Claus.

FATHER: That's too bad, Phil. He still believes in you.

PHIL: You're not talking about Santa Claus.

FATHER: Neither are you. You think you're going to find what you lost in that bottle?

PHIL (gulping down more booze): Maybe in the next one. I haven't tried all the bottles yet. But maybe I should get the Christmas spirit. Isn't this the time of year when all the little girls and boys suddenly start to behave?

FATHER: That's not the real secret of Christmas, Phil. Give it a try! Stop bending your elbow and start bending your knee!

*　　*　　*

The Story Behind the Film

Say One for Me was written by Robert O'Brien, the scion of a long line of Roman Catholic vaudevillians. He showed his story idea to director Frank Tashlin, who inevitably suggested Bing Crosby for the leading role. Crosby's own production company took over the project, and Bing originally wanted Frank Sinatra for the co-starring role of Tony the Heel. Ol' Blue Eyes wisely steered clear of this stinker, which left Ol' Baby Blue Eyes Bing to work with Debbie Reynolds and Bob Wagner.

Despite his extensive experience in ecclesiastical roles, Crosby suffered a horribly embarrassing moment on the first day of shooting. Walking onto the set, His Holiness tripped on his priest's cassock and fell flat on his face, as the cast and crew burst into hysterical laughter. His difficulties, however, were nothing when compared to Debbie Reynolds'. She claimed to be under "emotional strain" because of her recent divorce from Eddie Fisher. During one of her innumerable dance re-

hearsals she managed to trip and wrench her knee, and a blood clot resulted. Miss Reynolds wound up in the hospital, and for a while she couldn't eat and insisted she had ulcers. Doctors suggested that it was only an upset stomach, and eventually the star found her way back to the set. Near the end of production she commented, "It's a funny thing. I've pounded my poor feet so much that now I wear a size four shoe. I used to wear three and a half."

To make up for all the disappointments and frustrations, Bing Crosby needed some soothing, reassuring companionship during production. For that reason, he brought his oversized Labrador retriever onto the set with him on many occasions, much to the chagrin of his fellow cast and crew.

The only balm for such frayed tempers was sweet music, provided by songsmiths Sammy Cahn and James Van Heusen. These two have seldom come up with more eminently forgettable numbers, including "Say One for Me" (the inspiring title song), "The Spirit of Christmas," "The Girl Most Likely to Succeed," "I Couldn't Care Less," "You Can't Love 'Em All," and the classic cha-cha number with Debbie Reynolds, "Chico's Choo-Choo."

The Balance Sheet

In a forlorn attempt to sneak this turkey past the waiting critics, the studio moguls tried a unique innovation: the film was given a "half-premiere" while the filming was in progress. Members of the press were invited to the set, where a screening was held. This view of the incompleted masterpiece included such dramatic highlights as the "Chico's Choo-Choo" number. This particular bad medicine didn't go down any more smoothly because it was administered in stages: when the "full premiere" finally occurred, the critics panned the film. Box-office returns proved a major disappointment, and not even Father Crosby's prayers could prevent the film's losing money.

"Only once in three thousand years." Thank goodness!

SOLOMON AND SHEBA (1959)

Directed by: KING VIDOR
Written by: ANTHONY VEILLER, PAUL DUDLEY, AND GEORGE BRUCE
Produced by: TED RICHMOND
Story by: CRANE WILBUR
Music by: MARIO NASCIMBENE
Featuring: YUL BRYNNER, GINA LOLLOBRIGIDA, GEORGE SANDERS, MARISA PAVAN, JOHN CRAWFORD, LAURENCE NAISMITH, FINLAY CURRIE, DAVID FARRAR, JOSE NIETO, ALEJANDO REY, HARRY ANDREWS, JULIO PENA, MARUCHI FRESNO

United Artists

The Critics Rave

" . . . an animated comic strip utilizing live actors. The animation was done by King Vidor, the dialogue was presumably culled from a dictionary of clichés by four writers who, not to embarrass the Screen Writers Guild, we will not mention here, and the principal models for the animations were Yul Brynner, Gina Lollobrigida, and George Sanders. . . . The film may well owe a debt to society for its cosmic breaches of taste, morality, and intelligence. Penance is due."
—Hollis Alpert. *Saturday Review*

"The story is as old-fashioned as the creaking silent-film technique that has surrounded its making."

—*Cue*

"A flop . . . the queen dances like a college freshman involved for the first time in Modern Dance . . . as for [her] celebrated guile, she looks so patently sly that it's doubtful she would be able to fool Mortimer Snerd, let alone one of the wisest men in history. . . ."

—*Newsweek*

211

"Dialogue is often banal and bromides rub uneasy shoulders with Biblical quotations."
—*Variety*

" . . . a lavish display of hokum . . . the picture includes plenty of battling between Israelites and Egyptians. My old Boy Scout troop could have taken on the lot of them."
—John McCarten, *The New Yorker*

"Watch out it doesn't put you to sleep."
—Howard Thompson, *New York Times*

"Throughout, one has the feeling that if King Vidor, who directed, had just put his tongue firmly in one cheek, the whole thing might have come off well as a satire on spectacle. But as things are, one must say that *Solomon and Sheba* has all the defects but none of the excitements of the form. . . . The efforts at massiveness are ponderous enough but curiously ineffectual. . . . The dancing is awkward and visibly uncertain. . . . As for the battle scene, it is perhaps small of me to mention one Israelite spear tip flopping like a hunk of whale blubber as its bearer's arm wobbles."
—Paul V. Beckley, *New York Herald Tribune*

Plot Summary

Somewhere in the Sinai desert, Princes Solomon (Yul Brynner) and Adonijah (George Sanders) prepare Israelite troops for an Egyptian attack. Having watched a lot of Westerns, they group some tents in a circle and wait for the Egyptians unwittingly to attack the empty camp. Then the Israelite army rides down on the troops of Pharaoh, whooping like Apaches, brandishing tomahawks and shields emblazoned with the Star of David. Solomon rides around with a torch, setting Egyptian soldiers on fire. With such a fiendish assault the Egyptians never had a chance. The victorious Israelites prepare to leave for Jerusalem, when a sudden dust cloud appears on the horizon. Is that Annette Funicello in a '62 Chevy convertible? No, it's Gina Lollobrigida, the Queen of Sheba, in a chariot. With her bosoms abouncing, she drives up to Adonijah, insults him in a thick Italian accent, gives him a few lashes in

the face with her bullwhip, and then continues on her merry way.

In Jerusalem, King David is dying. You can tell because the music played in the background is a mixed chorus singing a mournful "Oo-oo-oo." King David (Finlay Currie), who looks like Santa Claus and speaks with a Scottish accent, summons his sons and the Elders of the Twelve Tribes of Israel to his bedside. He announces that he had a dream in which God appeared and told him that Solomon was to be the next ruler. Adonijah runs to his room and slams the door.

As King, Solomon grows a goatee and wears a colorful costume to show what a swinging and liberated monarch he is. He builds the Great Temple he had promised his father, but bases its design on a Holiday Inn in Tucscon, Arizona. Solomon may have been proverbially wise, but his tastes in clothing, furnishings, and architecture were abominable. The Star of David, the corporate logo of the Israelite empire, adorns everything in sight: swords, shields, chariots, flags, children, horses, etc. The production designers seemed untroubled by the historical record that shows the Star of David first came into use as a distinctive Jewish symbol in the seventeenth century, or more than two thousand years after the events in this film.

In Egypt, the Pharaoh fears an invasion from Israel, and recruits aid from his neighboring monarchs, including the Queen of Sheba. She promises to use her womanly guile to bring Solomon to his knees. In this case, womanly guile means wearing see-through chiffon negligees and bathing unabashedly in a tub the size of the Red Sea.

The Queen, trusty whip in hand, and her caravan of llamas, rugs, bathtubs, and negligees travel to Jerusalem and load Solomon with expensive gifts. In return, the King falls in love with her. He has a thing for whips, too, but he refuses to wear the chiffon negligees. However, the romance brings a strong protest from the Elders. These wise men and the prophet Nathan look as though they've lived their lives on benches and crumpled newspapers in Central Park. To demonstrate their anger, director Vidor has instructed these men to shake their fists, staves, beards, or all three whenever they have a chance to speak. The Elders command Solomon to send the pagan Queen away—what they really want, and need, is her bathtub. Even Adonijah is so enraged that he sends some assassins after Solomon. But the King of Israel is too quick for his attackers, and sets them on fire with a nearby torch. Besides having a thing for whips, Solomon is a pyromaniac. Reacting as any younger brother would, he banishes the elder Adonijah from the kingdom. Adonijah responds by making a pact with the Pharaoh.

Solomon is so busy trying on all his new things that he thinks of no one but himself and the Queen. He even permits her to hold one of her sacrilegious feasts in Jerusalem, and attends the after-dinner orgy as a guest of the house. This time, the Sheban *shikse* has replaced her regular chiffon with an iron brassiere, which is very alluring, if not subtle. Amid hundreds of scantily clad dancers doing the bunny hop to a bossa nova rhythm, the she-wolf seduces Solomon under a

Adonijah (George Sanders) accuses his brother, King Solomon (Yul Brynner), in a bitter exchange in Solomon *and* Sheba: *"You and your Sheban slut have defiled the fair name of Israel." The extras in the background to the right seem stunned at these words.*

bush. This annoys God to no end, and to express His displeasure He sends a few lightning bolts to knock down the Great Temple. All the Elders point their fingers at their naughty King and say, "Hum-mum-mum, you're in trouble." And the kingdom falleth into a state of disunity.

News arrives from the front that Egypt is preparing an attack. Solomon scrapes together a bedraggled army from his crumbling empire and heads for the sand-strewn hills of Sinai. In the first battle Solomon's army is virtually decimated, and the survivors scatter into the dunes.

Meanwhile, back in Jerusalem, the Queen of Sheba has developed guilt feelings. And that's not all. A quick rabbit test reveals that she's carrying the King's child. Somewhere along the line Solomon and Sheba must have put down their whips. The Queen creeps to the smashed altar of the Great Temple and prays to the God of the Hebrews, promising that if He'll take Solomon out of the mess he's in, she'll return to her country and renounce all gods but Jehovah. God (uncredited actor), with an effeminate voice and a British accent as thick as Commander Whitehead's, tells her the deal is on, and bids her "Cheerio." Sure enough, Solomon's soldiers miraculously return to their King, like ants converging on a sugar cube. Solomon announces proudly, "Set them to burnishing their shields. Let them shine like mirrors." He positions his army directly behind a deep gorge, and commands his men to flash their mirror-like shields into the eyes of the attacking Egyptians. The enemy plummets blindly to its death in the gorge, as Solomon collects a few souvenirs and prepares to return to Jerusalem.

In the Holy City, the people walk around moaning, "Woe unto us—the Egyptians have overthrown our Solomon." And we again hear the mournful mixed chorus's "Oo-oo-oo." Very touching. Adonijah has himself crowned and incites the crowds of mourning Israelites to stone the Queen of Sheba. As the crowd completes its bombardment of the buxom beauty, Solomon returns with his army and slays his brother in a fancy-dancy sword fight. He carries the bedraggled corpse of the Sheban sexpot into the Great Temple, mutters a prayer, and a light shines down from heaven. The mixed chorus changes its tune to "Oo-ah-oo-ah," the voice of God pronounces some biblical bromides, and the Queen is miraculously revived, just like Lazarus in the next Testament. She walks solemnly to her chariot, grabs her whip, and takes off for her homeland. Solomon prepares to rebuild the Temple, we hope with another architect.

Unforgettable Performances

There are so many foreign accents in this film that it could easily pass for the story of the Tower of Babel. Solomon is portrayed by an East European, Adonijah by an Englishman, the Queen of Sheba by an Italian, King David by a Scotsman, and both the Israelite and Egyptian troops are played by the Spanish army.

Yul Brynner certainly is versatile. As the King of Siam he sang and danced, and as the King of Israel he went to orgies and set people on fire. Brynner was signed on to the picture in such haste that it seems he had insufficient time to study his lines. He seemed to read all his dialogue from cue cards and doesn't understand the language he's speaking. To cover his ineptitude, he spends a lot of time looking heavenward, as if checking the weather or stopping a nosebleed. When lightning strikes in the orgy sequence and the King dramatically faces the heavens, one can almost imagine director Vidor yelling, "Okay, Yul, now look up!"

Upon first seeing George Sanders and Yul Brynner together, it's difficult to imagine that Sanders is supposed to be the warrior, and Brynner the poet. Sanders looks about sixty-eight years old, his paunch hangs out over the belt of his tunic, and his spindly legs seem hardly able to carry him around a barroom, let alone up a sand dune. He portrays Adonijah as if he were Henry VIII. Out of breath, he appears in one scene and sneers in impeccable English, "Sire, I have driven like the fury to attend this council, ever since your command reached me." Obviously, some half-wit casting directors decided that Sanders was regal by nature—hence his role here and in that other sandstorm epic, *King Richard and the Crusaders* (q.v.). The only aristocratic thing about Sanders, however, is his accent and his obvious disdain for everything going on around him.

When Gina Lollobrigida confronts Adonijah, she asks, "And whaat fay-ver cood an Eezreelite grant the Queeeen of Sheeeebah?" in accents not unlike Bela Lugosi's "I am Dracula. I beed you velcome." One wonders about this woman. In the "famous" bathtub sequence, she seems to take great pleasure in displaying her charismatic corpus to her nurse. When she emerges from the water she tells the woman, "Dry me," and then giggles as she gets a rubdown. Her performance suggests Little Sheba in a carnival midway (complete with jewel in navel), melded with Theda Bara.

Immortal Dialogue

PHARAOH: And how will you destroy Solomon?

SHEBA: It is said that Solomon is wise. But no matter how wise a man may be, he is still human. With a human weakness.

PHARAOH: Surely the way of a woman is beyond our understanding.

SHEBA: The way of a woman is simple, my lord. It is always to follow the way of a man.

❀ ❀ ❀

ABISHAG: How interesting your encampment is. Are your people always so carefree and gay?

SHEBA: We enjoy life and pleasure. Don't you?

ABISHAG: Oh yes, we do. But we are . . . an austere people. We tend to be more serious.

SHEBA: And your King . . . is he also serious?

ABISHAG: King Solomon has a great responsibility.

❀ ❀ ❀

SOLOMON: In the last few days I have shown you much of Israel. But you have not told me anything of your own country.

SHEBA: At this moment my own land seems . . . as distant as the stars.

SOLOMON: In my youth I used to dream of visiting all the faraway kingdoms of the earth.

SHEBA: And now, instead, the rulers of those countries come to you.

❀ ❀ ❀

SOLOMON: From the first, I knew that behind those lovely eyes is the brain of a very clever woman, who would never have traveled eight hundred leagues without a purpose. (Pause.)

SHEBA: You have found me out. How could I hope to deceive you? I have been trying to entrap you . . . with these (shakes her arms) . . . to bind you to me in soft chains, so that I may do with you as I will.

SOLOMON: Every woman demands a price from a man.

❀ ❀ ❀

SOLOMON: Nothing must come between us.

SHEBA: Not even our gods? I knew this moment would come, for the things we believe in are not the same.

SOLOMON: I had hoped that in time you would come to accept Jehovah.

SHEBA: As King of Israel, would you abandon the god of your people for mine?

SOLOMON: Still, I dared hope.

SHEBA: My love, I must leave Israel.

SOLOMON: Why? Why? I cannot let you go!

❀ ❀ ❀

ADONIJAH: You and your Sheban slut have defiled the fair name of Israel. I sought only to preserve our country from your contamination!

SOLOMON: Only because the blood of David flows through your veins as well as mine, I grant you your life—but I banish you from Israel forever.

❀ ❀ ❀

ELDER: I charge you, Solomon, to cleanse yourself of this iniquity you have permitted to spawn in Israel!

ANOTHER ELDER: Abjure this woman and her idolatries. Tear down the obscene abomination she has erected!

❀ ❀ ❀

GOD: But if he turn away and forsake my statutes, then will I pluck them up by the roots out of my land which I have given, and this house which is high shall be an astonishment to

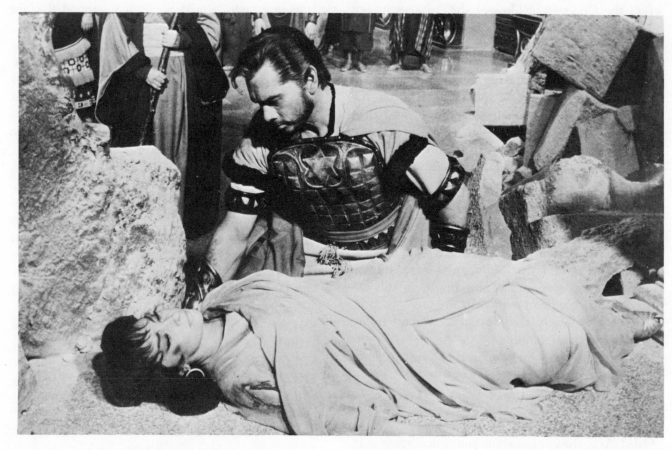

everyone who crosseth by it, so that he shall say, "Why has the Lord done naught onto this land, and onto this House?" And it shall be answered, "Because they forsook the Lord God of their fathers, which brought them forth out of the land of Egypt, and raised them on hollowed grounds, and worshiped them, and served them—therefore has he brought all this evil upon them."

—Gospel according to King Vidor

*   *   *

The Story Behind The Film

One can imagine a studio executive proposing his "brilliant" idea: "Let's make a Roman film—without the Romans! We'll make it about Jews . . . after all, Israel is a hot item in the news. We'll just throw in a lot of Jewish themes and symbols, and we'll have a blockbuster!" And indeed, the narrator at the beginning of the film (no, it is not the voice of God) solemnly intones, " . . . even then these boundaries [between Israel and Egypt] were kept ablaze with the fires of hatred

and conflict." A Jew's harp is plainly audible in the studio orchestra, and since Jews, according to religious tradition, always cover their heads, Yul Brynner covers his famous globe with a toupee.

At first, the filmmakers couldn't find a suitable location or the extras needed to portray the multitudes. "My Sheba [Lollobrigida] can't perform in the United States," reported executive producer Ed Small. "She has a six-year-old contract problem. Israel has gone modern and motorized, especially the army, handicapping our need for masses of horsemen. *Ben Hur* has Italy tied in knots. So we picked Spain, where horses and desert are available and where we're getting excellent official cooperation." Neo-fascist dictatorships do have their good points. Spain later lent its armed forces to the makers of *Patton*—the Spanish were happy to get the free military training. But how does one go about hiring the Spanish army for a movie? *S. and S.* producer Ted Richmond reported, "You go to the Minister of Defense, and tell him you need three thousand soldiers a day. He tells you that you'll have to pay their salaries, plus cost of transportation and food.

Yul Brynner as King Solomon mourns over the rock-pelted body of the Queen of Sheba (Gina Lollobrigida). For his role in Solomon and Sheba *Brynner donned a greasy hairpiece—the producers understood that traditional Jews always covered their heads.*

The army cost is a total of eighty thousand dollars. The same number of extras here in Hollywood would have cost us one million six hundred thousand." But the Spanish soldiers caused as many problems as they solved. For one, hardly any could speak English. Casting agents were sent to tourist areas in nearby cities, where they politely tapped British and American tourists on the back. The next thing these vacationers knew, they were wearing biblical robes and helmets, and enjoying speaking parts in a Hollywood epic. The Spanish troops, meanwhile, were so thrilled by their costumes, that they gave their helmets to their girl friends as souvenirs, and hapless costumers wound up driving around the countryside reclaiming studio property from bashful *señoritas.*

How King Vidor, the maker of such classics as *The Crowd, The Big Parade,* and *Hallelujah,* could have taken responsibility for this offensive mishmash of biblical bowdlerizing is a mystery. With 60 per cent of the film completed and in the can, Tyrone Power, originally cast as Solomon, was inconveniently stricken with a heart attack and died. If that was an omen, only Vidor would ignore it. The makers of the film were left with four alternatives. They could scrap the project and collect $2.5 million insurance; they could rewrite the script to end the movie approximately where the shooting left off; they could have Tyrone Power portray Solomon before David's death, and hire another star to portray him after; or they could start from scratch with a brand-new Solomon. They opted for this last course, helped by a record $1,229,172 insurance payment on Power's death, and secured the inimitable services of Yul Brynner.

Vidor commented that the film was based on "a very simple story, really, about the first kings of the Bible. We tried to make it in a way people could believe it was happening—not as a documentary, certainly, but with a feeling of conviction. Personally, I applied an artistic, not a technical yardstick; we had no technical experts on this! Using the Spanish army, we had three battles, designed and based on movement; used a brand-new idea in the last battle, how the Jews defeated the Egyptians. It was pure movies." And pure silliness. Screenwriter Arthur Hornblow added that the intention was to maintain a reverence for the story as it appeared in the Bible (the Bible [I Kings 10:1-13] says that the Queen of Sheba visited the court of Solomon and presented him with many gifts: "And king Solomon gave to the queen of Sheba all her desire, whatsoever she asked. . . ."). But to spread the blame around, Hornblow admitted that the biblical story was supplemented by quite a bit of outside material, particularly Arabic and Abyssinian myths. These legends hold that Menelik I, the first King of the Ethiopians and ancestor of Haile Selassie, was born of the union of Solomon and Sheba. Obviously the producers were hoping for a triumphant run in Addis Ababa. At the same time they wanted to protect their revenues in Biloxi, Mississippi, and so studio officials reassured the public about miscegenation. They declared that careful research proved that the Queen of Sheba was not black. This comes as no surprise to most scholars, but the fact that she was Italian has thrown many historians for a loop.

The Balance Sheet

Solomon and Sheba introduced a new presentation technique to motion-picture audiences, and the publicity for the film let everyone know about the "breakthrough": "The Sweeping Wonder of Super Technirama-70 Is the Revolutionary System That Turns Film into Real Life!" If that movie is real life, viewers would commit suicide by the thousands.

Advertisements featured Gina Lollobrigida and Yul Brynner in romantic embrace, underscored by the declarations "Behold! The Love Story of the Ages!" and "Behold! The Most Breathtaking Spectacle of All Time!" A record $1 million was spent on publicity alone. An ad in a large denominational newspaper said, "Attention, Religious Instructors! Bring the Biblical World of Solomon and Sheba to Exciting Life in Your Classroom! Informative Bible-Kit Available Free!" Simultaneously, secular media featured quite a different pitch. Describing Miss Lollobrigida, one ad related, "In Her Navel Is a Crescent-Shaped Ruby, Which Gleams and Glitters While She Performs the Orgiastic Dance Which Ends in Her Seduction of Solomon." Such two-facedness prompted the *Christian Herald* to ask, "This is for Sunday School? . . ." A studio spokesman responded to the complaints by casting them over his shoulder. Describing the ads as successful, he said, "We're very happy with the results. We wanted penetration. . . ." Well, yeah, so did Solomon when he first saw the Queen of Sheba. All in all, the film has grossed $5.5 million in the United States, and at least $10 million in Europe, where Lollobrigida and Brynner are matinee idols. At a $6 million production cost, *Solomon and Sheba* was hailed as a box-office smash. A paperback was published based on the film, as well as a comic book, but both seemed considerably less ludicrous than the film itself.

SPECIAL AWARD

The collected recordings of Xavier Cugat go to Granville Heathway, who receives prominent billing in the film as "Orgy-Sequence Adviser." Mr. Heathway, according to a studio official, "is an egghead Englishman who has studied every book and treatise on the subject of orgies." If he says that they did the bunnyhop as part of Sheban fertility rites, then it must be so.

The orgy in *Solomon and Sheba* was filmed at an estimated cost of $100,000, and was choreographed by Jaroslav Berger, ballet chief of Switzerland's Bern State Theater. Miss Lollobrigida rehearsed for a month to prepare for the dance, with among other things, a hula hoop. On screen, as the festivities begin, Miss Lollobrigida wiggles her hips and performs a mild striptease while Yul Brynner, looking very somber, follows her to a bush. Around them, 150 oil-skinned dancers stand on top of rocks, twisting about and flexing their muscles. The music, by Maestro Mario Nascimbene, suggests an overheated conga, complete with *forte* maracas and choral "OOMPH!" to accentuate the rhythm.

Mr. Heathway's expertise has also given us a few musclemen leaping pointlessly through the air. Other Sheban beauties are tossed skyward

like high school sophomores at their first beach party, and the papier-mâché set is reminiscent of *Hellzapoppin*. To intensify the eroticism and provide another realistic detail, the lighting is primarily in spectral shades of brown and green. Ten minutes of "Soul Train" on any given week is easily more erotic. The choreography here would make even Hermes Pan, who masterminded the dance sequences in *Lost Horizon* (q.v.), laughingly turn aside. The net result is perhaps the most amazing five minutes in the American cinema. No description could possibly do it justice. You'll have to see it to believe this one. Well done, Mr. Heathway (enjoy your records), and a special dishonorable mention to your sidekick, Mr. Berger. Thanks for the memories, guys.

Elvis Presley shows unbounded enthusiasm for his role as Mike McCoy—a rock 'n' roller singer/race car driver—in the 1966 musical thriller Spinout.

SPINOUT (1966)

Directed by: NORMAN TAUROG
Written by: THEODORE J. FLICKER and GEORGE KIRGO
Produced by: JOE PASTERNAK
Featuring: ELVIS PRESLEY, SHELLEY FA-BARES, DIANE McBAIN, DEBORAH WAL-LEY, CARL BETZ, WILL HUTCHINS

Metro-Goldwyn-Mayer

The Critics Rave

". . . foolish and altogether improbable. . . ."
—*Hollywood Reporter*

" . . . monotonously and unfailingly vacuous. . . . Apart from any other considerations, Elvis is now getting decidedly tubby. To be brutally frank he is becoming too old for such goings-on."
—Richard Davis, *Films and Filming*

"For Presley, immobility may signify maturity. He is pitching his act at some sort of adult audience—possibly adult chimpanzees . . . about all he does on the screen is waggle an aggressive guitar and, in an electronically reconstituted baritone, belt out a series of steamy lyrics. . . ."
—*Time*

"Strictly for Elvis' fans."
—Steven H. Scheuer, *Movies on TV*

Plot Summary

Mike McCoy (Elvis Presley) is a rock 'n' roll singer and race car driver. His troubles begin when *three* different women fall in love with him and want to marry him.

The first is Mike's very own female drummer, Les (Deborah Walley). She spends the film imi-

Elvis Presley proves irresistible to all the plump cuties in Spinout.

tating Jerry Lewis and protesting "I'm not a guy, I'm a girl" to the other members of Mike's band.

The next lovely is Diane McBain, portraying the author of books—*Ten Ways to Trap a Bachelor, Mating Habits of the Single Male*, and other literary masterpieces. Now she is in the process of writing a new book, *The Perfect American Male*, and she's considering rock 'n' roll singer/race car drivers. After all, what book is complete without them? Mike asks her, "When you find this Mr. Perfect, does he get some kind of award?" "Oh yes," is the vampy reply. "He gets me."

Now let's see. We have Mike being loved by a tomboy drummer who performs some mysterious rite called "goremay cookin'" for the rest of the band, and by an oversexed author. All that's missing is the misguided American teen-ager. Don't look now, 'cause here she comes. Her name is Cynthia Foxhugh (Shelley Fabares), and she is the daughter of multi-millionaire Howard Foxhugh, of Foxhugh Motors. Mr. Foxhugh shows up at a club where Mike and his group are playing and offers them $5,000 to sing one song to his daughter. At first Mike refuses. After all, he's an upstanding American who won't be pushed around by big business. He tells Mr. Foxhugh, "There's nothin' I enjoy more 'n singin' for a girl . . . but it's gotta be one that I pick." Notice that he refers to girls as "it" because in this film females are characterized exclusively by their buttocks, bosoms, and bikinis. "McCoy, you'll be there," Mr. Foxhugh promises as Mike and his

group drive away in their rare 1929 Duesenberg, towing a gleaming white Cobra race car. Despite the fact that the group scoots around in such expensive automobiles, they never stay in hotels. That would be too "establishment." Instead, they rough it and camp out in the wilds. Even so, it's difficult to maintain that "rustic" atmosphere when your campsite looks like an exhibit from Harrah's automobile museum.

True to his word, Mr. Foxhugh exerts mysterious influence on someone, and Mike's tour gets canceled. He has no choice but to pack up and go to the Foxhugh estate in Santa Barbara. But just then, twinkly ol' Diane McBain shows up to tell Mike that (surprise!) she's chosen him as her "perfect male." "You'll be the best husband a girl ever had," she tells him.

With Miss McBain panting after him like a hyena, Mike hightails it to the Foxhugh manor, and sings the one song (begrudgingly, mind you) to Cynthia Foxhugh. You can tell he doesn't like her because he sings her a song entitled "Am I Ready to Fall in Love with Yooooo . . ." with his eyes halfway closed and his lips two inches from hers. If he really liked her, he would have punched her in the arm like any self-respecting six-year-old. Cynthia tells Mike that she always gets everything she wants . . . she wanted him to sing for her, and he did—now she wants Mike to marry her.

Meanwhile, Mr. Foxhugh is interested only in Mike's driving one of his Foxhugh specials in an upcoming race. Mike, of course, won't have anything to do with Foxhugh or his daughter and stalks out. It's inspiring to see the uncompromising integrity of today's idealist young people. Foxhugh sends a cop named Tracy to throw Mike and his group out of town, but Tracy is a "goremay" cook too, and falls in love with Les (the drummer, remember?). Mike counters this display of police brutality (or bestiality) by moving into the house next door to Mr. Foxhugh. Don't ask how, it's a long story. There he has one pool party after another, all attended by hundreds of bikini-clad teeny-boppers doing the frug, watusi, twist, mashed potato, monkey, and the ever popular epileptic fit. In one scene, we see Mike in the background singing "My Beach Shack," while in the foreground a forty-times-life-sized bikinied tushy wiggles assertively.

Now for the denouement. At one of these wild parties, Diane McBain, Cynthia Foxhugh, and Les the drummer are present. So that you can remember what part each plays in the story, Mendelssohn's "Wedding March" is played on the glockenspiel whenever they appear on the screen. Les becomes so enraged by her competition that she rushes upstairs and puts on her best dress. She comes down looking like a senior high prom queen.

Just then, into the party come Mr. Foxhugh, who has taken a liking to Miss McBain and wants to marry her, Foxhugh's assistant, who wants to marry Cynthia, and Tracy the cop, who wants to marry Les. All three want to know Mike's intentions. But hold everything. There's only one way to solve any question of love and honor. That's right, a car race.

Mr. Foxhugh shows up at the race driving his own car. As Mike gets into his, one of his rivals pushes him down, jumps into the gleaming white Cobra, and zooms off. Cynthia shows up in her own sporty red sedan. With the other cars seemingly miles ahead, Mike borrows a car from a driver who dropped out, and speeds off to take the lead. Impossible? You bet. We see the usual spinarounds, cars crashing into haystacks, and of course, Mike wins. What the race decides is anyone's guess, but Mike marries all three women . . . Diane to Mr. Foxhugh, Les to Tracy the cop, and Cynthia to Mr. Foxhugh's assistant, whose name doesn't matter, anyway.

°　　°　　°

Unforgettable Performances

Spinout seemed to be a tiring exercise for the unhappy Elvis Presley. As *Time* magazine reported, " . . . he now sports a glossy something on his summit that adds at least five inches to his altitude and looks like a swatch of hot buttered yak wool." And his face finally expresses the pain of wearing those tight pants.

Perhaps Elvis' "maturity" is what attracts Diane McBain, the urbane but inane author of all those how-to-get-married-and-live-happily-ever-after books. She expresses the innocent curiosity of Rona Barrett and the sex appeal of the Burger King girl.

Deborah Walley is no newcomer to this kind of picture, being a veteran of the immortal *Beach Blanket Bingo*, *Gidget Goes Hawaiian*, and *It's a Bikini World*. For *Spinout*, she stamps her feet and fumes, and every other line she has is "I'm not a guy, I'm a girl." Yet she has a Beatles haircut and assumes the role of bossy manager of the singing group, so what does she expect?

Jimmy Hawkins and Jack Mullaney play Mike's lead guitarists, Larry and Curly. It can't be any coincidence that these goofs have the same names as two of the Three Stooges. They are so emasculated that they look as if they patterned their roles after the eunuchs in Plautus' comedies. They make funny faces, stomp on each other's toes, and leer at blond women in an abortive effort to amuse us.

Immortal Dialogue

Sparkling Repartee:

CYNTHIA: (after having run Elvis and his Cobra sports car off the road into a small lake): Hey! You're all wet! I saw you last night at the Crazy Club . . . you were great! You're cute!

MIKE: Naw, you're cute!

CYNTHIA: The way you sing, the way you drive, the way you get mad. Mike—I really go for you!

MIKE: I'm just about to go for you!

CYNTHIA: Ooh, I can hardly wait!

MIKE: If you're not outa here in about three seconds, I'm gonna put ya over mah knee, I'm gonna paddle your bottom until it's as red as that jalopy you're drivin'!

°　　°　　°

DIANE: That's right. And . . . as soon as I domesticate you . . . get you housebroken, you'll

be the best husband a girl ever had.
MIKE: Husband?

o   o   o

Song:

> Some like their women short,
> Some like 'em tall.
> I'll take 'em any size,
> Because I love 'em all!
>
> (Refrain)
> I'm just wild about smorgasbord,
> I gotta cravin' for smorgasbord.
> A little pinch here
> A little pinch there
> That's smorgasbord.
>
> Some like just Southern belles,
> They got a walk like mine.
> I go for all the bells,
> Except the weddin' kind.

The Story Behind the Film

The late Elvis Presley was born in 1935, and with the help of Colonel Tom Parker of RCA records, became the sensation of rock 'n' roll in 1955. His sex appeal was so potent that his hips were censored from his appearance on "The Ed Sullivan Show." He made his first film in 1956, *Love Me Tender*, at Twentieth Century-Fox.

Spinout was his twenty-second picture in ten years, his seventh picture for M-G-M, his sixth for director Norman Taurog, and his second for producer Joe Pasternak.

The film was originally titled *Never Say No*, then was changed to *Never Say Yes*, and finally to *Spinout*. The auto race scene was shot at Dodger Stadium. Two hundred extras and twenty-eight supporting actors were hired, and for the race, fifty autos and twelve custom racing cars were utilized.

In selecting one of Elvis' motion pictures for this book, the competition was intense.

Spinout seems particularly disreputable because of its ridiculous pandering to two of the classic adolescent dreams: drag racing and rock stardom. By throwing in a little beach-party spice, the producers hoped to come up with a perfect recipe for popular success. Digesting this concoction, however, is like dining on Fruit Loops cereal soaked in Coca-Cola, with a hefty side order of Screaming Yellow Zonkers (please hold the onions). In other words, spin out and throw up.

o   o   o

The Balance Sheet

In celebration of the tenth anniversary of Elvis' motion-picture debut, M-G-M staged a massive promotional campaign for *Spinout*. Exhibitors re-

1845-32

ceived elaborate *Spinout* kits distributed by M-G-M and RCA that promoted tie-ins between theaters and music stores. In the kits were Presley portraits, posters proclaiming, "It's Elvis!", flyers, tabloid heralds, booklets detailing Elvis' gold car on tour, plus a twenty-page M-G-M anniversary story on Presley, to be sent to local newspapers. Five thousand radio stations received copies of Presley's new single, "Spinout." Special displays and open-end interviews were arranged with *Spinout* co-stars Shelley Fabares, Deborah Walley, and Diane McBain, as well as director Tau-

rog. They all spoke in hushed, awed tones about the privilege of working with the Great Man.

Despite the regression factor inherent in Presley films (they never get any better). *Spinout* earned a hefty $529,632 in its first week. By the end of 1966 (it was released in November of that year), the film had made $1,770,000, with an anticipated revenue of $3 million.

Although *Spinout* received no critical praise, it did earn the Southern California Motion Picture Council Award for November 1966, in the family category recommended for all age groups.

Francis X. Bushman, former star of the silent screen, was recruited to play the part of Moses in Irwin Allen's dismally pretentious epic The Story of Mankind. *Please note the realistic set.*

THE STORY OF MANKIND (1957)

Directed by: IRWIN ALLEN
Written by: IRWIN ALLEN and CHARLES BENNETT
Based on the history by: HENDRIK WILLEM VAN LOON
Produced by: IRWIN ALLEN
Music by: PAUL SAWTELL
Featuring: RONALD COLMAN, VINCENT PRICE, FRANCIS X. BUSHMAN, HEDY LA-MARR, MARIE WILSON, PETER LORRE, VIRGINIA MAYO, REGINALD GARDINER, THE MARX BROTHERS, SIR CEDRIC HARD-WICKE, EDWARD EVERETT HORTON, DENNIS HOPPER, GEORGE E. STONE

Warner Brothers

The Critics Rave

"It is the kind of pontification that any kid who has ever dozed through a history class has learned to see through."
—Richard W. Nason, *New York Times*

"Unearthly. . . . A poor excuse to use a bunch of available actors in some of the weirdest casting ever committed."
—*Newsweek*

"In a Warner Brothers picture based dimly—very dimly—on a book by the late Hendrik van Loon, we have a West Coast interpretation of history as it might have been made if one of the Warner Brothers had been around to gas things up a little."
—*The New Yorker*

"Historical dud. . . . poor van Loon is probably standing in his grave and banging on his coffin in protest at the caricature to which his

The Devil (Vincent Price) and the Spirit of Man (Ronald Colman) debate the future of the human race in The Story of Mankind. *Various figures from history are summoned to present evidence.*

serious work has been reduced here."

   —S. A. Desick, *Los Angeles Examiner*

"Sophomoric. . . . The 'big names' parading through this schoolboyish charade are all made to look and sound foolish by the inane dialogue."

   —Jesse Zunser, *Cue*

"Laughable in juvenile results . . . poorly handled."

   —Leonard Maltin, *TV Movies*

"Amateurishly conceived and acted. . . . In *The Story of Mankind* a High Tribunal is called into session somewhere in heaven to decide whether or not we folks down here have done

anything to make us worth saving. It is my personal observation that if the High Tribunal ever catches this pictures, we're goners."

   —Philip K. Scheuer, *Los Angeles Times*

"Telling history on the screen can be like a bad joke told twice. You first have to find a handle, a gimmick."

   —Irwin Allen,
producer, director, and co-writer of *The Story of Mankind*

Plot Summary

Fifty-five seconds before the title of the film appears, the names of twenty-five stars are flashed separately on the screen in huge block letters, accompanied by fanfare and drumbeat. The viewer braces himself, expecting the worst—and he will not be disappointed.

We soon learn that man has discovered the "super-H-bomb" sixty years ahead of schedule, and a tribunal has been formed in heaven (one knows that it's heaven from the white sheets and dry ice) to decide whether or not man should be permitted to blow himself to smithereens. Sir Cedric Hardwicke presides over the High Tribunal of Outer Space, where the debate centers on the Devil (Vincent Price), who calls himself Mr. Scratch, and the Spirit of Man (Ronald Colman). Each drags up one historical event after another; the Devil conjures up the world's heavies, while the Spirit of Man responds with heroes, thus telling, in one hour and forty minutes, "the Story of Mankind." The Devil recalls Hedy Lamarr as Joan of Arc, Virginia Mayo as Cleopatra, Groucho Marx as Peter Minuit (the man who bought Man-

226

The Emperor Nero (played by Peter Lorre) enjoys an orgy before burning Rome to the ground. Other masterstrokes of casting in The Story of Mankind *include Hedy Lamarr as Joan of Arc, Virginia Mayo as Cleopatra, Dennis Hopper as Napoleon, and Harpo Marx as Sir Isaac Newton.*

hattan from the Indians for twenty-four dollars), Marie Wilson as Marie Antoinette, and Peter Lorre as Roman Emperor Nero. The Spirit of Man mentions Harpo Marx as Sir Isaac Newton, Dennis Hopper as Napoleon, Reginald Gardiner as Shakespeare, and Francis X. Bushman as Moses. Amazingly enough, neither advocate is cited for contempt of court in response to these lamentable examples of miscasting.

At long last the court reaches its decision, and the high judge intones: "In the matter of the Story of Mankind, it is the decision of the High Tribunal of Outer Space . . ." The camera pulls back so the audience can't hear what the decision is, and big red letters flash across the screen "Is This the End?" We can only hope so.

Unforgettable Performances

Said producer-director Irwin Allen, "We started out by paying them the compliment of playing a big part in history and then telling them we're not paying too much." Actors were paid $2,500 for what generally amounted to one day's work—consequently, the acting aspires to the dramatic heights of "General Hospital."

Memorable is Harpo Marx as Newton, playing the harp under a tree, and having not one, but a whole bushel of apples tumble down on his head. Groucho, too, emerges unscathed as Peter Minuit—every time the Indians offer him the peace pipe he offers them his cigar.

Peter Lorre as Nero is depicted as a Roman version of Marty. He's the guy who doesn't want to join in his friends' orgies because he's too shy (one can imagine the sort of dialogue: "What do you want to do tonight, Nero?" "I dunno, what do

you want to do tonight, Claudius?"). In desperation, Nero decides to go out on his porch and play his fiddle. Meanwhile, Rome has just been set ablaze, and Nero stays out on the porch, tears streaming down his face, proclaiming, "Burn, glorious Rome, burn! May this mantle of fire make you eternal." Poor Peter—for this he left Germany?

Somehow Vincent Price makes everything he does seem sinister, so he is saved any embarrassment. But Ronald Colman, in what proved to be the last role of his career, is so earnest that the most notable audience reaction is pity.

Immortal Dialogue

Opening Sequence (angels appear in the form of two stars):

FIRST ANGEL: This story here in the newspaper. . . . Some devilish fellow down on the earth has actually discovered the secret of the super-H-bomb!

SECOND ANGEL: That's impossible! . . . The super-H-bomb is not scheduled for invention by the Devil until the year . . . let's see . . . until . . . here it is . . . until the year . . . 2016. . . . Why, they're not ready or wise enough to handle it yet. . . . According to our heavenly statistics, if exploded now, the bomb would blow Man and his earth sky-high. No one would be left alive . . . everyone would be dead.

FIRST ANGEL: My, my, the housing shortage up here would be terrible! . . . What'll we do?

❊   ❊   ❊

LE MARQUIS DE VARENNES: They protest that they have no bread, Your Majesty!

MARIE ANTOINETTE: No bread indeed! Then let them eat cake!

*   *   *

Love Scene:
ANTONY: Cleopatra—my love! Why did you turn your ship from the fight? All your galleys have scattered—run before the foe—and just when the battle was almost won!
CLEOPATRA: I believed the battle was lost. Oh, do not blame me—what do I know of war?
ANTONY: But what about love?—Ours. If the worse came, we had sworn to die together.
CLEOPATRA: Aren't we together now, Antony?
ANTONY: With shame on our names.
CLEOPATRA: But with love for each other in our hearts. Believe me, my galley is swift . . . the Romans will never catch us. Come close to me, Antony.

The Story Behind the Film

The film is based on Hendrik van Loon's informal history of the same title, published in the 1920s. The book has been one of the best-selling paperbacks in publishing history.

The Story of Mankind was Irwin Allen's first film with people—his prior screen credits were *The Animal World* and the Academy Award-winning *The Sea Around Us*. Allen reported that: "I said to our research department, 'Find me the giants of history—those people who affected mankind more than anyone else.' We found four hundred so-called giants! Obviously, if we were to devote only a minute to each of these giants it would be impossible to tell the story. We boiled it down to fifty-six people."

While actors making "cameo" appearances were paid $2,500, Allen saved money by using discarded footage of battle scenes, the Boston Tea Party, and other disasters from older Warner Brothers films. He would have done better to have realized why the footage was discarded in the first place.

The ad campaign for this film was short-lived, but featured such alluring lines as "It Took Thirty Top Film Personalities to Tell This Story" and "The Book They All Talked About Is Now a Pic-ture They'll All Talk About." The latter is certainly true. While still in production, *Newsweek* magazine referred to the project as "the most pretentious-sounding movie in recent history."

The Balance Sheet

The Story of Mankind opened in Philadelphia on October 23, 1957. It earned a poor $8,000 the first week, a meager $5,000 the second, and closed in the third. It fared likewise in other major cities. In Des Moines, Iowa, Warner Brothers suggested that coupons, entitling students to a reduced admission price, be distributed in the Des Moines public schools. The school board rejected the proposal (the same stunt had been tried unsuccessfully with another film which came out around the same time, *The Ten Commandments*).

Undaunted by his colossal flop, Irwin Allen went on to make such commercial blockbusters as *The Towering Inferno* and *The Poseidon Adventure*. No comment.

SWAMP WOMEN (1955)

Directed by: ROGER CORMAN
Written by: DAVID STERN
Produced by: BERNARD WOOLNER
Music by: WILLIS HOLMAN
Featuring: MARIE WINDSOR, CAROLE MAT-
THEWS, BEVERLY GARLAND, JIL JARMYN,
TOUCH CONNORS, SUSAN CUMMINGS

American International Pictures

The Critics Rave

"Heavy-handed nonsense. . . ."
—Leonard Maltin, *TV Movies*

" . . . contrived. . . ."
—Steven H. Scheuer, *Movies on TV*

"A film called *Swamp Women*, which opened
yesterday, boasts in its credits that it was shot in
the scenic bayou country of Louisiana. The country is pretty, all right, but the story that is laid in
it gets bogged down in clichés and
apathy. . . ."
—S. A. Desick, *Los Angeles Examiner*

"Pic's chief asset is its exploitable tag; otherwise, it's just filler material. . . ."
—*Variety*

Plot Summary

Swamp Women opens with expressionist titles pic-
turing exotic women while a cool saxophone
blows some slow cocktail music. As this medley
ends, we are thrust into the heart of the film. Hold
on to your seats.

A policewoman named Lee (Carole Mathews)
is disguised as a convict and put into the prison
cell of the notorious Nardo gang, a trio of murder-

*A battle between Touch Connors and a man-eating
crocodile is presented with terrifying realism in*
Swamp Women. *If you look carefully at the very top
of this photo you can see the tiled edge of the swimming pool in which the sequence was filmed.*

ous (but buxom) women. Lee's mission—should we choose to accept it—is to find out where the gang has hidden a load of stolen diamonds. To accomplish her goal, she is to help the gang escape, and then join them to find out where the treasure is buried.

And now, introducing those women you love to hate, the Nardo girls. Josie (Marie Windsor), a blond with a ponytail, is the leader of the group. That's because she has the deepest voice. Then there's Billie (Jil Jarmyn). She's the curly blond flirt who will do anything for a man, even knit socks and wash his underwear. And finally there's Vera (Beverly Garland)—the *bad* girl. This redhead slinks around doing a Sheldon Leonard imitation (see *Daughter of the Jungle*), chews gum, and spews insults out of the corner of her mouth.

Once out of prison, the girls grab a boat and head for their hidden loot, somewhere in the Louisiana bayous. Though this film was shot in the real bayous, it was photographed in a way that makes the swamplands look as dangerous as the Jungle-Boat ride at Disneyland.

For all their toughness, the girlie gangsters don't seem to know much about boating, and their small craft sinks, leaving them stranded. Who should come putt-putting around the bend in a motor boat but a young geologist named Bob (Touch—a.k.a. Mike—Connors), his girl friend, and a guide. The Nardos wave them over, shoot the guide, knock out Bob with one slap, and toss the girl friend to the alligators.

The next hour or so is spent cruising around the bayous, with Bob tied up at one end of the boat, and the girls at the other end gawking at him. The cocktail music in the background is still playing, but none of the girls ask Bob to dance.

"The Nardo girls never run around in pants like a bunch of boys," our hoodlum honeys declare, and in order to ensure femininity, they make cutoffs out of their jeans. When the group beds down on dry marshland at night, the girls take turns making passes at the helpless geologist. First each tries to kiss him, then discovers that she's being watched by one of the others, and slaps poor Bob for being fresh. In one scene the girls bathe nude in a lagoon while Bob, untied, wanders around on shore whistling. Besides being a geologist, Bob is an idiot.

Finally, the diamonds are found. The gang digs, with bare hands, until they unearth a small black box. Inside are what look like several hundred rhinestones. Are these the famous diamonds? Or are they spangles that have fallen off Liberace's coat? You can tell that the girls know a lot about the value of such things. One of them takes a handful of the gems and gleefully throws it up in the air. Half the diamonds disappear into the swamp this way, but no one seems to notice.

Now that the diamonds are in hand, or in swamp, or wherever, greed sets in. Vera, the meanie, grabs the diamonds, steals the guns, and kidnaps Bob while the others are sleeping. She leaves the geologist tied up and climbs a nearby tree in order to pick off her former compatriots like a sniper. Her partners wake up, see what has happened, and toss a homemade spear into Vera's abdomen. Then Lee (who you'll recall is a cop) unties Bob and the two of them beat Josie and Billie unconscious just as a boatload of police arrives. In the final scene, the cocktail music swells as Lee and Bob walk arm in arm to greet the police captain and have some well-deserved martinis.

Unforgettable Performances

The unsung heroes of *Swamp Women* are the real swamp women, the alligators. In an alligator wrestling sequence (no swamp film is complete without one) the reptiles seem to be so heavily drugged that any sensitive viewer wants to boo the humans for beating up on them.

Roger Corman's interpretation of a female convict is a woman who acts like a man. A convict is a convict, after all. As a result, the members of the Nardo gang swagger around like the Dead End Kids, employ the hippest criminal lingo (words like "man," "dame," the immortal "sissy," etc.). So that we don't forget that these are women, however, the girls seem to have footballs under their blouses. "Getting busted" in the context of this film takes on a new definition—it means having one's chest inflated.

Touch Connors smiles a lot. When the women point their guns at him, when his tootsie-pie gets tossed to the alligators, and when the Nardos try to romance him, all he does is smile, smile, smile. He seems to be saying, "Oh boy, that was sure exciting. I wonder what's going to happen next!"

Immortal Dialogue

BOB'S GIRL FRIEND (before their capture): Oh, Bob, honey, you're just so strong and big and brave. I don't know what I'd do without you.

*   *   *

LEE: Look, if I bother you, go somewhere else!
JOSIE: Oh, cut it, cut it, I said!
VERA: Look, nobody talks to me like that! I'll kill that dame!

*   *   *

BILLIE: Oh, this stinkin' swamp water stinks!

*   *   *

Would-be Seduction Scene:
BOB: What can I do for you?
BILLIE: Anything you like.
BOB: What if I don't like?
BILLIE: You will.
VERA: You dirty little dumb broad!

The Story Behind the Film

Swamp Women, which used as alternate titles *Swamp Diamonds* and *Cruel Swamp*, was filmed on location in Louisiana bayous because it was cheaper than building a swamp at the studios. The movie was made in a mere twenty-two days, and it would seem that the producers saved on paper costs by not writing down any dialogue. A press release said that "Danger and death were just a slip away from the stars and technicians who made up the location unit for the filming of the Woolner Bros. romantic adventure-thriller *Swamp Women*." The real danger was not finishing before the money ran out.

The ads proclaimed that this was the first time the bayous received a starring role in a film. The cast and crew worked out of long, narrow rowboats which were manned by bayou natives—whoever they are. The special color cameras were mounted on a raft made of empty oil barrels and balsa wood. Occasionally this "thing" would nudge an alligator, causing the reptile to bare its teeth, thrash its tail, and yawn a couple of times. One can imagine director Corman leaning over the side of his boat (if he were present) and saying to the alligator, "Hold it . . . you're not in till the next scene! Go back to sleep."

A local citizen was hired to ride shotgun on the production. This lucky fellow was to guard against any irate animals who would try to attack the film crew. It appears that when Roger Corman is coming, everyone knows about it. The only time the sharpshooter's services were needed was when it was necessary to kill a ten-foot rattlesnake that was about to touch Touch Connors. Reports said that the rifleman killed the snake "with aplomb, planting a .38 bullet squarely in its head. And this was called for in the script!" It probably wasn't, but proved to be such an exciting bloody mess that it was written in.

To make the fight scenes between the women more realistic, a trainer named Jack Hayes was hired to teach the star actresses the art of fisticuffs. Hayes was said to be a "specialist in teaching women how to battle with guns, knives, and their fists." *Swamp Women* boasted no stand-ins for the fight sequences. This is an uncommon practice, for as Hayes said, "If an actress accidentally gets a facial or shoulder bruise, it can hold up production for two or three days. Hollywood has never learned to camouflage a bruise with make-up. Most of the fight scenes between women somehow don't turn out right on the screen. Women don't have the same muscular coordination as men. On film, the gals look like they're either playing volleyball or patty-cake. This leads the audience to laugh, something that every producer fears in an action-thriller." And the audience won't laugh at this? Good luck. Hayes, a former featherweight boxer, said, "I teach the girls how to roll with a punch, how to side-slip our heads just at the split second of impact, so that they look like they are actually being slugged." What fun. Hayes taught his girls very

well—in one lesson, Marie Windsor tossed him over her shoulder and knocked him unconscious for several minutes. No wonder Hayes is a *former* featherweight boxer.

The Balance Sheet

The poster art for this film is far more exciting than the film itself. Imagine such exciting proclamations: "Scarlet Women Out to Get Every Thrill They Could Steal!" And "Strips Down to Naked Fury!" And "Man Crazed Women . . . They Were All Bad Company!" And "They Invaded the Bayou with Guns, Scanty Clothes and One Man Between Them!" And so on. In Los Angeles, *Swamp Women* was billed with a film called *Gunslinger*, a woman's Western, where Beverly Garland portrays a town marshal who's handy with a gun. Together, this veritable women's film fest (or film fiasco) grossed a measly $8,400 in its first week, which also was its last week.

Swamp Women was one of the first films made by Roger Corman, who has over the years earned the title King of the "B's," even though he has said, "I don't make 'B' movies and nobody makes 'B' movies anymore." Okay, Roger. You can be the King of the "C's." Corman made most of his films in five to ten days with budgets of $30,000 to $40,000. One film, *Monster from the Ocean Floor*, was made for a paltry $12,000. Corman seems to be trying to set a record for film prolificacy, having directed more than fifty films in ten years and produced almost one hundred and fifty. His motto, apparently, is "Quality? What's that?" He has ground out such fine schlock masterpieces as *She-Gods of Shark Reef*, *Attack of the Crab Monsters*, *Viking Women and the Sea Serpent*, and *Teenage Caveman*.

Roger Corman received his B.A. from Stanford University, and his Master's in English from Oxford. In recent years he has even set up a $1,000 scholarship at the British university. He is responsible for having given Francis Ford Coppola, Peter Bogdanovich, Jack Nicholson, Peter Fonda, Martin Scorsese, Haskell Wexler, and Laszlo Kovacs their stars in Hollywood. Notice how all of these people have been praised for the artistic merits of their work? Apparently Corman has noticed too. He has repented for his past sins and now distributes films like Fellini's *Amarcord*, Truffaut's *The Story of Adele H.*, and Bergman's *Cries and Whispers*. Corman once said, "I think that had I had the chance to go to a film school I could have saved myself a lot of time and a lot of bother." You and us both.

If Touch Connors looks familiar in *Swamp Women*, it's because most audiences know him as Mike Connors, the star of television's "Mannix." "Touch" was the name he picked up playing bas-

232

Josie (Marie Windsor), left, is the leader of the all-girl Nardo gang, recently escaped from prison in Roger Corman's Swamp Women. Touch (Mike) Connors plays the young geologist, Bob, who along with his innocent girl friend, is kidnapped by the girlie gangsters. The film was advertised with the lines "Flaming Passions! Weird Adventure!"

ketball for UCLA. "Connors" was the name he picked up in Hollywood. His real name is Krekor Ohanion.

SPECIAL AWARD

A first-edition copy of Stanislavski's *My Life in Art* goes to Beverly Garland for her unique contribution to American culture.

Miss Garland, who describes her figure as "neat but not gaudy," began her acting career early. At age five she impersonated Cupid in a kindergarten play. While shooting an arrow into the hero's heart, her brief costume fell off and she was the hit of the show. Miss Garland went on to develop her talent as a klutz. There was the time "When I was a model at Magnin's and wore a dress backward all day without knowing it. And not to mention when I auditioned for the role of Mary Magdalene in a pilgrimage play and came up with the line, 'Hear, hear. The Mesa is coming.'" No, mountains don't move in the Bible. She had merely mispronounced the word "Messiah."

Miss Garland began her Hollywood career as a patient on the television series "Medic." She got the part when she was on her way to an interview for another film that needed a Marilyn Monroe type girl. Miss Garland dressed up like the sex kitten, but didn't get the part. However, the producers of "Medic" took one look at her and reportedly said, "Yes, you do look emaciated—as though you had leukemia. You're hired!" From then on she was type-cast as a hospital patient. "Why, it got to the point when they called me for a role that I figured I should bring my own hospital bed." In addition to *Swamp Women* and *Gunslinger*, she was featured in a number of other "B" movies. "You don't have to act in these pictures," she said. "All you have to do is possess a good pair of lungs. I can scream with more variations from shrill to vibrato than any other girl in pictures." And she screamed her way through films like *Made Not of This World, Beast from the Amazon, It Conquered the World,* and *A Killer Leopard.*

Her greatest artistic achievement, however, was back on television. One day a friend called and said, "Fred MacMurray is getting married on 'My Three Sons.' I'm asking my agent to suggest me for the part." Miss Garland says that when she put down the phone she thought, "If she can be Fred MacMurray's wife, why can't I?" She got the part, and probably lost a friend. But she had previous experience, having portrayed Bing Crosby's wife on his TV show. Her most recent film appearance was as the wife of Dana Andrews, in *Airport 1975* (q.v.).

In real life, Miss Garland is married to a man named Fillmore Crank. She was recently elected the mayor of North Hollywood.

SWING YOUR LADY (1938)

Directed by: RAY ENRIGHT
Written by: JOSEPH SCHRANK and MAURICE LEO
Adapted from the play by: KENYON NICHOLSON and CHARLES ROBINSON
Featuring: HUMPHREY BOGART, RONALD REAGAN, FRANK McHUGH, NAT PENDLETON, PENNY SINGLETON, LOUISE FAZENDA, ALLEN JENKINS, HUGH O'CONNELL, TOMMY BUPP, SONNY BUPP, DANIEL BOONE SAVAGE, THE WEAVER FAMILY

Warner Brothers

The Critics Rave

"Vulgar, ludicrous, irresponsible. . . ."
—B. R. Crisler, *New York Times*

"A definite tendency to vulgarity spoils a clever idea. Negative social value. Sound machine much too loud."
—American Legion Auxiliary

"This type of picture is limited in its appeal and will offend many."
—General Federation of Women's Clubs

"Humphrey Bogart's talents are wasted on a quite unworthy part. . . ."
—*Monthly Film Bulletin*

"Abysmal."
—Nathaniel Benchley, *Bogie*

"Noisy and mediocre."
—National Society of New England Women

"Hillbilly music and some amusing acting by Nat Pendleton cannot save from mediocrity this

Allen Jenkins, Frank McHugh, Nat Pendleton, and Humphrey Bogart enjoy the witty byplay in the 1938 Warner Brothers classic Swing Your Lady. *Bogart, who plays the corrupt manager of "rassler" Pendleton ("the Greek Hercules"), considered this his worst film performance.*

satire about a wrestling match in the backwoods. Suggestive innuendo."

—Daughters of the American Revolution

"A sorry vehicle. . . . As far as Bogart was concerned, the whole effort was tasteless and vulgar and he considered it his worst film performance."

—Alan G. Barbour, *Humphrey Bogart*

Plot Summary

Ed Hatch (Humphrey Bogart) is the manager of a simpleminded but good-natured "rassler" named Joe Skopapoulos (Nat Pendleton). This lumbering lummox is billed all over as "the Greek Hercules."

Our story opens as Ed and his crew roam around Hillbillyland in a jalopy, trying to scare up a match for Joe. But a foe tain't to be found. Suddenly (things always happen "suddenly"), the jalopy gets stuck in the mud. Ed calls for help, and who should bound over but a lady blacksmith named Sadie (Louise Fazenda). This "Herculette" single-handedly—but ever ever so daintily—lifts the car out of the mud onto dry terra firma. Guess what sort of scheme runs through the brain of money-minded manager Ed? That's right. He offers Sadie $100 if she can stay in the ring with Big Joe for thirty minutes. She has her eye on some bedroom furniture and hastily consents.

Joe begins a rigorous training program. But while skipping rope out on the road he happens upon Sadie's smithy, asks for a drink of water, and boom! Cupid drops his horseshoe on Big Joe's head. He refuses to fight the woman he loves (in the bedroom, maybe, in the ring, no). Sadie gets upset because she won't get the $100, or the bedroom furniture.

Soon an old beau of Sadie's stomps out of the hills firing bird shot, angered by the attention the Greek Hercules/American Idiot is paying to Sadie. Ed, that ol' wizard of finance, comes up with another brainstorm. He arranges a "battle of love" between Joe and the rival hillbilly, with the victor to be awarded the hand of Sadie and the rest of her too, if he wants it. Sadie of course would get her bedroom furniture.

Ed realizes that if Joe wins the match, he'll run off and marry Sadie, leaving the poor manager with nothing to manage but his girl friend, who hasn't kept her mouth closed since the film started. So Ed makes Joe promise to lose the match, and then tells Sadie that Joe is already married so that she won't want him, anyway.

The day of the match finally arrives, and all the citizens of Hillbillyland turn out in the their official hillbilly uniforms: soiled overalls and straw hats. They keep guzzling slugs of corn mash from jugs marked "XXX." When the jugs are empty, they become instruments in the Hillbilly Symphony Orchestra, being played like . . . well, like corn mash jugs.

And the battle begins. Everything goes as planned, with Joe looking bad and going down time after time. Out of the blue, or perhaps *Oedipus Rex*, a messenger appears. He bears a telegram which states that the winner of the match is to fight in Madison Square Garden the following week. Ed leaps up and gives a signal to Joe to win, and the big bruiser throws his opponent to the ground as if he were a piece of hog jowl. Joe rushes to his bumpkin babe, Sadie, but she wants nothing to do with him because she thinks he's a bigamist. Joe makes Ed tell her that it isn't true, and then announces that Sadie is going to come along with them to the Big Apple for the big fight. As the sun slowly sets on Hillbillyland, our story ends. As the lights in the theater come up and the audience begins to wake up, the first one to say "Play it again" gets punched in the mouth.

Unforgettable Performances

For that authentic hillbilly look, *Swing Your Lady* features the Weaver Family: Leon, Elvirey, and "Cicero." When it comes to singin' no one shatters glass the way the Weavers do. And when it comes to dressin' they do for rags and patches what Johnny Carson did for Stylish sports coats.

Louise Fazenda, a gangling veteran of the Mack Sennett studios (and the Spanish American War, from the looks of her), storms through this movie like a randy gorilla. She bears a striking resemblance to Snuffy Smith's wife, which must be how she attracted Nat Pendleton, the Greek Her-

236

cules, whose performance rivals the screen moronics of Lon Chaney, Jr., in *Of Mice and Men* and *North West Mounted Police* (q.v.). Also worthy of censure is Penny Singleton, whose comic abilities leave the viewer with a migraine headache.

The film was one of Humphrey Bogart's most ignoble efforts. His performance leaves no doubt that he knew it was bad while he was doing it. He approaches the role with all the self-willed enthusiasm of a sophomore halfback playing the final quarter of his big game with a fractured ankle. At times, Bogie's failing bravado reminds us of a late-night talk-show host with failing ratings, trying desperately to keep himself and his jokes on the air. ("Now that is funny. Isn't it? Isn't it?") The best that can be said for *Swing Your Lady* is that it had no permanent impact on Bogie's career.

The Weaver Family, Leon, "Cicero," and Elvirey, provide a touch of hillbilly humor in Swing Your Lady. The film was praised by the New York Times as "vulgar, ludicrous, irresponsible."

Immortal Dialogue

ED: Joe Skopapoulos, the ponderous pachyderm of grunt and groan, the Greek Hercules, is the next heavyweight champion of the world!

❉   ❉   ❉

SHINER: Lissen, if you're so hard up, try talkin' to yourself!
JOE: I did but I couldn't get no answers.

❉   ❉   ❉

MRS. DAVIS: My! You oughta see all them clothes she's got. Would you believe it—three pairs of shoes!
FIRST WOMAN: Great day! What's she want with three pair shoes?
SECOND WOMAN: She's only got two feet!

❉   ❉   ❉

SADIE: Say, mister! Who in the name o' Jerusalem air ye, anyway?
JOE: Joe Skopapoulos.
SADIE: Huh?
JOE? Skopapoulos—Skopapoulos!
SADIE (shaking head): Wut air ye—Eyetalian?
JOE: Naw, I'm of Greek accent.

❉   ❉   ❉

SADIE: Wal, shuck my corn!

❉   ❉   ❉

JOE: Hey—is your old man home?
SADIE: Naw—last I seen o' him, he wuz going out possum huntin'.
JOE: Ain't he liable to come in any minute?
SADIE: I don't reckon—that wuz eleven years ago.
JOE: Oh.

❉   ❉   ❉

OLLIE (examining Sadie all dressed up): Wal, I'll be a plumb catawampus!

❉   ❉   ❉

The Story Behind the Film

Swing Your Lady was one of about sixty films directed by Ray Enright, who also made such films as *Dancing Sweeties, Traveling Saleslady, Miss Pacific Fleet, Earthworm Tractors, Ready, Willing* and Able, The Singing Marine, Naughty but Nice, Brother Rat and a Baby, Sin Town, and Gung Ho! He may not have been able to direct, but no one could touch him when it came to making up titles.

Penny Singleton, who portrays Ed Hatch's girl friend, Cookie, later became known for her portrayals on film of Chic Young's comic-strip heroine, Blondie. ("God bless Chic Young," Miss Singleton was fond of saying.) Miss Singleton began her career at an early age, when she was known as Baby Dorothy in "one of those horrible kid acts." Her big break came when she played at New York's Winter Garden and befriended some of vaudeville's great showmen. "Jack Benny taught me all about timing," she recalled. She coined the name Penny because as a child she collected the one-cent pieces. She may have lacked financial sense, but then again, "Dollar" Singleton has a peculiar ring to it. When Hollywood called, Miss Singleton bleached her hair and headed West. "They threw parts at me Claire Trevor didn't want." Her big break came in 1938 when she played Blondie. She made films about the comic-strip character until 1950, with titles such as Blondie Meets the Boss, Blondie Goes Latin, and Blondie Hits the Jackpot. She married Hollywood producer Robert Sparks, creator of television's "Gunsmoke," "Perry Mason," "Have Gun—Will Travel," and "Rawhide."

In subsequent years, Miss Singleton became embroiled in Hollywood politics as president of the American Guild of Variety Artists (AGVA). Wal, shuck my corn!

The Balance Sheet

Swing Your Lady was a bomb all the way around. It didn't even make money! The film was painfully remembered by Humphrey Bogart. As Allen Eyles described it in Bogart: "The kind of roles that awaited Bogart on his return to the Warner lot suggest that he was in temporary disgrace, perhaps after feuding with Jack Warner. Bogart regarded Swing Your Lady as his worst film, and it probably was. . . ."

The Weaver Family was spotted in no time by those wonderful talent scouts at Republic Pictures, the makers of Daughter of the Jungle (q.v.) and Twilight on the Rio Grande (q.v.). The singing family was soon making a string of low-budget pictures of their own at Republic, and in no time at all, everyone lost interest in them.

THE TERROR OF TINY TOWN
(1938)

Directed by: SAM NEWFIELD
Written by: FRED MYTON
Added dialogue by: CLARENCE MARKS
Produced by: JED BUELL
Music and lyrics by: LEW PORTER
Featuring: BILLY CURTIS, YVONNE MORAY, LITTLE BILLY, BILLY PLATT, JOHNNY BAMBARY, CHARLES BECKER, JOSEPH HERBERT, NITA KREBS, GEORGE MINISTERI, KARL CASITZKY, FERN McDILL, W. H. O'DOCHARTY

Columbia Pictures

The Critics Rave

"Wild West drama played entirely by midgets. . . . As all the cast are midgets, the element of surprise is lost and the film tends to be just another Western. . . . Everybody seems to be riding everywhere."

—Monthly Film Bulletin

"Quaint. . . . Performed by the first all-midget cast ever to make a feature. . . . The hard-riding, two gun boys go buckety-buck on Shetland ponies. The heroine escapes the villain by running under the furniture instead of around it. . . . The formula drama has been given pint-sized treatment."

—Hollywood Reporter

"Contrived . . . doll-like personalities. . . . They sling mean six-guns in battles between hero and villains, indulge in miniature romance, promote the triumph of virtue over heavy odds and carry on all the other antics of the Western meller."

—Variety

Little Billy

"A Rollickin', Rootin', Tootin', Shootin' Drama of the Great Outdoors."

—Publicity for the film

Plot Summary

Move over, P. T. Barnum. Jed Buell is here with an army of trained midgets. And what better way to show off their talents than in a stirring, musical saga of the Old West? Hi ho, Peanut, and away!

The Terror of Tiny Town opens with an announcer of normal height introducing the film—his brief appearance marks the only time a full-sized person shows up on screen. Soon two midgets, sporting cowboy boots and gun belts, come up to him and begin arguing furiously as to who is the real star of the show. The announcer arbitrates. "Let's go through with the picture," he suggests, and before the audience can groan in protest the action has begun.

The citizens of Tiny Town are relaxing in a bar that looks like the place where the Munchkins in *The Wizard of Oz* might go after hours. The patrons enter by walking *under* the saloon doors and, once inside, they drink beer from steins as big as their heads. The bartender has an enormous baby curl pasted on his forehead, and the patrons of this recreational establishment all join in a song that goes, "Laugh your troubles away/ ah-ha-ha-ha-ha!"

If you were hoping that the "Terror" in this film was a green monster that ravages this miniature city and its inhabitants, you will be sorely disappointed. The Terror is a malevolent fella named Haines (portrayed by an actor known as Little Billy) who incites a feud between two families. Haines hopes that he can take over their ranches when the families have killed each other off. Then, of course, there's our hero, Pat (Billy Curtis), a dashing young midget who wears a hat shaped like an enormous banana. Pat senses that Haines is up to no good, and being a born pacifist, he gallops across the countryside trying to spread good feelings between the feuding families. His heroic dedication is depicted by repeatedly showing the same scene of Pat and his amigos riding off toward the horizon. After a while, it becomes evident that the property department has gone to some lengths in deciding which props to scale down to size and which to leave enormous (i.e.,

as is). For example, our little friends trot around on tiny Shetland ponies while their hitching posts tower over them. Whenever one of the cowpokes tries to hitch his "hoss" he practically hangs the poor animal in the process.

During the remainder of the film, we are introduced to several "fascinating" characters. We meet Pat's sweetheart (Yvonne Moray), a virtuous, curly-haired, orphaned maiden with dimples. Then there's the Terror's gun moll (Nita Krebs), a barroom songstress with an accent somewhere between Marlene Dietrich's and Boris Karloff's. She sings a song entitled "Hey, Look Out, I Wanna Make Love to You" as she comes gliding down a staircase. Perhaps the torrid musicality of this midget mademoiselle might give contemporary producers the idea for an X-rated novelty item—but let's not get into that. In *Tiny Town*, we also see a dim-witted cook (used as comic relief) who interminably chases a goose around a yard, trying to chop its head off for his next meal. For good measure, there's a midget barbershop quartet and even a midget black shoeshine boy—complete with Stepin Fetchit delivery. Some of this material is really so sad that the members of the audience feel guilty if they laugh. Inexplicably, a penguin wanders onto the set and overshadows the entire cast. In the film's gripping finale, courageous Pat finally succeeds in exposing Haines, the bite sized baddy, as the real source of trouble in the family feud. To clear up matters even more, Pat triumphantly blows up Haines in a log cabin with a stick of dynamite. Boy, these fellas sure are cute.

The problem is that for even the most kinky viewers, it becomes tiring to watch the little people slamming into huge doors or riding horses the size of puppies. We get the point after five minutes and can only begin thinking of new possibilites for specialty horse operas. Just imagine what kind of Western you could make *à la* Jed Beull, with a truckload of amputees, or what kind of showdown you could stage with an all-blind cast.

Unforgettable Performances

And we'll bet you thought Alan Ladd was short! What can we really say about a troupe of midgets whose acting ability is exceeded only by their height. At times, the viewer has the uncanny sensation that he is watching a Western in which Truman Capote acts, sings, dances, and plays all the major parts. The director, Sam Newfield, apparently gave his cast no other direction than "Look cute and act midgety!" And that they do. At times, the film resembles a below-average Our Gang comedy, in which the children try to talk after sucking on helium balloons all day. Even when the barroom temptress belts out "I Wanna Make Love to You" one wonders whether she is old enough. The biggest song of the film is a forgettable number called "The Wedding of Jack and Jill." As these little people waddle through the film spewing high-pitched, garbled dialogue, it seems that the actors are intended to be retarded as well as minuscule.

Immortal Dialogue

Opening Sequence:

PAT: I'm the hero! After this picture's out I'll be the biggest cowboy star in Hollywood!
HAINES: I'm the villain. I'm the toughest hombre that ever lived, and I ain't afraid o' the biggest one o' you. I'm the Terror of Tiny Town, and that's the star part.
PAT: That's what you think.
HAINES: Ye-eah. That's just what I think!
FULL-SIZED ANNOUNCER: Wait a minute! Men! Men! Wait a minute!

*   *   *

(In the saloon.)
SHERIFF: Howdy, Tex.
TEX: Hello, Sheriff.
SHERIFF: I'm warnin' you, Tex. Don't start no trouble in town.
TEX: I don't want no trouble. But I won't run away from it, neither!

*   *   *

FIRST MIDGET: I wonder who those hombres are?

SECOND MIDGET: Let's pick up the trail and see what they're up to!

*   *   *

BUCK: Dad, I jumped a bunch o' rustlers at work!
TEX: Rustlers!
BUCK: They left in such a hurry they forgot their branding iron.
TEX: (examines iron): Cheap Work Pete!
BUCK: That's the way I read it.
TEX: Why, that low-down ki-yoat!

The Story Behind the Film

Jed Buell, producer of *The Terror of Tiny Town*, certainly had an eye for bad taste. In 1939 he and *Tiny Town* writer Fred Myton, composer Lew Porter, and director Sam Newfield collaborated once again. This time the result was a film called *Harlem on the Prairie*. Guess what kind of novelty Western that was. We'll give you a hint: it was designed to play in as many as possible of the eight hundred Negro theaters then operating in the United States.

One wonders where someone like Mr. Buell gets his inspiration. According to one magazine, the idea for *Tiny Town* came in a blinding flash after a subordinate had quipped to Buell, "If this economy drive keeps on, we'll be using midgets for actors." Before long, Mr. Buell was advertising "Big Salaries for Little People." He collected midgets from all over the country, using agencies, advertisements, and radio broadcasts. A troupe of fourteen midgets arrived from Hawaii. Eventually he had secured the services of some sixty midgets, averaging 3'8" in height, and ranging in age from nineteen to sixty-five.

The film was shot on the Lazy A Ranch at Santa Susana, California. There were problems. Midgets didn't prove to be the greatest stuntmen. They were continually tumbling off their ponies, or lunging backward after firing their man-sized six-shooters. And of course, there were the inevitable attacks of sunburn and artistic temperament. Finally, at a cost of $100,000, the film was finished. It opened to a good-natured audience in Los Angeles in July of 1938. *Time* magazine reported that only once did the audience really howl: "when three foot nine hero Billy Curtis, pursuing three foot nine villain Little Billy, galloped off on a black pony, was soon scooting along on a white pony, finished the chase on the black." *Time* was quick to add that the "trouble with *The Terror of Tiny Town* . . . was that without a few normal-sized folks for contrast, midgets appear much like other people." What a shame for Mr. Buell, and for other who find humor in deformities.

The Balance Sheet

The Terror of Tiny Town proved a modest success. And what happens to all successful films with an unusual twist? SEQUELS! On July 20, 1938, *Weekly Variety* featured the following news item:

> PEE-WEES TO MAKE SERIES OF PICTURES
>
> Hollywood, July 19.
> Sol Lesser has closed a deal with Jed Buell for series of films using midget cast utilized in Buell's *Terror of Tiny Town*. Second picture to be started within thirty days will be based on lumber camp, with a grown-up heavy portraying mythical Paul Bunyan. Upon completion of this one Buell is leaving for Europe to round up additional midgets for future productions.

Whether the film was ever made is not known. At least it's not listed in Buell's filmography.

The star of *The Terror of Tiny Town*, Billy Curtis, is still a prominent Hollywood figure, appearing recently in the Twentieth Century-Fox film *Planet of the Apes*, with Charlton Heston. Apparently many midgets were cast in the film as child apes. Said Curtis, "It was a work bonanza for the little people. We got about four weeks. We're always happy to work for Twentieth, where we're treated well. Midgets have much dignity and pride." Mr. Curtis also enjoyed working again with Charlton Heston: "I've worked with him in a lot of pictures, *Ten Commandments*, *Greatest Show on Earth* included. He's a swell guy in my book." It's too bad that Mr. Curtis didn't have a chance to appear in another one of Heston's classics—*Airport 1975* (q.v.). It's surprising that the producers of that epic, having filled the screen with a musical nun and a cheerful kidney patient on a stretcher, missed the chance to entertain us with an inspirational midget.

Billy Curtis went on to explain how important to the film industry Hollywood's "little people" are. "We stand in for any kid entitled to a stand-in," Curtis revealed. "Result is fewer kids, fewer kids' mothers, and fewer teachers on the sets. And when there's a stunt to be done, we can do it." Curtis himself has been stand-in for child stars such as Shirley Temple, Margaret O'Brien, and Darryl Hickman. But alas, the midget industry has begun to dry up. "There's not too much work in films and TV, and now and then some will desert to circuses, although there aren't many of those left." Curtis went on to say that there is only a handful of midgets left who work steadily in movies and TV. "I call 'em the Big Eight," he said.

Billy Curtis and his sister Mary, also a midget, were the last to be born in a family of six children. Their parents and brothers and sisters all were of normal size. Billy attended Northwestern University until he was "yanked off campus and into show business." He began touring vaudeville houses in 1932 with his sister in an act called—of

all things—The Curtises. From vaudeville, Billy ventured into several other entertainment fields. "At one point," he said, grinning, "I had my own midget wrestling show. Later I refereed an astounding match between Gorgeous George and Burt Lancaster for a charity circus here in Los Angeles. Bob Hope was the announcer."

After arriving in Hollywood, Billy landed jobs in such films as *The Wizard of Oz, Lady in the Dark,* and *Saboteur.* Billy recalls that he "was married to a normal-sized woman twenty-five years ago. It ended in divorce. I have two chil-

dren, Tim, nineteen, who is over six feet tall, and Judy Elena, twenty-one, who is married and a mother. That makes me a grandfather." Billy's second marriage was a well-publicized match with Lois De Fee, a towering showgirl who was nearly 6' 8" tall. The marriage was annulled after three years. At the time, Billy was quoted as saying, "It was very serious with me." Billy now announces that "he's a bachelor and available." An omnipresent figure around the studios, cigar-chomping Billy Curtis has no intention of leaving or quitting. "I like Hollywood," he says.

Eighteen-year-old Shirley Temple (center) displays the signs of adolescent development in That Hagen Girl. *The film describes the tragic effects of small-town gossip which holds her to be the illegitimate daughter of slick young lawyer Ronald Reagan.*

THAT HAGEN GIRL (1947)

Directed by: PETER GODFREY
Written by: CHARLES HOFFMAN
From a novel by: EDITH ROBERTS
Produced by: ALEX GOTTLEIB
Music by: FRANZ WAXMAN
Featuring: RONALD REAGAN, SHIRLEY TEMPLE, RORY CALHOUN, LOIS MAXWELL, CONRAD JANIS

Warner Brothers

The Critics Rave

"Bomb! Lowest rating! An atrocious 'comedy' of Shirley Temple convinced she's Ronald Reagan's illegitimate daughter."
—Leonard Maltin, *TV Movies*

"An inept, all-thumbs scripting job that shows no comprehension of the problem. . . . Reagan walks through his role without conviction."
—*Weekly Variety*

"A bleak indiscretion . . . with a script which might have been written—and directed—by a second-rate amateur. . . . Ronald Reagan keeps as straight a face as he can while doing what must have struck him as the silliest job of his career. . . . But it is poor little put-upon Shirley who looks most ridiculous through it all. . . . They shouldn't do such things to Shirley. It's downright un-American!"
—Bosley Crowther, *New York Times*

"The plot grows monotonous; the players seem to move stolidly without a change of pace."
—John L. Scott, *Los Angeles Times*

245

"From a dull basic story idea *That Hagen Girl* develops into a dull screenplay. . . . Both Shirley Temple and Ronald Reagan do their level best but under the circumstances they cannot help but show their confusion from time to time."

      —*The Hollywood Reporter*

"Contrived. . . . In substance, there is a marked resemblance to afternoon radio serials."

        —*Film Daily*

"This is less a film than a series of false situations."

      —*Monthly Film Bulletin*

"One of Hollywood's most preposterous comedies."

    —Patrick McGilligan, *Take One*

"Pictures like this trash must be the reason Shirley is so happily retired."

    —Steven H. Scheuer, *Movies on TV*

Plot Summary

For years, the entire town of Jordan, Ohio, has been gossiping about the true origins of Mary Hagen (Shirley Temple). Apparently, Mary was adopted by the Hagens at the same time that young lawyer Tom Bates (Ronald Reagan) left town. The reason Tom took off was to separate himself from memories of his former fiancée—a lovely girl who suddenly lost her mind and ended up in a mental institution. Putting two and two together (and getting five) the biddies of the town decide that Mary Hagen is really the illegitimate daughter of Tom Bates and his demented lady love. They're biddies—no one ever said they were astute.

The gossip intensifies when Mary is nineteen and Tom unexpectedly returns to town to begin a law practice. As he's driving down the street one day in his spiffy new convertible, he nearly runs down Mary Hagen, who's crossing the street with a friend. Tom smiles, waves, and says, "Thank you, girls." Nice guy. Mary's friend takes a long gander at the handsome new fella. "Did you see

him? Dee-lishus!" she squeals. "Who was that?" asks Shirley-Mary. "I don't know," the friend answers. "Somebody I've never seen before. . . . I wonder who it could be." Think hard, girls. As Bates continues through town he is spotted by a flock of old biddies. "Isn't that . . . ?" asks one. "It most certainly is," answers another. "Darling, may I use your phone?" asks the first. "I'll be using it myself," the second gleefully exclaims. We are greeted by a montage of women picking up telephone receivers and yapping away. And if we still don't get the point, we are briefly shown a shot of chickens squawking in a coop. How artistic. How obvious. How stupid.

Poor Mary! Everyone begins staring at her, convinced that Tom has come back to town to be near his illegitimate daughter. At a school dance, everyone looks at her so hard that she runs away—leaving her boy friend (Rory Calhoun). She takes refuge in a corridor, where's she's later caught by the principal necking with Conrad Janis. (Shirley Temple does that?) The school's chief reprimands her: "The parents of the other students expect us to keep up the school's morals." So remember: *no kissing*. Especially Conrad Janis.

This little tragedy is followed by many others. Befriended by one of her teachers (Lois Maxwell), Mary gets the part of Juliet in the school's production of *Romeo and Juliet*. But the local citizens react with such outrage to the casting of a supposed b-b-b-bastard that the part is taken away from her. Mary is heartbroken, but at the last moment, when her substitute takes sick, Mary comes in and plays the part beautifully(?) without so much as a rehearsal. Tom Bates goes backstage to congratulate her—but never says anything about being her father.

Bates's main romantic interest is Mary's teacher (Lois Maxwell), who puts it to him bluntly. "Everyone in this town says that Mary Hagen is your daughter!" Tom is flabbergasted, and denies it stoutly. As far as the viewing audience is concerned, that settles that—all America knows that Ronald Reagan would never lie.

But the citizens of Jordan, Ohio, remain suspicious and plucky Mary determines to find things out for herself. She repeatedly asks her mother who she really is, and gets nothing but casual dismissals. Then one evening Mary returns home to find her mother dying. She rushes to the bedside, where the old lady looks at her with sad and knowing eyes. "There's another thing," the mother gasps. "It's about you. . . ." But naturally, Mrs. Hagen dies before she can get it out. Rats. Now we'll never know the truth.

To console Mary for her loss, Tom asks her to come along on his outings with Mary's teacher. Just the three of them—rowing on the lake, going to the movies, eating ice cream cones. It's good, clean American fun. (What do you expect from Shirley and Ronnie?) It looks like a healthy romance is developing between Tom and the teacher.

Then, more tragedy. Mary's boy friend (Rory Calhoun) runs off and marries another girl—the rumors about Mary's origins are too much for him. Mary is so distraught that she grabs Conrad Janis and goes dancing. Some men try to pick her up and a brawl ensues, resulting in Mary's expulsion from school. (We never find out exactly what happens to Conrad Janis.) Mary reacts to this setback the way any normal, healthy adolescent would react—she tries to commit suicide by drowning herself in a lagoon. Luckily, Tom happens by and fishes her out of the drink.

After her rescue life takes a turn for the better: a newspaper article reveals that this is not the first time Tom has proved himself a hero. With the article is a picture of Tom in military uniform, being awarded some sort of medal. The story reads, "In awarding the medal to Lieutenant Colonel Bates the President of the United States paid high tribute not only to the officer's long and distinguished conduct record, but to his magnificent organization which contributed so greatly to the successful launching of atomic warfare." Well, well, well. No wonder Ronald Reagan didn't want this film showing around while he was running for President (see SPECIAL AWARD). With this latest revelation, Tom Bates is now in good standing with the citizens of his town. And for a second plot twist—hold on to your seats—Tom's teacher girl friend tells him, "I don't think you two even realize how much you mean to each other. Now go to Mary and stop playing the father. You've been in love with the girl for weeks." (EEE-YEW! Are you listening, Dr. Freud?) Before we've fully recovered, Tom has invited Mary over for tea and told her that he has researched her past and found that she is indeed not his daughter—she was adopted by the Hagens from an orphanage in Evanston, Illinois. Too bad someone didn't come forward to tell us that in the beginning so we wouldn't have had to wade through all this molasses.

Tom promises to send Mary through college and take care of her for the rest of her days. In the final scene, we see Tom and Mary on a train pulling out of the station, waving happily. As the train disappears, one old man standing on the platform says to another, "Well, what're we gonna talk about now?" How about bad movies?

Unforgettable Performances

When you take off the tap shoes, the skimpy Raggedy-Ann dresses, the four-inch-long blond curls, and the Grand-Canyon-deep dimples, you still come up with Shirley Temple. For "On the Good Ship Lollipop" that's great, but as the star of a heart-wrenching melodrama? Portraying the tormented Mary Hagen, Miss Temple treats the whole affair as another animal cracker in her soup, or at worst a fly in the mustard. As the *New York Times*'s Bosley Crowther pointed out, "She acts with the mopish dejection of a school child who has just been robbed of a two-scoop ice cream cone. And when she performs, in the school play, some scenes from *Romeo and Juliet*—well!" Certainly this Shakespearean interlude, intended to showcase Miss Temple's dramatic range, must rank as one of the most hilarious high-camp moments in cinema history. Unfortunately, this is one role in which Shirley can't tap-dance her way out of trouble. In fact, she was not so embarrassed again until her unsuccessful race for Congress some twenty years later.

Rory Calhoun, endowed with one of the most prominent widow's peaks in show business, seems to be biting his lip throughout the movie . . . probably to keep from laughing. It's not every young actor who gets to walk out on an actress known since her childhood as America's Little Sweetheart.

The most sympathetic performance in this ridiculous film is turned in by Ronald Reagan. With his deadpan approach, he manages to convey to the audience the feeling that he, too, knows the film is absolutely absurd, and there's nothing anyone can do about it. His stolid, color-less, grin-and-bear-it performance is actually more reminiscent of his later rival Gerald Ford than it is of the smooth, professional Ronald Reagan we've all come to know so well.

Immortal Dialogue

(Mrs. Miller meets Mrs. Hagen on the street with the new baby.)

MRS. MILLER: Precious child. She's very sweet, but where in the world did she get that color hair and those eyes?

MRS. HAGEN: She was born with them.

* * *

GIRL FRIEND: Of course, it's only gossip . . . rumor. My mother said that nobody really knows.

MARY HAGEN: Knows what?

GIRL FRIEND: Who you are.

MARY: Who I am? I'm me, of course. Mary Hagen.

GIRL FRIEND: That's just it. Are you Mary Hagen, or are you . . . ?

MARY: What are you talking about?

* * *

MARY: Mother . . . who am I?

MRS. HAGEN: What did you say?

MARY: I said, who am I? Please tell me the truth.

MRS. HAGEN: Who are you? Why . . . why . . . you're Mary. Our girl. Didn't I have you baptized by the Reverend Sparland? Didn't I raise you like other girls' mothers?

* * *

DEWEY (Conrad Janis): How 'bout it? C'mon. Let's hit the high spots.

GIRL FRIEND: Why don't you go somewhere and catch yourself, you foul ball!

* * *

GIRL FRIEND: Mary, you're never gonna be happy if you're always gonna be sad! Now you've got nice teeth and you took two years of French. So why not try to see the bright side of things!

The Story Behind the Film

In the spring of 1945, Shirley Temple married the up-and-coming star John Agar (see *Jet Attack*), and in July of that year, on the set of *That Hagen Girl*, Shirl announced that she was expecting a baby in January. Whether the pregnancy had anything to do with her performance is anyone's guess. When asked what kind of career she had planned for her child, she quipped, "Are you kidding? It's going to have the career of a baby!" It was a better line than anything she was given to say in the film.

Ronald Reagan also had his share of disabilities during the production, including a case of near fatal pneumonia. His first day back on the set after a stint in the hospital involved his rescuing Miss Temple from a freezing cold lagoon. He went through with it (a real trouper, that Reagan!) but it hardly increased his fondness for a project that he already resented.

Miss Temple later referred to *That Hagen Girl* as her best adult film. "I'm not too proud of the movies I made as a grown-up except *That Hagen Girl*, which nobody remembers but which gave me a chance to act," she said. Unfortunately, we do remember, and fortunately, Miss Temple has changed her name and her career.

Ronald Reagan's recollections of the film are notably less pleasant. In his autobiography, *Where's the Rest of Me?*, he describes his long struggle to turn down the script, and laments his failure to do so. "Every so often now it pops up on 'The Late Late Show,' " he writes, "and I'm reminded of how right my first actor's instinct was and how wrong I was to go against that instinct and do the picture. . . . When Jack Warner called me in and laid it on the line regarding the big investment they had tied up in the screenplay and then asked me for my help as a personal favor, I was all out of arguments. . . . Even after I'd agreed to do the picture I tried to talk the director into a sixth rewrite that would have put Shirley in the arms of her schoolboy romance, Rory Calhoun, and matched me with a school-teacher in the story. Trying to put this over, I

Tom Bates (Ronald Reagan) and the troubled Mary Hagen (Shirley Temple) are united in the heartwarming conclusion of That Hagen Girl. *As Reagan observed in his autobiography: "You are left to guess as to whether we are married, just traveling together, or did I adopt her."*

spoke one sentence too many to Peter Godfrey, our director. I said, 'You know, people sort of frown on men marrying girls young enough to be their daughters.' He gave me a long, level look and answered quietly, 'I'm old enough to be my wife's father.' That didn't leave me much in the way of an answer." Actually, it left Ronnie up Hagen Creek without a paddle.

The Balance Sheet

As might be expected considering the quality of this film, its sneak preview turned out to be a disaster. The audience was hardly shy in expressing its displeasure. As Ronald Reagan recalls, "Came the moment on screen when I said to Shirley, 'I love you,' and the entire audience en masse cried, 'Oh, no!' I sat huddled in the darkness until I was sure the lobby would be empty. You couldn't have gotten me to face that audience for a million bucks. Before release the line was edited out of the picture, leaving us with a kind of oddball finish in which we climb on a train—Shir-

ley carrying a bouquet—and leave town. You are left to guess as to whether we are married, just traveling together, or did I adopt her. Maybe a late night TV sponsor can run a contest: 'Was I passionate or paternal to the present Mrs. Black?' " Judging from Reagan's performance, how about just impartial?

The moguls at Warner Brothers may have been worried by the sneak preview, but they moved forward anyway with a major promotional campaign for their film. One poster featured the tormented faces of Reagan and Temple on a flaming red background, with the caption: "Around Her Young Heart She Wore the Scarlet Letter of Another Woman's Shame." One gets the feeling that someone in the publicity department got *That Hagen Girl* mixed up with another movie. At the time of release, an ad in *Variety* proclaimed, "That Hagen Girl Is Going to Make a Big Name for Herself." Yes, she is—and it's going to be "mud." Warner Brothers was left with considerable egg on its face. *Variety*'s comment that the film was doing only "mild" business was the gentlest way of breaking the bad news. It did about $40,000 during its first week in *three* Los Angeles theaters. The film did weak business all across the country . . . *especially* in small towns.

In addition to *That Hagen Girl*, director Peter Godfrey was responsible for such other triumphs as *Make Your Own Bed, One Last Fling,* and *He's a Cockeyed Wonder.* We hope that his May-December marriage turned out better than his films.

For Ronald Reagan, *That Hagen Girl* marked a personal setback. He lost the lead part in *Rocky Mountain* to Errol Flynn because the studio believed he was somehow responsible for *Hagen*'s financial failure. Fortunately, Mr. Reagan has long since managed to escape the stigma attached to him by this film, and he has moved on to bigger and better roles.

SPECIAL AWARD

The J. Edgar Hoover Catch 'Em and Kill 'Em Award is hereby presented, with all due humility, to the authors of this volume, who managed to bring to light this skeleton in the closet of two prominent American politicians.

One would never guess that locating a print of a notoriously awful movie would be so difficult. One almost imagines some desperate film distributor standing on a street corner, trying to give prints of flops away. But in the case of *That Hagen Girl*, we found that we were up against . . . well, what seemed like organized suppression.

First of all, we had the presidential campaign of '76 to contend with. The FCC said that if *That Hagen Girl* or any other Ronald Reagan movie were shown, television stations would have to give equal time to Gerald Ford and show one of his movies.

Whenever we'd mention the film to an acquaintance, we'd get responses such as, "Oh yeah. I saw that on television a couple of years ago. It was terrible." It seemed as if everyone in the world had seen this film but us. We checked all television stations and all film libraries in Southern California. No one had a print, not even to show us *privately*. If the TV stations had once owned copies of this film which they showed regularly, then those copies had now mysteriously disappeared. Some rumors had it that Mr. Reagan had bought up all the prints himself to keep the film from being used against him politically. If a few nervous breakdowns were enough to ruin Thomas Eagleton's candidacy for national office, couldn't *That Hagen Girl* help destroy Ronald Reagan?

In general, we look with skepticism on paranoid conspiracy theories, but as we continued our search, our suspicions began to deepen. We soon learned that the film we were after, along with all postwar Warner Brothers films, had been sold to United Artists. Our inquiries to the Los Angeles office of that firm were met with a lot of embarrassed, or perhaps frightened silences. After calling several times we were finally told, "You better call New York about that."

So with fingers deftly crossed, we wrote to New York: to Mr. Robert Schwartz, vice-president of UA. We were sent the following reply:

Thank you very much for your letter of July 19th relative to a screening of the 1947 Warner Brothers picture *That Hagan* [sic] *Girl*.

There is a depository at the University of Wisconsin which includes a print of *That Hagan Girl,* and I am sure that if you write directly to the University indicating why you wish to view the picture they will permit you to do so, but this research must be done at the University of Wisconsin. I cannot permit you to view the picture in Los Angeles.

The University of Wisconsin! One would think that somewhere in those vast storage bastions in Hollywood there'd be one—just one—measly print of this lousy movie. Boy. Some people.

By this time we had a personal vendetta. We put on our Captain Ahab hats and wrote to the University of Wisconsin at Madison. We received no reply. Finally, we called long-distance and a special screening was arranged.

When we arrived at the film "depository" (what an appropriate title for *That Hagen Girl's* last resting place!) we were not permitted to use our tape recorders to help make a transcript of the film's dialogue. We were seated in a tiny room in front of a Steenbeck viewing machine, but fortunately we were allowed to run the film backward and forward to our hearts' content. And the cost of this screening—free. The plane fare to Wisconsin, however, made it one of the most expensive admission prices we had ever encountered.

Jerry Lewis shows his devotion to his fiancée, Janet Leigh, in the climactic party scene from Three on a Couch.

250

THREE ON A COUCH (1966)

Directed by: JERRY LEWIS
Written by: BOB ROSS and SAMUEL A. TAY-LOR
Produced by: JERRY LEWIS
Music by: LOUIS BROWN
Featuring: JERRY LEWIS, JANET LEIGH, JAMES BEST, MARY ANN MOBLEY, GILA GOLAN, LESLIE PARRISH, KATHLEEN FREEMAN, BUDDY LESTER, RENZO CESANA, FRITZ FELD, SCATMAN CROTHERS

Columbia Pictures

The Critics Rave

"Unintentionally *un*funny."
> —Leonard Maltin, *TV Movies*

"Most of it is just dull and even Jerry's moments of clowning are few and far between."
> —*Cue*

"Only incurable Jerry Lewis junkies will find something of value in *Three on a Couch.* . . . The star does four impersonations, all equally inept, epicene, and repulsive. Janet Leigh and Mary Ann Mobley are among the unfortunate females involved in this mess."
> —Judith Crist, *TV Guide to the Movies*

"No subtlety or depth. . . . The trouble with Mr. Lewis's impersonations is that he's done them all so many times, in one or more variations, that anyone who's seen two of his films has pretty well seen all of them."
> —Bosley Crowther, *New York Times*

"*Three on a Couch* seems to have been written on the 'Three Bears' principle: first, Papa Bear

says it, then Mama Bear says it, then Baby Bear says it. And every repetition is stretched out interminably. . . . The film lacks wit for the same reason that it lacks pathos—it has no sparkle, no mischief, no excess. . . . Extraordinarily plodding development . . . boring caricatures. . . . *Three on a Couch* is Jerry's tomb."

—Raymond Durgnat, *Films and Filming*

"Lowest rating. . . . Stay on your couch and don't bother with Jerry's."

—Steven H. Scheuer, *Movies on TV*

Plot Summary

Jerry Lewis plays Christopher Pride, an American artist who wins a prize of $10,000 to paint a mural in Paris. He wants to take his fiancée Liz (Janet Leigh) with him for a Paris honeymoon, but his sweetie refuses. She is a psychiatrist, and she refuses to leave her patients behind until they are "cured." It turns out that her patients are three beautiful young women who all hate men because of their previous love affairs. In desperation, Chris comes up with the "brilliant" idea of posing as three separate suitors and making the man-hating patients fall in love with him. That way, the girls will be cured and then Liz can accompany him to Paris. The underlying premise, of course, is that all young ladies become happy and healthy as soon as they develop any sort of interest in a man. As usual, Hollywood provides some marvelous insights into feminine psychology.

With the aid of a doctor friend, Ben (James Best), Jerry Lewis gets his chance to do a series of hackneyed impersonations while courting the females. When Chris asks Ben why he is taking so much time in helping him achieve his goal, Ben sincerely replies, "It's good for business. I want you and Liz to get married and have lots of babies so I can deliver them." First, Chris/Jerry dresses up as a cowboy named Ringo Raintree to attract Gila Golan, one of the three pretty patients. This girl goes for the rugged type (Jerry Lewis?) and immediately falls in love when she hears about Ringo's ranch. Next, Jerry imitates an athletic dolt named Warren, who wins the affection of a karate-chopping amazon (Mary Ann Mobley). Last, but not least, Chris has to capture the heart of a shy zoologist (Leslie Parrish) from the Old South. She is so frightened of men that Chris first dresses up as a woman in order to catch her attention. Outfitted in a red wig and extra-large dress, Chris talks of his (her?) cousin Rutherford who is an insect buff and arranges a meeting for the two. The three girls, all having met new boy friends, no longer need their psychiatrist, and Liz plans to leave for Paris with Chris.

To celebrate this triumph, Chris and Liz invite their best friend Ben over for cocktails, and the three join hands and dance a ring-around-the-rosy chanting, "We're going to Paris! We're going to Paris! We're going to Paris!" Liz's secretary arranges a surprise farewell party for them and naturally invites—who else?—the three mixed-up female patients, who are now all convinced that they are in love.

In the final party sequence, the crackling tension is provided by Jerry Lewis' attempts to hide from the three girls. At this point, the action manages to sink even lower than the inane level of the script, as the characters shout out their dialogue, often unintelligibly. Here, as in the rest of the film, director-producer-star Jerry Lewis makes every ten-second gag last at least six minutes. Some comic highlights include: Ben getting his arm caught in an elevator (always good for a million yuks), Chris bumping his nose on the elevator's doors (this is repeated three times), Liz's secretary spilling champagne in Chris's lap, and a wide variety of trips, falls, stumbles, and bumps.

Eventually, each of Liz's patients recognizes Chris as her own boy friend, and all three realize that they've been had. Naturally, Liz blows her stack. But the three patients insist that they have learned about men from the experience and still feel fine. Liz still refuses to speak to Chris until he threatens to commit suicide. Liz, thinking that he has actually done himself in, admits that she loved him and that he should have known it. But, ha ha, Chris didn't commit suicide after all! He's still alive and well. The film ends with all the major characters yukking it up, holding hands, and marching directly into the camera. What an uproarious finale. We haven't laughed so hard since our last automobile accident.

Unforgettable Performances

The most noteworthy aspect of Jerry Lewis' performance is his hair styling. His head seems to have been treated with a mixture of axle grease and Shinola shoe polish. Every strand drips with goo, and the ducktail in back of his head suggests that the waterfowl in question has been the victim of an oil spill. His impersonations—supposedly the highlight of his performance—would be enough to bore even a birthday party full of seven-year-olds. The only sequence in which Lewis manages to muster some enthusiasm for his own "antics" comes in the scene in which he plays the part of a woman. In that sequence, we hear him holding a dramatic dialogue with himself while struggling to free his body of nectarine breasts under his bra and other pertinences of drag. Believe it or not, Lewis looks more comfortable here than during his romantic clinches with Janet Leigh.

Ms. Leigh, as the dedicated lady psychiatrist and Jerry's fiancée, looks haggard and embarrassed. She is supposed to be a competent professional, but with her slight whining voice and cutie-pie mannerisms she would have been better cast as a proud housewife in a floor-wax commercial.

Danny Costello appears on screen for only 135 seconds, but in his role as a "ballroom singer" he manages to steal what little show there is. In his part, he is asked to sing the torch song "A Now and Later Love" (see IMMORTAL DIALOGUE), which, quite unintentionally, provides the film with its funniest moments. Costello belts out this number to the dancing couple of Jerry Lewis and Janet Leigh, and occasionally turns a knowing glance in their direction. Lewis' unforgettable ducktail dances past the camera as Ms. Leigh loves up his hair (sticky fingers!). Mr. Costello complements the absurd music and the limp, neo-big-band sound with a gaping mouth and a prominent view of throbbing tonsils.

Immortal Dialogue

(Chris learns from the French Ambassador that he has just won a prize for his art work.)

Christopher Pride (Jerry Lewis) offers a hearty greeting to his friends James Best and Gila Golan. Lewis himself produced and directed this tasteless story of a lady psychiatrist and her patients.

AMBASSADOR: Ze first prize is fifty thousand francs. In American money zat ees ten thousand dollars.
ATTACHÉ (adding): Give or take a little.
CHRIS: As long as you give, I'll take.

   * * *

(Chris greets Liz's secretary, Murphy.)
CHRIS: Hi, Murphy, you precious pussycat!

   * * *

Love Song: "A Now and Later Love"
 My love is a complete love
 A once only love.
 A love that makes my world
 Stand still.
 To some, it may seem strange—such a love
 Nothing on earth could ever change such a love.
 Who but the gods could have arranged such a love?
 It's a now and later love.

   * * *

(Mary Lou (Leslie Parrish) is confronted by a drunk at the party.)
MARY LOU: If y'all would 'scuse me, Ah'm lookin' for the doctor.
DRUNK: Oh, I happen to be a doctor, but I'm

not in surgery today. You see, I'm driving the ambulance. Say, what's your name?

MARY LOU: Ah do declare!

DRUNK: Clare. Oh, that's a pretty name!

The Story Behind the Film

Three on a Couch was Jerry Lewis' thirty-fourth starring role and the ninth motion picture he had directed. It was, however, his first film for Columbia Pictures. For the previous seventeen years he had worked for Paramount Pictures, but after his last Paramount project (*Boeing Boeing* with Tony Curtis) the relationship was terminated. It's unclear whether it was Lewis or the studio execs who really initiated the break, but after noting the horrid quality of *Boeing Boeing* we certainly have our suspicions.

For the man-hating patients in *Three on a Couch* Lewis picked three eminent beauties with no acting ability. They were Mary Ann Mobley, a former Miss America; Gila Golan, a former Miss Israel; and Leslie Parrish, the former NBC "color girl" whom the network used as "an example of the wonders to be seen on color television." James Best, who played Ben in the film, was on the verge of giving up acting forever until he received a part in *Three on a Couch*. It was his first intentionally comic role, and Best hoped—in vain—that the film would open up a new career for him.

Three on a Couch was shot at various California locations: West Los Angeles, near the ship SS *Roosevelt* in San Francisco, and in Arcadia. An entire Los Angeles city block was roped off for filming the department store sequence, and the interior shooting required six sound stages at Columbia Studios.

The Balance Sheet

Columbia Pictures launched a large promotional campaign to try to sell *Three on a Couch* to the public. Director-star Jerry Lewis appeared on numerous national talk shows, on which he issued bromides such as "Directing is a magnificent challenge. I like it. I intend to do more of it."

Other imaginative promotional techniques emphasized the number three (as in *Three on a Couch*). For instance, sidewalks around the theater where the picture was playing were stenciled with the number "3" for several blocks. A newspaper contest was suggested with prizes going to readers who circled the most "3's" printed in the classified-ad section. Triplets, naturally, would be allowed into the theater without charge.

The promotional wizards at Columbia also suggested that auditions could be held in the theater for children with the best impersonations of Jerry Lewis. (Kids below the age of eight must have been particularly well suited for this competition.) Even more obnoxious was the suggestion in the pressbook that in honor of the man-hating girls in the film, "a local 'We Hate Men Club' of girls who have been disappointed in love" should be formed. Interested women would leave their names and addresses in a designated box at the theater and they would later be invited to a get-together dinner at a local restaurant. Eventually a "debate" would be arranged, with a crusading member of the We Hate Men Club pitted against an angry male advocating the case of *women* haters." A couple of the girls from the club would also, at some point, march through the city proudly carrying a banner proclaiming "We Hate Men! Why? See *Three on a Couch*." Certainly anyone who did see that film would understand the antipathy of the "man haters" toward the sex of its producer-director-star.

The film was advertised with stirring lines such as "Move Over, Casanova!!! Here Comes the Greatest Lover of Them All!" or "Jerry's a Triple Threat Hero! Three-in-One Lover! He's got three love-starved lulus to handle . . . it isn't easy playing Threezy!" Domestically the film grossed over $2.5 million, turning in a fair profit.

Leslie Parrish, the former NBC "color girl," went on to a particularly interesting career, working on another spectacular film in 1973. This time she wasn't required to do any acting. Instead, she served as a research assistant for that celebrated bird dropping *Jonathan Livingston Seagull* (q.v.).

THE TRIAL OF BILLY JACK (1974)

Directed by: FRANK LAUGHLIN
Written by: FRANK and TERESA CHRISTINA
Produced by: JOE CRAMER
Featuring: TOM LAUGHLIN, DELORES TAYLOR, TERESA LAUGHLIN, VICTOR IZAY, RUSSELL LANE, GEO ANNE SOSA, LYNN BAKER, RILEY HILL, SPARKY WATT, GUS GREYMOUNTAIN, SACHEEN LITTLE-FEATHER, MICHAEL BOLLAND, BONG SOO HAN, WILLIAM WELLMAN, JR.

United Artists

The Critics Rave

"It is one of the longest, slowest, most pretentious and self-congratulatory ego trips ever put on film."
—Charles Champlin, *Los Angeles Times*

"Piece of dreck . . . scales the heights of amateur movie making with out-of-focus photography, sloppy editing, blurred sound track, and horse-opera distortion of historical events . . . three hours of illustrated mind rot."
—*Gallery*

"One of the biggest piles of pretentiousness ever made. Laughlin's once quiet Billy Jack has turned into an unbearably preachy Billy Jerk."
—John Barbour, *Los Angeles*

"Movie-Western clichés and wretched sentiment . . . padded out with an Ed Sullivan-like grab bag of variety acts. These range from stagy musical numbers that are multiracial equivalents of the grand finales of the old Garland-Rooney pictures to long mumbo-jumbo mystical sequences that only a Khalil Gibran devotee could find riveting."
—Frank Rich, *New Times*

In a touching moment from The Trial of Billy Jack, Carol (Teresa Laughlin) teaches a one-armed child (Michael Bolland) to play the guitar with his hook. Delores Taylor and Victor Izay ("Doc") look on from a distance.

"Twice as bad as the original 1971 film, and not just because it's an hour longer . . . scenes of revolting violence and banal blandness alternate against some very handsome scenery with an incoherence that only a mindless twelve-year-old could tolerate."

—Judith Crist, *New York*

"Unintentionally funny. New Left rhetoric, translated to the screen in the most juvenile manner imaginable . . . political brainwashing of the most irresponsible kind."

—Benjamin Stein, *Wall Street Journal*

"A repetitive, elephantine mock-epic . . . overlong . . . this sequel proved more of a trial for me than it was for Billy. . . ."

—Donald J. Mayerson, *Cue*

"A blindingly dumb and joyless movie. . . . The characters are faceless automatons who babble clichés. . . ."

—Vincent Canby, *New York Times*

"Feeble plot. . . . A little of everything is dropped in along the way, from Indian rights to mysticism . . . to a My Lai-style slaughter. Shoddily as they are staged, Billy Jack's fights are the only portions of the film with the slightest life at all."

—Jay Cocks, *Time*

"This film probably represents the most extraordinary display of sanctimonious self-aggrandizement the screen has ever known. . . . I fled the theater. . . . They've brought the worst of mass culture together with the worst of the counterculture."

—Pauline Kael, *The New Yorker*

Plot Summary

Jean Roberts (Delores Taylor), head of the famed Freedom School in Arizona, lies injured in a hospital bed. A reporter asks her about the "massacre" at the school in which Jean was wounded. Jean tells the reporter, "I wouldn't know where to begin," but goes on with her excruciating story anyway. In the truest Shakespearean sense, it proves "a tale/told by an idiot, full of sound and fury,/Signifying nothing."

In a series of flashbacks, we meet Billy Jack, an intense American Indian/Vietnam vet/kung fu expert with grim chubby cheeks and suspiciously light skin. Back in the original *Billy Jack* our hero murdered a sexual pervert who had brutally raped and beaten our friend Jean (everybody's favorite victim) and in the sequel the avenging Billy must stand trial for his life. In the midst of the trial he flashes back to his memories of the Vietnam war (giving us, thank you, a flashback within a flashback). We watch a graphic and bru-

Everybody's favorite victims, Jean (Delores Taylor) and Billy Jack (Tom Laughlin), are reunited in the tragic climax of The Trial of Billy Jack. *Billy was supposed to be dying at this point but apparently the prospect of the upcoming sequel—*Billy Jack Goes to Washington—*restored his will to live.*

tal massacre of civilians (the first in a series), but to show that B.J.—and presumably the filmmakers—disapprove of such activities, we see our noble savage hanging his head in shame and standing aside as the butchery proceeds. In other words, the bloodlust of the audience is appeased at the same time as its social conscience is stroked.

Though we now all know of Billy's laudable "sensitivity," Mr. Jack is eventually sentenced to from five to fifteen years in a penitentiary. To occupy our time as we wait for his release, we enjoy a leisurely review of the Freedom School. This noble institution was launched in an abandoned academy, and organized largely by the "kids" themselves, including a collection of bratty teeny-boppers, occasional orphans and cripples, a sprinkling of American Indians, former drug addicts, and New Left drop-outs. This mixed bag proves so successful that soon the school acquires its own newspaper, magazine, recording studio, television station, and small fleet of helicopters. Don't ask how or why: all this equipment is important to the plot. Meanwhile, the school replaces old-fashioned subjects such as reading and history with courses in tennis, Yoga, and belly dancing.

After five years in prison, Billy Jack is let off for good behavior and makes his way to the Freedom School and his old friends. He is welcomed back in a touching ceremony in the cafeteria. A spaced-out student named Carol (in real life Te-

resa Laughlin, daughter of producer-director-writer-star Tom Laughlin) sings a song she specially wrote for the occasion, "Shed a Tear." Billy also hooks up once more with his old Indian pals. How do we know they are Indians? They bear such authentic names as Turning Water, Little Uncle Tommyhawk, Blue Elk, Thunder Mountain, Little Bear, and Running Deer. One of the older and wiser Indians, known to everyone as "Grandfather," advises Billy to go on a spiritual journey, with the help of some readily available hallucinogenic drugs. On this journey, Billy encounters his "inner self" (actor Laughlin, his body painted in watercolors), "shadow demons" in the form of snakes and bats, and, naturally, a "Vision Maiden" who takes him on a mystical tour of violence through the ages.

While Billy is tripping out, his little buddies at the Freedom School are having a ball playing with their TV station. They make a series of what they themselves describe as "scorching exposés." Not only do the young sleuths at the school personally blow the lid off the Watergate cover-up (take note, Bernstein and Woodward), but they also discover bizarre conspiracies organized by the CIA, the FBI, the Senate, furniture store owners, jail wardens, all human beings over the age of thirty-five, and so forth. A couple of bigoted officials begin to worry about these "scorching exposés" and decide to do something about it. They brutally torture one of the young Indians until Billy Jack arrives on the scene and saves the day. Throwing off his shoes and socks, our hero does several karate kicks, a couple of kung fu kicks, and a half-dozen chorus line kicks for good measure. All this is accompanied by blood, guts, eyes, limbs, and saliva spurting onto the camera lens and bone-crunching sound effects on the sound track. It's a fun-filled frolic the whole family can enjoy!

The carnage proves too much for the government, and the National Guard is dispatched to occupy the campus. The students barricade themselves in their buildings, and as they await the inevitable apocalypse, they enjoy one of the most tasteless scenes in cinema history. One of the students at the Freedom School is a boy who is missing an arm: we are told that his father had ripped his arm clean off in a past fit of pique. Now the child has a metal, mechanical arm, but thanks to the inspirational aid of his fellow student Carol, this is hardly a handicap. Combining the best of Julie Andrews in *The Sound of Music* and Anne Bancroft in *The Miracle Worker*, Carol has taught the unfortunate child how to play the guitar with his hook! This little concert is intended to lift the spirits of the frightened students, but apparently the National Guardsmen are so offended by the gross display that they decide to exterminate everyone in sight. Oh boy, another massacre! In one particularly touching scene, we see the scared one-armed guitar-picker hugging his cute little rabbit when this hulking "pig" in a gas mask comes over and creams him. Jean Roberts, leader of the school, comes running out of the building with tears streaming down her face, pleading for peace and understanding. Bang, bang, bang. She gets it, and rolls around on the ground for a while. Billy Jack and Carol are also shot down. Finally, Blue Elk (you guessed it, one of the Indians) comes out with a group of his colleagues and informs the rampaging National Guardsmen that an obscure Indian treaty from the 1880s prohibits the Feds from setting foot on this soil. Disgruntled, the troops disperse and begin looking for some little old ladies to beat up.

We now cut back to the wounded Jean Roberts, still crying, in her hospital bed. The reporter by her side has just about fallen asleep when Jean announces that the students (what's left of them) will attempt to rebuild the Freedom School by go-

ing around and begging for money. Naturally, Billy Jack and Carol were only wounded, and the film ends with the central characters in wheelchairs going into their favorite chapel. An afterword is superimposed on the screen to make sure we get the message. It reads, "All We Are Saying Is Give Peace a Chance." Considering the bloody and horribly violent film we have just witnessed, this final touch reaches the nadir of hypocrisy.

Unforgettable Performances

Tom Laughlin's "characterization" of Billy Jack consists principally of inexplicable little smiles emitted periodically throughout the film. These smiles have nothing at all to do with the action on the screen or the emotions he is supposed to be expressing. Perhaps someone told Laughlin that American Indians were descended from Asiatic stock, so the star decided to play Billy J. as "inscrutable." Actually, Laughlin seems to express himself more readily with his feet than he does with his face: the martial arts kicks that he directs at assorted bad guys are his strongest statements in the film.

Delores Taylor, who in real life is Mrs. Tom Laughlin, plays Jean Roberts as if she were suffering from an unspeakably unpleasant allergy. Tears are constantly in her eyes, and she can seldom control an urge to sob. Enough water is generated by her hysterics to make the Arizona desert bloom—which would have been a better application of her lachrymosic virtuosity than this feeble attempt at acting.

Teresa Laughlin, the fifteen-year-old daughter of Tom Laughlin and Delores Taylor, plays Carol, the inspirational student leader at the Freedom School. Her singing is almost good enough to pass muster at a high school talent show, but her acting is out of the question. She communicates earnestness by raising her voice and communicates suffering by narrowing her eyes. Teresa seems to have inherited some of her mother's crying ability, and turns to that device when unable to think of anything better to do. Her few tears give her flat performance its only seasoning—a decidedly salty flavor.

Immortal Dialogue

(Billy Jack is questioned by his prosecutor at his trial.)

PROSECUTOR: Do you expect us to believe that you have absolutely no fear of the death penalty?

BILLY JACK: I have a lot of fear, but I have a lot more respect. Long ago, I learned that he's my constant companion. He eats with me, he walks with me, he even sleeps with me.

PROSECUTOR (not understanding him): I'm sorry, I must have missed something back there. Who is this faithful companion of yours?

BILLY JACK: Death.

(A startled buzz runs through the courtroom.)

*   *   *

Song: "*Shed a Tear*" (written by Teresa Laughlin)

> Shed a tear, Running Deer:
> Don't turn back, Billy Jack!
> I am crying
> Are you dying
> Just for me?
>
> You aren't an animal, you're a man;
> It wasn't fair, it just wasn't fair; . . .
>
> What will happen to you now?
> You've got to live, but I don't know how;
> I am crying
> Are you dying
> Just for me?

(Everyone listening suddenly bursts into tears.)

*   *   *

(Billy Jack is about to experience a mystical trip as he takes an ancient Indian ceremonial rite.)

BILLY JACK (speaking to a wise old Indian whom he calls Grandfather): Grandfather, I would be honored if you would teach me how to pierce the veil and go to that other world and make my own inward journey to find my own center. . . . I want to make the inward journey.

GRANDFATHER: Many cannot survive the dangerous inward journey; but if you do, in time you will come face to face with your own shadow. Then you will know what I mean.

*   *   *

(The students ascend the mountain to ask Blue Elk if they can talk to Billy Jack.)

MALE STUDENT: Aw, come on, Blue Elk! We came all the way up here just to see Billy!

BLUE ELK: I can't help that. You can't see him now. This is a gathering of medicine men. Some of them are using smoke from religious herbs and others are purifying themselves for Billy's sacred journey. The whole mountain is closed.

FEMALE STUDENT: You mean they purify themselves just to take drugs?

BLUE ELK: If one has not fasted or purified oneself thoroughly—or if outsiders interfere—the spirit would be angry and make Billy sick or even take him away.

FEMALE STUDENT (relating): You mean like when a kid's tripping out; or on a real bummer?

The Story Behind the Film

In an attempt to excuse the juvenile nature of this wretched film, the Laughlins gave direction credit to Frank Laughlin, their nineteen-year-old son. The screenplay was credited to "Frank and Teresa Christina." It just so happens that the three Laughlin children are named Frank, Teresa, and Christina. Coincidentally, the original *Billy Jack* was allegedly directed by a person named "T. C. Frank." All of this familial namesmanship is intended to be clever and heartwarming, but the Laughlins should have considered what they were doing to their own children. If they didn't want to take credit for their films, that's fine: after all, who could blame them? But to burden their innocent children with the official responsibility for these cinematic turkeys surely must qualify as a prime example of child abuse.

In addition to the Laughlin family, other celebrities involved with this film included Kathy Cronkite, daughter of Walter Cronkite, in her screen debut, and Alexandra Nicholson, a former world champion trampolinist. *The Trial of Billy Jack* was shot in several different Arizona locations, including Phoenix, Tucson, the Grand Canyon, Monument Valley, and Canyon de Chelly. To finance this grandiose indulgence, the Laughlins put up $2.5 million of their own money, and the estimated total production cost ran to $7.8 million. These costs were greatly inflated by Tom

Laughlin's well-publicized temper tantrums on the set. A former employee of Laughlin's told *Rolling Stone*: "There were times when you could see him revving up . . . you could tell when he was going to have one of his purges. He'd get sick of the film . . . he'd hate the film, then he'd get these psychosomatic colds and wouldn't be able to work for three days . . . and then he'd explode and just fire everyone. It was sort of purgation for him. Then he'd go through this orgy of interviewing and hire a whole new bunch." Laughlin himself once sheepishly admitted, "I'm too volatile. Either you really like me and want to work for me. Or you really are threatened by me and hate my guts."

One of the people who did keep his job throughout this project was William Beaudine, Jr., who served as production manager. Beaudine is the son of the celebrated William ("One Shot") Beaudine, director of some of the biggest stinkers in Hollywood's history. The senior Beaudine's "credits" include *Jesse James Meets Frankenstein's Daughter*, *Bela Lugosi Meets a Brooklyn Gorilla*, *The Ape Man*, *Voodoo Man*, and *Billy the Kid Versus Dracula*.

The music for *The Trial of Billy Jack* was composed and conducted by Elmer Bernstein. After a long period of producing great scores for reputable motion pictures, Bernstein had finally returned to the glories of his *Robot Monster* (q.v.) days.

The Balance Sheet

The film was previewed to audiences around the country in rough-cut prints. The most important of these previews was in North Hollywood, where the youthful crowd was nearly 100 per cent enthusiastic about the film. When finally released, the movie was advertised with the stirring lines "There Is Only One Word for Him—Courage" and "The Picture You've Been Waiting For." The film opened on November 13, 1974, in what *Variety* claimed "may be the largest national saturation launch of any pic in memory." In its first week, it played simultaneously in thirteen hundred theaters and grossed a record-breaking $11 million. Business was helped by inventive publicity stunts, such as arranging karate demonstrations in theater lobbies and having a theater staff wear In-

Billy Jack magically commands an eagle to drop from the sky and land on his arm. Tom Laughlin—writer, director, and star of the Billy Jack films—has demonstrated an even more miraculous ability: making tens of millions of dollars from a series of wretched, self-indulgent movies.

dian costumes. The movie went on to gross an astounding $35 million in the United States alone. In the foreign market, however, it did very poorly. Tom Laughlin claimed that the reason for this was that it "had been banned in almost every country in the world." Laughlin said he became "curious why it never did any business overseas. I was shown a list that it cannot play in this country, cannot play in that country. . . ." Included on the list of nations banning *The Trial of Billy Jack* were France, England, Germany, Italy, Spain, Sweden, and Portugal. This might not be "almost every country in the world" but it is certainly enough to make a difference. Laughlin naturally assumed that the State Department, or the CIA, or some other conspiratorial agency was behind it: that the "scorching exposés" featured so prominently in the film caused the U.S. government to try to persuade its allies to ban the film. As of this writing, the State Department was unavailable for comment on Laughlin's theory.

At the original preview in North Hollywood, a diehard Billy Jack fan eagerly asked Laughlin if he planned yet another sequel. Laughlin answered with his characteristic modesty and reserve, "As long as there's still madness running this country, as long as people are rummaging in garbage cans for food, you're goddamned right we'll make another one!" He might have added that as long as people are foolish enough to pay good money to see such films, his family will be glad to continue cleaning up on them. The planned sequel will be a remake of the Frank Capra-Jimmy Stewart 1930s classic *Mr. Smith Goes to Washington.* The new title, sure enough, will be *Billy Jack Goes to Washington.* In bidding for remake rights on *Mr. Smith,* Laughlin had to compete with folk singer John Denver, who reportedly was interested in using the format for a starring vehicle of his own. Instead, we may be treated to another delightful spectacle, featuring everyone's favorite ass-kicking Indian, battling his way for peace, freedom, and human dignity down the halls of Congress.

SPECIAL AWARD

The Clifford Irving Memorial Embattled Artist Award to Tom Laughlin, for his infamous and ill-conceived "Billy Jack Versus the Critics" campaign. When *The Trial of Billy Jack* was re-released for the summer of 1975, Laughlin sponsored an essay contest to answer the question, "Why is it that critics are so totally out of touch with the audiences they are paid to review for?" $100,000 in prizes were offered to contestants in full-page ads in the *New York Times,* the *Los Angeles Times,* and many other newspapers. These ads generally took the form of "open letters" from Tom Laughlin, featuring a photograph of our hero wearing his traditional broad-brimmed Billy Jack hat with its beaded Indian hatband. In the text of these letters, Laughlin compared his work to Shakespeare's, quoted Jesus ("Judge not, that ye be not judged"), and generally wallowed in self-pity concerning the horrible reviews his film had received. At one point he suggested that in the future, newspapers and magazines give filmmakers equal space to defend their work and respond to negative reviews. He went all the way back to elementary school in attacking the pundits he described as "critic-monsters." He wrote, "This put-down process begins in school when a teacher grades a pupil on his or her understanding of a given book. By grading

the student, the teacher is placing his or her own subjective value judgment on someone else's inner personal experience, whereas the student should be free to enjoy the inner experience the book aroused without the imposition of someone else's opinion." If it's good enough for the Freedom School, it's good enough for America. Right, Billy?

As an ad campaign, "Billy Jack Versus the Critics" totally backfired. *New York* magazine called the campaign a "total disaster . . . the re-release of *Trial,* too soon after its original opening, did a fast el floppo." In fact, the advertising program was such a catastrophe that the reissue of the film played in theaters for only a week before Laughlin himself withdrew it. As for the public's reaction to Laughlin's lofty ideals, one theater manager explained, "There was no way to measure the effect of the campaign pro or con, because there weren't enough people around at the theater to ask."

The grand prizewinner in the Billy Jack essay contest was a graduate student in psychology named Brant Cortright, who was also director of the Do It Now Foundation drug abuse program. Mr. Cortright won $25,000 in the form of a negotiable check painted on a 7' × 20' canvas. Subtlety and an unerring sense of proportion have not always been among Mr. Laughlin's most endearing characteristics. Countless other prizes were awarded to the eager contestants, including a series of "Lloyd's Deluxe AM Pocket Radios." One of the lucky winners of a portable radio was John Morgan Wilson, who subsequently wrote an article about his experience for *Take One* magazine. "The problem was," he recalled, "I felt that Billy Jack, in taking on the critics in his typically gutsy way, was making an ass out of himself. . . . I never saw the film myself. The reviews, as you know, were terrible." Mr. Wilson reported that another winner in the essay contest said, "I actually felt that *The Trial of Billy Jack* was the most abominable product I have consumed in several years."

Did any of this manage to discourage Tom Laughlin? Not on your life, it didn't. "I'm going to write a paperback book," he proclaimed, "taking on each critic, pulling out his reviews, proving the dichotomy between each critic and the preferences of the popular audience." Go get 'em, Billy!

Robert Hooks, a talented actor, was totally wasted as "Mr. T" in the dismal blacksploitation film Trouble Man. *As one in a series of violent, super-cool ghetto heroes he was only "more plastic, more bullet-proof and more improbable than his predecessors."*

Don't worry, censors. That's a shotgun he's holding in his left hand.

TROUBLE MAN (1972)

Directed by: IVAN DIXON
Written by: JOHN D. F. BLACK
Produced by: JOEL D. FREEMAN
Music by: MARVIN GAYE
Featuring: ROBERT HOOKS, PAUL WIN-
FIELD, RALPH WAITE, WILLIAM SMITH-
ERS, PAULA KELLY, JULIUS HARRIS, JAMES
"TEXAS BLOOD" BROWN

Twentieth Century-Fox

The Critics Rave

"The latest in a lengthening line of black ghetto heroes, Mr. T is, if anything, more handsome, more plastic, more bullet-proof and more improbable than his predecessors. He is also (as played, with unwarranted self-satisfaction, by Robert Hooks) so cool as to make one suspect it isn't Coke he is constantly drinking but anti-freeze. Everything else is according to the black superman formula, including the general characterlessness, the carefully choreographed but tiresome violence, and the unhelpful dialogue, which is even more reliant than usual on exhortations to "Stay loose!" and "Move your arse!" One has to delve deep to find a redeeming feature. . . ."
—Clyde Jeavons, *Monthly Film Bulletin*

"Hollywood will be in big trouble if it turns out many more films like *Trouble Man*. . . . Practically every sentence in *Trouble Man* contains one of a dozen faddish slang words. They pepper the script like litter. So 'Man, if you don't dig this super cool black . . . stay away from the box office, you M——' If you do choose to go, all you will discover is that *Trouble Man* is a big rip-off, copy cat in form and inept in execution. . . . Director Ivan Dixon takes the whole thing seriously which makes it seem merely ludicrous, but

can't even raise the temperature to 'alive' in the meager action sequences."
—Bridget Byrne, *Los Angeles Herald Examiner*

". . . predictable, bland narrative . . most of the violence is staged unimaginatively and quickly becomes frustratingly boring. . . ."
—Glenn Lovell, *Hollywood Reporter*

"*Trouble Man* is an extremely troubled attempt to cash in on the black-movie boom and still lay claim to a conscience of its own—and therein lies its only interest. Its plot, characters and trappings adhere obediently to the commandments laid down by *Shaft*, the Father Divine of the genre."
—Charles Michener, *Newsweek*

"I had hoped to be left, at least, with some memorable music; but apart from the title song, Marvin Gaye's sound track is of the type that, although in the earlier films of this new genre was refreshing, now seems to have fallen into a well-hackneyed framework of basic riffs."
—Stuart James, *Films and Filming*

"A caper of excessive violence."
—Wanda Hale, *New York Daily News*

". . . lacks the uptight frenzy usually associated with this genre."
—*Variety*

"If sequels are contemplated, it might not be a bad idea to take the character—and this entire genre—in the general direction of parody. Regrettably, the actresses have been given nothing to do except lounge around, look decorative and wait for Mr. T to drop by."
—Gary Arnold, *Washington Post*

"In the most mindless fashion, this commercial film neutralizes not revolution but all sorts of other less cataclysmic social changes. . . . On the one hand, the action is that of the conventional black private-eye film, but the scenery looks like the illustrations for a prospectus for Century City, where, if we are good and don't rock the boat, we may all be able to live some day. Either Century City, or someplace just like it. . . .

Trouble Man is a horrible movie, but it's worth thinking about."
—Vincent Canby, *New York Times*

Plot Summary

The protagonist in this film is called Mr. T. One assumes from the title that "T" stands for trouble. It could also stand for tired, tuberculosis, tetanus, *tuchus*, or tomato. All of these would be just as applicable as trouble. Mr. T is a private detective (you'll never see a blacksploitation film about a dentist). His office is in the back of a pool hall in a black ghetto of Los Angeles. We soon learn that T is wealthy. He zooms around in a white Lincoln Mark IV with burgundy interiors (although the true sign of wealth would be having a white chauffeur), has a closet full of fifty suits, one hundred shirts, and at least that many pairs of boxer shorts. All the people of the neighborhood come to his billiard-hall throne room for help and advice. If they were really smart they'd take a look at the way he lives and go into business for themselves.

One day Mr. T is visited by two thugs named Chalky (Paul Winfield) and Pete (Ralph Waite). Now, guess which one is black and which is white. If you guessed that Chalky was the whitey, you're wrong—that would be stereotyping, and we certainly can't have any of that in a blacksploitation film. Pete and Chalky run some traveling crap games. Someone is raiding the games, and they want Mr. T to find out who it is and tell them to quit it. T's investigations lead him to a rival crap gamer named Big. T and Big hold a summit meeting in the pool hall, some cops march in, take T's gun, and murder Big with it. Perhaps they want to frame Mr. T? Right on! And you can bet they're not real cops either. T pulls a gun out of a Coke (Coca-Cola, that is) machine and puts the weapon into the hand of Big's corpse to make it look as if the big man drew first. Yes sir, you've got to get up pretty early to fool Mr. T. Eventually T discovers that Chalky and Pete were responsible for the nasty attempt to set him up, and he goes after them. First he sends his girl friend and best friend out of town so that they won't get hurt. Then he steals some guns from the evidence room of the local police station, and heads for Chalky's lair, a laundry plant in Soul Town. T sneaks up the dumbwaiter (he knows he's not allowed to use the front stairs), confronts Chalky, and in no time at all, *boom! boom!* Chalky's brains are all over everything. Lucky they're in a laundry.

Now Mr. T goes after Pete, his white enemy, who lives in a Century City penthouse (hey, it looks like there's some inequality here!). When T arrives at the apartment building, he finds Pete's all-white army waiting for him. With a few blasts of his gun, T knocks off all of Pete's henchmen, who seem hesitant to shoot back at T because they may mess up his wardrobe and, this time, there's no laundry close at hand. Pete is upstairs in his mirrored bedroom, cowering under the sheets. T storms up the elevator, breaks into Pete's bedroom, and kills the hood. He sees the mirrors and can't resist shooting them up too—since shattering glass worked so well for Orson Welles (*The Lady From Shanghai*), why not use it again?

Later, T carefully replaces his guns at police headquarters so the records will show that all the bodies that have been showing up with bullet holes in them all over Los Angeles were shot with guns that were in storage.

In the final scene, T drives happily away with a young black policewoman. Now we know the real reason he sent his girl friend out of town. We would have left too, but we paid to get in.

Unforgettable Performances

Robert Hooks plays Mr. T as though he were a corporate lawyer gone berserk. His immaculate wardrobe, precise diction, and elegant bearing all suggest an Ivy League common room more than a Watts pool hall. To add a touch of brutal realism, however, Mr. Hooks periodically spews such hip expressions as "Freeze, motherfucker!" But the pronunciation is so clear that we might be listening to a UN interpreter.

William Smithers portrays a police captain always on Mr. T's tail, like a bloodhound. And that's exactly the way he delivers his dialogue . . . like a dog. He is a member of the scream school of acting. He barks all his words loudly as if he were speaking to a deaf audience. Not deaf, Mr. Smithers, just asleep.

Paula Kelly, as T's girl friend, is an exciting presence, and it's a shame to see her used as inanimate set decoration.

Immortal Dialogue

CHI: Chalky sent me to say he wanted to see you on some business, Mr. T.
MR. T: You go tell Chalky he can kiss my black ass.

❖   ❖   ❖

SAM: Mah bruthah . . . he's in da slammer . . . can't get nobody to go bond fo' him. He skipped one time, Mr. T.
MR. T: That son of a bitch skipped twice. Don't jive me, Sam.
SAM: Dat's why I came t'you, Mr. T. He wouldn't run on you.
MR. T: He run on me, I'd feed him his ass in pieces.

❖   ❖   ❖

PETE (on phone): This is Pete Cockrell. I want to talk with Chalky.
MR. T: This is T . . . Chalky's dead . . . now I'm coming to get your ass!

❖   ❖   ❖

Love Scene:
GIRL FRIEND: Should I be worried for you?
MR. T: Yeah, worry. That's real good for you and it helps a lot. Shit, baby, there's never nothin' to worry about. Be cool.
GIRL FRIEND: If I didn't love you, I wouldn't even ask, baby.
MR. T (leaving): Later.

❖   ❖   ❖

POOL HALL OWNER: Closin' time, bruthahs.
DUDE: Wha' kind o' jive is that, man? It's only ten-thirty . . . we got plenty o' tahm!
POOL HALL OWNER: Mr. T says it's closin' time, dude.
DUDE: What the hell, man, I can shoot all day tomorrah!

265

* * *

MR. T: What's happenin', Willy?

NEWS VENDOR WITH YIDDISH ACCENT: Dun't ask . . . also dun't hef daughters who marry schmuck husbands!

The Jive Behin' The Flick

To achieve what they called an "uninterrupted sense of realism," *Trouble Man*'s producers shot on locations around Los Angeles. The pool hall was found in Central Los Angeles, the laundry in Culver City, and the penthouse in Century City. For one scene, in which Robert Hooks plays a heavy game of pool (heavy—right on!), a real live hustler was found to play the part of his opponent. The hustler's name was James "Texas Blood" Brown (hey—Texas Blood—right on!). The pressbook adopted a sociological tone and explained that "Texas is his original home and Blood is an ethnic idiom meaning young, black man" (hey, pressbook—right on!).

The film was written by John D. F. Black and produced by Joel D. Freeman, both white (white on!). After these two hit it big on their creation *Shaft*, they founded their own company, JDF/B Productions, and made *Trouble Man* as their first feature. They hired the token black from television's "Hogan's Heroes," Ivan Dixon, to direct the film.

Writer (write on!) Black is the winner of the "coveted" Edgar Award, presented to him by the Mystery Writers of America for his script to a TV movie called *The Thief*. His other credits include *House of Monsters, Three Guns for Texas, Nobody's Perfect* (you can say that again), and *Survival*.

The Balance Sheet

Pressbooks proclaimed that *Trouble Man* was "definitely geared to both the black and white audience while, at the same time, preserving the ethnic validity of storyline and character." And just listen to the public-spirited advertising campaign that Hollywood encouraged for this baby:

"*Trouble Man* Hot Line. Working with a radio station or disc jockey or newspaper, try to set up a *Trouble Man* 'Hot Line' for people with troubles— legitimate problems they need help in solving. These might be potholes on a street or a runaround from city bureaucrats or some other injustice. Perhaps it's streetlights that need fixing or a phony store with gyp merchandise, etc. The station (or whatever you have tied in with) promotes the whole idea. The public is invited to call *Trouble Man* on the 'Hot Line' and get help with their troubles." It's very simple; they just send someone out to shoot whoever's bothering you. Ads also promoted tie-ins with men's clothiers: "*Trouble Man* Is Fashion. All the chicks will notice your——suit, or——shirt." And wear your bloodstains proudly. With a hot ad campaign like this one, *Trouble Man* raked in $1,083,752 in eight weeks. Right on! No write-off! How's that for blood money?

The film boasted quite a few fine talents, such as Robert Hooks, of the famed Negro Ensemble Company of New York; Ralph Waite, who received fine notices for his performances in *Five Easy Pieces* and television's "The Waltons"; and Paul Winfield, from the film *Sounder*. Paula Kelly, who portrayed Mr. T's woman, was trained at Juilliard's School of the Performing Arts, and was one of the first women to display her pubic hair in *Playboy* magazine.

266

TWILIGHT ON THE RIO GRANDE
(1948)

Directed by: FRANK McDONALD
Written by: STUART E. McGOWAN
Featuring: GENE AUTRY and CHAMPION, JR.,
THE WONDER HORSE OF THE WEST. With:
STERLING HOLLOWAY, ADELE MARA, BOB
STEELE, CHARLES EVANS, MARTIN GAR-
RALAGA, THE CASS COUNTY BOYS

Republic Pictures

The Critics Rave

"Gene Autry has seldom been concerned with as
sad a Western adventure as the one in which he is
paraded under the title of *Twilight on the Rio
Grande*. It is possible that the kids will like this,
although it is likely that even they will laugh
when Autry jumps his horse on the rear of a truck
to make good an escape. . . . The script al-
lows only for an exceedingly slow picture. Nothing Frank McDonald's direction can do seems to
speed it up. . . ."

—Hollywood Reporter

"Border jewel smuggling action-drama puts
musical numbers ahead of the script."

—Film Daily

Plot Summary

While on vacation in a Mexican border town,
Gene Autry (Gene Autry) and his sidekick Pokie
(Sterling Holloway) discover their good friend
Dusty Morgan has been knifed in the back. Gene
is understandably upset. He sets out with Pokie
and the Cass County Boys to find the murderer.

But first they pause at the cemetery to sing the title song, "Twilight on the Rio Grande," at Dusty's graveside. The Cass County Boys are a strange lot of cowpokes—they pack guitars, maracas, and accordions instead of guns.

While investigating the murder, Gene learns from U. S. Customs officials that Dusty was probably murdered by smugglers. They wanted to impersonate Gene's pal in order to bring contraband jewelry across the border. The smugglers have bought the jewelry from a mysterious group of refugees, "who have been persecuted and betrayed so much before they came here that they are afraid and mistrustful of everyone . . . even the police."

Gene Autry in a tense moment from Twilight on the Rio Grande. *Can goodness and decency prevail in an imperfect world?*

Gene and Pokie start looking for clues. They walk the street at night in front of the cantina where their pardner Dusty was last seen, and sure enough, zing!, a knife comes flying through the air, missing them by inches. Gene goes to investigate. He scales the balcony of the cantina and bursts in on the local *chanteuse*, Elena Del Rio (Adele Mara). She refuses to speak but makes an appointment to talk to Gene later.

They rendezvous in a small rustic churchyard, complete with lamplighter. There Miss Del Rio explains that her father was murdered in the town several months earlier with the same brand of knife that killed Dusty. She agrees to help Gene in any way she can. Gene, however, seems preoccupied with the lamplighter, who is making his rounds in the churchyard. Suddenly Gene bursts into song: "He made the night a little brighter, wherever he would go . . . the old lamplighter of long, long ago. . . . His snowy hair was so much whiter beneath the candle glow. . . ." Miss Del Rio and the lamplighter listen with embarrassed smiles, particularly when Gene sings about the "snowy hair." The lamplighter is as bald as Dick Wessel in *Dick Tracy Versus Cueball* (q.v.).

Gene returns to the cantina, and Pokie has

Sterling Holloway (comic relief) and the Cass County Boys (musical relief) consort with our hero, Gene Autry. If you can't pick out the hero in this picture, please look for the white hat.

some exciting news. Someone planted some jewels in his saddlebag. The owner of the cantina, Jake (cantina owners are always named Jake), pauses near Pokie and seems particularly interested in the jewels. After Gene and Pokie leave the cantina, a lazy Mexican woodchopper named Mucho Pesos (Martin Garralaga) tells them that the cantina owner made a suspicious phone call as soon as they left. (That's right, a phone call. This is the 1940s, not the 1880s. Since the Old West is "timeless," Gene can play an old-fashioned cowboy and still enjoy all the modern conveniences.) Gene hatches a scheme, brilliant in its simplicity, to find out whom Jake called. He takes Pokie and the Cass County Boys to the phone company, and explains to the operators that they want to audition for a gig over the phone, and they'd like to practice it once to see if it works. Out come the accordion, the guitars, and the maracas, and the group belts out a bebop tune, "Ol' Grandad." While the operators are distracted, Gene checks the company records, and finds that Jake called a lawyer in town named Henry Blackstone.

In the dead of night, Gene breaks into Blackstone's office, only to find the shifty attorney waiting for him. Blackstone turns out to be the head smuggler, and he hands Gene over to his hench-

men to be shot, but Gene makes a daring escape on horseback. The great thing about being a cowboy in the Forties is that you no longer have to depend on antiquated equipment like horses. Just as Gene is about to be recaptured by Blackstone's pursuing henchmen, Pokie drives by in a flatbed truck. Gene and his horse, Champion, Jr., "the Wonder Horse of the West," jump safely onto the vehicle and escape with ease. And what happened to Champion, Sr.? He must have missed the truck in the first take.

Now Gene has the goods on Jake and Blackstone. But these smugglers are still one jump ahead. They clobber Miss Del Rio and Mucho, who turns out to be an insurance investigator, and send Miss Del Rio to the American hospital across the border with some jewels hidden in her handbag. But Gene and his boys are waiting, and the fight we've all been waiting for ensues.

Cowboy fights are interesting in several respects. First, the participants never break their hands when they slug their opponents in the jaw, and no one ever gets knocked out. And no one bleeds, either. Despite the number of groans, smacking noises, and screams we hear, the cowboys keep getting up for more as if their jaws were made of sponge rubber. When Blackstone finally goes down and stays down, Jake pulls out his knives. Aha! So he's the one. Gene blocks all the knives with a chair, and Jake runs outside and steals a truck. Gene gives chase on horseback. Jake runs the truck into a fruit stand and lands on one of his own knives. What dramatic irony.

The film concludes with a sing-along at the cantina. Miss Del Rio has recovered admirably. She throws a knife at Gene to attract his attention, and it sticks in the wall just above his head. How charming. Then he leaps on stage and joins her for the closing number, another rendition of "Twilight on the Rio Grande." And as the sun sinks slowly in the west . . .

Unforgettable Performances

Gene Autry sure is a snappy dresser. He wears spotless cowboy shirts decorated with fanciful paisleys and handsome Farah slacks. He exudes good-guyism and speaks in the sort of deliberate, sweetly inflected monotone that nursery school teachers use in addressing their classes. Perhaps in preparing this role, Autry had a realistic expectation of the sort of audience he would draw.

Sterling Holloway has a voice like a broken train whistle. He tries to act dumb and succeeds. He attempts to add some comedy to the film, but when your character is named Pokie, you're doomed from the start.

Adele Mara pronounces her "Hs" so hard that she keeps blowing out all the candles in the room. Fortunately for the lamplighter, she speaks softly in that scene. Perhaps she feasted on garlic for lunch, and that is what caused the look of stoic endurance that Autry wears throughout the film.

Immortal Dialogue

Cowboy Humor:
POKIE: What time is it?
GENE: 'Bout noon.
CASS COUNTY BOY NO. 1: I sure slept.
CASS COUNTY BOY NO. 2: I didn't. That thunder kept me awake.
CASS COUNTY BOY NO. 3: That wasn't thunder—that was Jerry snoring.
CASS COUNTY BOY NO. 2: Aw, you're crazy!

* * *

MUCHO PESOS: Excuse mee, seenyor. Hugh are lookeeng for a leetle black-haired cowboy, no?
GENE: We are looking for a leetle black-haired cowboy, yes.

* * *

GENE: I'd like permission to carry a gun.
POLICE CAPTAIN: A gun? Why?
GENE: Because I'm joining in on this hunt, and it might come in handy.
POLICE CAPTAIN: I can appreciate how you feel, *señor*. But take my advice and go back to your ranch.
GENE: In other words, that's a polite way of sayin' no, isn't it?
POLICE CAPTAIN (laughs): Yes. This is a matter for the police.
GENE: I'm sorry, Captain. Gun or no gun, or whether you like it or not, I'm not leavin' this town until I find out who murdered my partner. Let's go, Pokie.

* * *

"Twilight on the Rio Grande"

When it's twilight on the Rio Grande,
Lazy shadows fall,
And soon recall
A midnight blue.

Time to bed the cattle down
'Neath the darkenin' sky.
Build a campfire, gather 'round!
And dream of days gone by.

The Story Behind the Film

Twilight on the Rio Grande takes place in a bizarre era best described by Richard Griffith and Arthur Mayer in their book *The Movies:* "The world of the new singing cowboys was a strange never-never land where the social conditions of 1880 rubbed shoulders with the costumes and dialogue of 1935." In other words, when a horse isn't fast enough, take a car.

Twilight is one of more than twenty films Gene Autry made for Republic Pictures, the company that brought you *Daughter of the Jungle* (q.v.).

Autry's promising career was interrupted by World War II. When he left the service, he attempted to have his contract terminated with Republic (judging by the quality of Republic's output, this seemed a reasonable action). Autry argued that while he was in the service, he had lost all his fans to another Republic cowboy star, Roy Rogers. Republic produced a ten-year-old girl named Faye Rizzo. She fondly demonstrated that despite his claims, Autry was still number one in the eyes of American youth. One can imagine Mr. Autry patting the girl kindly on the head for her admiration, and then kicking her in the seat of the pants for blowing his case. At any rate, he lost the judgment and received the maximum sentence—twenty-one more films for Republic Pictures according to the terms of his contract.

But Autry wasn't quite through with Republic Pictures. He later tried to enjoin them from selling his old movies to television stations on the grounds that it would cheapen his other TV ventures. Roy Rogers was in court with Republic for the same reason. Both actors lost, and on any day of the week the determined viewer can see any one of a number of wonderful films by these "singin' cowpokes." For the uninitiated who are unable to tell the two cowboys apart: Autry's horse is named Champion, while Roy Rogers' is named Trigger.

The Balance Sheet

Gene Autry is one of the most successful cowboy stars of all time. He is so beloved by fans that one little girl (no, not Faye Rizzo) hitchhiked all the way from Memphis to Los Angeles to move in with Autry and his wife. Another demanded that the Motion Picture Academy give Autry a special Oscar in a newly created Best Cowboy Actor category. According to "reliable fan-magazine surveys," he received more fan mail than any other picture personality, including forty-thousand letters in a single month. Autry shocked the world (or at least Tombstone, Arizona) when he became the first cowboy to kiss a woman on screen. The recipient of the famous smooch was Elena Verdugo in *A Little Spanish Town*. The extent of her injuries is not known.

Republic Pictures describes Gene's rise to stardom this way: "Gene Autry sang his way into motion pictures. In fact, from the time Gene was ten years old, he sang only to the cattle. Then joining a roving medicine show, he traveled through southern Oklahoma, singing while he dispensed cure-alls and patent medicines. In 1930, Gene began singing over radio station KVOO in Tulsa, Oklahoma. Billed as 'Oklahoma's Yodeling Cowboy,' his reputation began to spread. The Victor Record Company offered him a contract, which he accepted. An immediate sensation, he recorded in quick succession for every major company."

Autry used his recording and motion-picture successes as a springboard for more ambitious commercial enterprises. He first allowed his name to be used in a promotional venture when Sears, Roebuck manufactured a guitar carrying his endorsement in 1932. His royalty amounted to ten cents a guitar. Later in his career he owned two motion-picture companies, three radio stations, a television station, some hotels, a partnership in a huge cattle ranch in Arizona, and a major-league baseball team.

While he has long been able to preserve his good-guy image on the screen, his true-life adventures have not always lived up to his legendary pureheartedness. In 1953 a clock salesman charged Autry in a $10,000 battery suit. The salesman said that after his car collided with one driven by Autry, the cowboy "wantonly, maliciously, and outrageously" assaulted him. Autry was later named in a superior-court suit involving the 1958 Brussels World's Fair, where 150 cowboys and cowgirls were stranded in the Belgian capital after their rodeo, which was partly owned by Autry, went broke. Said Autry of the incident, "I think it was a combination of poor management and a bad break in the weather that caused the closing. . . . Since it rained almost every day, the people just didn't want to sit and get soaked watching our cowpokes wrestlin' steers. Unless someone comes up with some cash it will be a cold hard winter for some of the cowboys over there." Not as long as the cowpokes learn how to sing in Flemish and Walloon.

*From left to right, Barbara Parkins,
Sharon Tate, and Patty Duke in*
Valley of the Dolls, *a film which
has grossed more than $20 million.*

*Patty Duke, as the ill-fated star
Neely O'Hara, shows the unhappy
effects of too much pill-popping in*
Valley of the Dolls.

VALLEY OF THE DOLLS (1967)

Directed by: MARK ROBSON
Written by: HELEN DEUTSCH and DOROTHY KINGSLEY
Based on the novel by: JACQUELINE SUSANN
Produced by: DAVID WEISBART
Music by: JOHNNY WILLIAMS
Featuring: BARBARA PARKINS, PATTY DUKE, SHARON TATE, SUSAN HAYWARD, PAUL BURKE, TONY SCOTTI, MARTIN MILNER, CHARLES DRAKE, ALEX DAVION, LEE GRANT, JOEY BISHOP, GEORGE JESSEL, JACQUELINE SUSANN

Twentieth Century-Fox

The Critics Rave

"For out-and-out trash, few films have surpassed 1967's *Valley of the Dolls*. . . . It's a bowdlerized version of the Jacqueline Susann book which provided a mawkish, trite, cheap story and smut: the movie lacks the smut but compensates by being badly acted, badly photographed, and sleazily made, with a cheapjack production underlining the near-idiot literacy level of the script."

—Judith Crist, *TV Guide to the Movies*

"What a howl! . . . *Valley of the Dolls*, one of the most stupefyingly clumsy films ever made by alleged professionals, has no more sense of its own ludicrousness than a village idiot stumbling in manure."

—Joseph Morgenstern, *Newsweek*

". . . an unbelievably hackneyed and mawkish mishmash of backstage plots and *Peyton Place* adumbrations. . . . It's every bit as phony and old-fashioned as anything Lana Turner ever

did, and all a fairly respectful admirer of movies can do is laugh at it and turn away. . . ."
—Bosley Crowther, *New York Times*

"Lowest rating! . . . a piece of trash. Cheap, melodramatic mishmash. . . . You're doomed to a stupefying two hours if you watch."
—Steven H. Scheuer, *Movies on TV*

"Poor: Lowest rating! . . . Think of a showbiz cliché and *Valley of the Dolls* has it. . . ."
—*Monthly Film Bulletin*

"A thoroughly maladroit soap opera, whose innumerable iridescent suds are blown up ten times bigger than life and therefore become, even when they are meant to be tragic, laughable."
—Brendan Gill, *The New Yorker*

"The story is about girls who take all sorts of pills, but *Valley of the Dolls* offers only bromides. . . . Viewers are also not likely to feel anything—except numbness—after ingesting this film. . . ."
—*Time*

"Bomb: Lowest rating! Scattered unintentional laughs do not compensate for terribly written, acted, and directed adaptation of Jacqueline Susann novel. . . ."
—Leonard Maltin, *TV Movies*

"Ineptitude, inadequacy, and downright dishonesty characterize every aspect of this Mark Robson-David Weisbart production. . . ."
—Arthur Knight, *Saturday Review*

"Patty Duke is ghastly here. Sharon Tate is pretty, but that's about it. The men are all an uninteresting-looking lot. Sometimes you'll laugh in the wrong places at the script. There's a lot of talk about taking pills (dolls). But what kind of pills do you take to sit through a film like this?"
—*Cue*

Plot Summary

Valley of the Dolls tells the story of three young women who come to wicked old New York to "make the big time" but manage to get all messed up in the process.

Our first young lovely is Jennifer North (played by the late Sharon Tate). She knows that her only chance for success is peddling her body since her mother has convinced her (by telephone—it's the next best thing to being there) that she has no talent and so should concentrate on her bust exercises. The proud mother seems to ignore the fact that if Sharon Tate were to do any further bust exercises she'd have a tough time getting her belt on. While struggling along, Jen meets a young nightclub singer and marries him. But this unfortunate *chanteur* develops an incurable disease and must stop working. To pay for the best possible medical care, Jen goes to Paris and makes pornographic movies until she discovers a lump in one of her breasts. ("You see," we can hear Mom saying, "this is what happens when you let up on your bust exercises.") She soon learns that she harbors a malignant tumor and her doctor schedules a mastectomy. Since Jen faces a bleak future as a nudie star, she commits suicide.

Our next fair maiden is Anne Welles (Barbara Parkins). After arriving in the Big Apple from a small New England town, she gets a job with a theatrical law firm. She survives an on-again off-again love affair with her boss Lyon, a lawyer who always wanted to be a writer. Eventually she is "discovered" by a cosmetics firm, which decides to use her as their star TV model. She enjoys a dose of life at the top, takes a few too many pills, and finally recognizes the evils of show biz. She decides to return to quiet nights by the fireside and carefree ice-skating parties in her home town, where she lives happily ever after. There must be a moral in this somewhere.

Our third and most illustrious tootsie-pie is a budding actress named Neely O'Hara (Patty Duke). Neely gets a minor part in a Broadway show, playing alongside veteran star Helen Lawson (Susan Hayward). The older actress fears that the newcomer will upstage her, and orders Neely dropped from the cast. Does this discourage our plucky heroine? Not on your life! She wins a spot singing for a charity telethon and becomes the biggest star in Hollywood before you can say "cerebral palsy." The only fly in the ointment is Neely's growing addiction to "dolls"—pills of various kinds, be they amphetamines, barbiturates, or Carter's Little Liver Pills. When Patty Duke begins crying hysterically, "I gotta have a doll!" or "I've forgotten how to sleep without a doll!" she doesn't want a Raggedy Ann or a Barbie. Neely's burgeoning problem is depicted in one "artistic" montage showing Miss Duke singing, then popping pills; jogging, then popping pills; doing sit-ups, then popping pills; fencing, then popping pills. Why, for heaven's sake, is she taking all those pills—we're the ones who are throwing up! At any rate, the little buggers make her so uppity that she dumps her nice-guy husband, Mel (Martin Milner), and takes up with her suspiciously effeminate hairdresser, Ted Casablanca. Ted soon runs out on her, which provokes a nervous breakdown and a melodramatic sojourn in a sanitorium. Sympathetic cards and letters pour in from all over the world, and when Neely is fully recovered she gets a contract to star in a new Broadway musical. On opening night, however, she begins to worry that she might be upstaged by a minor character—just as Susan Hayward worried at the beginning of this soap opera (oh, the irony of it all). Neely flies off the handle at her beau of the moment, who walks out on her. The star gets drunk, is unable to act her part, and is replaced by an understudy. The show turns out to be a smash, the understudy becomes a big star (don't they always), and at the end of this movie we see poor Neely staggering down an alley behind the theater. She is ranting and raving, and to make the bathos complete, she begins rolling among the garbage cans. Perhaps in that particular environment she might find a print of this film.

Unforgettable Performances

Sharon Tate, a starlet with a lovely body and no acting ability, is cast here as Jennifer North, a starlet with a lovely body and no acting ability. Miss Tate succeeds in conveying her character's lack of talent, but when it comes to communicating suffering, love, or any other human emotion, she fails miserably.

Barbara Parkins as Anne Welles spends so much energy stepping in and out of various glamorous outfits and trying her level best to look "lovely" that she has neither the strength nor the time to vary the expressions on her face or the patterns of her speech. She puckers her lips so frequently that she would be better suited to advertising citrus fruit than beauty products.

Oh, Patty Duke. What ever happened to the good ol' days and the twin cousin with the accent? As Neely O'Hara, Miss Duke belts out one André Previn tune after another and her clumsy, unstylish singing is actually the best part of her performance. For the rest, she rolls her eyes and screams, suggesting that she is a victim of an amusement park fun house rather than a broken-down, suffering star. She's supposed to be sexy and attract men like flies, but in this film she might even have a tough time with the flies. She comes off looking as young as she did in her old TV show, only with less brains. *Cue* magazine aptly described her performance as ghastly, and writer Doug McClelland (author of Susan Hayward's life story) has characterized Miss Duke's efforts as "one of the screen's all-time worst performances."

Martin Milner, famous as a TV policeman, walks through his role as Neely's writer husband, Mel. His portrayal is so heavy and lifeless that even though he does not play a police officer this time, he still seems to be made of copper.

Immortal Dialogue

JENNIFER (on the telephone): You told me Gramp's been sick, Mother, and I know about the oil burner. (Pause.) Okay, I'll pawn the mink. He'll give me a couple of hundred for it. (Pause.) Mother, I know I don't have any talent, and I know all I have is a body, and I *am* doing my bust exercise. (Pause.) Goodbye, Mother. I'll wire you the money first thing in the morning. Goodbye. (Hangs up and starts performing calisthenics to expand her bust.). Oh! To hell with 'em! Let 'em droop!

       *   *   *

LYON: Do you realize, Miss Welles, that you are the most beautiful girl that ever left lipstick in my office?
ANNE: You like women, don't you?
LYON: I like career girls. We're compatible.
ANNE: There's a rumor they don't make very good wives.
LYON: Well, I'm not looking for a wife.
ANNE: You're fortunate you know yourself. I don't know who I am, or what I want.

       *   *   *

(Neely has bitter words with her writer husband, Mel.)

NEELY: You're not the breadwinner, either!

MEL: Maybe I better get off my rump and go back to New York. I can always get my old job back.

NEELY: Suit yourself. I'm too tired to argue. I'm gonna take a shower and get back to Ted Casablanca's.

MEL: You know, you're spending a lot more time than necessary with that fag.

NEELY: Ted Casablanca is not a fag! (Pause.) And I'm the dame who can prove it!

The Story Behind the Film

The film rights to the novel *Valley of the Dolls* by Jacqueline Susann were purchased by Twentieth Century-Fox before the book was even published. When Susann's potboiler became a smash best seller, the studio moguls knew they had a hot property on their hands and recruited an appropriate director. The man they selected was Mark Robson, who is also responsible for such cinematic masterpieces as *Peyton Place* (1957) and *Earthquake* (1974). Far more important (for publicity purposes) than the selection of a director was the choice of a cast. Twentieth Century considered such stars as Petula Clark, Raquel Welch, Ann-Margret, Candice Bergen, and Jill Ireland for the leading roles before casting the lesser actresses who finally made the film. Judy Garland was originally cast as Helen Lawson, the aging Broadway star, and to keep Garland on the project the studio made a number of concessions to her eccentricities—including providing her with a pool table in her own dressing room. Nevertheless, Garland backed out at the last minute, and it was announced that her role would be played by either Bette Davis or Tammy Grimes. Fortunately, these two veterans turned down the part, and Susan Hayward was stuck with it. It was certainly one of Miss Hayward's least noteworthy screen credits.

The film was shot on location in New York City and New England. For a rural ice-skating scene, more than one hundred inhabitants of Mount Kisco, New York, participated as extras. Men, women, children, and dogs were attracted by radio advertisements asking for "actors."

Another novelty extra in this film was Jacqueline Susann, author of the novel, who played an obnoxious reporter at Jennifer North's death scene. Miss Susann has been widely criticized for her shallow, commercial hack writing, but those who take notice of her brief performance in this film will understand why she turned to writing from her earlier career as an actress.

The Balance Sheet

The death toll among those prominently associated with this film is positively gruesome. Poor Sharon Tate, of course, became a victim of the Manson Gang in one of the most grisly murders in history. Author Jacqueline Susann, after writing several other best sellers, died of cancer in 1975. And David Weisbart, producer of the film, didn't even live to see the fruits of his labors. One afternoon, a few weeks after filming was completed, he played golf with director Mark Robson. In the midst of their game, Weisbart suffered a massive stroke and died on July 21, 1967. He was fifty-two.

For the survivors, however, this miserable film proved a financial triumph. It grossed more than $11 million in domestic rentals in its first five months. Though critics were unanimous in their condemnation, this turkey proved one of the biggest money-makers in Twentieth Century-Fox history up to that time. To date it has grossed more than $20 million in the United States and Canada.

Following the success of *Valley of the Dolls*, Fox determined to continue cashing in on this bad-taste bonanza. They hired Russ Meyer to direct a film called *Beyond the Valley of the Dolls*. In no sense was this film a sequel; it merely attempted to exploit the tried-and-true title. A double bill was later formed featuring the two *Dolls* on the same program—and any viewer who managed to sit through both gumdrops certainly is entitled to some sort of endurance award.

Jacqueline Susann was understandably upset with this unremunerative and unauthorized rip-off of her title. Miss Susann sued the studio, claiming that the new film misled her fans and that it injured sales of her latest novel, *The Love Machine*. The case wasn't settled until after Miss Susann's death, when the courts awarded more than $2 million in damages to her estate.

ZABRISKIE POINT (1970)

Directed by: MICHELANGELO ANTONIONI
Written by: MICHELANGELO ANTONIONI, FRED GARDNER, SAM SHEPARD, TONINO GUERRA, and CLARE PEPLOE
Produced by: CARLO PONTI
Music by: THE ROLLING STONES, PINK FLOYD, THE GRATEFUL DEAD, JERRY GARCIA, JOHN FAHEY, KALEIDOSCOPE, and THE YOUNGBLOODS
Featuring: MARK FRECHETTE, DARIA HALPRIN, ROD TAYLOR, PAUL FIX, G. D. SPRADLIN, BILL GARAWAY, KATHLEEN CLEAVER, MEMBERS OF THE OPEN THEATER OF JOE CHAIKIN

Metro-Goldwyn-Mayer

The Critics Rave

"Pathetic mess . . . *Zabriskie* is a disaster, but, as one might guess, Antonioni does not make an ordinary sort of disaster. . . . This is a huge, jerry-built, crumbling ruin of a movie. . . . There is not a new idea or a good idea in the entire movie—not even a small one."
—Pauline Kael, *The New Yorker*

"A small, sad shambles of a film that has obviusly been salvaged from a larger shambles. It's bad enough to give anti-Americanism a bad name. . . . Antonioni and his deep-think colleagues carry on like a befuddled Columbus who has just discovered Spain. . . . The burlesque is coarse, the radicalism infantile, the dialogue atrocious, and the performances are death barely warmed over. . . ."
—Joseph Morgenstern, *Newsweek*

"Hilariously awful . . . it is uninspired and phony. . . . Two of the worst performances of

Newcomers Daria Halprin and Mark Frechette in Michelangelo Antonioni's Zabriskie Point.

the decade. 'Sometimes I feel like screaming my head off!!' says the girl. I know exactly what she means."

           —Rex Reed, *Holiday*

"Incredibly simple-minded and obvious. The scenario might have been written by a first-year student in film school . . . awful."

           —*Time*

"So silly as almost to beggar description . . . about as credible as a Nixon pledge of integration

Mark Frechette in Antonioni's Zabriskie Point: *Boy, did he get a wrong number.*

. . . neither of the leads can act."

           —Charles E. Fager, *Christian Century*

"A big lie and totally alien."

           Mark Frechette, star of *Zabriskie Point*

"One of the 10 worst of 1970. Although Mr. Antonioni spent months traveling the country to research his film, he probably could have obtained the same insights by watching prime time American television for one week at the St. Regis Hotel and then shooting the entire film in Spain."

           —Vincent Canby, *New York Times*

"Hollywood's most expensive flop."

           Sam Shepard, co-writer of the film, predicting public response

Plot Summary

While a group of dissident students have a "rap" session, the camera pans aimlessly over them, desperately trying to establish a quality of *cinéma vérité*. The young rebels use "heavy" language like, "I don't have to prove my revolutionary cre-

dentials to you," and, "Right on!", and "Beautiful." Mark, one of the rebels, claims that he's ready to die for his cause. A fellow non-conformist asks, "Alone?", to which Mark coolly answers, "No—of boredom," and leaves the room. This is a foreshadowing of the cinema experience that lies ahead.

On the street, Mark witnesses a police raid on a library where several black revolutionaries are holed up. Most of the rebels rush out of the library with their hands up, but one of them fails to come out on time, and is shot down by a policeman. Next we hear a gunshot and the policeman falls to the ground. Mark may or may not have been the assassin; that is not resolved until the end of the film, and by then nobody cares.

On the lam from the police, Mark arrives at an airport. He steals a small private plane because, as he rationalizes, "I wanna get off the ground!" That's fine for him, because this film never does. Mark flies the plane flawlessly—he makes it look so easy that every boy and girl on the block will want to jump in a plane and fly it around for a while.

While flying over the desert, Mark spots a car below on the highway. With a youthful sense of humor, he repeatedly buzzes the car until it stops. Mark's plane runs out of gas, and he lands it (with the skill of a B-52 fighter-bomber pilot) right next to the highway. The girl in the car is named Daria, and she is driving to Phoenix, where her employer is having a business meeting. Daria agrees to give Mark a ride to a filling station so he can get more gas for his plane (and then buzz her car again). But on the way they stop off at Zabriskie Point, in Death Valley, California, for a little mufky-fufky.

The two walk the blazing sands of the desert exchanging some really heavy dialogue, man. When Daria sees some desert plants, she wonders, "How do these plants make it in the sand? They're so beautiful." Then she asks Mark, "Don't you feel at home here? It's so peaceful." To which Mark replies, "It's dead." Daria agrees (and so do the critics). "Okay," she says, "it's dead. Let's play death games." And so they chase each other around the dunes. Later, Daria lights up a marijuana joint and offers a hit to Mark, but he tells her that he's on a reality trip, and that, no thank you, he'd rather not. Finally, they make love at the bottom of a sand dune, and—lo and behold—the desert blossoms with hundreds of couples and triples miming copulation. They roll around in the dirt and the rock fissures, and then magically disappear. Mark comments, "I always knew it would be like this."

When Mark decides to return the plane, Daria warns that it might be risky, but Mark insists: "I need to take risks!" So that the craft won't be recognized, they paint the plane dark green with the help of a hermit, who not only just happens to be living out in the desert, but also happens to own some cans of dark green paint. With the plane sufficiently camouflaged (although it still looks like a plane), Mark flies back to the police-infested airport. The police are waiting for him because they believe he killed the cop at the beginning of the film. When Mark doesn't stop the plane immediately, they fire away and kill him.

Mark's death apparently receives a lot of publicity; at least enough for Daria to hear it announced on her car radio. She arrives at her boss's desert home in Phoenix, and with hatred of everything that represents the American system, she imagines the house blowing up repeatedly, and we see at least seven shots, from different angles, of its eruption. Next we are treated to a veritable cavalcade of explosions—a detonation of all the corrupt institutions in America. This blast-fest includes the blowing up of a whole library—including several books and magazines—assorted garden furniture, a clothes rack, a television set, a refrigerator, a loaf of Wonder bread, a cucumber, a Campbell's soup can, and a raw chicken. By this time one is tempted to blow up the screen and projector. And as if this weren't stupid enough, the destruction is enhanced by the "far out" Pink Floyd rock music thrown on the sound track. The film finally closes with an inspiring shot of a sunset fading into the distance, as we listen to a teen-exploitation song entitled "So Young." Ah, yes!

Unforgettable Performances

Mark Frechette, a non-actor who plays (fittingly enough) Mark, was a carpenter when he was approached by Antonioni's talent scouts. According to the M-G-M pressbook, he was spotted "standing at a bus stop in Cambridge, Massachusetts, swearing at a man who had thrown a geranium pot at a quarreling couple." Frechette got the part even though he had never heard of Antonioni and had never read the script. This is only too apparent in his performance. He tries to do a cool imitation of Peter Fonda, but he's so insecure with his part that he comes off more like Laurence Harvey in *King Richard and the Crusaders* (q.v.). Throughout the film he is seen standing with his hands on his hips trying to look concerned, but he really looks as though he can't think of anything to do in front of the camera. This is probably true, since Antonioni never discussed Mark's part with him at all. Frechette has remarked, "Our relationship was very futile."

Daria Halprin, another non-actor, was formerly an anthropology student at the University of California at Berkeley. From the start, she was Antonioni's first choice for the part of the girl. She tries to look cute, sexy, and sweet—all at the same time—and turns in the kind of performance that might only appeal to fifty-five-year-old divorced men. She was discovered by Antonioni himself when he saw her in *Revolution*. In that film she dances, and briefly reads from a book while in the nude. She dropped out of Berkeley after her freshman year to make Antonioni's film. After making *Zabriskie*, Daria entered a real-life relationship with co-star Mark Frechette. For a time they lived together in a Boston commune. In an interview with Wayne Warga of the *Los Angeles Times*, she was asked if she and Frechette would eventually marry. She replied, nudging Frechette, "One of these days. Right, pal?" Frechette coldly remarked, "Wrong. Maybe someday." Halprin insisted: "Well, when we have kids," to which Frechette replied, "In France they call them natural children, not bastards."

Halprin eventually did get married, though not to Frechette. In May 1972 she married Dennis Hopper, director and star of *Easy Rider* and *The Last Movie* (q.v.).

Immortal Dialogue

FELLOW RADICAL (after Mark encounters a girl on the street): Who was that?
MARK: A girl from my long-gone past.
FELLOW RADICAL: What's her name?
MARK: Alice—she's my sister.

＊　＊　＊

COP (booking a young radical in the pokey): Occupation?
REBEL: Associate professor of history.
COP: That's too long. I'll just put down clerk.

＊　　＊　　＊

MARK (walking into a store): Can I ask you a favor?
STOREOWNER: Shoot!
MARK: Would you trust me for the price of a sandwich?
STOREOWNER (sincerely): It's not that I don't trust you. But if I trusted you, I'd have to trust everybody in the whole world.
MARK (sulking): Yeah. . . .

＊　　＊　　＊

DARIA: Hey, guy, you want a smoke?
MARK: You know you're talking to a guy under discipline.
DARIA: What's that?
MARK: This group I was in had rules against smoking. They were into a reality trip.
DARIA: Wow! What a drag!

＊　　＊　　＊

DARIA: There's a thousand sides to everything, not just heroes and villains. . . . So anyway . . . so anyway . . . so anyway . . . So anyway ought to be one word. Like a place or a river. "So Anyway River."

＊　　＊　　＊

MARK: Would you like to go with me?
DARIA: Where?
MARK: Wherever I'm going.
DARIA: Are you *really* asking?
MARK: Is that your *real* answer?

The Story Behind the Film

This whole film is cluttered with clichéd symbols of "what's wrong" with America: billboards, freeways, the stock market, etc. But as we've all seen this sort of thing before, *Zabriskie Point* turns out to be as enlightening and stirring as the eleven o'clock news. In all his vapid cynicism, Antonioni missed one major fault in contemporary culture—that an American movie studio would provide $7 million for a wretched film by an overblown Italian filmmaker.

The film was based on a news item about a boy who stole a plane and was later shot down for trying to return it. Antonioni collaborated with two Americans on the screenplay: playwright Sam Shepard and Fred Gardner. The other conspirators were Tonino Guerra (co-writer of *L'Avventura* and *Amarcord*, not to mention the classic *A Place for Lovers* (q.v.)) and Clare Peploe. The score is comprised of selected songs by rock groups like Pink Floyd, the Grateful Dead, and the Rolling Stones.

During the actual filming, Mark Frechette had constant arguments with Antonioni. Frechette tried to turn the director on to his philosophy and stressed over and over again the importance of non-violence. However, Antonioni simply ignored the impotent radical. This later prompted Frechette to comment that the film was "a big lie and totally alien."

The filming of the orgy in Death Valley is especially interereresting, since more than one hundred persons participated in it. Half of them were from New York actor Joseph Chaikin's Open Theater, while the rest were made up of assorted hippies. The scene was rehearsed for two weeks, but Rangers were aroused (so to speak) and called the police. Next thing M-G-M knew, they had a grand jury case on their hands. It seems that Antonioni had unwittingly violated the Mann Act, which prohibits the import of women over state lines for immoral purposes. The case was later dismissed.

The Balance Sheet

When Wayne Warga asked Frechette what he thought about the rough notices the film received Frechette commented, "Who the hell wants to talk about that movie, anyway." Indeed, the film did open to incredible reviews from critics, and this time even the audiences didn't like it. The production cost was around $7 million; by the end of the second-run engagements the film had grossed a meager $891,918, making it one of the biggest money-losers of all time.

At its world premiere, *Zabriskie Point* was greeted with derisive howls. Counting on a teen-age acceptance of this trash, M-G-M promoted it as a "trip" movie. The advertising read, *"Zabriskie Point* Will Blow Your Mind!" The pressbook for the film boasts that as part of the advertising campaign, "a multi-colored pop-art painted plane" (resembling the one in the film) flew to nineteen cities on a nationwide publicity tour. Students of colleges in all cities came to affix their school decal or emblem to the fuselage.

SPECIAL AWARD

A wreath of unspoiled daisies and our Art-into-Life Sincerity Award are presented (posthumously) to Mark Frechette for his off-camera follow-up to *Zabriskie Point*.

After *Zabriskie Point*, Mark made a film in Yugoslavia called *Man Against* (about a World War I poet), and one in Italy by the name of *Many Wars Ago* (directed by Francesco Rosi). After these excursions, Mark went to Boston to reside at the Fort Hill commune near Elliot Park with Daria Halprin.

Infuriated by Watergate, Frechette, along with two other members of his commune, robbed the Brigham Circle Branch of the New England Merchant National Bank. One of the robbers, Christopher Thien, was "pointlessly" shot down by a policeman at the scene of the crime. Thien died on his way to the Brigham Hospital. Frechette was sentenced to six to fifteen years at the Walpole State Prison. When later asked why he had robbed the bank, Frechette explained, "I am afflicted by a political conscience. We did it as a revolutionary act of political protest. We had been watching the Watergate hearings on television and we saw John Dean tell the truth and we saw Mitchell and Stans lie about it. We saw the American people sinking deeper and deeper into apathy and we felt an intense rage. They did not know the truth and did not want to know the truth. We know the truth and wanted to show it to them. Because banks are federally insured, robbing that bank was a way of robbing Richard Nixon without hurting anybody." Gee, Frechette puts on a better act in real life.

He later said, "There was no way to stop what was going to happen. We just reached the point where all that the three of us really wanted to do was hold up a bank. And besides," he added, "standing there with a gun, cleaning out a teller's cage—that's about as fuckin' honest as you can get, man!"

While in prison, Frechette directed a dramatization of the White House transcripts for presentation at the Norfolk Correctional Institute in Massachusetts and other prisons around the country. He was killed in a reported accident in 1975—he was found after morning exercise with a 150-pound barbell lying across his throat in Norfolk State Prison. He was twenty-seven.

APPENDIX

In preparing our list of the Fifty Worst Films we have tried to be as thorough and thoughtful as possible. Nevertheless, we realize that our subjective choices hardly represent the final word on bad films. In order to present our readers with some alternative opinions, we asked a number of prominent critics to submit their own nominations for the most notable stinkers in cinema history. Their unedited responses are included in this Appendix. In those cases in which our guest critics selected a film that appears in this book, we have noted with an asterisk their agreement with our choices.

CHARLES CHAMPLIN: *Los Angeles Times*

The Salzburg Connection (1972)
°*A Place for Lovers (1969)*
Hammersmith Is Out (1972)
Mother, Jugs and Speed (1976)

You must understand that I don't see the worst films except by accident. Life is too short, and I can take suffering or leave it alone.

ROGER EBERT: *Chicago Sun-Times*

Several of the worst films of all time are:
°*Lost Horizon (1973 Version)* (particularly the fertility dance, which was cut from the film after the initial audience hilarity)

Tidal Wave (in which the special effects apparently consisted of mud on the bottom of a bathtub, stirred up by a garden hose)
Now About All These Women (which demonstrated that it took one of the world's greatest directors [Bergman] to make one of the world's worst comedies)
Superstooges Versus the Wonderwomen (the ads promised: "See! Anthropoidal Pogo Sticks!")
Mame (the movie of the musical of the movie of the play of the novel)
°*Jonathan Livingston Seagull*

LEO LERMAN: *Vogue*

Three of my favorite worst films are:
The Egyptian (1954)
Madame X (1966) (with Lana Turner)
Beyond the Forest (1949) (with Bette Davis)

FRED W. McDARRAH: *The Village Voice*

A Warm December
Charlie One-Eye
°*Lost Horizon (1973 Version)*
The Nickel Ride
Dark Star
Alfredo, Alfredo
The Don Is Dead
Erotic Adventures of Zorro
Grizzly
Virility
Salsa
Inserts
Sweet Movie

283

FRANK RICH: *New York Post*

Last Summer (1969)
Myra Breckinridge (1970)
Mandingo (1975)
*Oh Dad, Poor Dad, Mama's Hung You In The Closet And
    I'm Feeling So Sad (1967)*
At Long Last Love (1975)

For me, a worst film can't be any mediocre movie, but
must be a movie that is *both* atrociously made and philosophically ridiculous—a merging of form and content, as it
were.

KEVIN THOMAS: *Los Angeles Times*

The Adventures (1970) (a kind of trash potboiler to end
    all trash potboilers)
Blood Feast (1963) (still the grisliest, sickest picture I
    ever saw)
Snuff (1976) (not as grisly as *Blood Feast* but consistently
    wretched in all areas)

KENNETH TURAN: staff writer with the *Washington
    Post* and film critic for *The Progressive*

Since no absolute standards seem to exist for bad, let alone
"worst" films, I have chosen the ten films that drove me
wildest with aggravation, that filled me to bursting with
cranky animosity toward the people who made them. In
no particular order:

The Last Movie (1971) (directed by Dennis Hopper)
The Trial of Billy Jack (1974) (directed by Tom Laugh-
    lin)
Coming Apart (1969) (directed by Milton Moses
    Ginsberg)
Play It As It Lays (1972) (directed by Frank Perry)
Death Wish (1974) (directed by Michael Winner)
The Long Goodbye (1973) (directed by Robert Altman)
Johnny Got His Gun (1971) (directed by Dalton
    Trumbo)
The Oscar (1966) (directed by Russell Rouse)
Black Gunn (1972) (directed by Robert Hartford-Davis)
Beyond the Valley of the Dolls (1970) (directed by Russ
    Meyer)

(Perennial worsts: anything by Lina Wertmuller
                     anything by Peter Bogdanovich)

ARCHER WINSTEN: *New York Post*

I do recall a couple of pictures I writhed through within
the past couple of years. Surely they would lead any
Worst List:

Pink Flamingoes (1972)
The Texas Chainsaw Massacre (1974)

YOUR BALLOT

for the grand, exalted WORST FILMS POLL

- - - - - - - - - - - - - - - - - -

Please list those films which you consider to be the worst
movies you have ever seen. Provide as many or as few
titles as you wish. Your nominations will be tabulated, and
the results will be reported in subsequent editions of this
book.

MY OWN LIST OF THE WORST FILMS OF
ALL TIME—

NAME _____

ADDRESS _____

PLEASE MAIL TO:

WORST FILMS POLL
c.o. Michael Medved
610 South Venice Boulevard
Number 4094
Venice, California 90291

INDEX